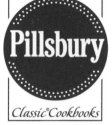

The Best of
CLASSIC®
COOKBOOKS

Pillsbury
Classic® Cookbooks

The Best of CLASSIC® COOKBOOKS

275 RECIPES FROM 20 YEARS OF PILLSBURY'S BEST-SELLING COOKING MAGAZINE

THE PILLSBURY COMPANY

CLARKSON POTTER/PUBLISHERS
NEW YORK

Published by Clarkson Potter/Publishers, 201 East 50th
Street, New York, New York 10022.
Member of the Crown Publishing Group.

Random House Inc. New York, Toronto, London, Sydney,
Auckland
www.randomhouse.com

CLARKSON N. POTTER, POTTER, and colophon are
registered trademarks of Random House, Inc.

Classic Cookbooks is a registered trademark of The Pillsbury
Company.

Bundt is a registered trademark of Northland Aluminum
Products, Inc., Minneapolis, MN.

Printed in Japan

Design by Julie Baker Schroeder

Library of Congress Cataloging-in-Publication Data
Pillsbury—best of classic cookbooks : 275 recipes from
20 years of Pillsbury's best-selling cooking magazine /
The Pillsbury Company. — 1st ed.
    Includes index.
    1. Cookery. I. Pillsbury Company.
TX714.P548   1998
641.5—dc21   98-28784
                           CIP

ISBN 0-609-60377-9

10 9 8 7 6 5 4 3 2

Credits

PILLSBURY: THE BEST OF CLASSIC® COOKBOOKS
The Pillsbury Company

Publisher: Sally Peters
Publication Manager: Diane B. Anderson
Senior Editor: Jackie Sheehan
Senior Food Editor: Andi Bidwell
Recipe Editors: Nancy Lilleberg, Grace Wells
Contributing Writer: Mary Caldwell
Photography: Glenn Peterson Photography, Graham Brown Photography,
    Tad Ware Photography, The Studio Central
Food Stylists: Lynn Boldt, JoAnn Cherry, Janice Cole, Sharon Harding,
    Cindy Ojczyk, Barb Standal
Recipe Typist: Michelle Barringer

PILLSBURY PUBLICATIONS
Publisher: Sally Peters
Publication Managers: Diane B. Anderson, William Monn
Senior Editors: Elaine Christiansen, Jackie Sheehan
Senior Food Editor: Andi Bidwell
Test Kitchen Coordinator: Pat Peterson
Circulation Manager: Karen Goodsell
Circulation Coordinator: Rebecca Bogema
Recipe System Administrator: Bev Gustafson
Recipe System Coordinator: Nolan Vaughan
Recipe Production Specialist: Mary Prokott
Publication Secretary: Jackie Ranney

CLARKSON POTTER/PUBLISHERS
The Crown Publishing Group

President and Publisher: Chip Gibson
Vice President-Editorial Director: Lauren Shakely
Senior Editor: Katie Workman
Assistant Editor: Erica Youngren
Designer: Julie Baker Schroeder
Executive Managing Editor: Laurie Stark
Managing Editor: Amy Boorstein
Senior Production Manager: Jane Searle
Publicist: Wendy Schuman

Frontispiece: Home-Style Roasted Vegetables, page 191
Cover: Parsley-Potato Topped Oven Swiss Steak, page 123

CONTENTS

HERE, BY POPULAR DEMAND

We have collected the very best of the best: more than 275 of the most outstanding recipes ever published in Pillsbury CLASSIC® COOKBOOKS. You'll find start-to-finish instructions for great home-cooked family meals and successful special-occasion entertaining, from appetizers through dessert.

Since the CLASSIC COOKBOOKS' debut in 1979, more than 80 million copies have been sold. We've earned our position as America's favorite cookbook magazine thanks to our carefully tested and always dependable recipes, which emphasize easy-to-find ingredients and simple cooking instructions for dishes that earn rave reviews from family and guests.

Producing each issue of the magazine doesn't happen in the seclusion of our editorial offices. Staff members are in continual dialogue with our readers through surveys, reader correspondence and ongoing research on food trends, so that the magazine's editorial mission keeps pace with your interests and needs.

Cooking styles have evolved over the years. Today's recipes are shorter, quicker and leaner, and the pantry of the 1990s and beyond includes couscous, pesto and other "new" choices. CLASSIC cookbook readers seek balance between contemporary flavors and familiar favorites, and have a special appreciation for recipes that update traditional dishes with a simple "twist."

To ensure your success in the kitchen, we include with our recipes practical information on cooking techniques and ingredients. It's easy to see at a glance how long it will take to prepare and cook a recipe, and suggestions for freezing, garnishing or modifying dishes, as well as tips for entertaining with ease and flair, are sprinkled throughout the book.

If you're new to the CLASSIC COOKBOOKS family, welcome. We're confident you'll find this one of the most useful recipe collections ever. If you're one of our many loyal readers who has collected dozens of issues over the years, you'll be pleased to have so many of your favorite recipes in one handy volume.

HAPPY COOKING!

Corn and Clam Chowder, page 205; Waldorf Chicken Salad, page 49;
Grilled Walleye with Pecan Butter, page 154; Whole Wheat Sugar Cookies, page 259

Sweet-Sour Cocktail Meatballs, page 23

APPETIZERS

A GOOD FIRST COURSE AT A SIT-DOWN DINNER WHETS THE APPETITE FOR THE MEAL TO COME; AT AN INFORMAL GATHERING, AN ASSORTMENT OF HOT AND COLD HORS D'OEUVRES MAKES A DELIGHTFUL MIX-AND-MATCH PARTY MENU. THIS CHAPTER OFFERS FABULOUS SPECIALTIES FOR EITHER. SOME CAN BE MADE IN ADVANCE; OTHERS COME TOGETHER QUICKLY AT THE LAST MINUTE.

ACAPULCO SUNSET SPREAD

prep time: 20 min. • yield: 16 servings

The addition of shrimp gives this Mexican-inspired appetizer a touch of class. Save fat and calories by choosing baked tortilla chips instead of deep-fried.

1 (16-oz.) can refried beans

½ cup salsa

1 (8-oz.) pkg. ⅓-less-fat cream cheese (Neufchâtel), softened

1 avocado, pitted, peeled and chopped

1 tablespoon fresh lime juice

½ lb. frozen shelled, deveined, cooked small shrimp, thawed

1 tomato, chopped

Fresh cilantro, if desired

1 (14½-oz.) pkg. tortilla chips

1 In medium bowl, combine beans and salsa; mix well. Spread bean mixture onto large serving plate.

2 In food processor bowl with metal blade or blender container, combine cream cheese, avocado and lime juice; process until well blended. Spread cream cheese mixture over bean mixture.

3 Top with shrimp and tomato; garnish or sprinkle with cilantro. Serve with tortilla chips.

Nutrition Information Per Serving

Serving Size: ¹⁄₁₆ of Recipe

Calories	230	Calories from Fat	110
		% Daily Value	
Total Fat	12 g	18%	
Saturated	4 g	20%	
Cholesterol	40 mg	13%	
Sodium	420 mg	18%	
Total Carbohydrate	22 g	7%	
Dietary Fiber	4 g	16%	
Sugars	1 g		
Protein	8 g		
Vitamin A	8%	Vitamin C	6%
Calcium	6%	Iron	8%

Dietary Exchanges: 1½ Starch, ½ Lean Meat, 2 Fat OR 1½ Carbohydrate, ½ Lean Meat, 2 Fat

AVOCADO

Avocado gives body, color and rich flavor to the Acapulco Sunset Spread featured here. In the market, you'll most likely find Fuerte avocados with smooth, shiny green skin or the bumpy-skinned Hass variety, which turn black when ripe. Ripe avocados yield to gentle pressure.

For either kind, slit the avocado top to bottom, gently twisting the two halves apart and removing the pit with a spoon. A serrated grapefruit spoon is effective for removing the pit and separating the flesh from the skin. Inside, the flesh ranges from pale yellow to deep green. To prevent discoloration, rub the cut edges or toss the cut-up flesh with lemon or lime juice.

Cook's Notes

WARM ROASTED PEPPER AND ARTICHOKE SPREAD

prep time: 15 min. (ready in 40 min.) • yield: 3¼ cups

This spread is a good candidate for preparing early in the day of the party, then refrigerating until it's time to pop it in the oven. Just before serving, sprinkle the top of the spread with minced fresh parsley or green onions.

1 cup grated Parmesan cheese

½ cup fat-free mayonnaise or salad dressing

1 (8-oz.) pkg. cream cheese, softened

1 small garlic clove

1 (14-oz.) can artichoke hearts, drained, finely chopped

⅓ cup finely chopped roasted red bell peppers (from 7.25-oz. jar)

1 Heat oven to 350° F. In food processor bowl with metal blade, combine Parmesan cheese, mayonnaise, cream cheese and garlic; process until smooth.

2 Place mixture in large bowl. Add artichoke hearts and roasted peppers; blend well. Spread in ungreased 9-inch quiche dish or glass pie pan.

3 Bake at 350° F. for 20 to 25 minutes or until thoroughly heated. Serve warm with crackers, cut-up fresh vegetables or snack bread slices.

Nutrition Information Per Serving
Serving Size: 1 Tablespoon

Calories	25	Calories from Fat	20
		% Daily Value	
Total Fat	2 g	3%	
Saturated	1 g	5%	
Cholesterol	5 mg	2%	
Sodium	85 mg	4%	
Total Carbohydrate	1 g	1%	
Dietary Fiber	0 g	0%	
Sugars	0 g		
Protein	1 g		
Vitamin A	2%	Vitamin C	2%
Calcium	4%	Iron	0%

Dietary Exchanges: ½ Fat

RED PEPPERS

Red bell peppers are actually green bell peppers left to ripen on the vine. They have more sugar than green peppers, so they're sweeter and slightly more tender. Sometimes a little chopped red bell pepper is just the right garnish for an appetizer or main dish.

Roasting peppers brings out their sweetness. Place whole peppers under the broiler or on the grill, turning the peppers to blacken the skin evenly. When the peppers have cooled, peel off the skin, remove the seeds and ribs and cut up the flesh.

Purchased roasted peppers, available in jars or by bulk in the deli department, come in two basic styles: those packed in olive oil and those in vinegar.

Cook's Notes

Taco Dip

TACO DIP

prep time: 20 min. • yield: 12 servings

Under the shredded Cheddar, chopped tomatoes, green onions, olives and chiles, you'll find a smooth, rich blend of avocado dip and cream cheese.

1 (8-oz.) pkg. cream cheese, softened

1 (8-oz.) container sour cream

1 (6-oz.) container frozen avocado dip, thawed

1 teaspoon lemon juice

4 drops hot pepper sauce

2 cups shredded lettuce

1 (2 1/4-oz.) can chopped ripe olives, drained

1 (4.5-oz.) can chopped green chiles, drained

4 green onions, sliced

1 tomato, peeled, seeded and chopped

4 oz. (1 cup) shredded Cheddar cheese

1 In small bowl, combine cream cheese, sour cream, avocado dip, lemon juice and hot pepper sauce; beat at low speed until well blended. Spread mixture on large serving plate.*

2 Top evenly with all remaining ingredients. Serve with tortilla chips.

Tip: *Cream cheese mixture can be made several hours ahead; store in refrigerator. Just before serving, top with all remaining ingredients.

Calories	220	Calories from Fat	170
		% Daily Value	
Total Fat	19 g	29%	
Saturated	12 g	60%	
Cholesterol	50 mg	17%	
Sodium	380 mg	16%	
Total Carbohydrate	5 g	2%	
Dietary Fiber	1 g	4%	
Sugars	2 g		
Protein	8 g		
Vitamin A	15%	Vitamin C	10%
Calcium	20%	Iron	4%

Dietary Exchanges: 1 Vegetable, 1 High-Fat Meat, 2 Fat

TIPS FOR SERVING APPETIZERS

- Determine what you'll need for serving dishes and utensils and arrange them on the table the night before the party.
- Serve foods on several small platters (refilling when necessary) rather than one large platter, which looks desolate and picked over when food is partially gone.
- Place some dishes on sturdy pedestals to provide interesting height variations.
- Hot hors d'oeuvres are best while still warm. Arrange platters of cold appetizers on a serving table, but circulate warm appetizers among the guests.

Cook's Notes

DILLY DIP

prep time: 10 min. (ready in 2 hr. 10 min.) • yield: 2 cups

This classic party dip gets its incomparable richness from a blend of sour cream and real mayonnaise. If you prefer a lighter mixture, substitute reduced-fat or nonfat sour cream and mayonnaise.

1½ cups sour cream

⅔ cup mayonnaise

2 tablespoons instant minced onion

2 tablespoons dried parsley flakes

2 tablespoons dried dill weed

1 teaspoon celery salt or seasoned salt

4 drops green food color

1 In small bowl, combine all ingredients; mix well. Cover; refrigerate at least 2 hours to blend flavors.

2 Serve with cut-up fresh vegetables.

Nutrition Information Per Serving
Serving Size: 1 Tablespoon

Calories	60	Calories from Fat	50
		% Daily Value	
Total Fat	6 g	9%	
Saturated	2 g	10%	
Cholesterol	10 mg	3%	
Sodium	90 mg	4%	
Total Carbohydrate	1 g	1%	
Dietary Fiber	0 g	0%	
Sugars	1 g		
Protein	0 g		
Vitamin A	2%	Vitamin C	0%
Calcium	0%	Iron	0%

Dietary Exchanges: 1½ Fat

CRESCENT-WRAPPED GOUDA

prep time: 10 min. (ready in 45 min.) • yield: 8 servings

This party appetizer is deceptively simple to make and definitely sensational to serve. Add color to the serving platter by surrounding the crescent-wrapped cheese with ripe olives, parsley sprigs or strips of red, yellow and green bell peppers.

1 (7-oz.) round natural Gouda cheese

1 (8-oz.) can refrigerated crescent dinner rolls

1 egg, beaten

1 Heat oven to 350° F. Cut cheese round in half horizontally to form 2 rounds; remove wax.

2 Separate dough into 4 rectangles; firmly press perforations to seal. Place 2 rectangles, 3 inches apart, on ungreased cookie sheet. Place 1 cheese round on center of each rectangle. Place 1 remaining rectangle on top of each cheese round. Press dough around cheese; fold bottom edges over top edges. Gently stretch dough to form a rim around cheese; press to seal completely. Brush with beaten egg.

3 Bake at 350° F. for 18 to 22 minutes or until golden brown. Cool 10 minutes before serving.

Nutrition Information Per Serving
Serving Size: ⅛ of Recipe

Calories	200	Calories from Fat	120
		% Daily Value	
Total Fat	13 g	20%	
Saturated	6 g	30%	
Cholesterol	55 mg	18%	
Sodium	430 mg	18%	
Total Carbohydrate	12 g	4%	
Dietary Fiber	0 g	0%	
Sugars	2 g		
Protein	9 g		
Vitamin A	4%	Vitamin C	0%
Calcium	20%	Iron	4%

Dietary Exchanges: 1 Starch, 1 High-Fat Meat, ½ Fat OR 1 Carbohydrate, 1 High-Fat Meat, ½ Fat

APPLE CHEESE BALL

prep time: 15 min. (ready in 2 hr. 15 min.) • yield: 1 ¾ cups

Plain "water biscuit" crackers best show off the spiced, faintly sweet flavor of the cheese mixture. For easier spreading, let the cheese ball stand at room temperature for 15 to 30 minutes prior to serving.

1 (8-oz.) pkg. cream cheese, softened

4 oz. (1 cup) shredded Cheddar cheese

¼ teaspoon cinnamon

¾ cup finely chopped dried apples

⅓ cup finely chopped nuts

1 bay leaf

1 cinnamon stick, halved

1 In large bowl, combine cream cheese, Cheddar cheese and cinnamon; beat until well blended. Stir in apples.

2 Shape mixture into ball; roll in nuts. Insert bay leaf and cinnamon stick on top of ball to resemble stem and leaf of apple. Refrigerate 2 hours or until firm. Serve with crackers. Store in refrigerator up to 2 weeks.

Nutrition Information Per Serving
Serving Size: 1 Tablespoon

Calories	60	Calories from Fat	45
		% Daily Value	
Total Fat	5 g	8%	
Saturated	3 g	15%	
Cholesterol	15 mg	5%	
Sodium	50 mg	2%	
Total Carbohydrate	2 g	1%	
Dietary Fiber	0 g	0%	
Sugars	1 g		
Protein	2 g		
Vitamin A	4%	Vitamin C	0%
Calcium	4%	Iron	0%

Dietary Exchanges: 1 Fat

BAKED BRIE AND BRANDIED MUSHROOMS

prep time: 20 min. • yield: 16 servings

Garlic and brandy flavor a blend of meaty mushrooms and crisp almonds, a nice counterpoint to the richly melting cheese below.

1 tablespoon margarine or butter

2 tablespoons slivered almonds

1 cup chopped fresh mushrooms

2 garlic cloves, minced

1 tablespoon brandy

1 teaspoon chopped fresh tarragon or
    ¼ teaspoon dried tarragon leaves

⅛ teaspoon pepper

1 (8-oz.) round Brie cheese

2 sprigs fresh tarragon, if desired

Baked Brie and Brandied Mushrooms

1 Heat oven to 375° F. Melt margarine in medium skillet over medium heat. Add almonds; cook and stir 2 to 3 minutes or until almonds are browned. Stir in mushrooms, garlic, brandy, tarragon and pepper. Cook and stir 1 to 2 minutes or until mushrooms are tender. Remove from heat.

2 Place cheese in ungreased decorative shallow baking dish or 8- or 9-inch pie pan; spoon mushrooms over top.

3 Bake at 375° F. for 10 to 12 minutes or until cheese is soft. Garnish with tarragon sprigs. Serve as a dip or spread with melba toast rounds or crackers.

Nutrition Information Per Serving
Serving Size: 1/16 of Recipe

Calories	60	Calories from Fat	45
		% Daily Value	
Total Fat	5 g	8%	
Saturated	3 g	15%	
Cholesterol	15 mg	5%	
Sodium	100 mg	4%	
Total Carbohydrate	1 g	1%	
Dietary Fiber	0 g	0%	
Sugars	0 g		
Protein	3 g		
Vitamin A	2%	Vitamin C	0%
Calcium	4%	Iron	0%

Dietary Exchanges: 1/2 High-Fat Meat

Cook's Notes

ALL ABOUT ALMONDS

It may seem strange to learn that an almond is a first cousin to the peach, unless you've split a woody peach pit open and seen the seed kernel inside—it indeed resembles an almond nutmeat. Almonds are native to West Asia and are widely cultivated in the Mediterranean and California.

Unshelled almonds can be stored in a cool place for up to six months. Store shelled almonds in the refrigerator for up to three months or in the freezer for up to six months.

EASY PESTO PINWHEELS

prep time: 30 min. • yield: 16 appetizers

Made with three purchased ingredients, these showy spirals are so easy that you might actually be embarrassed if anyone asks for the recipe! They're equally good as a party appetizer or as a bread accompaniment for a meal.

1 (8-oz.) can refrigerated crescent dinner rolls

1/3 cup purchased pesto

1/4 cup chopped roasted red bell peppers (from 7.25-oz. jar)

1 Heat oven to 350° F. Unroll dough into 2 long rectangles. Firmly press perforations to seal. Spread rectangles with pesto to within 1/4 inch of edges. Sprinkle with roasted peppers.

2 Starting at shortest side, roll up each rectangle; pinch edges to seal. Cut each roll into 8 slices. Place, cut side down, on ungreased cookie sheet.

3 Bake at 350° F. for 13 to 17 minutes or until golden brown. Immediately remove from cookie sheet. Serve warm.

Nutrition Information Per Serving
Serving Size: 1 Appetizer

Calories	60	Calories from Fat	35
		% Daily Value	
Total Fat	4 g	6%	
Saturated	1 g	5%	
Cholesterol	0 mg	0%	
Sodium	125 mg	5%	
Total Carbohydrate	6 g	2%	
Dietary Fiber	0 g	0%	
Sugars	1 g		
Protein	1 g		
Vitamin A	0%	Vitamin C	4%
Calcium	0%	Iron	0%

Dietary Exchanges: 1/2 Starch, 1/2 Fat OR 1/2 Carbohydrate, 1/2 Fat

CROSTINI WITH BEEF AND CAPER MAYONNAISE

prep time: 30 min. • yield: 24 appetizers

For even more pungent crostini, add a clove of chopped garlic to the olive oil and heat the mixture in the microwave for about 20 seconds before brushing it onto the bread.

24 slices baguette or small French bread (¼ to ½ inch thick)

2 tablespoons olive oil

½ cup mayonnaise

¼ cup grated Parmesan cheese

2 tablespoons chopped fresh chives

2 to 4 tablespoons drained capers

¼ teaspoon garlic powder

½ lb. thinly sliced cooked roast beef (from deli), cut into 24 pieces

2 Italian plum tomatoes, cut into 24 thin slices

Chopped fresh chives, if desired

1 Heat oven to 350°F. Place bread slices on ungreased cookie sheet; brush lightly with oil. Bake at 350°F. for 8 to 10 minutes or until crisp. Cool 5 minutes or until completely cooled.

2 Meanwhile, in small bowl, combine mayonnaise, cheese, 2 tablespoons chives, capers and garlic powder; mix well. Spread mayonnaise mixture on bread slices; top with roast beef and tomato slice. Garnish with chives.

Nutrition Information Per Serving
Serving Size: 1 Appetizer

Calories	90	Calories from Fat	50
		% Daily Value	
Total Fat	6 g	9%	
Saturated	1 g	5%	
Cholesterol	10 mg	3%	
Sodium	230 mg	10%	
Total Carbohydrate	6 g	2%	
Dietary Fiber	0 g	0%	
Sugars	1 g		
Protein	3 g		
Vitamin A	0%	Vitamin C	0%
Calcium	2%	Iron	2%

Dietary Exchanges: ½ Starch, 1 Fat OR ½ Carbohydrate, 1 Fat

CAPERS

Capers are the flower buds of bushes grown in the Mediterranean and parts of Asia. The buds range in size from very small (considered the best) to as large as the tip of your little finger. Capers are picked and sun-dried, then pickled in a vinegar brine. They are sold in small glass jars and can be found in the condiment or pickle section of supermarkets. Capers add a bright, briny burst of flavor to recipes. Stir capers in just before serving so they don't lose their punch. If you wish, rinse them before using to remove excess salt.

Quick Chocolate-Banana Muffins, page 33
and Fruity Orange Refrigerator Muffins, page 32

EASY VEGETABLE PIZZA

prep time: 20 min. (ready in 2 hr. 10 min.) •
yield: 60 appetizers

Baked, cooled crescent roll dough makes a convenient crust for this cross between a pizza and conventional crudité-and-dip tray.

2 (8-oz.) cans refrigerated crescent dinner rolls

1 (8-oz.) pkg. cream cheese, softened

½ cup sour cream

1 teaspoon dried dill weed

⅛ teaspoon garlic powder

20 small fresh broccoli florets

20 cucumber or zucchini slices

10 cherry tomatoes, halved

2 tablespoons tiny fresh parsley sprigs, if desired

1 Heat oven to 375°F. Unroll dough into 4 long rectangles. Place crosswise in ungreased 15 × 10 × 1-inch baking pan; press over bottom and 1 inch up sides to form crust. Firmly press perforations to seal.

2 Bake at 375°F. for 13 to 17 minutes or until golden brown. Cool 30 minutes or until completely cooled.

3 In small bowl, combine cream cheese, sour cream, dill and garlic powder; blend until smooth. Spread evenly over cooled crust. Cover; refrigerate 1 to 2 hours.

4 To serve, cut into 1-inch squares. Garnish each square as desired with broccoli, cucumber, tomatoes and parsley.

Nutrition Information Per Serving
Serving Size: 1 Appetizer

Calories	45	Calories from Fat	25
		% Daily Value	
Total Fat	3 g	5%	
Saturated	1 g	5%	
Cholesterol	5 mg	2%	
Sodium	70 mg	3%	
Total Carbohydrate	3 g	1%	
Dietary Fiber	0 g	0%	
Sugars	1 g		
Protein	1 g		
Vitamin A	4%	Vitamin C	4%
Calcium	0%	Iron	0%

Dietary Exchanges: ½ Vegetable, ½ Fat

VEGETABLE VARIETY

In addition to the vegetables specified in the Easy Vegetable Pizza recipe, let your imagination and seasonal availability determine other choices. Some ideas:

- Blanched chopped green beans, roasted red pepper strips and ripe olives
- Chopped tomatoes, cooked fresh corn kernels and diced red onion
- Chopped fresh spinach, sliced mushrooms and diced bell peppers
- Small cauliflower florets, carrot slices and chopped green onions

Cook's Notes

ROASTED CHICKEN NACHOS

prep time: 25 min. • yield: 8 servings

Beans, salsa with chunks of chicken, plus tortilla chips turn a favorite snack into a heartier first course. If you're a fan of hot and spicy foods, spice up the salsa with a few drops of hot pepper sauce.

8 oz. tortilla chips

¾ cup chunky style salsa

1 (15-oz.) can black beans, drained, rinsed

3 frozen charbroiled mesquite chicken breast patties, thawed, chopped

1 tomato, chopped

8 oz. (2 cups) finely shredded Mexican natural cheese blend

1 Heat oven to 400°F. Line 15×10×1-inch baking pan with foil. Spread half of tortilla chips evenly in foil-lined pan.

2 In medium bowl, combine salsa and beans; mix well. Spoon half of bean mixture over chips. Top with half each of chicken, tomato and cheese. Repeat layers.

3 Bake at 400°F. for 12 to 14 minutes or until cheese is melted. Serve immediately.

Nutrition Information Per Serving
Serving Size: ⅛ of Recipe

Calories	360	Calories from Fat	170
		% Daily Value	
Total Fat	19g	29%	
Saturated	8g	40%	
Cholesterol	40mg	13%	
Sodium	780mg	33%	
Total Carbohydrate	29g	10%	
Dietary Fiber	4g	16%	
Sugars	2g		
Protein	18g		
Vitamin A	10%	Vitamin C	4%
Calcium	25%	Iron	8%

Dietary Exchanges: 2 Starch, 1½ Medium-Fat Meat, 2 Fat OR
2 Carbohydrate, 1½ Medium-Fat Meat, 2 Fat

SHRIMP AND PINEAPPLE KABOBS

prep time: 25 min. • yield: 12 kabobs

To prepare a fresh pineapple, use a sharp knife to slice off the spiky green top. Cut the fruit in quarters from top to bottom, then trim away the hard core, and cut the fruit away from the skin.

2 medium green bell peppers, cut into 24 (1-inch) pieces

24 (1- to 1½-inch) chunks fresh pineapple

12 uncooked medium shrimp, shelled, deveined

½ cup purchased sweet-and-sour sauce

½ teaspoon dry mustard

2 teaspoons chopped fresh chives or 1 teaspoon freeze-dried chives

1 On each of twelve 4- to 6-inch wooden skewers, thread 1 pepper piece, 1 pineapple chunk, 1 shrimp, 1 pineapple chunk and 1 pepper piece. Place kabobs on broiler pan.

2 In small bowl, combine remaining ingredients; mix well. Brush kabobs with sweet-and-sour mixture.

3 Broil 4 to 6 inches from heat for 3 minutes. Turn kabobs; brush with remaining mixture. Broil an additional 2 to 4 minutes or until shrimp turn pink.

Nutrition Information Per Serving
Serving Size: 1 Kabob

Calories	40	Calories from Fat	0
		% Daily Value	
Total Fat	0g	0%	
Saturated	0g	0%	
Cholesterol	10mg	3%	
Sodium	75mg	3%	
Total Carbohydrate	9g	3%	
Dietary Fiber	1g	3%	
Sugars	6g		
Protein	1g		
Vitamin A	2%	Vitamin C	20%
Calcium	0%	Iron	2%

Dietary Exchanges: ½ Starch OR ½ Carbohydrate

Crab Roll-Ups

CRAB ROLL-UPS

prep time: 15 min. (ready in 30 min.) • yield: 36 appetizers

"Imitation" crabmeat, an economical and easy-to-use alternative to the real crustacean, is made of mild whitefish plus flavorings.

4 oz. cream cheese, softened

2 tablespoons mayonnaise or salad dressing

2 teaspoons prepared horseradish

½ avocado, pitted, peeled and chopped

6 (8-inch) flour tortillas

1 (8-oz.) pkg. flaked imitation crabmeat (surimi)

¾ cup chopped red bell pepper

⅓ cup sliced green onions

1 (2¼-oz.) can sliced ripe olives, drained

1 In food processor bowl with metal blade or blender container, combine cream cheese, mayonnaise, horseradish and avocado; process on high speed until well mixed.

2 Spread cream cheese mixture evenly over tortillas. Top each tortilla with crabmeat, bell pepper, onions and olives. Roll up each tortilla; wrap securely in plastic wrap. Refrigerate at least 15 minutes or overnight.

3 To serve, slice rolls diagonally into ¾-inch-thick slices.

Nutrition Information Per Serving
Serving Size: 1 Appetizer

Calories	60	Calories from Fat	25
		% Daily Value	
Total Fat	3 g	5%	
Saturated	1 g	5%	
Cholesterol	5 mg	2%	
Sodium	110 mg	5%	
Total Carbohydrate	5 g	2%	
Dietary Fiber	0 g	0%	
Sugars	1 g		
Protein	2 g		
Vitamin A	4%	Vitamin C	8%
Calcium	0%	Iron	2%

Dietary Exchanges: ½ Starch, ½ Fat OR ½ Carbohydrate, ½ Fat

SAUSAGE SNACK WRAPS

prep time: 10 min. (ready in 25 min.) • yield: 48 snacks

Here's a super easy rendition of "pigs in blankets," a longtime party favorite. Set out custard cups filled with different styles of mustard—grainy brown, mild yellow, horseradish-spiked—and let guests sample their favorites.

2 (8-oz.) cans refrigerated crescent dinner rolls

48 fully cooked cocktail smoked sausage links or hot dogs

1 Heat oven to 375°F. Separate dough into 8 triangles. Cut each triangle lengthwise into thirds. Place sausages on shortest side of each triangle. Roll up, starting at shortest side; roll to opposite point. Place on ungreased cookie sheets.

2 Bake at 375°F. for 12 to 15 minutes or until golden brown. If desired, serve warm with ketchup and mustard.

Nutrition Information Per Serving
Serving Size: 1 Snack

Calories	100	Calories from Fat	60
		% Daily Value	
Total Fat	7 g	11%	
Saturated	2 g	10%	
Cholesterol	10 mg	3%	
Sodium	310 mg	13%	
Total Carbohydrate	4 g	1%	
Dietary Fiber	0 g	0%	
Sugars	1 g		
Protein	4 g		
Vitamin A	0%	Vitamin C	0%
Calcium	0%	Iron	2%

Dietary Exchanges: ½ Starch, ½ High-Fat Meat, ½ Fat OR ½ Carbohydrate, ½ High-Fat Meat, ½ Fat

TEX-MEX DEVILED EGGS

prep time: 30 min. (ready in 1 hr. 30 min.) •

yield: 12 deviled eggs

Deviled eggs were a must at parties decades ago. This version brings the dish up to date by spicing the mayonnaise—egg yolk filling with fresh cilantro, a hot chile and chili powder.

6 eggs

1 tablespoon finely chopped green onions

1 tablespoon chopped fresh cilantro or parsley

1 small serrano or jalapeño chile, seeded, finely chopped

¼ cup mayonnaise or salad dressing

1 teaspoon prepared mustard

1 oz. (¼ cup) shredded Cheddar cheese

Chili powder

1 Place eggs in medium saucepan; cover with cold water. Bring to a boil. Reduce heat; simmer about 15 minutes.

2 Immediately drain; run cold water over eggs to stop cooking. Peel eggs. Cut tips off both ends of each egg to create a flat surface for eggs to stand on. Cut each egg in half crosswise.

3 Remove yolks; place in small bowl and mash. Add onions, cilantro, chile, mayonnaise and mustard; blend well.

4 Spoon about 1 tablespoon yolk mixture into each egg half. Top each with cheese. Sprinkle with chili powder. Cover; refrigerate at least 1 hour or until serving time.

Nutrition Information Per Serving
Serving Size: 1 Deviled Egg

Calories	80	Calories from Fat	60
		% Daily Value	
Total Fat	7 g	11%	
Saturated	2 g	10%	
Cholesterol	110 mg	37%	
Sodium	80 mg	3%	
Total Carbohydrate	1 g	1%	
Dietary Fiber	0 g	0%	
Sugars	1 g		
Protein	4 g		
Vitamin A	6%	Vitamin C	15%
Calcium	4%	Iron	2%

Dietary Exchanges: ½ Medium-Fat Meat, 1 Fat

HOT CHILES

Serrano chiles have a smooth skin, bright green color and very hot taste. They have slightly pointed tips and are smaller and slimmer than jalapeños.

Jalapeño chiles have smooth, medium-to-dark green skin that turns dark red when ripe. Jalapeños range from hot to very hot in taste. (Taste all chiles warily if you're a novice.) They have rounded tips and are about 2 to 2½ inches long and ¾ to 1 inch in diameter.

Jalapeño, serrano and other varieties of hot chiles contain the colorless irritant capsaicin, which gives them their hot bite. Direct contact with capsaicin can irritate skin and eyes. Wear rubber or plastic gloves (or slip a plastic bag over your hands) when handling hot peppers, and avoid touching your face or eyes. Scrub the knife and cutting board when you're finished. If peppers do come in contact with your skin or eyes, wash the area well with soap and water or flush your eyes with running water.

Cook's Notes

STUFFED REUBEN MUSHROOMS

prep time: 25 min. (ready in 50 min.) • yield: 16 appetizers

The leftover mushroom stems in this recipe can be added to soups or sautéed with onions to top a burger or mashed potatoes. Or, slice them for use in an omelet.

16 large fresh mushrooms

¼ lb. thinly sliced cooked corned beef

⅓ cup sauerkraut, drained

3 tablespoons purchased Thousand Island salad dressing

2 oz. (½ cup) finely shredded Swiss cheese

1 teaspoon chopped fresh or freeze-dried chives

1 Heat oven to 350°F. Brush mushrooms or wipe clean with damp cloth. Remove stems from mushrooms; discard or reserve stems for another use.

2 Fold and fit 1 slice of corned beef inside mushroom cap. Top with 1 teaspoon sauerkraut, ½ teaspoon salad dressing and about 1 teaspoon cheese. Place in ungreased 15 × 10 × 1-inch baking pan. Repeat with remaining mushrooms. Sprinkle with chives.

3 Bake at 350°F. for 20 to 25 minutes or until thoroughly heated.

Nutrition Information Per Serving
Serving Size: 1 Appetizer

Calories	45	Calories from Fat	25
		% Daily Value	
Total Fat	3 g	5%	
Saturated	1 g	5%	
Cholesterol	10 mg	3%	
Sodium	120 mg	5%	
Total Carbohydrate	1 g	1%	
Dietary Fiber	0 g	0%	
Sugars	1 g		
Protein	3 g		
Vitamin A	0%	Vitamin C	0%
Calcium	4%	Iron	2%

Dietary Exchanges: ½ High-Fat Meat

CURLED RIBBON STREAMERS

Decorate your tables with colorful curled ribbon streamers for a festive look that instantly says "party!" Long curled ribbon streamers can be draped over tables; shorter streamers can be placed between individual place settings or between serving dishes on a buffet table.

To make curled ribbon streamers, you'll need a sharp scissors and two or three different colors of curling ribbon that coordinate with your color scheme.

- Cut the curling ribbon into desired lengths. For long table streamers, use about 2 yards. For shorter streamers for end tables or balloon bouquets, try 1-yard lengths.
- Pull the ribbon across the sharp edge of the scissors to form curls, then arrange the streamers as desired, anchoring the ends with tape.

SPICED ORANGE CHICKEN DRUMMIES

prep time: 50 min. • yield: 24 appetizers

Apricot or peach preserves can substitute for the orange marmalade, if you prefer. The sauce also makes a fine glaze for a roasted whole chicken or turkey breast.

SAUCE
1 tablespoon grated orange peel

3 teaspoons dry mustard

1 teaspoon ginger

½ teaspoon salt

⅛ teaspoon ground red pepper (cayenne)

2 tablespoons red wine vinegar

1 medium onion, quartered

¾ cup orange marmalade

CHICKEN
24 chicken wings

1 GRILL DIRECTIONS: Heat grill. In food processor bowl with metal blade or blender container, combine all sauce ingredients. Process until smooth.

Spiced Orange
Chicken Drummies

2 To prepare 1 drummie, using scissors or sharp knife, cut through skin and cartilage connecting the 2 larger sections of 1 chicken wing. If desired, reserve the 2-part wing-tip section for stock or soup.

3 Using small knife, cut tendons to loosen and scrape cartilage loose from cut end of drummie. Holding drummie in 1 hand, push meat and skin to top of bone. Shape into a compact ball. Repeat with remaining chicken wings.

4 When ready to grill, oil grill rack. Place chicken on gas grill over low heat or on charcoal grill 4 to 6 inches from medium coals. Cook 15 to 30 minutes or until chicken is fork-tender and juices run clear, turning once and brushing chicken frequently with sauce. Bring any remaining sauce to a boil; serve with chicken.

TIP: To broil chicken, place on greased broiler pan; broil 4 to 6 inches from heat using times above as a guide, turning once and brushing frequently with sauce.

Nutrition Information Per Serving			
Serving Size: 1 Appetizer			
Calories	130	Calories from Fat	60
		% Daily Value	
Total Fat	7 g	11%	
Saturated	2 g	10%	
Cholesterol	30 mg	10%	
Sodium	80 mg	3%	
Total Carbohydrate	7 g	2%	
Dietary Fiber	0 g	0%	
Sugars	5 g		
Protein	9 g		
Vitamin A	0%	Vitamin C	0%
Calcium	0%	Iron	2%

Dietary Exchanges: ½ Fruit, 1 High-Fat Meat OR ½ Carbohydrate, 1 High-Fat Meat

HOW TO MAKE CHICKEN DRUMMIES

Chicken "drummies" don't come from a little, bitty breed of chicken, but from one section of a regular chicken wing. Try this easy two-step technique for a new take on chicken wings.

STEP 1

With a sharp knife or scissors, cut through the skin and cartilage connecting the two larger sections of a chicken wing. (The two-part wing-tip section can be frozen and used for soup meat or to make chicken stock.) Use a small knife to scrape the cartilage loose from the cut joint of the remaining section.

STEP 2

To form the drummies, hold the section in one hand and

push the meat and skin to the top of the bone, shaping them into a compact ball. Repeat with remaining wings.

CHINESE SPARE RIBLETS

prep time: 30 min. (ready in 3 hr. 30 min.) • yield: 6 servings

A sweet glaze flavored with five-spice powder makes these pork riblets irresistible.

⅓ cup soy sauce

⅓ cup plum jelly

2 tablespoons water

2 tablespoons dry sherry

2 garlic cloves, minced

1 teaspoon Chinese five-spice powder

2 lb. pork spareribs, cut into 1½-inch pieces

1 In small saucepan, combine all ingredients except spareribs. Cook over low heat, stirring until jelly is melted. Cool.

2 Trim any excess fat from spareribs; place spareribs in resealable plastic bag. Pour marinade into bag. Squeeze out air; seal. Refrigerate 2 to 3 hours to marinate, turning bag several times.

3 Heat oven to 450°F. Line shallow baking pan with foil. Remove spareribs from plastic bag; reserve marinade. Place spareribs, meaty side down, in foil-lined pan; cover. Bake at 450°F. for 30 minutes.

4 Reduce oven temperature to 350°F. Remove pan from oven. Uncover; drain liquid from spareribs. Turn meaty side up. Brush spareribs with reserved marinade. Bake uncovered at 350°F. for 30 minutes.

5 Drain liquid if necessary. Brush again with marinade. Bake an additional 10 to 15 minutes or until tender and no longer pink. Discard any remaining marinade.

Nutrition Information Per Serving
Serving Size: ⅙ of Recipe

Calories	290	Calories from Fat	160
		% Daily Value	
Total Fat	18 g	28%	
Saturated	7 g	35%	
Cholesterol	70 mg	23%	
Sodium	980 mg	41%	
Total Carbohydrate	14 g	5%	
Dietary Fiber	0 g	0%	
Sugars	9 g		
Protein	18 g		
Vitamin A	0%	Vitamin C	0%
Calcium	4%	Iron	10%

Dietary Exchanges: 1 Fruit, 2½ High-Fat Meat OR
1 Carbohydrate, 2½ High-Fat Meat

HOW MANY APPETIZERS DO YOU NEED?

When calculating how many appetizers you'll need for a party, consider:

- Time of day the party will occur—If the appetizers are in place of a meal, prepare enough to compensate (at least six to eight appetizer portions per person).
- Length of party—Increase the amount and variety of food as the time increases.
- Guests' food preferences—Are many people dieting? Any known allergies or special dietary restrictions?
- Occasion—If the guests are active, they'll probably eat more.
- Number of recipes you want to make—people eat more when there are more offerings.

Cook's Notes

SWEET-SOUR COCKTAIL MEATBALLS

prep time: 25 min. (ready in 50 min.) •
yield: 72 meatballs; 18 servings

PICTURED ON PAGE 2

If you wish, use ground turkey as a substitute for some of the ground beef or pork in this traditional crowd pleaser. Baking rather than panfrying the meatballs frees up the cook for other tasks.

1 (20-oz.) can pineapple chunks, drained, reserving liquid

¾ cup unseasoned dry bread crumbs

⅛ teaspoon garlic powder

1 egg, slightly beaten

1 lb. ground beef

½ lb. ground pork

1¼ cups sugar

2 tablespoons cornstarch

1 teaspoon chicken-flavor instant bouillon

1 cup liquid (remaining pineapple liquid plus water)*

½ cup ketchup

½ cup vinegar

1 garlic clove, minced

1 small green bell pepper, cut into ½-inch pieces

1 small tomato, cut into wedges, if desired

1 Heat oven to 375°F. Measure ⅓ cup reserved pineapple liquid; set remaining liquid and pineapple aside. In large bowl, combine ⅓ cup pineapple liquid, bread crumbs and garlic powder; blend well. Add egg and ground meats; mix well. Shape into 1-inch balls; place on ungreased 15 × 10 × 1-inch baking pan.

2 Bake at 375°F. for 20 to 25 minutes or until browned and thoroughly baked.

3 Meanwhile, in medium saucepan, combine sugar, cornstarch and bouillon; mix well. Add 1 cup liquid, ketchup, vinegar and garlic; cook and stir over medium-high heat until thickened and bubbly. Add pineapple chunks and bell pepper; cook until thoroughly heated.

4 With slotted spoon, transfer hot cooked meatballs to 2-quart casserole or serving dish. Spoon warm bell pepper mixture over meatballs; mix gently. Garnish with tomato wedges.

TIP: *A 6-oz. can pineapple juice plus water to make 1 cup can be substituted for pineapple liquid.

Nutrition Information Per Serving			
Serving Size: 4 Meatballs			
Calories	190	Calories from Fat	50
		% Daily Value	
Total Fat	6 g	9%	
Saturated	2 g	10%	
Cholesterol	35 mg	12%	
Sodium	200 mg	8%	
Total Carbohydrate	27 g	9%	
Dietary Fiber	1 g	2%	
Sugars	20 g		
Protein	8 g		
Vitamin A	2%	Vitamin C	8%
Calcium	2%	Iron	6%

Dietary Exchanges: ½ Starch, 1½ Fruit, 1 Medium-Fat Meat OR
2 Carbohydrate, 1 Medium-Fat Meat

Crostini with Beef and Caper Mayonnaise

BREADS

FRESH FROM THE OVEN, HOME-MADE BREAD IS A SIMPLE, HOMESPUN PLEASURE THAT'S DELIGHTFULLY EASY TO ACHIEVE, WHETHER YOU HAVE THE TIME TO PREPARE A YEAST BREAD FROM SCRATCH OR PREFER TO USE PURCHASED DOUGH AS A STARTING POINT. RECIPES IN THIS CHAPTER RANGE FROM SWEET CINNAMON ROLLS (PAGE 36) TO QUICK CHEESE BURST BISCUITS (PAGE 28) TO LOAVES SPECIALLY FORMULATED FOR BREAD MACHINES.

CRANBERRY AND ORANGE SCONES

prep time: 20 min. (ready in 45 min.) • yield: 8 scones

Here's a great way to showcase the tangy combo of cranberry and orange. In this case, dried cranberries and orange peel join forces in tender, sweet biscuits that also feature vanilla milk chips.

SCONES

1¾ cups all-purpose flour

¼ cup sugar

2 teaspoons baking powder

¼ teaspoon baking soda

¼ teaspoon salt

¼ cup butter

½ cup sweetened dried cranberries

Cranberry and
Orange Scones

½ cup vanilla milk chips

1 teaspoon grated orange peel

½ cup low-fat vanilla yogurt

⅓ cup buttermilk*

TOPPING
1 to 2 tablespoons buttermilk or milk

1 tablespoon sugar

½ teaspoon grated orange peel

1 Heat oven to 375°F. Grease cookie sheet. In large bowl, combine flour, ¼ cup sugar, baking powder, baking soda and salt; mix well.

2 With pastry blender or fork, cut in butter until mixture resembles coarse crumbs. Stir in cranberries, vanilla milk chips and 1 teaspoon orange peel. Add yogurt and ⅓ cup buttermilk; stir just until moistened.

3 Shape dough into ball; place on greased cookie sheet. Roll or pat dough into 8-inch round. Cut into 8 wedges; do not separate. Brush with 1 to 2 tablespoons buttermilk. In small bowl, combine 1 tablespoon sugar and ½ teaspoon orange peel. Sprinkle over dough.

4 Bake at 375°F. for 15 to 20 minutes or until edges begin to turn golden brown. Cool 5 minutes. Cut into wedges. Serve warm or cool.

TIP: *To substitute for buttermilk, use 1 teaspoon vinegar or lemon juice plus milk to make ⅓ cup.

High Altitude (Above 3,500 feet):
Increase flour to 2 cups. Bake as directed above.

Nutrition Information Per Serving
Serving Size: 1 Scone

Calories	290	Calories from Fat	90
		% Daily Value	
Total Fat	10 g	15%	
Saturated	6 g	30%	
Cholesterol	20 mg	7%	
Sodium	320 mg	13%	
Total Carbohydrate	46 g	15%	
Dietary Fiber	1 g	4%	
Sugars	23 g		
Protein	5 g		
Vitamin A	4%	Vitamin C	0%
Calcium	15%	Iron	8%

Dietary Exchanges: 2 Starch, 1 Fruit, 1½ Fat OR 3 Carbohydrate, 1½ Fat

CRANBERRIES

This naturally tart, crimson berry is a native North American fruit and a traditional item on holiday menus. Before the Pilgrims ventured to the New World, Native Americans put the versatile cranberry plant to good use as a deer-meat preserver, medicinal salve, colorful dye for rugs and blankets, even as a symbol of peace.

- At the market, choose berries that are brightly colored, plump and firm.
- Store fresh cranberries in the refrigerator if you plan to use them within a week or two. Freeze berries to prolong quality.
- Wash berries just before use. Place them in a colander and rinse under cold running water. Pick off any stems, and discard mushy or shriveled berries.
- Do not thaw frozen cranberries before stirring them into a recipe; doing so may turn the dough pink.
- In the past few years, another cranberry option has become available, too. Dried cranberries, available in most supermarkets as well as in specialty stores, look like red raisins but have a sharper, tangier edge to the flavor. Because cranberries' natural flavor verges on sour, the dried version is sold presweetened. They're a bit more expensive than raisins, but offer a slightly more sophisticated flavor; the two may be used interchangeably in most any recipe.

CHEESE BURST BISCUITS

prep time: 20 min. • yield: 10 biscuits

These biscuits offer a warm and cheesy alternative to crackers as a soup partner. During baking, a little bit of cheese may pop out of the cuts in the biscuit tops.

1 (12-oz.) can refrigerated flaky biscuits

2½ oz. American or Cheddar cheese, cut into ten ¾-inch cubes

1 tablespoon milk

1 teaspoon sesame, caraway or poppy seed

1 Heat oven to 400°F. Separate dough into 10 biscuits. Partially separate each biscuit into 2 layers; insert 1 cheese cube. Press edge to seal well. Place filled biscuits on ungreased cookie sheet.

2 Cut a deep "X" on top of each biscuit. Brush with milk; sprinkle with sesame seed.

3 Bake at 400°F. for 10 to 12 minutes or until golden brown. Serve warm.

Cheese Burst Biscuits

Calories	140	Calories from Fat	60
		% Daily Value	
Total Fat	7 g	11%	
Saturated	2 g	10%	
Cholesterol	5 mg	2%	
Sodium	460 mg	19%	
Total Carbohydrate	14 g	5%	
Dietary Fiber	1 g	2%	
Sugars	2 g		
Protein	4 g		
Vitamin A	0%	Vitamin C	0%
Calcium	6%	Iron	4%

Dietary Exchanges: 1 Starch, 1½ Fat OR 1 Carbohydrate, 1½ Fat

JALAPEÑO CORN BISCUITS

prep time: 20 min. • yield: 18 biscuits

For a less zesty version of this biscuit recipe, substitute regular Monterey Jack cheese, also known as California Jack or simply Jack.

1¼ cups all-purpose flour

¾ cup cornmeal

3 teaspoons baking powder

½ teaspoon salt

½ cup shortening

1 cup milk

4 oz. (1 cup) shredded Monterey Jack cheese with jalapeño chiles

1 Heat oven to 450°F. Grease 2 cookie sheets. In large bowl, combine flour, cornmeal, baking powder and salt; mix well.

2 With a pastry blender or fork, cut in shortening until mixture resembles coarse crumbs. Add milk and cheese; stir just until dry ingredients are moistened. Drop dough by generous tablespoonfuls onto greased cookie sheets.

3 Bake at 450°F. for 8 to 12 minutes or until light golden brown. Serve warm.

High Altitude (Above 3,500 feet): No change.

Calories	130	Calories from Fat	70
		% Daily Value	
Total Fat	8 g	12%	
Saturated	3 g	15%	
Cholesterol	5 mg	2%	
Sodium	180 mg	8%	
Total Carbohydrate	11 g	4%	
Dietary Fiber	1 g	2%	
Sugars	1 g		
Protein	3 g		
Vitamin A	2%	Vitamin C	0%
Calcium	10%	Iron	4%

Dietary Exchanges: 1 Starch, 1½ Fat OR 1 Carbohydrate, 1½ Fat

ALL-PURPOSE FLOUR

All-purpose flour is milled from the inner part of the wheat kernel and contains neither the germ (the sprouting part) nor the bran (the outer coating). Since 1940, enriching all-purpose flour with thiamin, riboflavin, niacin and iron has been encouraged by the U.S. Food and Drug Administration. All-purpose flour is available bleached or unbleached. Bleached flour has been whitened by a bleaching agent. Both are suitable for all kinds of baking.

Cook's Notes

HERB PULL-APART BREAD

prep time: 10 min. (ready in 30 min.) • yield: 8 servings

Refrigerated breadstick dough makes short work of preparing a savory bread that goes great with chili or stew.

1 (11-oz.) can refrigerated soft breadsticks

1 tablespoon margarine or butter, melted

¼ teaspoon dried basil leaves

¼ teaspoon dried thyme leaves

1 Heat oven to 350° F. Separate dough into 8 rounds; do not unroll. Place rounds on cookie sheet, slightly overlapping as shown in diagram.

2 In small bowl, combine margarine, basil and thyme. Brush margarine mixture over top of loaf. Bake at 350° F. for 15 to 20 minutes or until golden brown. Serve warm.

Nutrition Information Per Serving
Serving Size: ⅛ of Recipe

Calories	120	Calories from Fat	25
		% Daily Value	
Total Fat	3 g	5%	
Saturated	1 g	5%	
Cholesterol	0 mg	0%	
Sodium	300 mg	13%	
Total Carbohydrate	18 g	6%	
Dietary Fiber	1 g	2%	
Sugars	2 g		
Protein	3 g		
Vitamin A	0%	Vitamin C	0%
Calcium	0%	Iron	6%

Dietary Exchanges: 1 Starch, ½ Fat OR 1 Carbohydrate, ½ Fat

PULL-APART FLAVOR VARIATIONS

B asil and thyme is just one flavor combination for the soft breadstick dough. Other possibilities include:

- Garlic powder and black pepper
- Hot chili powder
- Oregano, salt and pepper
- Sage and marjoram
- Dill weed
- Minced fresh garlic and fresh parsley
- Cinnamon, nutmeg and sugar

RUM BUTTER BISCUIT PULL-APART

prep time: 20 min. (ready in 45 min.) • yield: 12 servings

Baked in a buttery rum-caramel mixture and accented with nuts and fragrant spices, these tender biscuit pieces are hard to resist!

¾ cup firmly packed brown sugar

¼ teaspoon cinnamon

¼ teaspoon nutmeg

⅛ teaspoon cloves

½ cup butter, melted

1 teaspoon rum extract

2 (7-oz.) cans refrigerated buttermilk biscuits

½ cup chopped nuts

1 Heat oven to 375° F. Grease 12-cup Bundt® or 10-inch tube pan. In small bowl, combine brown sugar, cinnamon, nutmeg, cloves, butter and rum extract; blend well.

2 Separate each can of biscuit dough into 10 biscuits. Cut each biscuit into quarters. Place half of biscuits in greased pan. Spoon ½ cup of the butter mixture over biscuits. Sprinkle with ¼ cup of the nuts. Repeat with remaining biscuits, butter mixture and nuts.

3 Bake at 375°F. for 20 to 25 minutes or until golden brown. Cool 3 minutes; invert onto serving plate. To serve, pull apart. Serve warm.

Nutrition Information Per Serving			
Serving Size: ¹⁄₁₂ of Recipe			
Calories	240	Calories from Fat	110
		% Daily Value	
Total Fat	12 g	18%	
Saturated	5 g	25%	
Cholesterol	20 mg	7%	
Sodium	400 mg	17%	
Total Carbohydrate	30 g	10%	
Dietary Fiber	1 g	3%	
Sugars	15 g		
Protein	3 g		
Vitamin A	6%	Vitamin C	0%
Calcium	2%	Iron	8%

Dietary Exchanges: 1 Starch, 1 Fruit, 2 Fat OR 2 Carbohydrate, 2 Fat

PINEAPPLE-ZUCCHINI BREAD

prep time: 20 min. (ready in 2 hr. 30 min.) •
yield: 1 (16-slice) loaf

Although zucchini is most often served as a vegetable, its mild flavor has made it a popular "secret" ingredient in many cakes and sweet breads; it adds moisture and texture. It's a good foil for the sweet spices and nuts in this fruity bread topped with a shimmering glaze.

BREAD
1 cup firmly packed brown sugar

½ cup margarine or butter, softened

1 cup shredded zucchini

1 (8-oz.) can crushed pineapple in unsweetened juice, undrained, reserving 1 tablespoon liquid

2 eggs, slightly beaten

2 cups all-purpose flour

1 teaspoon baking soda

1 teaspoon cinnamon

¼ teaspoon salt

¼ teaspoon allspice

½ cup chopped nuts

GLAZE
½ cup powdered sugar

1 tablespoon reserved pineapple liquid

1 teaspoon corn syrup

¼ teaspoon cinnamon

1 Heat oven to 350°F. Grease and flour bottom only of 9 × 5-inch loaf pan. In large bowl, combine brown sugar and margarine; beat until light and fluffy. Stir in zucchini, pineapple and eggs. Add flour, baking soda, 1 teaspoon cinnamon, salt and allspice to zucchini mixture; mix well. Fold in nuts. Spread evenly in greased and floured pan.

2 Bake at 350°F. for 60 to 70 minutes or until toothpick inserted in center comes out clean. Cool 10 minutes. Remove from pan.

3 In small bowl, combine all glaze ingredients; blend until smooth. Spoon over warm loaf. Cool on wire rack for 1 hour or until completely cooled. Wrap tightly; store in refrigerator for up to 1 week or in freezer for up to 2 months.

High Altitude (Above 3,500 feet):
Bake at 375°F. for 55 to 65 minutes.

Nutrition Information Per Serving			
Serving Size: 1 Slice			
Calories	220	Calories from Fat	80
		% Daily Value	
Total Fat	9 g	14%	
Saturated	1 g	5%	
Cholesterol	25 mg	8%	
Sodium	190 mg	8%	
Total Carbohydrate	32 g	11%	
Dietary Fiber	1 g	4%	
Sugars	19 g		
Protein	3 g		
Vitamin A	6%	Vitamin C	2%
Calcium	2%	Iron	8%

Dietary Exchanges: 1 Starch, 1 Fruit, 2 Fat OR 2 Carbohydrate, 2 Fat

FRUITY ORANGE REFRIGERATOR MUFFINS

prep time: 20 min. (ready in 3 hr. 40 min.) • yield: 30 muffins

PICTURED ON PAGE 24

Rich with texture from whole-bran cereal and dried fruit, this muffin batter is great to have on hand for baking a warm treat in the morning. Mix the batter in advance and bake just the amount needed.

1½ cups all-purpose flour

1 cup whole wheat flour

2 cups shreds of whole bran cereal

1½ cups sugar

1¼ teaspoons baking soda

1 teaspoon baking powder

½ teaspoon salt

¼ teaspoon allspice

1 tablespoon grated orange peel

2½ cups buttermilk*

½ cup oil

2 eggs, slightly beaten

1 (6-oz.) pkg. dried fruit bits

1 In large bowl, combine all-purpose flour, whole wheat flour, cereal, sugar, baking soda, baking powder, salt, allspice and orange peel; mix well. Add buttermilk, oil and eggs; blend well. Stir in fruit bits. Cover tightly; refrigerate at least 3 hours or up to 2 weeks.

2 When ready to bake, heat oven to 400°F. Grease desired number of muffin cups or line with paper baking cups. Stir batter; fill greased muffin cups ¾ full.

3 Bake at 400°F. for 18 to 20 minutes or until toothpick inserted in center comes out clean. Immediately remove from pan. Serve warm.

TIP: *To substitute for buttermilk, use 2 tablespoons plus 1½ teaspoons vinegar or lemon juice plus milk to make 2½ cups.

High Altitude (Above 3,500 feet): No change.

Nutrition Information Per Serving
Serving Size: 1 Muffin

Calories	150	Calories from Fat	35
		% Daily Value	
Total Fat	4 g	6%	
Saturated	1 g	5%	
Cholesterol	15 mg	5%	
Sodium	140 mg	6%	
Total Carbohydrate	25 g	8%	
Dietary Fiber	2 g	8%	
Sugars	14 g		
Protein	3 g		
Vitamin A	6%	Vitamin C	2%
Calcium	6%	Iron	6%

Dietary Exchanges: 1 Starch, ½ Fruit, 1 Fat OR 1½ Carbohydrate, 1 Fat

MUFFIN PANS

To date, muffin pans have not been manufactured with an absolutely standard size. The cup size of older muffin pans tends to be larger than more recently manufactured pans. Both old and new are likely to yield smaller muffins than the mega-sized treats found in many bakeries.

Smaller muffin pans and those with a dark metal finish will require less baking time. Fill the muffin cups ⅔ to ¾ full with batter. To check for doneness, insert a toothpick into the center of the muffin. If the toothpick comes out clean, the muffin is done.

Cook's Notes

QUICK CHOCOLATE-BANANA MUFFINS

prep time: 15 min. (ready in 40 min.) • yield: 14 muffins

PICTURED ON PAGE 24

Is it a muffin or a cupcake? You decide! To gild the lily, sprinkle the batter with sugar before baking.

2 oz. unsweetened chocolate

1 cup buttermilk*

⅓ cup oil

1 (14-oz.) pkg. banana quick bread mix

¼ cup unsweetened cocoa

1 (6-oz.) pkg. (1 cup) semi-sweet chocolate chips

2 eggs, slightly beaten

1 Heat oven to 400° F. Grease 14 muffin cups or line with paper baking cups.** In small saucepan over low heat, melt unsweetened chocolate, stirring constantly. Stir in 3 tablespoons of the buttermilk and 1 tablespoon of the oil; blend well.

2 In large bowl, combine bread mix and cocoa; mix well. Add remaining buttermilk, remaining oil, chocolate mixture, chocolate chips and eggs. Stir just until dry ingredients are moistened. Spoon batter into greased muffin cups.

3 Bake at 400° F. for 18 to 22 minutes or until tops spring back when lightly touched. Immediately remove from muffin cups. Serve warm or cool.

TIPS: *To substitute for buttermilk, use 1 tablespoon vinegar or lemon juice plus milk to make 1 cup.

**Muffins can be baked in 48 miniature muffin cups. Prepare as directed above. Bake at 375° F. for 10 to 14 minutes.

High Altitude (Above 3,500 feet): No change.

Nutrition Information Per Serving
Serving Size: 1 Muffin

Calories	270	Calories from Fat	120
		% Daily Value	
Total Fat	13 g	20%	
Saturated	5 g	25%	
Cholesterol	30 mg	10%	
Sodium	190 mg	8%	
Total Carbohydrate	33 g	11%	
Dietary Fiber	2 g	8%	
Sugars	19 g		
Protein	4 g		
Vitamin A	0%	Vitamin C	0%
Calcium	4%	Iron	8%

Dietary Exchanges: 1 ½ Starch, ½ Fruit, 2 ½ Fat OR 2 Carbohydrate, 2 ½ Fat

FREEZING MUFFINS, BREADS AND BISCUITS

Many of these foods lose quality when refrigerated but actually freeze well. Bake as directed and cool completely, then freeze in an airtight container or wrapper. Before serving, allow them to thaw at room temperature, slightly unwrapped, for 2 to 3 hours. Serve warm or at room temperature. To reheat, wrap them in foil and heat at 350° F. for 10 to 15 minutes or until warmed through. Or, wrap in paper towels and microwave briefly.

Cook's Notes

ALMOND FRUIT CRESCENT COFFEE CAKE

prep time: 20 min. (ready in 50 min.) • **yield: 16 servings**

Refrigerated crescent rolls "doctored" with a rich almond filling become an impressive coffee cake to include in your holiday entertaining.

COFFEE CAKE
⅔ cup ground almonds

¼ cup sugar

2 tablespoons all-purpose flour

2 tablespoons margarine or butter, softened

2 teaspoons grated lemon peel

¾ teaspoon almond extract

⅓ cup mixed candied fruit

2 (8-oz.) cans refrigerated crescent dinner rolls

GLAZE
½ cup powdered sugar

¼ teaspoon almond extract

2 to 3 teaspoons milk

GARNISH
2 tablespoons sliced almonds

1 Heat oven to 375°F. In medium bowl, combine ground almonds, sugar, flour, margarine, lemon peel and ¾ teaspoon almond extract; blend well. Stir in candied fruit.

Almond Fruit Crescent Coffee Cake

2 Unroll dough; separate into 16 triangles. Sprinkle about 1 tablespoon almond mixture on each triangle. Starting with shortest side of triangle, roll loosely to opposite point. Place 9 rolls, point side down, in spoke fashion in ungreased 9-inch pie pan. Place remaining 7 rolls, point side down, around edge of pan.

3 Bake at 375°F. for 20 to 30 minutes or until deep golden brown and center is no longer doughy. Remove from oven; let stand 5 minutes. Remove from pan.

4 In small bowl, blend all glaze ingredients, adding enough milk for desired drizzling consistency. Drizzle over warm coffee cake. Garnish with sliced almonds. Serve warm.

Nutrition Information Per Serving
Serving Size: 1/16 of Recipe

Calories	190	Calories from Fat	90
		% Daily Value	
Total Fat	10 g	15%	
Saturated	2 g	10%	
Cholesterol	0 mg	0%	
Sodium	240 mg	10%	
Total Carbohydrate	22 g	7%	
Dietary Fiber	1 g	4%	
Sugars	11 g		
Protein	3 g		
Vitamin A	0%	Vitamin C	0%
Calcium	2%	Iron	4%

Dietary Exchanges: 1 Starch, 1/2 Fruit, 2 Fat OR 1 1/2 Carbohydrate, 2 Fat

PETITE CARAMEL PECAN ROLLS

prep time: 15 min. (ready in 45 min.) • yield: 16 rolls

Here's a shortcut for "sticky buns" made with refrigerated rolls.

1/4 cup firmly packed brown sugar

1/4 cup margarine or butter, softened

2 tablespoons light corn syrup

1 (8-oz.) can refrigerated crescent dinner rolls

2 tablespoons sugar

1/2 teaspoon cinnamon

1/4 cup finely chopped pecans

1 Heat oven to 375°F. In small bowl, combine brown sugar, margarine and corn syrup; blend well. Spread in bottom of ungreased 8- or 9-inch round cake pan.

2 Separate dough into 4 rectangles; firmly press perforations to seal. In small bowl, combine sugar and cinnamon; sprinkle mixture evenly over rectangles. Sprinkle 1 tablespoon of the pecans on each rectangle.

3 Starting at shorter side, roll up each rectangle; pinch edges to seal. Cut each roll into 4 slices. Place, cut side down, over brown sugar mixture in pan.

4 Bake at 375°F. for 20 to 27 minutes or until golden brown. Cool in pan 1 minute; invert onto serving platter or foil. Serve warm or cool.

Nutrition Information Per Serving
Serving Size: 1 Roll

Calories	120	Calories from Fat	60
		% Daily Value	
Total Fat	7 g	11%	
Saturated	1 g	5%	
Cholesterol	0 mg	0%	
Sodium	150 mg	6%	
Total Carbohydrate	13 g	4%	
Dietary Fiber	0 g	0%	
Sugars	7 g		
Protein	1 g		
Vitamin A	2%	Vitamin C	0%
Calcium	0%	Iron	2%

Dietary Exchanges: 1/2 Starch, 1/2 Fruit, 1 Fat OR 1 Carbohydrate, 1 Fat

SOFTENING BROWN SUGAR

To soften brown sugar that's hardened, place it in a baking pan in a 350°F. oven for 5 minutes, or on a microwave-safe plate in a microwave oven on LOW for 2 minutes. The sugar will soften, but must be used immediately or it will quickly harden again. To prevent rehardening, place brown sugar in an airtight container along with a slice of fresh bread.

HOW TO MAKE CINNAMON ROLLS

There's no deep, dark secret to making fresh-from-the-oven cinnamon rolls. Just follow the instructions in the recipe and the yeast will come alive. Two easy steps come next—rolling and cutting the dough.

STEP 1

On a lightly floured surface, use a rolling pin or your fingers to roll or pat the dough into a 20 × 16-inch rectangle. Spread the dough with softened margarine and sprinkle it evenly with the cinnamon-sugar mixture. Starting with the 16-inch side, roll the dough rectangle up tightly. Press the long edge firmly into the dough to seal the seam.

STEP 2

Mark the roll every inch, using a ruler as a guide. To cut the dough into slices, use a sharp knife, or place a 12-inch piece of heavy-duty thread or dental floss under the roll where you want to make the cut. Then pull the thread ends up so they criss-cross at the top. Pull the thread ends quickly to cut through the dough. Place the rolls, cut side down, in a greased pan. Let rise, bake and frost the rolls as directed in the recipe.

CINNAMON ROLLS

prep time: 45 min. (ready in 3 hr.) • yield: 16 rolls

Set aside a leisurely weekend morning to prepare these delicious cinnamon-scented rolls for brunch.

ROLLS
6 to 7 cups all-purpose flour

½ cup sugar

2 teaspoons salt

2 pkg. active dry yeast

1 cup water

1 cup milk

½ cup margarine or butter

1 egg

FILLING AND GLAZE
¼ cup margarine or butter, softened

½ cup sugar or firmly packed brown sugar

2 teaspoons cinnamon

¾ cup powdered sugar

1 tablespoon margarine or butter, softened

¼ teaspoon vanilla

1 to 2 tablespoons milk

1 In large bowl, combine 2 cups flour, ½ cup sugar, salt and yeast; mix well. In small saucepan, heat water, 1 cup milk and ½ cup margarine until very warm (120 to 130°F.). Add warm liquid and egg to flour mixture; blend at low speed until moistened. Beat 3 minutes at medium speed.

2 By hand, stir in an additional 3 cups flour until dough pulls cleanly away from sides of bowl.

3 On floured surface, knead in remaining 1 to 2 cups flour until dough is smooth and elastic, 5 to 10 minutes.

4 Place dough in greased bowl; cover loosely with plastic wrap and cloth towel. Let rise in warm place (80 to 85°F.) until light and doubled in size, 45 to 60 minutes.

5 Generously grease 13 × 9-inch pan. Punch down dough several times to remove all air bubbles. On lightly floured surface, roll out dough to 20 × 16-inch rectangle. Spread with ¼ cup margarine. In small bowl, combine ½ cup sugar and cinnamon; blend well. Sprinkle over dough.

6 Starting with 16-inch side, roll up tightly, pressing edges to seal. Cut into 16 slices. Arrange slices, cut side down, in greased pan. Cover; let rise in warm place until light and doubled in size, 35 to 45 minutes.

7 Heat oven to 375°F. Uncover dough. Bake 25 to 30 minutes or until golden brown. Immediately remove from pan; place on wire rack. Cool 5 minutes.

8 In small bowl, combine powdered sugar, 1 tablespoon margarine, vanilla and enough milk for desired drizzling consistency; blend until smooth. Drizzle over warm rolls. Serve warm.

TIP: For Whole Wheat Cinnamon Rolls, substitute whole wheat flour for half of the all-purpose flour.

High Altitude (Above 3,500 feet): No change.

Nutrition Information Per Serving
Serving Size: 1 Roll

Calories	360	Calories from Fat	90
		% Daily Value	
Total Fat	10 g	15%	
Saturated	2 g	10%	
Cholesterol	15 mg	5%	
Sodium	390 mg	16%	
Total Carbohydrate	61 g	20%	
Dietary Fiber	2 g	8%	
Sugars	20 g		
Protein	7 g		
Vitamin A	10%	Vitamin C	0%
Calcium	4%	Iron	15%

Dietary Exchanges: 2 ½ Starch, 1 ½ Fruit, 1 ½ Fat OR
4 Carbohydrate, 1 ½ Fat

Whole Wheat Cinnamon Rolls

HONEY ALMOND TWIST

prep time: 45 min. (ready in 2 hr. 30 min.) •
yield: 3 (16-slice) loaves

Go ahead and pour another cup of coffee. These stunning pretzel-shaped loaves, topped with an almond-honey glaze, have a cinnamon filling that is great for a coffee break. The loaves freeze beautifully, too.

BREAD
6 to 7 cups all-purpose flour

1/2 cup sugar

2 teaspoons salt

2 pkg. active dry yeast

1 cup water

1 cup milk

1/2 cup margarine or butter

1 egg

FILLING
1/3 cup sugar

1 teaspoon cinnamon

3 tablespoons margarine or butter, softened

GLAZE
1/4 cup sugar

1/4 cup honey

2 tablespoons margarine or butter

1/2 cup slivered almonds

1 In large bowl, combine 2 cups flour, 1/2 cup sugar, salt and yeast; mix well. In small saucepan, heat water, milk and 1/2 cup margarine until very warm (120 to 130° F.). Add warm liquid and egg to flour mixture; blend at low speed until moistened. Beat 3 minutes at medium speed.

2 By hand, stir in an additional 3 cups flour until dough pulls away from sides of bowl.

3 On floured surface, knead in remaining 1 to 2 cups flour until dough is smooth and elastic, about 5 minutes.

4 Place dough in greased bowl; cover loosely with plastic wrap and cloth towel. Let rise in warm place (80 to 85°F.) until light and doubled in size, about 45 minutes.

5 Grease 2 cookie sheets. Punch down dough several times to remove all air bubbles. In small bowl, combine 1/3 cup sugar and cinnamon; set aside. Divide dough into 3 equal parts.

6 On lightly floured surface, roll each part into 25 × 6-inch rectangle. Spread each with 1 tablespoon margarine. Sprinkle with sugar-cinnamon mixture. Starting with longer side, roll up tightly; pinch edges to seal. Twist each roll, stretching slightly. Form into pretzel shape; tuck ends under to seal. Place on greased cookie sheets. Cover; let rise in warm place until doubled in size, about 30 minutes.

7 Heat oven to 350° F. Uncover dough. Bake 20 to 30 minutes or until deep golden brown. Immediately remove from cookie sheets; place on wire racks.

8 In small saucepan, combine all glaze ingredients. Bring to a boil, stirring constantly. Spoon hot glaze over warm loaves, completely covering tops and sides.

High Altitude (Above 3,500 feet):
Decrease each rise time by 15 minutes. Bake as directed above.

Nutrition Information Per Serving
Serving Size: 1 Slice

Calories	130	Calories from Fat	35
		% Daily Value	
Total Fat	4 g	6%	
Saturated	1 g	5%	
Cholesterol	5 mg	2%	
Sodium	130 mg	5%	
Total Carbohydrate	21 g	7%	
Dietary Fiber	1 g	3%	
Sugars	7 g		
Protein	3 g		
Vitamin A	4%	Vitamin C	0%
Calcium	0%	Iron	6%

Dietary Exchanges: 1 Starch, 1/2 Fruit, 1/2 Fat OR 1 1/2 Carbohydrate, 1/2 Fat

DILLY CASSEROLE BREAD

prep time: 25 min. (ready in 2 hr. 50 min.) • yield: 1 (18-slice) loaf

Try this fragrant loaf and you'll see why the judges awarded its creator, Leona Schnuelle of Nebraska, the $25,000 Grand Prize in the 1960 Pillsbury Bake-Off® Contest. Cottage cheese and egg in the dough yield a loaf with a pale yellow interior and moist texture.

    2 to 2⅔ cups all-purpose flour

    2 tablespoons sugar

    2 to 3 teaspoons instant minced onion

    2 teaspoons dill seed

    1 teaspoon salt

    ¼ teaspoon baking soda

    1 pkg. active dry yeast

    ¼ cup water

    1 tablespoon margarine or butter

    1 cup creamed cottage cheese

    1 egg

    2 teaspoons margarine or butter, melted

    ¼ teaspoon coarse salt, if desired

1 In large bowl, combine 1 cup flour, sugar, onion, dill seed, 1 teaspoon salt, baking soda and yeast; mix well.

2 In small saucepan, heat water, 1 tablespoon margarine and cottage cheese until very warm (120 to 130°F.). Add warm liquid and egg to flour mixture; blend at low speed until moistened. Beat 3 minutes at medium speed.

3 By hand, stir in remaining 1 to 1⅔ cups flour to form a stiff batter. Cover loosely with greased plastic wrap and cloth towel. Let rise in warm place (80 to 85°F.) until light and doubled in size, 45 to 60 minutes.

4 Generously grease 1½- or 2-quart casserole. Stir down batter to remove all air bubbles. Turn into greased casserole. Cover; let rise in warm place until light and doubled in size, 30 to 45 minutes.

5 Heat oven to 350°F. Uncover dough. Bake 30 to 40 minutes or until deep golden brown and loaf sounds hollow when lightly tapped. Immediately remove from casserole; place on wire rack. Brush warm loaf with melted margarine; sprinkle with coarse salt.

FOOD PROCESSOR DIRECTIONS: 1 In small bowl, dissolve yeast in ¼ cup *warm* water (105 to 115°F.). In food processor bowl with metal blade, combine 2 cups flour, sugar, onion, dill seed, 1 teaspoon salt, baking soda and 1 tablespoon margarine; cover and process 5 seconds. Add cottage cheese and egg; process about 10 seconds or until blended.

2 With machine running, pour yeast mixture through feed tube. Continue processing until blended, about 20 seconds or until mixture pulls away from sides of bowl and forms a ball, adding additional flour if necessary. Carefully scrape dough from blade and bowl; place in greased large bowl. Cover; let rise. Continue as directed above.

High Altitude (Above 3,500 feet):
Bake at 375°F. for 35 to 40 minutes.

Nutrition Information Per Serving
Serving Size: 1 Slice

Calories	100	Calories from Fat	20
		% Daily Value	
Total Fat	2 g	3%	
Saturated	1 g	5%	
Cholesterol	15 mg	5%	
Sodium	230 mg	10%	
Total Carbohydrate	16 g	5%	
Dietary Fiber	1 g	3%	
Sugars	2 g		
Protein	4 g		
Vitamin A	0%	Vitamin C	0%
Calcium	0%	Iron	6%

Dietary Exchanges: 1 Starch, ½ Fat OR 1 Carbohydrate, ½ Fat

HERBED OATMEAL PAN BREAD

prep time: 30 min. (ready in 1 hr. 45 min.) • **yield: 16 servings**

Cutting through the dough before baking makes this bread easy to separate into individual portions.

BREAD
2 cups water

1 cup rolled oats

3 tablespoons butter

3¾ to 4¾ cups all-purpose flour

¼ cup sugar

2 teaspoons salt

2 pkg. active dry yeast

1 egg

HERB BUTTER
1 tablespoon grated Parmesan cheese

½ teaspoon dried basil leaves

¼ teaspoon dried oregano leaves

¼ teaspoon garlic powder

6 tablespoons butter, melted

1 Bring water to a boil in medium saucepan; stir in rolled oats. Remove from heat; stir in 3 tablespoons butter. Cool to 120 to 130°F.

2 In large bowl, combine 1½ cups flour, sugar, salt and yeast; mix well. Add rolled oats mixture and egg; blend at low speed until moistened. Beat 3 minutes at medium speed.

3 By hand, stir in an additional 1¾ cups to 2½ cups flour to form stiff dough. On floured surface, knead in ½ to ¾ cup flour until dough is smooth and elastic, about 5 minutes. Shape dough into ball; cover with large bowl. Let rest 15 minutes.

4 Grease 13 × 9-inch pan.* Punch down dough several times to remove all air bubbles. Press into greased pan. Using very sharp knife, cut diagonal lines 1½ inches apart, cutting completely through dough. Repeat in opposite direction creating diamond pattern. Cover loosely with greased plastic wrap and cloth towel.** Let rise in warm place (80 to 85°F.) until light and doubled in size, about 45 minutes.

5 Heat oven to 375°F. Uncover dough. Redefine cuts by poking tip of knife into cuts until knife hits bottom of pan; do not pull knife through dough. In small bowl, combine Parmesan cheese, basil, oregano and garlic powder; mix well. Set aside. Spoon 4 tablespoons of the butter over cut dough.

6 Bake at 375°F. for 15 minutes. Brush remaining 2 tablespoons butter over bread. Sprinkle with Parmesan cheese–herb mixture. Bake for an additional 10 to 15 minutes or until golden brown. Serve warm or cool.

TIPS: *Two 8- or 9-inch square pans or one 8-inch and one 9-inch square pan can be substituted for 13 × 9-inch pan. When using 2 square pans, one pan can be baked and the other refrigerated for baking the next day.

**To bake at a later time, at this point let stand at room temperature for 20 minutes. Remove cloth towel. Refrigerate 2 to 24 hours. Remove plastic wrap from dough; let stand at room temperature 30 minutes. Bake as directed above.

High Altitude (Above 3,500 feet): No change.

Nutrition Information Per Serving
Serving Size: 1/16 of Recipe

Calories	240	Calories from Fat	70
		% Daily Value	
Total Fat	8 g	12%	
Saturated	4 g	20%	
Cholesterol	30 mg	10%	
Sodium	350 mg	15%	
Total Carbohydrate	35 g	12%	
Dietary Fiber	2 g	8%	
Sugars	4 g		
Protein	6 g		
Vitamin A	6%	Vitamin C	0%
Calcium	0%	Iron	10%

Dietary Exchanges: 2 Starch, ½ Fruit, 1 Fat OR 2½ Carbohydrate, 1 Fat

RYE BREAD

prep time: 30 min. (ready in 2 hr. 45 min.) •
yield: 2 (22-slice) loaves

Because rye flour contains less gluten (protein) than all-purpose flour, it yields a loaf with a denser texture. For this bread, 1 to 2 tablespoons of caraway seed can be stirred into the dough, if you wish.

2 pkg. active dry yeast

1 cup warm water

1 cup warm milk

½ cup molasses

¼ cup shortening, melted

2 teaspoons salt

3 to 3½ cups all-purpose flour

3 cups medium rye flour

1 tablespoon water

1 egg yolk

1 In small bowl, dissolve yeast in 1 cup warm water (105 to 115° F.). In large bowl, combine warm milk (105 to 115° F.), molasses, shortening and salt; blend well. Stir in dissolved yeast. Add 2 cups all-purpose flour; blend at low speed until moistened. Beat 3 minutes at medium speed.

2 By hand, stir in 3 cups rye flour and an additional ¾ to 1 cup all-purpose flour until dough pulls cleanly away from sides of bowl.

3 On floured surface, knead in remaining ¼ to ½ cup all-purpose flour until dough is smooth and elastic, about 5 minutes.

4 Place dough in greased bowl; cover loosely with greased plastic wrap and cloth towel. Let rise in warm place (80 to 85° F.) until light and doubled in size, 45 to 60 minutes.

5 Grease 2 cookie sheets. Punch down dough several times to remove all air bubbles. Divide dough into 2 parts; shape into balls. Shape dough into two 12-inch oblong loaves; round ends. Place on greased cookie sheets.

6 With sharp knife, make four ¼-inch-deep diagonal slashes on top of each loaf. Cover; let rise in warm place until doubled in size, 20 to 30 minutes.

7 Heat oven to 350° F. Uncover dough. In small bowl, combine 1 tablespoon water and egg yolk; beat well. Brush over loaves. Bake at 350° F. for 35 to 45 minutes or until loaves sound hollow when lightly tapped. Immediately remove from cookie sheets; cool on wire racks.

High Altitude (Above 3,500 feet):
Decrease first rise time by 15 to 30 minutes; decrease second rise time by 10 minutes. Bake as directed above.

Nutrition Information Per Serving
Serving Size: 1 Slice

Calories	90	Calories from Fat	20
		% Daily Value	
Total Fat	2 g	3%	
Saturated	0 g	0%	
Cholesterol	5 mg	2%	
Sodium	100 mg	4%	
Total Carbohydrate	16 g	5%	
Dietary Fiber	1 g	4%	
Sugars	3 g		
Protein	2 g		
Vitamin A	0%	Vitamin C	0%
Calcium	0%	Iron	4%

Dietary Exchanges: ½ Starch, ½ Fruit, ½ Fat OR 1 Carbohydrate, ½ Fat

HEARTY HONEY GRANOLA BREAD

yield: 1 loaf

For an after-school snack, serve slices of this bread with honey. It also makes a fabulous choice for the classic peanut butter and jelly sandwich.

	SMALL LOAF (8 slices)	LARGE LOAF (12 slices)
Water	¾ cup + 2 tbls.	1¼ cups
Margarine or butter	1 tablespoon	2 tablespoons
Honey	1 tablespoon	1½ tablespoons
Bread flour	1½ cups	2¼ cups
Whole wheat flour	½ cup	¾ cup
Low-fat granola	¼ cup	⅓ cup
Instant nonfat dry milk	1 tablespoon	2 tablespoons
Salt	¾ teaspoon	1¼ teaspoons
Active dry yeast	1 teaspoon	2 teaspoons

1 If bread machine typically uses 2 cups flour, use small loaf recipe. If machine uses 3 cups flour, use large loaf recipe.

2 Follow manufacturer's directions for loading ingredients into machine. Measure ingredients carefully.

3 Select regular, rapid or delayed-time bake cycle and follow manufacturer's directions for starting machine.

High Altitude (Above 3,500 feet):
For small loaf, increase liquid by 1 to 2 tablespoons and decrease yeast by ¼ to ½ teaspoon. For large loaf, increase liquid by 1½ to 3 tablespoons and decrease yeast by ¼ to ¾ teaspoon. Continue as directed above.

Nutrition Information Per Serving			
Serving Size: 1 Slice from Large Loaf			
Calories	170	Calories from Fat	25
		% Daily Value	
Total Fat	3 g	5%	
Saturated	0 g	0%	
Cholesterol	0 mg	0%	
Sodium	260 mg	11%	
Total Carbohydrate	30 g	10%	
Dietary Fiber	2 g	8%	
Sugars	4 g		
Protein	5 g		
Vitamin A	2%	Vitamin C	0%
Calcium	2%	Iron	10%

Dietary Exchanges: 2 Starch, ½ Fat OR 2 Carbohydrate, ½ Fat

CARROT-ONION-DILL BREAD

yield: 1 loaf

Shredded carrots give this machine-baked bread a slight sweetness that's a good balance for the dill and the onion.

	SMALL LOAF (8 slices)	LARGE LOAF (12 slices)
Water	¾ cup	1¼ cups
Shredded carrots	⅓ cup	½ cup
Bread flour	2 cups	3 cups
Instant nonfat dry milk	1 tablespoon	2 tablespoons
Sugar	1 teaspoon	2 teaspoons
Salt	1 teaspoon	1¼ teaspoons
Margarine or butter	1 tablespoon	2 tablespoons
Dried dill weed	⅛ teaspoon	¼ teaspoon
Dried minced onion	1 tablespoon	1½ tablespoons
Active dry yeast	1¼ teaspoons	2 teaspoons

1 If bread machine typically uses 2 cups flour, use small loaf recipe. If machine uses 3 cups flour, use large loaf recipe.

2 Follow manufacturer's directions for loading ingredients into machine. Measure ingredients carefully.

3 Select regular, rapid or delayed-time bake cycle and follow manufacturer's directions for starting machine.

High Altitude (Above 3,500 feet):

For small loaf, increase liquid by 1 to 2 tablespoons and decrease yeast by ¼ to ½ teaspoon. For large loaf, increase liquid by 1 ½ to 3 tablespoons and decrease yeast by ¼ to ¾ teaspoon. Continue as directed above.

Nutrition Information Per Serving
Serving Size: 1 Slice from Large Loaf

Calories	160	Calories from Fat	25
		% Daily Value	
Total Fat	3 g	5%	
Saturated	0 g	0%	
Cholesterol	0 mg	0%	
Sodium	250 mg	10%	
Total Carbohydrate	27 g	9%	
Dietary Fiber	1 g	4%	
Sugars	2 g		
Protein	5 g		
Vitamin A	30%	Vitamin C	0%
Calcium	0%	Iron	10%

Dietary Exchanges: 2 Starch OR 2 Carbohydrate

BREAD MACHINE SUCCESS

When making homemade bread by hand, you can be somewhat flexible in your measuring. Bread machines are more particular. To turn out a good loaf, follow these tips:

- Measure *exactly*.
- Purchase yeast in a wide-mouthed jar for easiest measuring.
- Add ingredients in the order specified by the recipe.
- Bread flour works better than all-purpose flour in most cases because it is specially formulated to give the desired elasticity and structure needed to properly raise and bake bread.

Cook's Notes

Salmon Summer Fruit Salad, page 61

SALADS

THOUGH "SALAD" MOST OFTEN CONJURES UP IMAGES OF LEAFY GREENS, THE TERM IS TRULY MORE FAR-REACHING (JUST "LEAF" THROUGH THIS CHAPTER AND SEE). THERE'S A SALAD FOR ANY COURSE OF THE MEAL. AS A SIDE DISH, LITE LAYERED VEGETABLE SALAD (PAGE 74) OR CAULIFLOWER SALAD WITH ORANGE VINAIGRETTE (PAGE 70) EXCELS. FOR MAIN-COURSE SALADS, THERE'S GRILLED CHICKEN TACO SALAD (PAGE 46) OR MARINATED VERMICELLI SALAD (PAGE 62).

45

GRILLED CHICKEN TACO SALAD

prep time: 30 min. • yield: 4 servings

Flattening the chicken breast with a meat mallet or rolling pin (or even a 1-pound can) makes the meat a uniform thickness for grilling. Save fat and calories by choosing baked tortilla chips instead of deep-fried.

DRESSING
1/3 cup purchased reduced-calorie French salad dressing

1/3 cup chunky style salsa

1/4 cup sliced green onions

SALAD
4 boneless, skinless chicken breast halves

1/2 teaspoon chili powder

1/4 teaspoon garlic powder

4 cups shredded lettuce

2 medium tomatoes, chopped

4 oz. (1 cup) shredded reduced-fat Cheddar cheese

1/2 cup (1 oz.) tortilla chips

1/4 cup nonfat sour cream

1 GRILL DIRECTIONS: In small bowl, combine all dressing ingredients; blend well. Refrigerate until serving time.

2 Heat grill. To flatten each chicken breast half, place, boned side up, between 2 pieces of plastic wrap or waxed paper. Working from center, gently pound chicken with flat side of mallet or rolling pin until about 1/4 inch thick; remove wrap. Repeat with remaining chicken breast halves. Sprinkle chicken with chili powder and garlic powder.

3 When ready to grill, place chicken on gas grill over medium heat or on charcoal grill 4 to 6 inches from medium-high coals. Cook 8 to 10 minutes or until chicken is fork-tender and juices run clear, turning once.

4 To serve, arrange lettuce, tomatoes and cheese on 4 individual plates. Cut chicken crosswise into slices; place over lettuce mixture. Arrange tortilla chips around edge of each plate. Spoon dressing over each salad. Top with sour cream.

TIP: To broil chicken, place on broiler pan; broil 4 to 6 inches from heat using times above as a guide.

Nutrition Information Per Serving
Serving Size: 1/4 of Recipe

Calories	340	Calories from Fat	120
		% Daily Value	
Total Fat	13 g	20%	
Saturated	6 g	30%	
Cholesterol	90 mg	30%	
Sodium	710 mg	30%	
Total Carbohydrate	18 g	6%	
Dietary Fiber	2 g	8%	
Sugars	9 g		
Protein	37 g		
Vitamin A	30%	Vitamin C	25%
Calcium	25%	Iron	10%

Dietary Exchanges: 1 Starch, 5 Very Lean Meat, 1 1/2 Fat
OR 1 Carbohydrate, 5 Very Lean Meat, 1 1/2 Fat

PASTA AND FRUIT CHICKEN SALAD

prep time: 30 min. (ready in 1 hr. 30 min.) •
yield: 6 (1¼-cup) servings

This is a good way to use up yesterday's grilled or roasted chicken for a delicious meal that seems anything but leftover. Pineapple, melon and grapes punctuate the salad with color and bursts of juicy flavor.

5 oz. (2 cups) uncooked rotini (spiral pasta) or elbow macaroni

1 cup mayonnaise or salad dressing

1½ teaspoons dry mustard

½ teaspoon paprika

¼ teaspoon salt

⅛ teaspoon pepper

1 (20-oz.) can pineapple chunks, drained, reserving 3 tablespoons liquid

2 cups cubed cooked chicken

1 cup melon balls or cubes

1 cup seedless green grapes, halved

1 Cook rotini to desired doneness as directed on package. Drain; rinse with cold water to cool.

2 Meanwhile, in large bowl, combine mayonnaise, dry mustard, paprika, salt, pepper and reserved 3 tablespoons pineapple liquid; blend well.

3 Add cooked rotini, pineapple, chicken, melon and grapes to mayonnaise mixture; mix gently to coat. Cover; refrigerate 1 hour to blend flavors.

Nutrition Information Per Serving
Serving Size: 1¼ Cups

Calories	510	Calories from Fat	300
		% Daily Value	
Total Fat	33 g	51%	
Saturated	5 g	25%	
Cholesterol	65 mg	22%	
Sodium	340 mg	14%	
Total Carbohydrate	35 g	12%	
Dietary Fiber	2 g	8%	
Sugars	18 g		
Protein	18 g		
Vitamin A	25%	Vitamin C	25%
Calcium	4%	Iron	15%

Dietary Exchanges: 1 Starch, 1½ Fruit, 2 Lean Meat, 5 Fat OR
2½ Carbohydrate, 2 Lean Meat, 5 Fat

COOKED CHICKEN

Cooking chicken to have on hand for quick meals takes only minutes with the help of the microwave.

For 2 to 2½ cups of cubed, cooked chicken, place 2 whole chicken breasts (1½ to 2 lb.) in a 12 × 8-inch microwave-safe dish; cover the chicken with microwave-safe waxed paper. Microwave on HIGH for 8 to 10 minutes or until chicken is no longer pink and juices run clear, turning the dish a half turn and rearranging the chicken halfway through cooking. Cool chicken and cut it into cubes or bite-sized pieces.

Cooked chicken can be used immediately, refrigerated one to two days or tightly wrapped and frozen for up to six months.

Waldorf Chicken Salad

WALDORF CHICKEN SALAD

prep time: 20 min. • yield: 4 servings

Including cubed cooked chicken transforms the classic apple-celery-walnut combination into a satisfying main dish salad. Use both red and green apples, unpeeled, for pleasing color contrast.

DRESSING
1 (8-oz.) container low-fat plain yogurt

2 tablespoons honey

¼ teaspoon ginger

SALAD
2 cups cubed cooked chicken

1 cup chopped apple

1 cup seedless red grapes, halved

½ cup thinly sliced celery

½ cup raisins

4 lettuce leaves, if desired

2 tablespoons chopped walnuts

1 In small bowl, combine all dressing ingredients; blend well.

2 In large bowl, combine all salad ingredients except lettuce and walnuts. Pour dressing over salad; toss gently to coat.

3 To serve, arrange lettuce on 4 individual plates. Spoon salad over lettuce. Sprinkle with walnuts.

Nutrition Information Per Serving
Serving Size: ¼ of Recipe

Calories	350	Calories from Fat	80
		% Daily Value	
Total Fat	9 g	14%	
Saturated	2 g	10%	
Cholesterol	65 mg	22%	
Sodium	115 mg	5%	
Total Carbohydrate	41 g	14%	
Dietary Fiber	3 g	12%	
Sugars	35 g		
Protein	25 g		
Vitamin A	4%	Vitamin C	15%
Calcium	15%	Iron	10%

Dietary Exchanges: 2 ½ Fruit, 3 ½ Lean Meat OR 2 ½ Carbohydrate, 3 ½ Lean Meat

CHICKEN YIELDS

To determine how much uncooked chicken you'll need for a recipe that calls for cubed cooked chicken, follow these guidelines:

- One 2½- to 3-pound fryer yields 2½ to 3 cups.
- Two whole chicken breasts (1½ lb. with skin and bones, ¾ lb. without) yield about 2 cups.
- One 5-ounce can of chunk chicken (drained and flaked) yields 1 cup.
- Cooked turkey can be substituted for cooked chicken in any recipe.

WILD RICE CHICKEN SALAD

prep time: 30 min. (ready in 2 hr. 30 min.) •
yield: 6 (1-cup) servings

Wild rice is actually a type of grass rather than a true rice. It has a nuttier flavor and chewier texture than white rice.

SALAD
⅔ cup uncooked wild rice

2 cups water

3 cups cubed cooked chicken

¼ cup chopped green bell pepper

¼ cup sliced green onions

2 cups cubed fresh pineapple or 1 (20-oz.) can pineapple chunks, drained

¼ cup slivered almonds, toasted if desired*

DRESSING
½ cup oil

3 tablespoons lemon juice

2 teaspoons sugar

1 teaspoon salt

¼ teaspoon pepper

⅛ teaspoon dried tarragon leaves

1 In medium saucepan, combine wild rice and water. Bring to a boil, stirring occasionally. Reduce heat; cover tightly and simmer 40 to 50 minutes or until rice is tender and liquid is absorbed.

2 Meanwhile, in large bowl, combine chicken, bell pepper and onions. In jar with tight-fitting lid, combine all dressing ingredients; shake well.

3 Add cooked rice to salad; toss gently. Add dressing; toss to coat. Cover; refrigerate at least 2 hours to blend flavors.

4 Just before serving, fold in pineapple. Sprinkle with almonds.

TIP: *To toast almonds, spread on cookie sheet; bake at 350° F. for 5 to 7 minutes or until golden brown, stirring occasionally. Or spread in thin layer in microwave-safe pie pan. Microwave on HIGH for 4 to 7 minutes or until golden brown, stirring frequently.

Nutrition Information Per Serving
Serving Size: 1 Cup

Calories	420	Calories from Fat	230
		% Daily Value	
Total Fat	26 g	40%	
Saturated	4 g	20%	
Cholesterol	60 mg	20%	
Sodium	420 mg	18%	
Total Carbohydrate	23 g	8%	
Dietary Fiber	3 g	12%	
Sugars	7 g		
Protein	24 g		
Vitamin A	0%	Vitamin C	25%
Calcium	4%	Iron	10%

Dietary Exchanges: 1 Starch, ½ Fruit, 3 Lean Meat, 3 Fat OR
1½ Carbohydrate, 3 Lean Meat, 3 Fat

TURKEY SALAD POLYNESIAN

prep time: 25 min. • yield: 8 (1¼-cup) servings

Poultry's mild flavor nicely complements the sweet-sour Polynesian-style dressing. The recipe works equally well with roasted turkey or chicken or a chunk of deli turkey.

SALAD
8 oz. (2½ cups) uncooked mostaccioli (tube-shaped pasta)

2 cups cubed cooked turkey

¾ cup sliced celery

¾ cup chopped walnuts

¼ cup thinly sliced green onions

1 (11-oz.) can mandarin orange segments, drained

1 (8-oz.) can pineapple tidbits in unsweetened juice, drained, reserving 2 tablespoons liquid for dressing

DRESSING

½ cup reduced-calorie mayonnaise or
  salad dressing

⅓ cup light sour cream

2 tablespoons reserved pineapple liquid

½ teaspoon salt

1 Cook mostaccioli to desired doneness as
directed on package. Drain; rinse with cold water
to cool.

2 In large bowl, combine cooked mostaccioli
and all remaining salad ingredients. In small bowl,
combine all dressing ingredients; blend well. Pour
dressing over salad; stir gently to coat.

Nutrition Information Per Serving
Serving Size: 1¼ Cups

Calories	330	Calories from Fat	140
		% Daily Value	
Total Fat	15 g	23%	
Saturated	3 g	15%	
Cholesterol	35 mg	12%	
Sodium	300 mg	13%	
Total Carbohydrate	32 g	11%	
Dietary Fiber	2 g	8%	
Sugars	8 g		
Protein	16 g		
Vitamin A	8%	Vitamin C	20%
Calcium	6%	Iron	10%

Dietary Exchanges: 1½ Starch, ½ Fruit, 1½ Lean Meat, 2 Fat OR
2 Carbohydrate, 1½ Lean Meat, 2 Fat

WILTED SPINACH SALAD WITH SMOKED TURKEY

prep time: 20 min. • yield: 4 (1¼-cup) servings

*The hot bacon-flavored dressing slightly warms and
softens the spinach greens. If you wish, garnish each
serving with wedges of hard-cooked egg.*

4 cups torn fresh spinach

2 cups cubed smoked turkey

1 cup sliced fresh mushrooms

½ cup shredded carrot

¼ cup slivered almonds, toasted if desired*

3 slices bacon, cut into ½-inch pieces

⅓ cup vinegar

1 tablespoon honey

¼ teaspoon salt

⅛ teaspoon pepper

1 In large bowl, combine spinach, turkey, mushrooms, carrot and almonds. Set aside.

2 Cook bacon in small skillet over medium heat
until crisp. Remove bacon from skillet; drain on
paper towels.

3 Reserve 2 tablespoons drippings in skillet. Add
vinegar, honey, salt and pepper; cook and stir until
hot. Pour over spinach mixture; toss gently. Sprinkle with bacon. Serve immediately.

TIP: *To toast almonds, spread on cookie sheet;
bake at 350°F. for 5 to 7 minutes or until golden
brown, stirring occasionally. Or spread in thin
layer in microwave-safe pie pan. Microwave on
HIGH for 4 to 7 minutes or until golden brown,
stirring frequently.

Nutrition Information Per Serving
Serving Size: 1¼ Cups

Calories	190	Calories from Fat	70
		% Daily Value	
Total Fat	8 g	12%	
Saturated	1 g	5%	
Cholesterol	30 mg	10%	
Sodium	900 mg	38%	
Total Carbohydrate	12 g	4%	
Dietary Fiber	3 g	12%	
Sugars	6 g		
Protein	18 g		
Vitamin A	150%	Vitamin C	20%
Calcium	8%	Iron	15%

Dietary Exchanges: ½ Starch, 1 Vegetable, 2 Lean Meat, ½ Fat OR
½ Carbohydrate, 1 Vegetable, 2 Lean Meat, ½ Fat

APPLE BEEF SALAD

prep time: 15 min. • yield: 3 (1⅓-cup) servings

Be sure to rinse the spinach as many times as necessary, always lifting the spinach out of the water to let grit settle to the bottom before changing the water. Or, purchase packaged prewashed spinach.

DRESSING

¼ cup apple juice

3 tablespoons oil

2 tablespoons cider vinegar

2 teaspoons lemon juice

SALAD

2 cups packed torn fresh spinach

6 oz. thinly sliced roast beef (from deli), cut into 2 × 1-inch strips

1 medium apple, chopped

½ cup peanuts

1 In jar with tight-fitting lid, combine all dressing ingredients; shake well.

2 In medium bowl, combine all salad ingredients. Add dressing to salad; toss to coat.

Nutrition Information Per Serving
Serving Size: 1⅓ Cups

Calories	390	Calories from Fat	240
		% Daily Value	
Total Fat	27 g	42%	
Saturated	4 g	20%	
Cholesterol	25 mg	8%	
Sodium	710 mg	30%	
Total Carbohydrate	17 g	6%	
Dietary Fiber	4 g	16%	
Sugars	9 g		
Protein	20 g		
Vitamin A	50%	Vitamin C	25%
Calcium	6%	Iron	15%

Dietary Exchanges: 1 Starch, 1 Vegetable, 2 Lean Meat, 4 Fat OR
1 Carbohydrate, 1 Vegetable, 2 Lean Meat, 4 Fat

DEFINING VINEGARS

- Cider vinegar is sweet and smooth tasting. Since cooking enhances its sweetness, it's often used for hot dressings.
- White vinegar has a harsh flavor and is most often used in pickling but occasionally in salads.
- Red or white wine vinegars are smooth and mild in flavor. They work well in vinaigrette dressings.
- Rice wine vinegar, widely used in Asian cooking, is slightly sweet.
- Fruit-flavored vinegars are not sweet per se, but have a fruity flavor that combines well with fruit salads and mild meats such as poultry and pork.
- Herb-flavored vinegars enhance the flavor of milder lettuces such as iceberg, Boston or leaf lettuce.
- Balsamic vinegar is a wine-based Italian vinegar with a mellow, full-bodied, slightly sweet flavor and dark brown color. It complements bitter greens such as arugula, chicory or radicchio, and is also a good condiment for meat.

DELI BEEF AND VEGGIE SALAD

prep time: 25 min. • yield: 4 (1½-cup) servings

Adapt this recipe to suit the meat you have on hand: leftover roast beef, grilled steak, roasted chicken breasts or even panfried pork chops can be sliced and tossed with this easy-mix salad.

12 oz. thinly sliced roast beef (from deli), cut into ½-inch strips

⅓ cup purchased zesty Italian salad dressing

2 cups thinly sliced carrots

2 cups (6 oz.) fresh snow pea pods, cut in half on diagonal

1 small cucumber, sliced

1 small tomato, cut into wedges, if desired

1 Place roast beef in large serving bowl. Pour dressing over beef; mix well. Let stand 10 minutes to marinate.

2 In medium saucepan, bring 4 cups water to a boil. Add carrots; return to a boil. Boil 2 minutes. Add pea pods; cook an additional minute.

3 Drain vegetables; immediately plunge into ice water to chill. Drain thoroughly; place vegetables in bowl with beef mixture. Add cucumber; toss lightly. Garnish with tomato wedges.

Nutrition Information Per Serving
Serving Size: 1 1/2 Cups

Calories	260	Calories from Fat	110
		% Daily Value	
Total Fat	12 g	18%	
Saturated	2 g	10%	
Cholesterol	40 mg	13%	
Sodium	1050 mg	44%	
Total Carbohydrate	17 g	6%	
Dietary Fiber	4 g	16%	
Sugars	10 g		
Protein	21 g		
Vitamin A	350%	Vitamin C	60%
Calcium	6%	Iron	20%

Dietary Exchanges: 1/2 Starch, 2 Vegetable, 2 Very Lean Meat, 2 Fat OR 1/2 Carbohydrate, 2 Vegetable, 2 Very Lean Meat, 2 Fat

PASTA AND BEAN ANTIPASTO SALAD

prep time: 25 min. • yield: 5 servings

Radiatore—a chunky, ruffly type of pasta—has oodles of nooks and crannies to soak up the dressing from the bean salad. When fresh herbs are available, substitute 1 1/2 teaspoons minced fresh basil and 3/4 teaspoon minced fresh oregano for the dried.

4 oz. (1 1/2 cups) uncooked pasta nuggets (radiatore)

1 (15-oz.) can three bean salad, chilled, undrained

1 small red bell pepper, cut into 1-inch pieces

4 oz. (1 cup) provolone cheese, cubed

1 (2.5-oz.) pepperoni stick, halved lengthwise, cut into 1/4-inch pieces

1/2 teaspoon dried basil leaves

1/4 teaspoon dried oregano leaves

1/8 teaspoon pepper

4 cups purchased mixed salad greens

1 Cook pasta to desired doneness as directed on package. Drain; rinse with cold water to cool.

2 Meanwhile, in medium bowl, combine all remaining ingredients except salad greens.

3 Add cooked pasta to bean salad mixture; toss gently. Place salad greens on serving platter or in shallow bowl. Spoon pasta and bean mixture over greens. To serve, toss gently.

Nutrition Information Per Serving
Serving Size: 1/5 of Recipe

Calories	310	Calories from Fat	120
		% Daily Value	
Total Fat	13 g	20%	
Saturated	6 g	30%	
Cholesterol	25 mg	8%	
Sodium	840 mg	35%	
Total Carbohydrate	34 g	11%	
Dietary Fiber	5 g	20%	
Sugars	11 g		
Protein	15 g		
Vitamin A	45%	Vitamin C	50%
Calcium	25%	Iron	15%

Dietary Exchanges: 2 Starch, 1 Vegetable, 1 High-Fat Meat, 1/2 Fat OR 2 Carbohydrate, 1 Vegetable, 1 High-Fat Meat, 1/2 Fat

Ham-Pecan Tossed Salad

HAM-PECAN TOSSED SALAD

prep time: 20 min. • yield: 5 (1 ½-cup) servings

Sweet and crunchy caramelized pecans and fruit make this spinach–iceberg lettuce salad ideal for a special luncheon. Pass a basket of assorted small rolls or miniature muffins as an accompaniment.

DRESSING
¼ cup oil

2 tablespoons cider vinegar

1 tablespoon sugar

SALAD
3 cups torn iceberg lettuce

3 cups torn fresh spinach

2 cups cubed cooked ham

1 cup seedless red grapes, halved

¼ cup sliced green onions

1 (11-oz.) can mandarin orange segments, chilled, drained

½ cup caramelized pecan halves*

1 In small jar with tight-fitting lid, combine all dressing ingredients; shake well.

2 In large bowl, combine all salad ingredients except pecans; toss gently. Pour dressing over salad; toss to coat.

3 Just before serving, add pecans; toss gently.

TIP: *To make caramelized pecans, in small heavy saucepan, heat ¼ cup sugar over medium-high heat for 4 minutes or until sugar melts, stirring constantly. Add ½ cup pecan halves; stir until coated. Remove from heat. Pour onto waxed paper. Cool completely; break apart.

Nutrition Information Per Serving
Serving Size: 1 ½ Cups

Calories	360	Calories from Fat	190
		% Daily Value	
Total Fat	21 g	32%	
Saturated	3 g	15%	
Cholesterol	25 mg	8%	
Sodium	830 mg	35%	
Total Carbohydrate	29 g	10%	
Dietary Fiber	4 g	16%	
Sugars	24 g		
Protein	14 g		
Vitamin A	60%	Vitamin C	50%
Calcium	6%	Iron	10%

Dietary Exchanges: 1 ½ Fruit, 1 Vegetable, 1 ½ Lean Meat, 3 ½ Fat OR
1 ½ Carbohydrate, 1 Vegetable, 1 ½ Lean Meat, 3 ½ Fat

PECAN FACTS

Pecans are native American nuts that grow on a species of hickory tree. Rich and buttery in flavor, they're prized for their taste and texture. Most pecans are grown in the southern United States, with Georgia the leading producer. Pecans have a fat content of more than 70%, higher than any other nut. Because of this high fat content, store pecans carefully to prevent them from becoming rancid. Store unshelled pecans in an airtight container in a cool, dry place for up to six months. Store shelled pecans in an airtight container in the refrigerator for up to three months or in the freezer for up to six months.

ASIAN PORK SALAD

prep time: 20 min. • yield: 4 (1-cup) servings

If you wish, sprinkle the salad with toasted sesame seed before serving. Mung bean sprouts or sliced water chestnuts can be used in place of the celery.

SALAD

2 cups thin strips cooked pork

½ cup cashew halves or pieces

2 carrots, cut into matchstick pieces
    (about 1 cup)

1 stalk celery, cut into matchstick pieces
    (about ¾ cup)

1 bunch green onions, cut into ½-inch
    pieces (about ½ cup)

Fresh spinach leaves

DRESSING

⅓ cup oil

¼ cup rice vinegar or white vinegar

2 tablespoons soy sauce

1 teaspoon ginger

¼ teaspoon pepper

1 In medium bowl, combine all salad ingredients except spinach.

2 In jar with tight-fitting lid, combine all dressing ingredients; shake well. Pour half of dressing over salad; toss gently to mix.

3 To serve, line 4 individual plates with spinach. Spoon salad over spinach. Pass remaining dressing.

Nutrition Information Per Serving
Serving Size: 1 Cup

Calories	410	Calories from Fat	290
		% Daily Value	
Total Fat	32 g	49%	
Saturated	6 g	30%	
Cholesterol	50 mg	17%	
Sodium	1170 mg	49%	
Total Carbohydrate	14 g	5%	
Dietary Fiber	3 g	12%	
Sugars	4 g		
Protein	17 g		
Vitamin A	230%	Vitamin C	20%
Calcium	6%	Iron	45%

Dietary Exchanges: ½ Starch, 2 Vegetable, 2 Lean Meat, 5 Fat OR
½ Carbohydrate, 2 Vegetable, 2 Lean Meat, 5 Fat

NIÇOISE SALAD

prep time: 35 min. (ready in 2 hr. 35 min.) • yield: 8 servings

This colorful salad of seasoned cold vegetables, hard-cooked eggs and fish originated in the French Riviera city of Nice.

DRESSING

2 tablespoons chopped green onions

2 tablespoons chopped fresh parsley

½ teaspoon dried dill weed

¼ teaspoon garlic salt

1 (0.7-oz.) pkg. Italian salad dressing mix

¾ cup oil

¼ cup red wine vinegar

SALAD

4 medium potatoes, cooked, peeled and
    sliced

1 lb. (3 cups) cut fresh green beans,
    cooked, drained

3 eggs

Lettuce leaves

1 (15½-oz.) can pink salmon, drained,
    skin and bones removed, flaked*

2 tomatoes, peeled, cut into 8 wedges

½ cup pitted ripe olives, quartered

1 In jar with tight-fitting lid, combine all dressing ingredients; shake well.

2 In medium bowl, pour ¼ cup of the dressing over cooked potatoes; toss to coat. Cover; refrigerate at least 2 hours. In another bowl, pour ¼ cup of the dressing over cooked green beans; toss to coat. Cover; refrigerate 1 to 2 hours.

3 Place eggs in small saucepan; cover with cold water. Bring to a boil. Reduce heat; simmer about 15 minutes. Immediately drain; run cold water over eggs to stop cooking. Peel eggs; cut into quarters.

4 To serve, line large serving platter with lettuce leaves. Spoon potatoes onto center of plate. Arrange salmon over potatoes. Spoon green beans around potatoes. Alternately place egg quarters and tomato wedges over beans. Garnish with olives. Pour remaining dressing over salad.

TIP: *Two 9¼-oz. cans tuna, drained and flaked, can be substituted for salmon.

Nutrition Information Per Serving
Serving Size: ⅛ of Recipe

Calories	390	Calories from Fat	240
		% Daily Value	
Total Fat	27 g	42%	
Saturated	4 g	20%	
Cholesterol	100 mg	33%	
Sodium	710 mg	30%	
Total Carbohydrate	23 g	8%	
Dietary Fiber	4 g	16%	
Sugars	4 g		
Protein	14 g		
Vitamin A	15%	Vitamin C	40%
Calcium	4%	Iron	15%

Dietary Exchanges: 1 Starch, 1 Vegetable, 1½ Lean Meat, 4½ Fat OR
1 Carbohydrate, 1 Vegetable, 1½ Lean Meat, 4½ Fat

DILLED SHRIMP AND RICE

prep time: 25 min. (ready in 1 hr. 25 min.) •
yield: 4 (1 ¼-cup) servings

Squeezing fresh lemon over the salad immediately before serving keeps the fresh citrus tang at the forefront instead of allowing it to be absorbed and muted by the rice.

1 cup uncooked regular long-grain white rice

¼ cup white wine vinegar

¼ cup oil

3 teaspoons dried dill weed

½ teaspoon salt

¼ teaspoon pepper

¼ cup chopped green onions

¼ cup sliced radishes

½ lb. shelled deveined cooked medium shrimp

½ lb. fresh snow pea pods, blanched*

Lemon

1 Cook rice as directed on package.

2 Meanwhile, in jar with tight-fitting lid, combine vinegar, oil, dill, salt and pepper; shake well. Pour 2 tablespoons of the dressing over hot rice; toss gently. Cover; refrigerate 1 hour or until chilled.

3 In medium bowl, combine chilled rice, onions, radishes, shrimp and remaining dressing; toss to combine. On large serving platter or individual plates, arrange pea pods, spoke fashion, around outside edge of plate. Spoon rice mixture into center of pea pods.

4 Just before serving, lightly squeeze fresh lemon juice over salad. If desired, garnish with fresh dill and green onions.

TIP: *To blanch snow pea pods, cook in boiling water for 30 to 60 seconds or until crisp-tender. Remove from boiling water and immediately plunge into ice water until cold. Drain.

Nutrition Information Per Serving
Serving Size: 1 ¼ Cups

Calories	380	Calories from Fat	140
		% Daily Value	
Total Fat	15 g	23%	
Saturated	2 g	10%	
Cholesterol	110 mg	37%	
Sodium	400 mg	17%	
Total Carbohydrate	44 g	15%	
Dietary Fiber	3 g	12%	
Sugars	3 g		
Protein	17 g		
Vitamin A	6%	Vitamin C	50%
Calcium	8%	Iron	30%

Dietary Exchanges: 3 Starch, 1 Very Lean Meat, 2 ½ Fat
OR 3 Carbohydrate, 1 Very Lean Meat, 2 ½ Fat

DILL WEED

A member of the parsley family, dill weed is the thin feathery leaves of the dill plant. Commonly used to give pickles their characteristic flavor, dill weed can also be used to flavor fish, vegetable dishes and salads.

Dried dill, like other dried herbs, loses flavor and intensity over time; it's best to purchase it in small quantities. Date containers with the month and year purchased, and store them away from heat and light. Replace after one year.

If even small containers of herbs are more than you can reasonably use, split one with a friend, or purchase the desired amount from a natural food co-op where herbs and spices are available in bulk.

Cook's Notes

SHRIMP AND ORZO SALAD

prep time: 30 min. • yield: 4 (1 ½-cup) servings

For a pretty presentation, scoop the salad into hollowed-out beefsteak tomatoes. Or, garnish the top of each salad with strips of roasted red bell peppers.

7 oz. (1 cup) uncooked orzo or rosamarina (rice-shaped pasta)

1 (12-oz.) pkg. frozen ready-to-cook shrimp

¾ cup frozen sweet peas

⅓ cup olive or vegetable oil

2 tablespoons white wine vinegar

1 garlic clove, minced

½ teaspoon salt

⅛ teaspoon pepper

½ cup pitted kalamata olives, quartered

⅓ cup chopped red onion

1 red bell pepper, chopped

1 Anaheim chile, seeded, sliced

2 tablespoons chopped fresh cilantro

1 Cook orzo to desired doneness as directed on package, adding shrimp and peas during last 2 to 3 minutes of cooking time; cook until shrimp turn pink. Drain; rinse with cold water to cool.

2 Meanwhile, in small jar with tight-fitting lid, combine oil, vinegar, garlic, salt and pepper; shake well to blend.

3 In large bowl, combine cooked orzo, shrimp and peas with olives, onion, bell pepper, chile and cilantro; mix well. Pour dressing over salad; toss to mix.

Nutrition Information Per Serving
Serving Size: 1 ½ Cups

Calories	510	Calories from Fat	220
		% Daily Value	
Total Fat	24 g	37%	
Saturated	3 g	15%	
Cholesterol	125 mg	42%	
Sodium	720 mg	30%	
Total Carbohydrate	51 g	17%	
Dietary Fiber	3 g	12%	
Sugars	5 g		
Protein	22 g		
Vitamin A	30%	Vitamin C	100%
Calcium	6%	Iron	25%

Dietary Exchanges: 3 Starch, 1 Vegetable, 1 ½ Very Lean Meat, 4 Fat OR
3 Carbohydrate, 1 Vegetable, 1 ½ Very Lean Meat, 4 Fat

GRILLED TUNA VINAIGRETTE

prep time: 50 min. • yield: 5 servings

Balsamic vinegar, an Italian specialty that's aged in wood, mellows the flavor of the dressing. Use red wine vinegar for a salad with brighter, tarter notes.

DRESSING

½ cup olive oil

½ cup balsamic vinegar or red wine vinegar

2 tablespoons chopped fresh parsley

1 teaspoon dried dill weed

1 teaspoon Dijon mustard

2 garlic cloves, finely chopped

2 to 3 drops hot pepper sauce

SALAD

3 medium unpeeled red potatoes (about 1 lb.)

2 cups fresh green beans or frozen cut green beans

1 egg

1 lb. fresh tuna steaks

Fresh spinach leaves

3 Italian plum tomatoes

¼ cup sliced green onions

1 GRILL DIRECTIONS: In jar with tight-fitting lid, combine all dressing ingredients; shake well. In small saucepan, cook potatoes in small amount of water for 15 to 25 minutes or until tender. Cool slightly; slice.

2 Meanwhile, wash and trim fresh beans; break into 1-inch lengths. In medium saucepan, bring ½ cup water to a boil. Add beans; cook 5 to 10 minutes or until crisp-tender. Drain; cool.

3 In nonmetal bowl, pour ½ cup of the dressing over warm sliced potatoes. Cover; set aside.

4 Place egg in small saucepan; cover with cold water. Bring to a boil. Reduce heat; simmer about 15 minutes. Immediately drain; run cold water over egg to stop cooking. Peel egg. Refrigerate until serving time.

5 Heat grill. When ready to grill, oil grill rack. Place tuna on gas grill over medium heat or on charcoal grill 4 to 6 inches from medium coals. Cook 10 minutes per inch of thickness or until fish flakes easily with fork, turning once halfway through cooking.

6 To serve, line large platter with spinach leaves. Arrange marinated potatoes in a circle on spinach, 1 inch from outer edge of platter. Spoon cooked green beans into center. Flake grilled tuna; arrange over green beans.

7 In small saucepan, heat remaining dressing until warm; pour over salad. Mash egg with fork or press through sieve; sprinkle over tuna. Slice tomatoes lengthwise; arrange around edge of platter. Sprinkle salad with onions.

TIP: To broil tuna, place on oiled broiler pan; broil 4 to 6 inches from heat using times above as a guide.

Nutrition Information Per Serving
Serving Size: ⅕ of Recipe

Calories	460	Calories from Fat	250
		% Daily Value	
Total Fat	28 g	43%	
Saturated	5 g	25%	
Cholesterol	75 mg	25%	
Sodium	85 mg	4%	
Total Carbohydrate	26 g	9%	
Dietary Fiber	4 g	16%	
Sugars	3 g		
Protein	26 g		
Vitamin A	70%	Vitamin C	35%
Calcium	6%	Iron	20%

Dietary Exchanges: 1½ Starch, 3 Very Lean Meat, 5 Fat OR
1½ Carbohydrate, 3 Very Lean Meat, 5 Fat

SALMON SUMMER FRUIT SALAD

prep time: 25 min. • yield: 4 (1½-cup) servings

PICTURED ON PAGE 44

Tender leaf and Bibb lettuces make a pretty background for salmon, nectarines and fresh raspberries.

DRESSING

2 green onions, or 1 shallot, chopped

1 tablespoon chopped fresh dill or
   1 teaspoon dried dill weed

1 tablespoon chopped fresh parsley or
   1 teaspoon dried parsley flakes

5 tablespoons raspberry vinegar

1 tablespoon olive or vegetable oil

1 tablespoon honey

½ teaspoon lemon juice

SALAD

3 cups torn leaf lettuce

2 cups torn Bibb lettuce

1 (7.5-oz.) can pink salmon, drained, skin
   and bones removed

2 medium nectarines, sliced

½ cup fresh raspberries

1 In small bowl, combine all dressing ingredients; beat with wire whisk until blended.

2 In large bowl, combine all salad ingredients except raspberries. Drizzle with dressing; toss gently to coat. Gently fold in raspberries.

Nutrition Information Per Serving
Serving Size: 1½ Cups

Calories	170	Calories from Fat	50
		% Daily Value	
Total Fat	6 g	9%	
Saturated	1 g	5%	
Cholesterol	15 mg	5%	
Sodium	250 mg	10%	
Total Carbohydrate	18 g	6%	
Dietary Fiber	3 g	12%	
Sugars	13 g		
Protein	10 g		
Vitamin A	35%	Vitamin C	35%
Calcium	6%	Iron	8%

Dietary Exchanges: ½ Starch, ½ Fruit, 1 Lean Meat, 1 Fat OR
1 Carbohydrate, 1 Lean Meat, 1 Fat

OLIVE OIL

P rized for its contribution to salads and cooked dishes, olive oil is the cornerstone of Italian and other Mediterranean cooking. It is graded according to acidity levels. The highest quality of oil will have the least amount of acid and the best, most intense flavor. Olive oils range in color from golden to greenish; in general, the deeper the color, the more intense the olive flavor.

"Extra-virgin" olive oil, the highest quality and most expensive, comes from the first pressing of the olives. Reserve extra-virgin oil for uncooked dishes such as salads, or to sprinkle onto warm foods just before serving.

"Pure" olive oil (sometimes labeled "virgin") comes from subsequent pressings of the olives. It's less expensive and most suitable for cooking.

Stored in a cool, dark place, olive oil will keep up to six months. In the refrigerator, it can be stored for up to one year; however, it becomes cloudy and thick when chilled. Let refrigerated olive oil warm to room temperature before using it.

MARINATED VERMICELLI SALAD

prep time: 20 min. (ready in 4 hr. 20 min.) •
yield: 6 (1 ⅓-cup) servings

Vermicelli—very thin spaghetti—cooks quickly. Watch it carefully while it boils to make sure it remains al dente. Regular spaghetti may be used instead.

8 oz. uncooked vermicelli

1 medium tomato, cubed

1 medium cucumber, coarsely chopped

½ cup chopped green bell pepper

1 (4-oz.) can sliced ripe olives, drained

¼ cup chopped red onion

2 tablespoons salad supreme seasoning

½ cup purchased zesty Italian salad dressing

Marinated Vermicelli Salad

1 Cook vermicelli to desired doneness as directed on package. Drain; rinse with cold water to cool.

2 Meanwhile, in large bowl, combine all remaining ingredients except salad dressing.

3 Add cooked vermicelli and salad dressing to salad; toss gently to mix. Refrigerate at least 4 hours or overnight to blend flavors.

Nutrition Information Per Serving
Serving Size: 1 1/3 Cups

Calories	270	Calories from Fat	100
		% Daily Value	
Total Fat	11 g	17%	
Saturated	2 g	10%	
Cholesterol	0 mg	0%	
Sodium	860 mg	36%	
Total Carbohydrate	35 g	12%	
Dietary Fiber	3 g	12%	
Sugars	4 g		
Protein	7 g		
Vitamin A	6%	Vitamin C	25%
Calcium	6%	Iron	15%

Dietary Exchanges: 2 Starch, 1 Vegetable, 2 Fat OR 2 Carbohydrate, 1 Vegetable, 2 Fat

LEMONY LEEKS AND PASTA SALAD

prep time: 35 min. (ready in 2 hr. 35 min.) •
yield: 6 (1 1/3-cup) servings

Make this salad up to two days ahead of time, but stir in the capers just before serving so they retain their vinegary bite.

1 large lemon

1/4 cup olive or vegetable oil

1 cup slivered almonds

3 cups sliced leeks

3 tablespoons capers, drained

1/2 teaspoon salt

1/8 teaspoon pepper

1 red bell pepper, roasted, cut into strips★

1 yellow bell pepper, roasted, cut into strips★

8 oz. (3 1/2 cups) uncooked bow tie pasta

1 Remove peel from lemon using zester or grater; set aside. Cut white pith from lemon; discard. Cut lemon into 1/4-inch slices; set aside.

2 In large skillet, heat oil over high heat until hot. Add almonds; cook and stir 30 seconds or until light brown. With slotted spoon, remove almonds from skillet. Set aside.

3 To same skillet, combine lemon slices, lemon peel, leeks, capers, salt and pepper; cook and stir 1 minute or until vegetables are crisp-tender. Remove from heat. Remove lemon slices; discard. Stir in bell peppers and almonds. Cover; refrigerate at least 2 hours or until chilled.

4 Cook pasta to desired doneness as directed on package. Drain; rinse with cold water to cool.

5 In large serving bowl, combine pasta and vegetable mixture; toss gently.

TIP: ★Two 7.25-oz. jars roasted red bell peppers, drained, can be substituted for roasted red and yellow peppers.

Nutrition Information Per Serving
Serving Size: 1 1/3 Cups

Calories	370	Calories from Fat	160
		% Daily Value	
Total Fat	18 g	28%	
Saturated	2 g	10%	
Cholesterol	0 mg	0%	
Sodium	270 mg	11%	
Total Carbohydrate	42 g	14%	
Dietary Fiber	4 g	16%	
Sugars	5 g		
Protein	9 g		
Vitamin A	15%	Vitamin C	70%
Calcium	8%	Iron	20%

Dietary Exchanges: 2 1/2 Starch, 1 Vegetable, 3 Fat OR 2 1/2 Carbohydrate, 1 Vegetable, 3 Fat

FRUIT 'N YOGURT PASTA SALAD

prep time: 25 min. (ready in 1 hr. 25 min.) •
yield: 10 (½-cup) servings

Long-grain rice or orzo pasta can stand in for the shell pasta. Or, omit the pasta altogether and serve the fruit as a dessert or afternoon snack.

- 4 oz. (1 cup) uncooked small shell pasta or macaroni rings
- 1 (11-oz.) can mandarin orange segments, drained
- 1 (8-oz.) can pineapple chunks, drained
- 1 cup halved green grapes
- 1 (6-oz.) container low-fat lemon yogurt
- 1 tablespoon sugar
- 1 cup halved strawberries

1 Cook macaroni to desired doneness as directed on package. Drain; rinse with cold water to cool.

2 In medium bowl, combine cooked macaroni and all remaining ingredients except strawberries; mix gently to coat. Cover; refrigerate 1 to 2 hours to blend flavors.

3 Just before serving, stir in strawberries.

Fruit 'n Yogurt
Pasta Salad

Calories	110	Calories from Fat	10
		% Daily Value	
Total Fat	1 g	2%	
Saturated	0 g	0%	
Cholesterol	0 mg	0%	
Sodium	10 mg	0%	
Total Carbohydrate	21 g	7%	
Dietary Fiber	1 g	4%	
Sugars	12 g		
Protein	3 g		
Vitamin A	4%	Vitamin C	30%
Calcium	4%	Iron	4%

Dietary Exchanges: ½ Starch, 1 Fruit OR 1½ Carbohydrate

Cook's Notes

YOGURT'S NUTRITIONAL PROFILE

Yogurt is one of the richest sources of calcium. An 8-ounce container of plain nonfat yogurt has 110 calories and contains about 100 mg more calcium than the same amount of milk. Yogurt can be a better choice for people who cannot drink milk.

Read yogurt labels carefully because protein, fat and calorie content can vary. For flavored varieties, compare the amount of sugar or artificial sweetener.

1-CUP SERVING	GRAMS OF FAT	CALORIES	CALCIUM
plain nonfat yogurt	0	110	400 mg
plain skim milk yogurt	Less than 1	125	450 mg
plain 2% fat yogurt	3.5	145	415 mg
plain whole milk yogurt	7	140	275 mg

BANANA SALAD WITH PEANUTS

prep time: 15 min. • yield: 10 servings

Romaine lettuce is recommended for this salad because it's substantial enough to maintain its character when paired with the rich dressing, which would overwhelm more delicate greens. Chicory makes a good substitution. The slight bitterness balances the sweetness of the dressing and the fruit.

DRESSING

½ cup mayonnaise or salad dressing

¼ cup peanut butter

¼ cup honey

SALAD

6 cups torn romaine lettuce

3 bananas, sliced

2 apples, cubed

½ cup raisins

½ cup peanuts

1 In small bowl, combine all dressing ingredients; blend well.

2 To serve, in large bowl, combine all salad ingredients; toss gently. Serve salad immediately with dressing.

Nutrition Information Per Serving
Serving Size: ¹⁄₁₀ of Recipe

Calories	280	Calories from Fat	140
		% Daily Value	
Total Fat	16 g	25%	
Saturated	3 g	15%	
Cholesterol	5 mg	2%	
Sodium	130 mg	5%	
Total Carbohydrate	29 g	10%	
Dietary Fiber	3 g	12%	
Sugars	21 g		
Protein	5 g		
Vitamin A	20%	Vitamin C	20%
Calcium	4%	Iron	6%

Dietary Exchanges: 2 Fruit, ½ High-Fat Meat, 2½ Fat OR 2 Carbohydrate, ½ High-Fat Meat, 2½ Fat

COOL 'N CREAMY FRUIT SALAD

prep time: 15 min. • yield: 16 (1/2-cup) servings

Serve this dessert-style salad in saucer-shaped champagne glasses or pretty glass bowls. Ladle it over slices of angel food cake for an easy shortcake.

- 1 (20-oz.) can chunk pineapple in unsweetened juice, undrained
- 1 (11-oz.) can mandarin orange segments, undrained
- 2 bananas, sliced
- 2 cups halved strawberries
- 1½ cups halved seedless green grapes
- 1 cup fresh or frozen blueberries, thawed, drained
- 1 (3.4-oz.) pkg. instant vanilla pudding and pie filling mix
- ¼ to ½ cup granola, pecan halves or whole almonds, if desired

1 Drain pineapple and orange segments, reserving liquid in small bowl. In large bowl, combine all fruit.

2 Sprinkle pudding mix into reserved liquid; mix until combined and slightly thickened. Fold into fruit until well combined. Sprinkle with granola.

Nutrition Information Per Serving
Serving Size: ½ Cup

Calories	110	Calories from Fat	10
		% Daily Value	
Total Fat	1 g	2%	
Saturated	0 g	0%	
Cholesterol	0 mg	0%	
Sodium	95 mg	4%	
Total Carbohydrate	25 g	8%	
Dietary Fiber	2 g	8%	
Sugars	20 g		
Protein	1 g		
Vitamin A	4%	Vitamin C	50%
Calcium	0%	Iron	2%

Dietary Exchanges: ½ Starch, 1 Fruit OR 1½ Carbohydrate

GREENS AND PEACH SALAD

prep time: 15 min. • yield: 8 servings

Peaches come in two basic varieties: freestone and cling. Freestone are easiest to handle when you need sliced peaches for a recipe because the pit comes out easily. Smooth-skinned nectarines can be used in place of peaches in most recipes.

POPPY SEED DRESSING
⅓ cup sugar

½ teaspoon salt

½ teaspoon dry mustard

3 tablespoons vinegar

1 teaspoon finely chopped onion

½ cup oil

2 teaspoons poppy seed

SALAD
2 teaspoons lemon juice

2 cups (2 medium) sliced peeled fresh peaches

3 cups torn leaf lettuce

3 cups torn fresh spinach

¼ cup slivered almonds, toasted*

1 In blender container or food processor bowl with metal blade, combine sugar, salt, mustard, vinegar and onion. Cover; blend until combined. With machine running, add oil in a slow, steady stream, blending until thick and smooth. Add poppy seed; blend a few seconds to mix. Refrigerate until ready to serve.

2 Sprinkle lemon juice over peach slices; reserve ½ cup for garnish. In large serving bowl, combine remaining peaches, lettuce and spinach; toss gently. Arrange reserved peach slices over greens mixture. Sprinkle with almonds. Serve dressing with salad.

TIP: *To toast almonds, spread on cookie sheet; bake at 350° F. for 5 to 7 minutes or until golden brown, stirring occasionally. Or spread in thin layer in microwave-safe pie pan. Microwave on HIGH for 4 to 7 minutes or until golden brown, stirring frequently.

Nutrition Information Per Serving
Serving Size: $1/8$ of Recipe

Calories	220	Calories from Fat	140
		% Daily Value	
Total Fat	16 g	25%	
Saturated	2 g	10%	
Cholesterol	0 mg	0%	
Sodium	150 mg	6%	
Total Carbohydrate	16 g	5%	
Dietary Fiber	2 g	8%	
Sugars	13 g		
Protein	2 g		
Vitamin A	40%	Vitamin C	20%
Calcium	6%	Iron	6%

Dietary Exchanges: 1 Fruit, 1/2 Vegetable, 3 Fat OR 1 Carbohydrate, 1/2 Vegetable, 3 Fat

SOUTHERN CITRUS SALAD

prep time: 20 min. • yield: 8 servings

Use your favorite combination of greens in this refreshing salad; even spinach works well.

3 cups torn leaf lettuce

3 cups torn iceberg lettuce

2 grapefruit, peeled, sectioned

3 oranges, peeled, sectioned

1 avocado, peeled, pitted and sliced

$1/4$ cup slivered almonds, toasted if desired*

1 cup purchased poppy seed salad dressing

In large serving bowl, toss leaf and iceberg lettuce. Arrange grapefruit, oranges, avocado and almonds over greens. Serve with dressing.

TIP: *To toast almonds, spread on cookie sheet; bake at 350° F. for 5 to 7 minutes or until golden brown, stirring occasionally. Or spread in thin layer in microwave-safe pie pan. Microwave on HIGH for 4 to 7 minutes or until golden brown, stirring frequently.

Nutrition Information Per Serving
Serving Size: $1/8$ of Recipe

Calories	290	Calories from Fat	180
		% Daily Value	
Total Fat	20 g	31%	
Saturated	3 g	15%	
Cholesterol	10 mg	3%	
Sodium	230 mg	10%	
Total Carbohydrate	24 g	8%	
Dietary Fiber	4 g	16%	
Sugars	17 g		
Protein	3 g		
Vitamin A	20%	Vitamin C	70%
Calcium	6%	Iron	6%

Dietary Exchanges: 1/2 Starch, 1 Fruit, 4 Fat OR 1 1/2 Carbohydrate, 4 Fat

SECTIONING CITRUS

To prepare citrus for salads, use a sharp paring knife. Working over a bowl to catch the juices, peel the fruit all around, cutting just deeply enough to expose the flesh. Make V-shaped cuts between the membranes to release the fruit's flesh into the bowl below. The chewy membranes and bitter pith will be left behind and can be discarded; the salad will contain morsels of juicy, tender citrus.

COOK'S NOTES

STAR-STUDDED WATERMELON

prep time: 45 min. • yield: 30 (²/₃-cup) servings

If you can find fresh star fruit (also called carambola) in your market, cut them crosswise for star-shaped slices that further the theme of this naturally sweet salad.

1 large watermelon

20 cups cut-up fresh or canned fruit⋆

1 To carve melon bowl, cut off top ⅓ of melon. Cut thin slice from bottom of melon so it will sit flat, being careful not to cut through to melon flesh. Scoop out watermelon, leaving ½- to 1-inch-thick shell.

2 With pen or pencil, trace around a 1- to 2-inch star-shaped cookie cutter or adhesive-backed vinyl-coated paper pattern held at cut edge of melon, spacing stars as desired.

3 With small sharp knife, cut ¾ of the way around each star, cutting out 3 star points. Wrap melon bowl in plastic wrap to keep moist. Refrigerate until ready to fill with cut-up fruit.

TIPS: ⋆Use fresh fruits that are in season, such as watermelon, cantaloupe, honeydew, pineapple, strawberries, grapes, peaches, oranges, apples, bananas and blueberries. Use fruits with a variety of shapes and colors.

Orange juice concentrate can be drizzled over or tossed lightly with fruit. Fruits such as bananas, apples and peaches should be sprinkled with orange or lemon juice to prevent discoloration.

NUTRITION INFORMATION: Not possible to calculate because of recipe variables.

Star-Studded Watermelon

HOW TO CARVE A MELON BOWL

Whether you choose the "trace 'n cut" or "paste 'n trace" technique for carving a melon, the resulting fruit bowl is sure to be the star of your picnic buffet.

STEP 1

Select a uniformly shaped melon and wash it. Cut off the top ⅓ of the melon. Cut a thin slice from the bottom so the melon will sit flat, being careful not to cut into the red pulp. Scoop out the melon pulp, leaving a ½- to 1-inch shell.

STEP 2

With a pen and pencil, trace around a 1- to 2-inch star-shaped cookie cutter or adhesive-backed vinyl-coated paper pattern held at the cut edge of the melon, spacing stars as desired. With a sharp, small pointed knife, cut ¾ of the way around each star, cutting out 3 star points.

PINEAPPLE COLESLAW

prep time: 15 min. (ready in 1 hr. 15 min.) •
yield: 8 (½-cup) servings

This fruity version of traditional coleslaw is creamy and crunchy. Tart apples such as Granny Smith are especially good in the salad.

DRESSING
½ cup sour cream

½ cup mayonnaise

1 tablespoon finely chopped onion

2 teaspoons sugar

1 teaspoon lemon juice

SALAD
3 cups shredded green cabbage

1 cup chopped unpeeled apple

1 cup shredded carrots

1 (8-oz.) can pineapple tidbits, drained

1 In small bowl, combine all dressing ingredients; blend well.

2 In large bowl, combine all salad ingredients; toss gently. Pour dressing over salad; mix well. Cover; refrigerate at least 1 hour or until serving time.

Nutrition Information Per Serving
Serving Size: ½ Cup

Calories	170	Calories from Fat	130
		% Daily Value	
Total Fat	14g	22%	
Saturated	4g	20%	
Cholesterol	15mg	5%	
Sodium	95mg	4%	
Total Carbohydrate	10g	3%	
Dietary Fiber	2g	8%	
Sugars	8g		
Protein	1g		
Vitamin A	80%	Vitamin C	20%
Calcium	4%	Iron	2%

Dietary Exchanges: ½ Fruit, 3 Fat OR ½ Carbohydrate, 3 Fat

STRAWBERRY SPINACH SALAD WITH YOGURT POPPY SEED DRESSING

prep time: 10 min. • yield: 4 servings

The poppy seed dressing also makes a nice topping for sliced bananas and pineapple chunks.

DRESSING

4 teaspoons honey

½ cup low-fat strawberry yogurt

½ teaspoon poppy seed

SALAD

3 cups torn fresh spinach

2 cups sliced strawberries

¼ cup chopped pecans

1 In small bowl, combine all dressing ingredients; blend well.

2 Line 4 individual salad plates with spinach. Arrange strawberries over spinach. Sprinkle each with 1 tablespoon pecans. Drizzle dressing over salad.

Nutrition Information Per Serving
Serving Size: ¼ of Recipe

Calories	150	Calories from Fat	50
		% Daily Value	
Total Fat	6 g	9%	
Saturated	1 g	5%	
Cholesterol	0 mg	0%	
Sodium	50 mg	2%	
Total Carbohydrate	21 g	7%	
Dietary Fiber	4 g	16%	
Sugars	15 g		
Protein	4 g		
Vitamin A	60%	Vitamin C	100%
Calcium	10%	Iron	10%

Dietary Exchanges: 1 Fruit, 1 Vegetable, 1½ Fat OR 1 Carbohydrate, 1 Vegetable, 1½ Fat

SELECTING STRAWBERRIES

Strawberries should be firm, plump and fully red with a notable fragrance. For the best flavor, use berries within two days. Very large strawberries may make impressive garnishes but they can be hollow and not very flavorful.

To preserve freshness, wash and hull strawberries just before you're ready to use them. Store berries in the refrigerator for up to two days. For longer storage, rinse and hull the berries, then freeze them in a single layer on a baking tray or plate. When they're firm, transfer the frozen berries to a plastic container or resealable freezer bag and keep them in the freezer for up to four months.

1 pound of fresh berries = about 1 quart (about 4 cups)

1 pint fresh berries = about 2 cups

CAULIFLOWER SALAD WITH ORANGE VINAIGRETTE

prep time: 20 min. (ready in 2 hr. 20 min.) • yield: 12 (1-cup) servings

Cauliflower is a creamy-colored cousin of broccoli and is endowed with the same healthful cruciferous qualities. Don't bother peeling the zucchini for this salad unless the skin seems tough.

VINAIGRETTE

⅓ cup oil

¼ cup orange juice

2 tablespoons tarragon vinegar or cider vinegar

1 teaspoon dried tarragon leaves

1 teaspoon grated orange peel

½ to 1 teaspoon salt

½ teaspoon coarse ground black pepper

SALAD

2 cups bite-sized fresh cauliflower florets

2 small zucchini, sliced (2 cups)

½ cup sliced green onions

½ cup halved pitted ripe olives, drained

8 cups torn mixed salad greens

1 In jar with tight-fitting lid, combine all vinaigrette ingredients; shake well.

2 To partially cook cauliflower, plunge into rapidly boiling water for 1 to 2 minutes; drain. Place in large bowl. Pour vinaigrette over warm cauliflower. Add zucchini, onions and olives; toss gently. Cover; refrigerate at least 2 hours to blend flavors.

3 To serve, add salad greens to cauliflower mixture; toss gently.

Nutrition Information Per Serving
Serving Size: 1 Cup

Calories	90	Calories from Fat	60
		% Daily Value	
Total Fat	7 g	11%	
Saturated	1 g	5%	
Cholesterol	0 mg	0%	
Sodium	240 mg	10%	
Total Carbohydrate	5 g	2%	
Dietary Fiber	2 g	8%	
Sugars	3 g		
Protein	1 g		
Vitamin A	20%	Vitamin C	25%
Calcium	2%	Iron	2%

Dietary Exchanges: 1 Vegetable, 1½ Fat

Cauliflower Salad with Orange Vinaigrette

GARDEN VEGETABLE ROTINI SALAD

prep time: 20 min. (ready in 3 hr. 20 min.) •
yield: 15 (²⁄₃-cup) servings

There's no choice during the winter but to peel the heavily waxed skin of typical supermarket cucumbers. In summer, however, farmer's market cucumbers have tender, edible skin. To add a decorative edge to the cucumber slices, peel the skin off in strips, then slice.

8 oz. (2½ cups) uncooked rotini (spiral pasta)

½ cup thinly sliced red onion

2 medium tomatoes, chopped (2½ cups)

1 medium cucumber, chopped (2 cups)

1 medium yellow summer squash, halved, sliced (2 cups)

¼ to ⅓ cup salad supreme seasoning

1 (8-oz.) bottle zesty Italian salad dressing

1 Cook rotini to desired doneness as directed on package. Drain; rinse with cold water until cool.

2 Meanwhile, in large bowl, combine all remaining ingredients. Add cooked rotini; toss until well coated. Cover; refrigerate at least 3 hours. Stir gently before serving.

Nutrition Information Per Serving
Serving Size: ²⁄₃ Cup

Calories	100	Calories from Fat	25
		% Daily Value	
Total Fat	3 g	5%	
Saturated	1 g	5%	
Cholesterol	0 mg	0%	
Sodium	340 mg	14%	
Total Carbohydrate	16 g	5%	
Dietary Fiber	1 g	4%	
Sugars	3 g		
Protein	3 g		
Vitamin A	4%	Vitamin C	15%
Calcium	2%	Iron	6%

Dietary Exchanges: 1 Starch, ½ Fat OR 1 Carbohydrate, ½ Fat

TOMATO AND MOZZARELLA CHEESE SALAD

prep time: 15 min. (ready in 2 hr. 15 min.) • yield: 6 servings

Vidalia onions are naturally sweet. Marinating them in this recipe mellows the flavor further and adds subtle onion nuances to the dressing.

DRESSING
⅓ cup white wine vinegar

3 tablespoons olive or vegetable oil

1 teaspoon sugar

½ teaspoon dried basil leaves

¼ teaspoon salt

½ teaspoon lemon juice

SALAD
1 medium Vidalia or other sweet onion, thinly sliced

2 medium tomatoes, sliced

4 oz. mozzarella cheese, thinly sliced

2 tablespoons chopped fresh parsley

1 In small bowl, combine all dressing ingredients; blend well. Place onion slices in 8-inch square (2-quart) baking dish; pour dressing over onion. Cover; refrigerate at least 2 hours or until serving time.

2 Remove onion from dressing. Arrange onion, tomatoes and cheese on serving platter or 6 individual salad plates. Spoon dressing over salad. Sprinkle with parsley.

Calories	130	Calories from Fat	90
		% Daily Value	
Total Fat	10 g	15%	
Saturated	3 g	15%	
Cholesterol	10 mg	3%	
Sodium	190 mg	8%	
Total Carbohydrate	5 g	2%	
Dietary Fiber	1 g	3%	
Sugars	3 g		
Protein	6 g		
Vitamin A	10%	Vitamin C	20%
Calcium	15%	Iron	2%

Dietary Exchanges: 1 Vegetable, ½ Medium-Fat Meat, 1 ½ Fat

ALL-TIME FAVORITE POTATO SALAD

prep time: 25 min. (ready in 1 hr. 25 min.) •
yield: 5 (½-cup) servings

Scrub the potatoes thoroughly before boiling. When the cooked potatoes are cool enough to handle, it's easy to peel off just the thin outer skin and none of the flesh. However, peeling potatoes needn't be a precursor to making potato salad. If you use tender new red potatoes, you can leave the skins on for added color.

3 eggs

3 to 4 medium potatoes, cooked, peeled and cubed

2 stalks celery, chopped

1 small onion or 6 green onions, chopped

¼ cup chopped pickle or pickle relish

¾ cup mayonnaise or salad dressing

1 tablespoon prepared mustard

1 teaspoon salt

⅛ teaspoon pepper

1 Place eggs in small saucepan; cover with cold water. Bring to a boil. Reduce heat; simmer about 15 minutes.

2 Immediately drain; run cold water over eggs to stop cooking. Peel eggs; chop.

3 In large bowl, combine eggs, potatoes, celery, onion and pickle. In small bowl, combine mayonnaise, mustard, salt and pepper; blend well.

4 Add dressing to salad; mix well. Cover; refrigerate at least 1 hour or until serving time.

Calories	400	Calories from Fat	270
		% Daily Value	
Total Fat	30 g	46%	
Saturated	5 g	25%	
Cholesterol	145 mg	48%	
Sodium	790 mg	33%	
Total Carbohydrate	27 g	9%	
Dietary Fiber	3 g	12%	
Sugars	6 g		
Protein	6 g		
Vitamin A	6%	Vitamin C	15%
Calcium	4%	Iron	6%

Dietary Exchanges: 2 Starch, 5 ½ Fat OR 2 Carbohydrate, 5 ½ Fat

KEEP COOL, KEEP SAFE

Toting the potato salad or other perishables to a picnic?

- Keep cold foods cold and minimize the time they spend out of the cooler at the picnic site.

- Pack the most perishable foods closest to the ice.

- If possible, pack the foods you will eat first on top, so you can work your way down during the meal.

- Store the cooler in a shady area at the picnic site. Boost insulation qualities by covering the cooler with a thick folded towel or blanket.

- Avoid unnecessary opening of the cooler by packing beverages in a separate cooler.

- Remove small quantities of food at a time and place the storage containers back in the cooler as soon as possible.

Cook's Notes

LITE LAYERED VEGETABLE SALAD

prep time: 30 min. (ready in 8 hr. 30 min.) •
yield: 12 servings

This make-ahead salad is a great party choice, whether you're the host trying to minimize last-minute fussing or a guest who's contributing to the potluck.

1 head lettuce, torn into bite-sized pieces (about 10 cups)

½ cup chopped green onions

¾ cup reduced-calorie mayonnaise

½ cup light sour cream

½ cup sliced celery

½ cup chopped green bell pepper

1½ cups frozen sweet peas, cooked, cooled

1 cup halved cherry tomatoes

¾ cup finely shredded fresh Romano or Parmesan cheese

4 slices bacon, crisply cooked, crumbled

1 In large bowl or 13 × 9-inch pan, layer lettuce and onions.

2 In small bowl, combine mayonnaise and sour cream; blend well. Spoon ½ cup of the mayonnaise mixture evenly over onions.

3 Top with celery, bell pepper, peas and tomatoes. Spread remaining mayonnaise mixture over top. Sprinkle with cheese and bacon. Cover; refrigerate at least 8 hours or overnight. If desired, toss before serving.

Nutrition Information Per Serving
Serving Size: ¹/₁₂ of Recipe

Calories	80	Calories from Fat	35
		% Daily Value	
Total Fat	4 g	6%	
Saturated	2 g	10%	
Cholesterol	10 mg	3%	
Sodium	160 mg	7%	
Total Carbohydrate	7 g	2%	
Dietary Fiber	2 g	8%	
Sugars	3 g		
Protein	5 g		
Vitamin A	8%	Vitamin C	15%
Calcium	10%	Iron	4%

Dietary Exchanges: 1 Vegetable, ½ High-Fat Meat

Lite Layered Vegetable Salad

Orange-Hoisin Glazed Roasted
Chicken and Vegetables, page 94

POULTRY

P OULTRY IS A FAVORITE OF BEGINNING COOKS AND EXPERIENCED CHEFS ALIKE. ITS MILD FLAVOR LENDS ITSELF EQUALLY WELL TO PLAIN OR FANCY PREPARATIONS (ALL DELICIOUS); IT'S GREETED ENTHUSIASTICALLY BY BOTH YOUNG AND OLD; AND IT'S AMONG THE MOST ECONOMICAL PER SERVING OF MEATS. WHAT COULD BE BETTER? TURN THE PAGE TO BEGIN YOUR INTRODUCTION TO AN ARRAY OF CHICKEN AND TURKEY DISHES FOR GRILLING AND BAKING AS WELL AS FOR PANFRYING AND SLOW COOKING.

EASY CHICKEN PARMIGIANA

prep time: 30 min. • yield: 4 servings

To heighten color contrast, sprinkle the finished dish with chopped fresh basil, oregano and/or parsley, in addition to the ripe olives. Pass extra grated Parmesan cheese and hot pepper flakes.

6 oz. (2 cups) uncooked penne (medium pasta tubes)

¼ cup grated Parmesan cheese

¼ cup unseasoned dry bread crumbs

4 boneless, skinless chicken breast halves

1 tablespoon oil

1 (14.5-oz.) can Italian-style tomatoes with olive oil, garlic and spices, undrained

1 small zucchini, cut into 1½-inch-long thin strips

2 tablespoons chopped ripe olives

1 Cook pasta to desired doneness as directed on package. Drain; cover to keep warm.

2 Meanwhile, in shallow bowl, combine cheese and bread crumbs; mix well. Coat chicken breast halves with cheese mixture. Heat oil in large skillet over medium-high heat until hot. Add chicken; cook 3 to 5 minutes on each side or until browned.

3 Stir in tomatoes and zucchini. Bring to a boil. Reduce heat to low; cover and simmer 12 to 15 minutes or until chicken is fork-tender and juices run clear, stirring and turning chicken occasionally. Serve chicken mixture with pasta. Sprinkle with olives.

Nutrition Information Per Serving
Serving Size: ¼ of Recipe

Calories	430	Calories from Fat	110
		% Daily Value	
Total Fat	12 g	18%	
Saturated	3 g	15%	
Cholesterol	80 mg	27%	
Sodium	800 mg	33%	
Total Carbohydrate	43 g	14%	
Dietary Fiber	3 g	12%	
Sugars	7 g		
Protein	37 g		
Vitamin A	10%	Vitamin C	10%
Calcium	15%	Iron	20%

Dietary Exchanges: 2 Starch, 2 Vegetable, 4 Very Lean Meat, 1½ Fat
OR 2 Carbohydrate, 2 Vegetable, 4 Very Lean Meat, 1½ Fat

CHICKEN WITH PASTA AND PESTO

prep time: 20 min. • yield: 4 (1½-cup) servings

Along with Christopher Columbus, pesto sauce is one of Genoa, Italy's claims to fame. The wonderfully rich sauce is made with basil leaves, garlic, olive oil, Parmesan cheese and usually pine nuts or blanched almonds.

5 oz. (2 cups) uncooked medium shell pasta

1 tablespoon oil

4 boneless, skinless chicken breast halves, cut into 1-inch pieces

1 (14-oz.) can artichoke hearts, drained, quartered

½ cup purchased pesto

½ cup chopped tomato

1 oz. (¼ cup) shredded fresh Parmesan cheese

1 Cook pasta to desired doneness as directed on package. Drain; cover to keep warm.

2 Meanwhile, heat oil in large skillet over medium-high heat until hot. Add chicken; cook and stir 4 to 5 minutes or until browned and no longer pink.

3 Stir in artichoke hearts, pesto and pasta. Cook an additional 1 to 2 minutes or until thoroughly heated, stirring constantly. Sprinkle with tomato and Parmesan cheese.

Nutrition Information Per Serving
Serving Size: 1 ½ Cups

Calories	520	Calories from Fat	220
		% Daily Value	
Total Fat	24 g	37%	
Saturated	5 g	25%	
Cholesterol	80 mg	27%	
Sodium	450 mg	19%	
Total Carbohydrate	38 g	13%	
Dietary Fiber	5 g	20%	
Sugars	4 g		
Protein	39 g		
Vitamin A	10%	Vitamin C	15%
Calcium	20%	Iron	20%

Dietary Exchanges: 2 Starch, 1 Vegetable, 4 ½ Very Lean Meat, 4 Fat OR
2 Carbohydrate, 1 Vegetable, 4 ½ Very Lean Meat, 4 Fat

Chicken with Pasta and Pesto

CHICKEN FETTUCCINE WITH SUN-DRIED TOMATOES

prep time: 40 min. • yield: 4 (1¼-cup) servings

Inspired by Mediterranean ingredients, this skillet supper successfully teams the pungent flavors of rosemary, garlic, goat cheese and sun-dried tomatoes.

1 (3-oz.) pkg. sun-dried tomatoes, chopped

1 cup boiling water

¼ cup pine nuts

2 tablespoons olive or vegetable oil

3 boneless, skinless chicken breast halves (about 1 lb.), cut into bite-sized strips

2 garlic cloves, minced

½ teaspoon dried rosemary leaves, crushed

1 (9-oz.) pkg. refrigerated uncooked fettuccine

2 cups chopped fresh spinach

⅓ cup crumbled goat cheese (chèvre)

1 In small bowl, combine tomatoes and boiling water; let stand 10 minutes.

2 Meanwhile, heat large skillet over medium-high heat until hot. Add pine nuts; cook and stir until golden brown. Remove from skillet; set aside.

3 Heat oil in same skillet over medium-high heat until hot. Add chicken; cook and stir 4 to 5 minutes or until chicken is no longer pink. Add garlic; cook 30 seconds. Stir in tomato mixture and rosemary. Bring to a boil. Reduce heat; simmer 3 to 4 minutes to blend flavors.

4 Meanwhile, cook fettuccine to desired doneness as directed on package.

5 Add spinach to chicken mixture; cook 1 minute or until spinach just begins to wilt. Drain fettuccine; return to saucepan or place in serving bowl. Add chicken mixture; toss gently to mix. Sprinkle with cheese and pine nuts.

Nutrition Information Per Serving
Serving Size: 1¼ Cups

Calories	510	Calories from Fat	170
		% Daily Value	
Total Fat	19 g	29%	
Saturated	5 g	25%	
Cholesterol	125 mg	42%	
Sodium	580 mg	24%	
Total Carbohydrate	49 g	16%	
Dietary Fiber	5 g	20%	
Sugars	8 g		
Protein	35 g		
Vitamin A	45%	Vitamin C	20%
Calcium	10%	Iron	35%

Dietary Exchanges: 3 Starch, 1 Vegetable, 3½ Very Lean Meat, 3 Fat OR
3 Carbohydrate, 1 Vegetable, 3½ Very Lean Meat, 3 Fat

PICCATA CHICKEN

prep time: 30 min. • yield: 4 servings

Often paired with veal, piccata-style lemon-pepper sauce has a bright fresh flavor that works well with chicken, too. Stirring the parsley into the sauce just before serving keeps the herb's color and taste vibrant.

4 boneless, skinless chicken breast halves

¼ cup all-purpose flour

¼ teaspoon salt

¼ teaspoon white pepper

2 tablespoons oil

½ cup chicken broth

2 teaspoons Worcestershire sauce

¼ teaspoon dried marjoram leaves

2 tablespoons fresh lemon juice

¼ cup chopped fresh parsley

1 Place 1 chicken breast half between 2 pieces of plastic wrap or waxed paper. Working from center, gently pound chicken with flat side of meat mallet or rolling pin until about ¼ inch thick; remove wrap. Repeat with remaining chicken breast halves.

2 In shallow bowl, combine flour, salt and pepper. Coat chicken breast halves with flour mixture. Heat oil in large skillet over medium-high heat until hot. Add chicken; cook 3 to 5 minutes on each side or until golden brown, fork-tender and juices run clear.

3 Remove chicken from skillet; cover to keep warm. Add broth, Worcestershire sauce and marjoram to skillet; cook and stir 1 to 2 minutes. Stir in lemon juice and parsley. Serve over chicken.

Nutrition Information Per Serving
Serving Size: ¼ of Recipe

Calories	230	Calories from Fat	90
		% Daily Value	
Total Fat	10 g	15%	
Saturated	2 g	10%	
Cholesterol	75 mg	25%	
Sodium	320 mg	13%	
Total Carbohydrate	7 g	2%	
Dietary Fiber	0 g	0%	
Sugars	0 g		
Protein	28 g		
Vitamin A	4%	Vitamin C	10%
Calcium	2%	Iron	8%

Dietary Exchanges: ½ Starch, 4 Very Lean Meat, 1 Fat OR
½ Carbohydrate, 4 Very Lean Meat, 1 Fat

SAGE AND ROSEMARY CHICKEN STRIPS

prep time: 20 min. • yield: 4 servings

Serve the herbed chicken in a pita pocket with a dollop of sour cream or plain yogurt and some chopped fresh tomato or chopped bell pepper.

⅓ cup all-purpose flour

½ teaspoon onion powder

¼ teaspoon salt

¼ teaspoon dried rosemary leaves, crushed

⅛ teaspoon ground sage

4 boneless, skinless chicken breast halves, cut into long, thin strips

1 tablespoon oil

1 In shallow bowl, combine flour, onion powder, salt, rosemary and sage; mix well. Generously coat chicken pieces with flour mixture.

2 Heat oil in large skillet over medium-high heat until hot. Add chicken; reduce heat to medium. Cook and stir 8 to 10 minutes or until lightly browned on all sides and no longer pink.

Nutrition Information Per Serving
Serving Size: ¼ of Recipe

Calories	210	Calories from Fat	60
		% Daily Value	
Total Fat	7 g	11%	
Saturated	1 g	5%	
Cholesterol	75 mg	25%	
Sodium	200 mg	8%	
Total Carbohydrate	8 g	3%	
Dietary Fiber	0 g	0%	
Sugars	0 g		
Protein	28 g		
Vitamin A	0%	Vitamin C	0%
Calcium	0%	Iron	8%

Dietary Exchanges: ½ Starch, 4 Very Lean Meat, ½ Fat
OR ½ Carbohydrate, 4 Very Lean Meat, ½ Fat

GARDEN CHICKEN SAUTÉ

prep time: 20 min. • yield: 4 (1 ¼-cup) servings

Colorful and quick to make, this one-dish meal provides familiar flavors that everyone at your table will love.

2 teaspoons olive or vegetable oil

2 boneless, skinless chicken breast halves, cut into 1-inch pieces

2 garlic cloves, minced

2 cups water

2 (3-oz.) pkg. chicken-flavor ramen noodle soup mix

2 teaspoons dried Italian seasoning

1 cup fresh baby carrots, cut in half crosswise

2 cups sliced zucchini

1 Heat oil in large nonstick skillet over medium-high heat until hot. Add chicken and garlic; cook and stir 4 to 5 minutes or until chicken is browned.

2 Stir in 2 cups water, seasoning packets from soup mixes, Italian seasoning and carrots. Bring to a boil. Reduce heat; cover and cook 6 to 7 minutes or until carrots are crisp-tender.

3 Gently break each block of noodles in half; add noodles and zucchini to skillet. Bring to a boil. Boil, uncovered, 5 to 6 minutes or until zucchini is tender and noodles are cooked, separating noodles gently as they soften.

Nutrition Information Per Serving
Serving Size: 1 ¼ Cups

Calories	320	Calories from Fat	110
		% Daily Value	
Total Fat	12 g	18%	
Saturated	5 g	25%	
Cholesterol	35 mg	12%	
Sodium	710 mg	30%	
Total Carbohydrate	33 g	11%	
Dietary Fiber	2 g	8%	
Sugars	4 g		
Protein	19 g		
Vitamin A	180%	Vitamin C	10%
Calcium	6%	Iron	10%

Dietary Exchanges: 2 Starch, 1 Vegetable, 1 ½ Very Lean Meat, 2 Fat OR
2 Carbohydrate, 1 Vegetable, 1 ½ Very Lean Meat, 2 Fat

RAMEN NOODLES

Ramen noodles are Japanese instant-style noodles shaped like curly strands of spaghetti. Traditional versions are deep-fried and thus higher in fat than the same amount of regular pasta; lower-fat versions of ramen have become available in recent years. The noodles are usually sold in packages that also contain a packet of dehydrated broth mix. Ramen noodles can be found in your supermarket's soup section.

Cook's Notes

Garden Chicken Sauté

LIGHT LEMON CHICKEN

prep time: 20 min. • yield: 4 servings

Slightly sweet and somewhat tart, the lemony sauce gets an added flavor dimension from dry sherry and soy sauce.

4 cups cooked white rice (cooked as directed on package)

2 lemons

2 teaspoons cornstarch

1 teaspoon sugar

½ cup chicken broth

2 tablespoons dry sherry

2 tablespoons soy sauce

1 tablespoon oil

4 boneless, skinless chicken breast halves, cut into ¼-inch strips

½ teaspoon salt

⅛ teaspoon pepper

6 to 8 green onions, cut diagonally into 1½-inch pieces

1 red bell pepper, cut into ¼-inch strips

1 (4.5-oz.) jar sliced mushrooms, drained

1 While rice is cooking, cut ⅛-inch-thick strips of lemon peel from half of 1 lemon. Set aside. Slice other half and reserve for garnish. Squeeze juice from second lemon. In small bowl, combine cornstarch and sugar. Add 2 tablespoons lemon juice, broth, sherry and soy sauce; blend well. Set aside.

2 Heat oil in large skillet or wok over medium-high heat until hot. Add chicken; sprinkle with salt and pepper. Cook and stir 3 to 4 minutes or until chicken is no longer pink. Remove from skillet; cover to keep warm.

3 Add onions, bell pepper and mushrooms to skillet. Cook and stir 1 minute. Add lemon juice mixture to vegetables; cook and stir 1 to 2 minutes or until thickened. Return chicken to skillet; add lemon strips. Cook and stir 1 minute. Serve with rice. Garnish with lemon slices.

Nutrition Information Per Serving
Serving Size: ¼ of Recipe

Calories	430	Calories from Fat	60
		% Daily Value	
Total Fat	7 g	11%	
Saturated	2 g	10%	
Cholesterol	75 mg	25%	
Sodium	1090 mg	45%	
Total Carbohydrate	57 g	19%	
Dietary Fiber	4 g	16%	
Sugars	4 g		
Protein	34 g		
Vitamin A	15%	Vitamin C	70%
Calcium	8%	Iron	20%

Dietary Exchanges: 3 ½ Starch, 1 Vegetable, 3 Very Lean Meat, ½ Fat OR
3 ½ Carbohydrate, 1 Vegetable, 3 Very Lean Meat, ½ Fat

TYPES OF WHITE RICE

White rice is milled to remove the hull and bran coating. Vitamins and minerals are then added to most white rice to replace nutrients lost in the milling process.

White rice is available in three grain sizes: long, medium and short. *Long-grain rice* is long and thin, and the grains remain separate when cooked, making it the perfect choice for pilafs. *Medium-grain rice* is plump (but not round) and slightly more moist and tender than long-grain rice when cooked. Long or medium-grain white rice may be used when a recipe calls for regular white rice. *Short-grain rice* has almost round grains that have a higher starch content than the long or medium varieties. When cooked, short-grain rice tends to be softer, stickier and more moist. It is the preferred rice in Asia because it's easy to eat with chopsticks.

SKILLET CHICKEN CHOW MEIN

prep time: 30 min. • yield: 4 (1-cup) servings

This Chinese-American specialty is chock-full of colorful fresh vegetables. We've specified amounts, but feel free to substitute according to what's seasonally available. Other good choices include chopped bok choy or Chinese cabbage, snow pea pods or canned water chestnuts.

1 tablespoon oil

1 lb. boneless, skinless chicken breast halves, cut into ¾-inch pieces

1 cup sliced carrots

½ cup sliced celery

½ cup coarsely chopped green bell pepper

½ cup coarsely chopped onion

1 cup chicken broth

3 tablespoons soy sauce

2 teaspoons sugar

½ teaspoon garlic powder

½ teaspoon grated gingerroot or ⅛ teaspoon ginger

8 oz. (4 cups) fresh bean sprouts

2 tablespoons cornstarch

¼ cup cold water

1 cup chow mein noodles

1 Heat oil in large skillet or wok over medium-high heat until hot. Add chicken; cook and stir 3 to 5 minutes or until browned.

2 Add carrots, celery, bell pepper, onion, broth, soy sauce, sugar, garlic powder and gingerroot; mix well. Bring to a boil. Reduce heat to low; simmer 5 minutes or until vegetables are crisp-tender and chicken is no longer pink. Stir in bean sprouts; cook an additional 2 to 4 minutes or until thoroughly heated.

3 In small bowl, combine cornstarch and water; blend well. Gradually stir into mixture in skillet. Cook and stir over medium heat until sauce is bubbly and thickened. Sprinkle with chow mein noodles.

Nutrition Information Per Serving
Serving Size: 1 Cup

Calories	310	Calories from Fat	90
		% Daily Value	
Total Fat	10 g	15%	
Saturated	2 g	10%	
Cholesterol	70 mg	23%	
Sodium	1140 mg	48%	
Total Carbohydrate	24 g	8%	
Dietary Fiber	3 g	12%	
Sugars	7 g		
Protein	31 g		
Vitamin A	170%	Vitamin C	30%
Calcium	4%	Iron	15%

Dietary Exchanges: 1 Starch, 2 Vegetable, 3 ½ Very Lean Meat, 1 ½ Fat OR
1 Carbohydrate, 2 Vegetable, 3 ½ Very Lean Meat, 1 ½ Fat

Cook's Notes

THAWING FROZEN CHICKEN

When boneless, skinless chicken breasts are on sale, stock up. Wrap the breasts individually in plastic wrap, then pop them in a resealable plastic bag. Later, remove exactly the amount you need.

For optimum food safety, thaw frozen chicken gradually in the refrigerator, never at room temperature. Place the frozen wrapped chicken on a tray in the refrigerator and allow about 12 hours to defrost 2 to 3 pounds of chicken.

Many of us, however, prefer last-minute microwave thawing. Each microwave manufacturer has specific instructions for defrosting foods; some microwaves have "smart" defrost features that calculate time automatically when you punch in the food's weight and type. Microwave thawing may defrost unevenly, so cook foods right away to eliminate the possibility of bacterial growth.

MEXICALI CHICKEN AND RICE CASSEROLE

prep time: 20 min. (ready in 1 hr. 50 min.) • yield: 8 servings

Covering the casserole tightly helps retain the steam that cooks the rice as it bakes. When in season, leftover corn-on-the-cob kernels can be used in place of the frozen corn.

- 1 tablespoon oil
- 1 cup chopped onions
- ½ cup chopped green bell pepper
- 1 garlic clove, minced
- 1 (15.5-oz.) can light red kidney beans, drained
- 1 (14.5-oz.) can whole tomatoes, undrained, cut up
- 1 (14½-oz.) can ready-to-serve chicken broth
- 1 (4.5-oz.) can diced green chiles, undrained
- 2 cups frozen whole kernel corn
- ¾ cup uncooked regular long-grain white rice
- 1 teaspoon chili powder
- ½ teaspoon salt
- ½ teaspoon pepper
- 2 tablespoons all-purpose flour
- 1 teaspoon garlic salt
- 3 teaspoons paprika
- 3 to 3½ lb. cut-up frying chicken, skin removed if desired

1　Heat oven to 375°F. Heat oil in Dutch oven or large saucepan over medium-high heat until hot. Add onions, bell pepper and garlic; cook and stir until vegetables are tender. Add beans, tomatoes, broth, chiles, corn, rice, chili powder, salt and pepper; mix well. Pour mixture into ungreased 13 × 9-inch (3-quart) baking dish.

2　In resealable food storage plastic bag, combine flour, garlic salt and paprika; shake to mix. Add chicken; shake to coat. Place chicken pieces over rice mixture; press lightly into rice. Cover tightly with foil.

3　Bake at 375°F. for 1 to 1¼ hours or until chicken is fork-tender and juices run clear, rice is tender and liquid is absorbed. Remove foil; bake an additional 15 minutes or until chicken is browned.

Nutrition Information Per Serving
Serving Size: ⅛ of Recipe

Calories	330	Calories from Fat	70
		% Daily Value	
Total Fat	8 g	12%	
Saturated	2 g	10%	
Cholesterol	55 mg	18%	
Sodium	900 mg	38%	
Total Carbohydrate	38 g	13%	
Dietary Fiber	5 g	20%	
Sugars	5 g		
Protein	26 g		
Vitamin A	25%	Vitamin C	30%
Calcium	6%	Iron	20%

Dietary Exchanges: 2½ Starch, 2½ Lean Meat OR 2½ Carbohydrate, 2½ Lean Meat

LIGHT SOUR CREAM CHICKEN ENCHILADAS

prep time: 15 min. (ready in 50 min.) • yield: 6 servings

Mild green chiles add flavor, not fire. You can increase the heat of the enchiladas by substituting jalapeño chiles for the mild ones.

1 (8-oz.) container light sour cream

1 (8-oz.) container nonfat plain yogurt

1 ($10\frac{3}{4}$-oz.) can condensed 98% fat-free cream of chicken soup with $\frac{1}{3}$ less sodium

1 (4.5-oz.) can diced green chiles, undrained

12 (6- or 7-inch) white corn or flour tortillas

4 oz. (1 cup) shredded reduced-fat Cheddar cheese

$1\frac{1}{2}$ cups chopped cooked chicken

$\frac{1}{4}$ cup sliced green onions

1 Heat oven to 350°F. Spray 13 × 9-inch (3-quart) baking dish with nonstick cooking spray. In medium bowl, combine sour cream, yogurt, soup and chiles; mix well.

2 Spoon about 3 tablespoons sour cream mixture down center of each tortilla. Reserve $\frac{1}{4}$ cup of the cheese; sprinkle tortillas with remaining cheese, chicken and onions. Roll up; place in sprayed dish. Spoon remaining sour cream mixture over tortillas. Cover with foil.

3 Bake at 350°F. for 25 to 30 minutes or until hot and bubbly. Remove foil; sprinkle with reserved $\frac{1}{4}$ cup cheese. Bake uncovered for an additional 5 minutes or until cheese is melted. If desired, garnish with shredded lettuce and chopped tomatoes.

Nutrition Information Per Serving
Serving Size: $\frac{1}{6}$ of Recipe

Calories	340	Calories from Fat	110
		% Daily Value	
Total Fat	12 g	18%	
Saturated	6 g	30%	
Cholesterol	60 mg	20%	
Sodium	750 mg	31%	
Total Carbohydrate	37 g	12%	
Dietary Fiber	3 g	12%	
Sugars	7 g		
Protein	22 g		
Vitamin A	20%	Vitamin C	15%
Calcium	35%	Iron	8%

Dietary Exchanges: 2 ½ Starch, 2 Lean Meat, 1 Fat OR 2 ½ Carbohydrate, 2 Lean Meat, 1 Fat

CASSEROLES AND BAKING DISHES

"Casserole" usually refers to a dish that's deep, round and ovenproof. It generally has handles and a tight-fitting glass or ceramic cover.

A "baking dish" is usually square or rectangular, shallow and ovenproof. Foil is generally used when covering is required.

To substitute one type of dish for another, use the following guide:

$1\frac{1}{2}$-quart = 10 × 6-inch

2- to 2½-quart = 12 × 8- or 9-inch square

3-quart = 13 × 9-inch

Often, the size of the casserole or baking dish is stamped on the bottom. If not, you can determine the volume by measuring the amount of water it holds when filled.

Grease casseroles and baking dishes with nonstick cooking spray or solid shortening to make cleanup a snap.

CHICKEN PAPRIKASH POT PIE

prep time: 35 min. (ready in 1 hr. 20 min.) • yield: 6 servings

Chicken paprikash, a richly sauced Hungarian tradition, meets the down-home pot pie. To cut calories in this recipe, omit the bottom crust.

1 (15-oz.) pkg. refrigerated pie crusts

4 slices bacon, cut into 1/2-inch pieces

3/4 lb. boneless, skinless chicken breast halves, cut into 1/2-inch pieces

1 cup coarsely chopped onions

1 cup coarsely chopped red or green bell pepper

1 cup sliced carrots

1 cup frozen sweet peas

1/2 cup sour cream

1 (12-oz.) jar home-style chicken gravy

3 tablespoons cornstarch

3 teaspoons paprika

1 Heat oven to 425° F. Prepare pie crust as directed on package for *two-crust pie* using 9-inch pie pan.

2 In large skillet over medium heat, cook bacon until crisp. Reserve 1 tablespoon drippings with bacon in skillet.

3 Add chicken to skillet; cook and stir until no longer pink. Add onions, bell pepper and carrots; cook and stir until vegetables are tender. Stir in peas.

4 In small bowl, combine all remaining ingredients; mix well. Stir into chicken mixture in skillet. Spoon into crust-lined pan. Top with second crust and flute edges; cut slits or small designs in several places on top of crust.

5 Bake at 425° F. for 30 to 35 minutes or until crust is golden brown. Cover edge of crust with strips of foil after 10 to 15 minutes of baking to prevent excessive browning. Let stand 10 minutes before serving.

Nutrition Information Per Serving
Serving Size: 1/6 of Recipe

Calories	550	Calories from Fat	270
		% Daily Value	
Total Fat	30 g	46%	
Saturated	12 g	60%	
Cholesterol	65 mg	22%	
Sodium	750 mg	31%	
Total Carbohydrate	52 g	17%	
Dietary Fiber	3 g	12%	
Sugars	7 g		
Protein	19 g		
Vitamin A	160%	Vitamin C	45%
Calcium	8%	Iron	10%

Dietary Exchanges: 3 Starch, 1 Vegetable, 1 Very Lean Meat, 5 1/2 Fat OR
3 Carbohydrate, 1 Vegetable, 1 Very Lean Meat, 5 1/2 Fat

BAKED CHICKEN BREASTS SUPREME

prep time: 15 min. (ready in 9 hr. 25 min.) • yield: 12 servings

Sprinkle chopped fresh parsley or a little more paprika on the chicken just before serving to enhance the color.

2 cups sour cream

3 tablespoons lemon juice

1 tablespoon Worcestershire sauce

2 teaspoons celery salt

2 teaspoons paprika

1/2 teaspoon salt

1/2 teaspoon pepper

4 garlic cloves, minced

12 bone-in chicken breast halves, skin removed

1 3/4 cups unseasoned dry bread crumbs

1/3 cup margarine or butter

1 In large bowl, combine sour cream, lemon juice, Worcestershire sauce, celery salt, paprika, salt, pepper and garlic; mix well. Add chicken to sour cream marinade, covering each piece well. Cover; refrigerate 8 hours or overnight.

2 Heat oven to 350° F. Lightly grease two 15 × 10 × 1-inch baking pans or two 13 × 9-inch pans. Remove chicken from sour cream marinade; discard marinade. Coat chicken with bread crumbs. Arrange in single layer in greased pans. In small saucepan, melt margarine; spoon evenly over chicken.

3 Bake at 350° F. for 60 to 70 minutes or until chicken is fork-tender and juices run clear.

Nutrition Information Per Serving
Serving Size: 1/12 of Recipe

Calories	260	Calories from Fat	100
		% Daily Value	
Total Fat	11 g	17%	
Saturated	3 g	15%	
Cholesterol	75 mg	25%	
Sodium	360 mg	15%	
Total Carbohydrate	12 g	4%	
Dietary Fiber	0 g	0%	
Sugars	1 g		
Protein	29 g		
Vitamin A	8%	Vitamin C	0%
Calcium	6%	Iron	10%

Dietary Exchanges: 1 Starch, 3 1/2 Lean Meat OR 1 Carbohydrate, 3 1/2 Lean Meat

IS IT DONE?

To check smaller pieces of poultry (stir-fry-sized pieces, for example) for doneness, break apart the largest piece of meat with a spoon or knife. When there's no longer any pink in the center, it's fully cooked. To check the doneness of large pieces of poultry (breasts, whole birds or whole tenderloins), pierce the thickest portion of the meat with a fork. When the juice that appears is a clear, pale yellow without a pink tinge, and the flesh is fork-tender, the meat is fully cooked.

GARLIC 'N HERB OVEN-FRIED CHICKEN

prep time: 15 min. (ready in 1 hr. 10 min.) • yield: 4 servings

Buttermilk's role is threefold in this recipe. It allows the crumb coating to adhere to the chicken; it adds a tangy flavor; and it boosts the moistness of the meat. The chicken emerges from the oven with an appealing crisp, browned exterior, without the fat or labor-intensive preparation of deep-frying.

1 cup unseasoned dry bread crumbs

1/4 cup finely chopped fresh parsley

1 (.75-oz.) pkg. dry garlic-herb salad dressing mix

1 cup buttermilk

3 to 3 1/2 lb. cut-up frying chicken

2 tablespoons margarine or butter, melted

1 Heat oven to 400° F. In medium bowl, combine bread crumbs, parsley and salad dressing mix; mix well.

2 Place buttermilk in shallow bowl. Dip chicken pieces in buttermilk; coat with crumb mixture. Place chicken, skin side up, in ungreased 13 × 9-inch pan. Drizzle margarine evenly over chicken.

3 Bake at 400° F. for 50 to 55 minutes or until chicken is fork-tender and juices run clear.

Nutrition Information Per Serving
Serving Size: 1/4 of Recipe

Calories	420	Calories from Fat	150
		% Daily Value	
Total Fat	17 g	26%	
Saturated	4 g	20%	
Cholesterol	115 mg	38%	
Sodium	1130 mg	47%	
Total Carbohydrate	24 g	8%	
Dietary Fiber	1 g	4%	
Sugars	6 g		
Protein	43 g		
Vitamin A	10%	Vitamin C	6%
Calcium	15%	Iron	20%

Dietary Exchanges: 1 1/2 Starch, 5 1/2 Lean Meat OR 1 1/2 Carbohydrate, 5 1/2 Lean Meat

Herb Cheese-Stuffed Chicken Breasts

HERB CHEESE-STUFFED CHICKEN BREASTS

prep time: 20 min. (ready in 1 hr.) • yield: 4 servings

Feta cheese, fresh herbs, olives and tomatoes impart Mediterranean flair to boneless chicken breasts. Serve the chicken with green beans and crusty dinner rolls, or over pasta, such as fettuccine.

4 boneless, skinless chicken breast halves

2 oz. feta cheese, crumbled (½ cup)

¼ cup chopped fresh parsley

2 teaspoons chopped fresh oregano or ¼ teaspoon dried oregano leaves

2 tablespoons olive or vegetable oil

2 (14.5-oz.) cans Italian-style diced tomatoes, undrained

¼ cup sliced ripe olives

4 teaspoons cornstarch

1 Heat oven to 350°F. Using sharp knife, cut 3-inch slit in meaty side of each chicken breast half to form pocket.

2 In medium bowl, combine feta cheese, parsley, oregano and oil; mix well. Gently spoon half of filling into each pocket. Place chicken in ungreased 13 × 9-inch (3-quart) baking dish.

3 In another medium bowl, combine tomatoes, olives and cornstarch; mix well. Pour over chicken.

4 Bake at 350°F. for 35 to 40 minutes or until chicken is fork-tender and juices run clear.

Nutrition Information Per Serving			
Serving Size: ¼ of Recipe			
Calories	320	Calories from Fat	130
		% Daily Value	
Total Fat	14 g	22%	
Saturated	4 g	20%	
Cholesterol	85 mg	28%	
Sodium	750 mg	31%	
Total Carbohydrate	18 g	6%	
Dietary Fiber	3 g	12%	
Sugars	5 g		
Protein	31 g		
Vitamin A	30%	Vitamin C	35%
Calcium	15%	Iron	15%

Dietary Exchanges: ½ Starch, 2 Vegetable, 4 Very Lean Meat, 2 Fat OR ½ Carbohydrate, 2 Vegetable, 4 Very Lean Meat, 2 Fat

HOW TO MAKE STUFFED CHICKEN BREASTS

So simple, so special, stuffed chicken breasts are a snap to make. Start with boneless, skinless breast halves, then just stuff, bake and serve them.

STEP 1

Using a sharp knife, make a 3-inch cut in the meaty side of each chicken breast half to form a pocket.

STEP 2

Gently spoon ¼ of the cheese and herb filling into each pocket, pushing filling with the back of a spoon into the back of the pocket.

GARLIC AND LEMON ROASTED CHICKEN

prep time: 15 min. (ready in 1 hr. 55 min.) • **yield: 4 servings**

The lemon will release its juice more readily if you roll it on the counter with the palm of your hand before halving. To add an herbal nuance to the chicken, stir a tablespoon of chopped fresh rosemary or thyme into the lemon juice mixture.

2 lemons, halved

2 tablespoons margarine or butter, melted

1 tablespoon minced garlic

¼ teaspoon salt

⅛ teaspoon pepper

1 (3- to 3½-lb.) whole frying chicken

1 Heat oven to 375° F. Squeeze 1 lemon to yield ¼ cup juice; reserve remaining 2 lemon halves. In small bowl, combine lemon juice and all remaining ingredients except chicken; mix well.

2 Remove giblets from chicken; remove as much fat as possible. Rinse and drain chicken. Pat dry inside and out with paper towels. Brush lemon mixture over chicken skin and inside cavity. Place chicken, breast side up, on rack in shallow roasting pan. Place reserved lemon halves inside chicken cavity.

3 Bake at 375° F. for 1¼ to 1½ hours. Chicken is done when drumstick moves easily up and down and twists in socket, and when chicken is fork-tender and juices run clear. Let stand 5 to 10 minutes before serving.

Nutrition Information Per Serving
Serving Size: ¼ of Recipe

Calories	420	Calories from Fat	240
		% Daily Value	
Total Fat	27 g	42%	
Saturated	7 g	35%	
Cholesterol	135 mg	45%	
Sodium	330 mg	14%	
Total Carbohydrate	2 g	1%	
Dietary Fiber	0 g	0%	
Sugars	0 g		
Protein	43 g		
Vitamin A	10%	Vitamin C	6%
Calcium	4%	Iron	10%

Dietary Exchanges: 6 Lean Meat, 2 Fat

HANDLING UNCOOKED CHICKEN

Uncooked chicken can carry harmful bacteria. A few simple kitchen rules will help you serve chicken safely.

- Wash your hands before and after handling raw chicken.
- Wash raw chicken in cold water and pat it dry before cooking.
- Clean all utensils and cutting surfaces touched by raw chicken with hot soapy water and rinse thoroughly. It's best to use a cutting board with a hard surface. If you use a wooden cutting board, pay special attention to the crevices.
- Never transfer cooked chicken on the same platter that has held uncooked chicken until the platter has been washed thoroughly with hot, soapy water.

Garlic and Lemon
Roasted Chicken

ORANGE-HOISIN GLAZED ROASTED CHICKEN AND VEGETABLES

prep time: 10 min. (ready in 55 min.) • yield: 4 servings

PICTURED ON PAGE 76

Serve rice with this Asian-accented chicken.

CHICKEN AND VEGETABLES
4 bone-in chicken breast halves (with skin)

½ cup water

2 cups fresh baby carrots

2 cups fresh or frozen sugar snap peas

GLAZE
¼ cup orange marmalade

2 tablespoons hoisin sauce

1 tablespoon oil

¼ teaspoon salt

1 Heat oven to 425° F. Arrange chicken, skin side up, in ungreased 15 × 10 × 1-inch baking pan.

2 In small bowl, combine all glaze ingredients; mix well. Brush about 2 tablespoons glaze over chicken. Bake at 425° F. for 25 minutes.

3 Meanwhile, in medium saucepan, bring water to a boil. Add carrots; bring to a boil. Cover; simmer 8 to 10 minutes or until carrots are crisp-tender. Drain.

4 Add carrots and sugar snap peas to baking pan. Brush chicken and vegetables with remaining glaze. Bake an additional 15 to 20 minutes or until chicken is fork-tender, juices run clear and vegetables are tender.

Nutrition Information Per Serving
Serving Size: ¼ of Recipe

Calories	330	Calories from Fat	100
		% Daily Value	
Total Fat	11 g	17%	
Saturated	3 g	15%	
Cholesterol	80 mg	27%	
Sodium	400 mg	17%	
Total Carbohydrate	27 g	9%	
Dietary Fiber	4 g	16%	
Sugars	18 g		
Protein	31 g		
Vitamin A	100%	Vitamin C	6%
Calcium	8%	Iron	10%

Dietary Exchanges: 1 Fruit, 2 Vegetable, 4 Lean Meat OR 1 Carbohydrate, 2 Vegetable, 4 Lean Meat

STORING CHICKEN

Fresh uncooked chicken can be stored in the coldest part of the refrigerator for up to two days after purchase.

Chicken purchased in an airtight plastic bag or plastic-wrapped on a tray can be safely stored in its original packing. Set it on a plate or seal in a larger plastic bag to prevent drips.

If the wrapping is torn or if the chicken has been wrapped in butcher paper, rewrap it in plastic wrap or place it in a plastic bag (squeezing all the air out before sealing) prior to refrigerating.

Cook's Notes

ROASTED CHICKEN AND VEGETABLES PROVENÇAL

prep time: 30 min. (ready in 1 hr. 35 min.) • yield: 4 servings

Roasting the chicken together with vegetables and herbs lets the flavors mingle. Serve the casserole with a tossed salad and warmed French bread.

8 small new red potatoes, quartered

1 small yellow summer squash, cut into 1-inch pieces

1 small zucchini, cut into 1-inch pieces

1 red bell pepper, cut into 1-inch pieces

1 medium red onion, cut into eighths

1 (8-oz.) pkg. fresh mushrooms

¼ cup olive oil

2 teaspoons dried basil leaves

2 teaspoons dried thyme leaves

½ teaspoon salt

½ teaspoon coarse ground black pepper

3 garlic cloves, minced

3 to 3½ lb. cut-up frying chicken, skin removed

1 Heat oven to 375° F. In ungreased 13 × 9-inch (3-quart) baking dish, combine potatoes, squash, zucchini, bell pepper, onion and mushrooms.

2 In small bowl, combine oil, basil, thyme, salt, pepper and garlic; mix well. Brush half of oil mixture on vegetables. Place chicken pieces, meaty side up, over vegetables. Brush chicken with remaining oil mixture.

3 Bake at 375° F. for 45 minutes. Baste with pan juices; bake an additional 15 to 20 minutes or until chicken is fork-tender and juices run clear, and vegetables are tender. Baste with pan juices before serving.

Nutrition Information Per Serving
Serving Size: ¼ of Recipe

Calories	550	Calories from Fat	220
		% Daily Value	
Total Fat	24 g	37%	
Saturated	5 g	25%	
Cholesterol	115 mg	38%	
Sodium	390 mg	16%	
Total Carbohydrate	41 g	14%	
Dietary Fiber	7 g	28%	
Sugars	7 g		
Protein	43 g		
Vitamin A	30%	Vitamin C	80%
Calcium	10%	Iron	30%

Dietary Exchanges: 2 ½ Starch, 1 Vegetable, 5 Lean Meat, 1 Fat OR
2 ½ Carbohydrate, 1 Vegetable, 5 Lean Meat, 1 Fat

Cornish Hens with
Apple-Raisin Stuffing

CORNISH HENS WITH APPLE-RAISIN STUFFING

prep time: 20 min. (ready in 1 hr. 35 min.) • yield: 8 servings

Apple jelly and margarine give tasty game hens a beautifully browned, shimmering exterior. Currant jelly works as well.

STUFFING

3 tablespoons margarine or butter

1/2 cup chopped green onions

1 red baking apple, unpeeled, chopped

4 cups unseasoned dry bread cubes

1/2 cup raisins

1/4 teaspoon salt

1/4 teaspoon allspice

1/4 cup apple juice

CORNISH HENS

4 (1 1/2-lb.) Cornish game hens

1/4 teaspoon salt

1/8 teaspoon pepper

1/4 cup apple jelly

2 tablespoons margarine or butter

1 Heat oven to 350° F. Melt 3 tablespoons margarine in large skillet over medium-high heat. Add onions and apple; cook and stir until tender. Stir in remaining stuffing ingredients.

2 Split each game hen in half. Sprinkle lightly with salt and pepper. Spread stuffing in ungreased 15 × 10 × 1-inch baking pan. Place game hens, skin side up, over stuffing. In small saucepan over low heat, melt jelly with 2 tablespoons margarine. Brush over game hens.

3 Bake uncovered at 350° F. for 1 to 1 1/4 hours or until game hens are fork-tender and juices run clear.

Nutrition Information Per Serving
Serving Size: 1/8 of Recipe

Calories	400	Calories from Fat	140
		% Daily Value	
Total Fat	16 g	25%	
Saturated	4 g	20%	
Cholesterol	100 mg	33%	
Sodium	430 mg	18%	
Total Carbohydrate	29 g	10%	
Dietary Fiber	2 g	8%	
Sugars	15 g		
Protein	34 g		
Vitamin A	8%	Vitamin C	4%
Calcium	6%	Iron	15%

Dietary Exchanges: 1 Starch, 1 Fruit, 4 1/2 Lean Meat, 1/2 Fat OR
2 Carbohydrate, 4 1/2 Lean Meat, 1/2 Fat

CORNISH GAME HENS

The smallest and youngest of poultry commercially available in the United States, Cornish hens are four to six weeks old and weigh between 3/4 and 2 pounds. Depending on the size of the bird (and appetites of the diners), a single bird may serve one or two people. The hens are sweeter and more tender than older chickens, and usually more expensive, too.

To split the birds before cooking, use a sharp, heavy knife to cut along either side of the backbone. Spread the bird out flat on the cutting surface, using the knife to cut through the breast bone to separate the bird into two pieces.

Twenty-Garlic Chicken Dinner

TWENTY-GARLIC CHICKEN DINNER

prep time: 10 min. (ready in 7 hr. 10 min.) • yield: 4 servings

Because garlic loses its raw harshness and takes on a mellow, almost nutty character as it bakes, the large number of garlic cloves will not be overpowering. Roasted in its skin, the extra garlic makes a wonderful spread for accompanying mashed potatoes, bread, crackers or vegetables.

1 (3- to 3 1/2-lb.) whole frying chicken

1 teaspoon salt

1 teaspoon paprika

1/2 teaspoon pepper

1 teaspoon olive oil

1 large onion, sliced

1 medium bulb garlic (about 20 cloves)

Instant mashed potatoes for 4 servings

1 Remove giblets from chicken; remove as much fat as possible. Rinse and drain chicken. Pat dry inside and out with paper towels.

2 In small bowl, combine salt, paprika, pepper and oil; mix to form paste. Spread evenly over chicken.

3 Place onion in 3 1/2- or 4-quart slow cooker. Place chicken, breast side up, over onion. Separate garlic into cloves; do not peel cloves. Place garlic cloves in and around chicken.

4 Cover; cook on low setting for at least 7 hours or until chicken is fork-tender and juices run clear.

5 Ten minutes before serving, prepare mashed potatoes as directed on package.

6 With slotted spoon, remove chicken, onion and garlic from slow cooker. Cut chicken into pieces to serve. Squeeze 4 cooked garlic cloves onto mashed potatoes; mix well. Reserve remaining cooked garlic cloves to spread on bread or vegetables.

Nutrition Information Per Serving
Serving Size: 1/4 of Recipe

Calories	570	Calories from Fat	260
		% Daily Value	
Total Fat	29 g	45%	
Saturated	8 g	40%	
Cholesterol	140 mg	47%	
Sodium	930 mg	39%	
Total Carbohydrate	30 g	10%	
Dietary Fiber	3 g	12%	
Sugars	4 g		
Protein	47 g		
Vitamin A	20%	Vitamin C	10%
Calcium	10%	Iron	15%

Dietary Exchanges: 2 Starch, 5 1/2 Medium-Fat Meat OR 2 Carbohydrate, 5 1/2 Medium-Fat Meat

SLOW-COOKED SUCCESS

- For easiest cleaning, purchase a slow cooker with a removable insert so you don't have to worry about splashing the cord with dishwater.
- Slow cookers hold in moisture more than other cooking methods. Don't add more liquid than specified in the recipe.
- Slow cooking is supposed to be slow, but you may delay the process unnecessarily if you remove the lid too often or too soon.
- Seasonings sometimes fade in the slow cooker. Taste before serving and add more seasonings if needed.

Cook's Notes

EASY JERK CHICKEN

prep time: 15 min. (ready in 24 hr. 55 min.) • yield: 6 servings

Traditional "jerk" preparations, a Jamaican specialty, depend on long, slow cooking to let the spicy complexity of the seasoning mixture permeate the meat. Our version cooks quickly on the grill or under the broiler, relying instead on extended marinating to flavor the chicken.

MARINADE
½ cup chopped onion

⅓ cup firmly packed brown sugar

2 jalapeño chiles, seeded, chopped

2 garlic cloves, minced

1 tablespoon apple pie spice

½ cup red wine vinegar

⅓ cup olive oil

1 teaspoon hot pepper sauce

CHICKEN
3 to 3½ lb. cut-up frying chicken, skin removed

1 GRILL DIRECTIONS: In ungreased 12 × 8-inch (2-quart) baking dish or resealable food storage plastic bag, combine all marinade ingredients; blend well. Add chicken; turn to coat. Cover dish or seal bag. Refrigerate at least 24 hours, turning occasionally.

2 Heat half of gas grill to medium heat, or place charcoal along one side of charcoal grill and heat until coals are hot. Lightly oil unheated side of grill rack.

3 When ready to grill, remove chicken from marinade; reserve marinade. Place chicken pieces on oiled grill. Cover grill; cook 30 to 40 minutes or until chicken is fork-tender and juices run clear, brushing chicken with marinade and turn-ing twice during cooking. Discard any remaining marinade.

TIP: To broil chicken, place on broiler pan; broil 4 to 6 inches from heat using times above as a guide.

Nutrition Information Per Serving			
Serving Size: ⅙ of Recipe			
Calories	200	Calories from Fat	80
		% Daily Value	
Total Fat	9 g	14%	
Saturated	2 g	10%	
Cholesterol	75 mg	25%	
Sodium	75 mg	3%	
Total Carbohydrate	4 g	1%	
Dietary Fiber	0 g	0%	
Sugars	3 g		
Protein	25 g		
Vitamin A	0%	Vitamin C	10%
Calcium	2%	Iron	8%

Dietary Exchanges: ½ Fruit, 3 Lean Meat OR ½ Carbohydrate, 3 Lean Meat

HONEY MUSTARD CHICKEN

prep time: 1 hr. 10 min. • yield: 4 servings

Sweet glazes are brushed on grilled meats near the end of the cooking time to prevent the glaze from burning.

GLAZE
½ cup apple juice

3 tablespoons Dijon mustard

2 tablespoons oil

2 tablespoons honey

½ teaspoon salt

Dash pepper

CHICKEN
3 to 3½ lb. cut-up or quartered frying chicken, skin removed if desired

1 GRILL DIRECTIONS: Heat grill. In small bowl, combine all glaze ingredients; blend well. Set aside.

2 When ready to grill, place chicken, skin side down, on gas grill over low heat or on charcoal

grill 4 to 6 inches from medium coals. Cook 45 to 60 minutes or until chicken is fork-tender and juices run clear, turning often and brushing frequently with glaze during last 15 minutes of cooking. Bring any remaining glaze to a boil. Serve with chicken.

TIP: To bake chicken in oven, place, skin side down, in 13 × 9-inch (3-quart) baking dish. Bake at 350° F. for 30 minutes. Remove most of pan juices; turn chicken. Bake an additional 15 to 25 minutes, brushing with glaze as directed above.

Nutrition Information Per Serving
Serving Size: ¼ of Recipe

Calories	490	Calories from Fat	260
		% Daily Value	
Total Fat	29 g	45%	
Saturated	7 g	35%	
Cholesterol	135 mg	45%	
Sodium	680 mg	28%	
Total Carbohydrate	13 g	4%	
Dietary Fiber	0 g	0%	
Sugars	12 g		
Protein	43 g		
Vitamin A	6%	Vitamin C	0%
Calcium	4%	Iron	15%

Dietary Exchanges: 1 Fruit, 6 Lean Meat, 2 Fat OR 1 Carbohydrate,
6 Lean Meat, 2 Fat

TERIYAKI GRILLED CHICKEN KABOBS

prep time: 30 min. (ready in 2 hr. 30 min.) • yield: 4 kabobs

The sweet marinade is made with brown sugar, soy sauce, sherry and seasoning. It tenderizes the meat and promotes browning as it cooks. Serve the kabobs on a bed of rice with a salad of tender leaf lettuce.

MARINADE
2 tablespoons brown sugar

3 tablespoons soy sauce

2 tablespoons dry sherry

1 tablespoon oil

¼ teaspoon ginger

⅛ teaspoon garlic powder

KABOBS
8 boneless, skinless chicken thighs

1 large red bell pepper, cut into 8 pieces

1 medium zucchini, cut into 8 pieces

8 (1- to 2-inch) chunks fresh pineapple or 8 canned pineapple chunks

1 GRILL DIRECTIONS: In ungreased 12 × 8-inch (2-quart) baking dish or resealable food storage plastic bag, combine all marinade ingredients. Cut chicken thighs in half; add to marinade. Cover dish or seal bag. Refrigerate at least 2 hours to marinate, turning chicken once.

2 Heat grill. Drain chicken, reserving marinade. Alternately thread chicken, bell pepper, zucchini and pineapple onto four 12-inch metal skewers.

3 When ready to grill, place kabobs on gas grill over medium heat or on charcoal grill 4 to 6 inches from medium-high coals. Cook 15 to 20 minutes or until chicken is no longer pink, turning often and brushing frequently with reserved marinade. Discard any remaining marinade.

TIP: To broil chicken, place on broiler pan; broil 4 to 6 inches from heat using times above as a guide.

Nutrition Information Per Serving
Serving Size: 1 Kabob

Calories	280	Calories from Fat	120
		% Daily Value	
Total Fat	13 g	20%	
Saturated	3 g	15%	
Cholesterol	100 mg	33%	
Sodium	300 mg	13%	
Total Carbohydrate	12 g	4%	
Dietary Fiber	2 g	8%	
Sugars	8 g		
Protein	29 g		
Vitamin A	35%	Vitamin C	70%
Calcium	4%	Iron	10%

Dietary Exchanges: ½ Fruit, 1 Vegetable, 4 Lean Meat OR ½ Carbohydrate,
1 Vegetable, 4 Lean Meat

SIZZLING CHICKEN FAJITAS

prep time: 45 min. (ready in 2 hr. 45 min.) • yield: 4 servings

Cumin, chili powder and lime work their Tex-Mex magic as the chicken cooks in foil packets on the grill or in the oven.

4 teaspoons chili powder

1 teaspoon cumin

½ teaspoon salt

4 garlic cloves, minced

¼ cup lime juice

4 boneless, skinless chicken breast halves, cut into ½-inch strips

2 red or yellow bell peppers, seeded, cut into rings

2 small onions, thinly sliced, separated into rings

8 (8- to 10-inch) flour tortillas

1 GRILL DIRECTIONS: In large bowl, combine chili powder, cumin, salt, garlic and lime juice; mix well. Add chicken, bell pepper and onions; stir to coat. Cover bowl; refrigerate at least 2 hours to marinate, turning once.

2 Heat grill. Cut four 18 × 12-inch pieces of heavy-duty foil. Remove chicken and vegetables from marinade; discard marinade. Place ¼ of chicken and vegetables on each piece of foil. Wrap each packet securely using double-fold seals, allowing room for heat expansion. Place tortillas on another sheet of heavy-duty foil; wrap securely.

3 When ready to grill, place packets on gas grill over medium heat or on charcoal grill 4 to 6 inches from medium coals. Cook chicken and vegetables 10 to 15 minutes or until chicken is no longer pink and vegetables are crisp-tender. Cook tortillas 2 to 3 minutes or until warm.

4 Serve each chicken and vegetable packet with 2 tortillas. If desired, top tortillas with shredded lettuce, sour cream, guacamole and salsa.

TIP: To bake packets, place on cookie sheet. Bake at 425° F. Bake chicken and vegetable packets for 15 to 20 minutes; bake tortilla packet for 3 to 5 minutes.

Nutrition Information Per Serving
Serving Size: ¼ of Recipe

Calories	520	Calories from Fat	100
		% Daily Value	
Total Fat	11 g	17%	
Saturated	2 g	10%	
Cholesterol	75 mg	25%	
Sodium	670 mg	28%	
Total Carbohydrate	67 g	22%	
Dietary Fiber	5 g	20%	
Sugars	5 g		
Protein	37 g		
Vitamin A	45%	Vitamin C	90%
Calcium	15%	Iron	30%

Dietary Exchanges: 4 Starch, 1 Vegetable, 3 Very Lean Meat, 1½ Fat OR
4 Carbohydrate, 1 Vegetable, 3 Very Lean Meat, 1½ Fat

RECIPE PREPARATION SHORTCUT

Ingredients such as diced onion or chopped bell pepper can be prepared ahead of time. Seal them in plastic bags; label and refrigerate them up to three days. For longer storage, freeze them up to one month. Spread the vegetables in a single layer in a shallow baking pan, cover with plastic wrap and freeze. When frozen, break into pieces and place in a freezer bag or freezer-proof container. When needed in a recipe, add the required amount of onion or bell pepper without thawing.

Sizzling
Chicken Fajitas

TURKEY WILD RICE CASSEROLE

prep time: 15 min. (ready in 2 hr. 15 min.) • yield: 6 servings

To maximize moistness, the turkey tenderloins are baked whole over the wild rice mixture. Cut them into slices before serving.

RICE
1 cup uncooked wild rice, rinsed

½ cup chopped onion

3 cups water

SAUCE
3 tablespoons margarine or butter

3 tablespoons all-purpose flour

¼ teaspoon salt

⅛ teaspoon pepper

¾ cup chicken broth

½ cup milk

CASSEROLE
½ cup chopped carrot

½ cup chopped celery

½ teaspoon dried sage leaves

2 (½- to ¾-lb.) fresh turkey breast
   tenderloins

¼ teaspoon salt

1 teaspoon dried parsley flakes

⅛ teaspoon paprika

1 In medium saucepan, combine wild rice, onion and water. Bring to a boil. Reduce heat to low; cover and simmer 50 to 60 minutes or until rice is tender and water is absorbed. Set aside.

2 Melt margarine in medium saucepan over medium heat. Stir in flour, ¼ teaspoon salt and pepper. Cook until mixture is smooth and bubbly,

stirring constantly. Gradually stir in broth and milk, cooking until mixture boils and thickens, stirring constantly. Remove from heat.

3 Heat oven to 350°F. In ungreased 12 × 8-inch (2-quart) baking dish, combine cooked rice mixture, sauce, carrot, celery and sage; mix well. Place turkey breast tenderloins over rice. Sprinkle with ¼ teaspoon salt, parsley and paprika. Cover with foil.

4 Bake at 350°F. for 1 to 1¼ hours or until turkey is no longer pink. To serve, cut turkey breast tenderloins crosswise into ½-inch-thick slices.

Nutrition Information Per Serving
Serving Size: ⅙ of Recipe

Calories	300	Calories from Fat	60
		% Daily Value	
Total Fat	7 g	11%	
Saturated	2 g	10%	
Cholesterol	75 mg	25%	
Sodium	410 mg	17%	
Total Carbohydrate	27 g	9%	
Dietary Fiber	2 g	8%	
Sugars	3 g		
Protein	33 g		
Vitamin A	60%	Vitamin C	4%
Calcium	6%	Iron	15%

Dietary Exchanges: 2 Starch, 3 ½ Very Lean Meat, ½ Fat
OR 2 Carbohydrate, 3 ½ Very Lean Meat, ½ Fat

SAGE ADVICE

Sage is the traditional seasoning for the Thanksgiving turkey as well as any number of poultry dishes. The fresh herb can be readily identified by its velvety, gray-green leaves, which are aromatic and whose flavor intensifies when the herb is dried.

Two forms of dried sage are available in the supermarket. Rubbed sage is subjected to minimal grinding and is fluffy. It should be crushed slightly when used in a recipe. Ground sage has been finely ground to a powder and is ready to use. Because the flavor of ground sage is highly concentrated, the amount needed for recipes is reduced.

Cook's Notes

Turkey Wild Rice Casserole

TURKEY SPAGHETTI BAKE

prep time: 40 min. (ready in 1 hr. 20 min.) • yield: 6 servings

Ground turkey is a delicious alternative to ground beef in this family-pleasing casserole.

1 (7-oz.) pkg. spaghetti, broken into thirds

1 lb. ground turkey

½ cup chopped onion

1 garlic clove, minced

2 teaspoons sugar

1 teaspoon dried oregano leaves

½ teaspoon dried basil leaves

½ teaspoon salt

¼ teaspoon pepper

1 (28-oz.) can tomatoes, undrained, cut up

1 (6-oz.) can tomato paste

1 (4-oz.) can mushroom pieces and stems, drained

4 oz. (1 cup) shredded mozzarella cheese

⅓ cup grated Parmesan cheese

1 Cook spaghetti to desired doneness as directed on package. Drain.

2 Meanwhile, heat oven to 375°F. In large saucepan or Dutch oven, brown ground turkey with onion and garlic; drain if necessary. Stir in sugar, oregano, basil, salt, pepper, tomatoes, tomato paste and mushrooms. Bring to a boil. Reduce heat; cover and simmer 20 minutes, stirring occasionally. Remove from heat; stir in cooked spaghetti.

3 Place half of spaghetti mixture in ungreased 13 × 9-inch (3-quart) baking dish; sprinkle with mozzarella cheese. Top with remaining spaghetti mixture; sprinkle with Parmesan cheese.* Bake at 375°F. for 30 to 40 minutes or until bubbly.

TIP: *At this point, casserole can be covered and refrigerated several hours. Bake as directed above.

Nutrition Information Per Serving
Serving Size: ⅙ of Recipe

Calories	410	Calories from Fat	120
		% Daily Value	
Total Fat	13 g	20%	
Saturated	5 g	25%	
Cholesterol	70 mg	23%	
Sodium	1020 mg	43%	
Total Carbohydrate	44 g	15%	
Dietary Fiber	4 g	16%	
Sugars	7 g		
Protein	30 g		
Vitamin A	30%	Vitamin C	35%
Calcium	30%	Iron	25%

Dietary Exchanges: 2 ½ Starch, 1 Vegetable, 2 ½ Medium-Fat Meat OR 2 ½ Carbohydrate, 1 Vegetable, 2 ½ Medium-Fat Meat

LASAGNA ROLL-UPS

prep time: 30 min. (ready in 1 hr. 20 min.) • yield: 8 servings

Rolling the filling up in individual noodles simplifies serving. Freeze individual portions for a quick lunch or supper at a later date.

SAUCE
½ lb. ground turkey

2 garlic cloves, minced

1 (32-oz.) jar spaghetti sauce

2 teaspoons dried Italian seasoning

½ teaspoon fennel seed, if desired

FILLING
8 uncooked lasagna noodles

1 cup low-fat part-skim ricotta or cottage cheese

½ cup shredded carrot

1 (9-oz.) pkg. frozen spinach in a pouch, thawed, squeezed to drain*

2 egg whites or 1 egg

¼ teaspoon salt

TOPPING
4 oz. (1 cup) shredded mozzarella cheese

1 Heat oven to 350° F. In large skillet, brown turkey and garlic; drain, if necessary. Stir in remaining sauce ingredients; simmer about 15 minutes, stirring occasionally.

2 Meanwhile, cook lasagna noodles to desired doneness as directed on package. Drain; rinse with hot water.

3 In small bowl, combine ricotta cheese, carrot, spinach, egg whites and salt; mix well. Spread each cooked lasagna noodle with generous ¼ cup spinach filling to within 1 inch of 1 short end. Roll up firmly toward unfilled end.

4 Reserve 1½ cups of sauce. Pour remaining sauce in ungreased 12 × 8-inch (2-quart) baking dish. Arrange roll-ups, seam side down, in sauce. Pour reserved sauce over roll-ups. Cover tightly with foil.

5 Bake at 350° F. for 30 to 40 minutes or until hot and bubbly. Sprinkle with mozzarella cheese. Bake uncovered for an additional 3 to 5 minutes or until cheese is melted. Let stand 5 minutes before serving.

TIP: *To quickly thaw spinach, cut small slit in center of pouch; microwave on HIGH for 2 to 3 minutes or until thawed. Remove spinach from pouch; squeeze dry with paper towels.

Nutrition Information Per Serving
Serving Size: ⅛ of Recipe

Calories	280	Calories from Fat	90
		% Daily Value	
Total Fat	10 g	15%	
Saturated	4 g	20%	
Cholesterol	40 mg	13%	
Sodium	760 mg	32%	
Total Carbohydrate	29 g	10%	
Dietary Fiber	3 g	12%	
Sugars	2 g		
Protein	19 g		
Vitamin A	70%	Vitamin C	20%
Calcium	25%	Iron	15%

Dietary Exchanges: 2 Starch, 1½ Medium-Fat Meat OR 2 Carbohydrate, 1½ Medium-Fat Meat

Lasagna Roll-Ups

TURKEY MEATBALL STROGANOFF SUPPER

prep time: 30 min. • yield: 4 servings

For convenience, the noodles are cooked in the sauce and the meal is served right from the skillet.

MEATBALLS
1 lb. ground turkey

¼ cup unseasoned dry bread crumbs

1 teaspoon dried parsley flakes

½ teaspoon onion powder

¼ teaspoon salt

¼ teaspoon nutmeg

⅛ teaspoon pepper

1 egg, slightly beaten

1 tablespoon oil

STROGANOFF
1 (14½-oz.) can ready-to-serve chicken broth

½ cup water

¼ teaspoon salt

⅛ teaspoon nutmeg

⅛ teaspoon pepper

5 oz. (2½ cups) uncooked wide egg noodles

1½ cups frozen sweet peas

½ cup sour cream

1 In medium bowl, combine all meatball ingredients except oil; mix well. Shape into twelve 1½-inch meatballs.

2 Heat oil in large skillet over medium-high heat until hot. Add meatballs; cook and stir until well browned. Drain well.

3 Add broth, water, ¼ teaspoon salt, ⅛ teaspoon nutmeg and ⅛ teaspoon pepper. Bring to a boil. Stir in egg noodles and peas. Reduce heat to low; cover and simmer 10 minutes or until egg noodles are tender and meatballs are thoroughly cooked, stirring occasionally. Stir in sour cream.

Nutrition Information Per Serving
Serving Size: ¼ of Recipe

Calories	520	Calories from Fat	220
		% Daily Value	
Total Fat	24 g	37%	
Saturated	8 g	40%	
Cholesterol	185 mg	62%	
Sodium	860 mg	36%	
Total Carbohydrate	40 g	13%	
Dietary Fiber	3 g	12%	
Sugars	4 g		
Protein	35 g		
Vitamin A	10%	Vitamin C	8%
Calcium	10%	Iron	25%

Dietary Exchanges: 2½ Starch, 4 Medium-Fat Meat, ½ Fat OR
2½ Carbohydrate, 4 Medium-Fat Meat, ½ Fat

EASY TURKEY DIVAN

prep time: 20 min. (ready in 55 min.) • yield: 10 servings

Here's an imaginative way to use up leftover Thanksgiving turkey.

7½ cups frozen cut broccoli

1 (10¾-oz.) can condensed cream of chicken soup

1 (10¾-oz.) can condensed cream of mushroom soup

½ cup mayonnaise

2 tablespoons prepared mustard

⅛ teaspoon pepper

4 cups cubed cooked turkey

4 oz. (1 cup) shredded Cheddar cheese

1 (2.8-oz.) can french-fried onions

1 Heat oven to 350°F. Spray 13 × 9-inch (3-quart) baking dish with nonstick cooking spray. Cook broccoli as directed on package for minimum cooking time.

2 Meanwhile, in large bowl, combine soups, mayonnaise, mustard and pepper; mix well.

3 Drain broccoli; arrange in sprayed baking dish. Add turkey; toss gently. Pour soup mixture over top, spreading evenly over broccoli and turkey. Sprinkle with cheese.

4 Bake at 350°F. for 30 minutes or until hot and bubbly. Sprinkle with onions; bake an additional 5 minutes or until onions are lightly browned.

Nutrition Information Per Serving
Serving Size: 1/10 of Recipe

Calories	360	Calories from Fat	220
		% Daily Value	
Total Fat	24 g	37%	
Saturated	7 g	35%	
Cholesterol	65 mg	22%	
Sodium	730 mg	30%	
Total Carbohydrate	12 g	4%	
Dietary Fiber	2 g	8%	
Sugars	2 g		
Protein	23 g		
Vitamin A	15%	Vitamin C	35%
Calcium	15%	Iron	10%

Dietary Exchanges: 1/2 Starch, 1 Vegetable, 3 Lean Meat, 3 Fat OR
1/2 Carbohydrate, 1 Vegetable, 3 Lean Meat, 3 Fat

TURKEY POT ROAST WITH VEGETABLES

prep time: 30 min. (ready in 2 hr. 30 min.) • yield: 8 servings

Prepare this roast, then relax while your supper is cooking. Serve the pan juices with the turkey and potatoes.

1 (2- to 3-lb.) fresh boneless turkey breast roast or 3- to 4-lb. fresh bone-in turkey breast roast

2 medium sweet potatoes, peeled, cubed

2 medium russet potatoes, peeled, cubed

1 (8-oz.) pkg. frozen cut green beans, slightly thawed

1 (4.5-oz.) jar whole mushrooms, drained

1/2 cup chicken broth

1 tablespoon margarine or butter, melted

1/2 teaspoon dried thyme leaves

1/2 teaspoon dried rosemary leaves, crushed

1/4 teaspoon salt

1/8 teaspoon pepper

1 Heat oven to 350°F. Place turkey breast roast, skin side up, in ungreased 13 × 9-inch (3-quart) baking dish. Arrange sweet potatoes, russet potatoes, green beans and mushrooms around turkey.

2 In small bowl, combine broth and remaining ingredients; drizzle over turkey and vegetables. Insert meat thermometer in turkey breast roast. Cover tightly with foil.

3 Bake at 350°F. for 1 1/2 to 2 hours or until internal temperature of turkey is 170°F. and vegetables are fork-tender, basting once with pan juices.

Nutrition Information Per Serving
Serving Size: 1/8 of Recipe

Calories	260	Calories from Fat	25
		% Daily Value	
Total Fat	3 g	5%	
Saturated	1 g	5%	
Cholesterol	105 mg	35%	
Sodium	310 mg	13%	
Total Carbohydrate	18 g	6%	
Dietary Fiber	3 g	12%	
Sugars	3 g		
Protein	41 g		
Vitamin A	130%	Vitamin C	20%
Calcium	4%	Iron	15%

Dietary Exchanges: 1 Starch, 1/2 Vegetable, 5 Very Lean Meat OR
1 Carbohydrate, 1/2 Vegetable, 5 Very Lean Meat

QUICKEST-EVER TURKEY POT PIE

prep time: 40 min. • yield: 6 servings

The crust bakes separately while you prepare the filling.

1 refrigerated pie crust (from 15-oz. pkg.)

6 tablespoons margarine or butter

⅓ cup all-purpose flour

¼ teaspoon dried marjoram leaves

⅛ teaspoon pepper

1 cup milk

1 (10½-oz.) can condensed chicken broth

3 cups cubed cooked turkey or chicken

1 (1-lb.) pkg. frozen mixed vegetables, thawed*

1 Heat oven to 450°F. Prepare pie crust as directed on package for *one-crust baked shell.* Place crust on ungreased cookie sheet.

2 Invert 2-quart casserole over crust. With sharp knife, trace and cut around casserole rim; remove casserole. Trim an additional ¼ inch from edge of casserole-shaped crust. Using small cookie cutter or sharp knife, cut holes in crust. Cut additional shapes out of dough scraps, if desired; arrange over crust. Bake at 450°F. for 9 to 11 minutes or until light golden brown.

3 Meanwhile, melt margarine in large saucepan. Stir in flour, marjoram and pepper; cook until mixture is smooth and bubbly, stirring occasionally. Gradually stir in milk and broth; cook until mixture boils and thickens, stirring constantly.

4 Add chicken and vegetables. Cook 10 to 15 minutes or until vegetables are tender, stirring occasionally. Spoon mixture into casserole; place baked crust on top.

TIP: *To quickly thaw frozen vegetables, place unopened vegetable pouch in warm water for 20 minutes.

Nutrition Information Per Serving
Serving Size: ⅙ of Recipe

Calories	470	Calories from Fat	230
		% Daily Value	
Total Fat	25 g	38%	
Saturated	7 g	35%	
Cholesterol	65 mg	22%	
Sodium	670 mg	28%	
Total Carbohydrate	34 g	11%	
Dietary Fiber	3 g	12%	
Sugars	3 g		
Protein	27 g		
Vitamin A	40%	Vitamin C	8%
Calcium	8%	Iron	15%

Dietary Exchanges: 2 Starch, 1 Vegetable, 2 ½ Lean Meat, 3 ½ Fat OR
2 Carbohydrate, 1 Vegetable, 2 ½ Lean Meat, 3 ½ Fat

DEALING WITH TURKEY LEFTOVERS

Poultry is among the most perishable of meats and should be handled carefully before and after cooking.

After the turkey has been served, refrigerate any leftover turkey within two hours. (All stuffing should be removed from the bird before the meal is served.) Cool large amounts of leftover turkey quickly by dividing it into several small containers. Cover and refrigerate it immediately. Turkey will keep in the refrigerator for up to four days, or freeze it in moistureproof containers for up to two months.

Cook's Notes

Quickest-Ever Turkey Pot Pie

Oven-Roasted
Pork 'n Vegetables, page 138

BEEF, VEAL, PORK & LAMB

TRENDS COME AND GO, BUT MEAT STILL HOLDS A PLACE OF HONOR AT AMERICAN TABLES. ACCORDINGLY, THE FOLLOWING PAGES INCLUDE ALL MANNER OF BEEF RECIPES, FROM QUICK CANTONESE BEEF CHOW MEIN (PAGE 119) TO SLOW-COOKED BEEF BURGUNDY (PAGE 125), PLUS AN ASSORTMENT OF APPEALING PREPARATIONS FOR PORK, VEAL AND LAMB. TREAT GUESTS TO PORK CHOPS WITH CORN STUFFING (PAGE 134), FOR EXAMPLE, OR GRILL UP A MESS OF HOT AND SWEET GLAZED RIBS (PAGE 142) FOR A FAMILY PICNIC.

STEAK STIR-FRY WITH MIXED MUSHROOMS AND TOMATOES

prep time: 35 min. • yield: 4 (1-cup) servings

The stir-frying technique comes from Asian cooking, but the ingredients here have a definite Italian accent. A mix of porcini and cremini mushrooms complements the steak slices and piquant vinegar-tomato blend.

½ oz. (⅔ cup) dried porcini mushrooms

1½ cups boiling water

¼ cup beef broth

2 tablespoons balsamic or red wine vinegar

2 teaspoons cornstarch

2 tablespoons margarine or butter

1 lb. beef flank or boneless top sirloin steak, cut lengthwise into 2-inch-wide strips, thinly sliced

½ teaspoon salt

¼ teaspoon coarse ground black pepper

1 (5½-oz.) pkg. fresh cremini mushrooms, thinly sliced (2 cups)

4 Italian plum tomatoes, thinly sliced

1 tablespoon chopped fresh parsley

1 In medium bowl, soak porcini mushrooms in boiling water for 20 minutes. Drain, reserving ¼ cup liquid. Set mushrooms aside.

2 In small bowl, combine reserved mushroom liquid, broth, vinegar and cornstarch; blend well. Set aside.

3 Melt 1 tablespoon of the margarine in large skillet or wok over medium-high heat. Add beef strips, salt and pepper; cook and stir 2 to 3 min-

utes or until beef is browned. Remove from skillet; cover to keep warm.

4 In same skillet, melt remaining 1 tablespoon margarine over medium heat. Add porcini and cremini mushrooms; cook and stir 3 minutes.

5 Stir broth mixture until smooth; add to skillet. Cook and stir until sauce is thickened and bubbly. Add beef and tomatoes; cook and stir until thoroughly heated. Sprinkle with parsley.

Nutrition Information Per Serving
Serving Size: 1 Cup

Calories	240	Calories from Fat	130
		% Daily Value	
Total Fat	14 g	22%	
Saturated	5 g	25%	
Cholesterol	45 mg	15%	
Sodium	430 mg	18%	
Total Carbohydrate	9 g	3%	
Dietary Fiber	2 g	8%	
Sugars	1 g		
Protein	19 g		
Vitamin A	10%	Vitamin C	15%
Calcium	0%	Iron	15%

Dietary Exchanges: 1 Vegetable, 2 ½ Lean Meat, 1 ½ Fat

STIR-FRY SAVVY

Stir-frying originated in China as a way to conserve scarce cooking fuel. By cutting food into small pieces, it cooks quickly.

- Cut foods into uniformly sized pieces to ensure even cooking.
- Drain canned ingredients thoroughly, patting them dry with paper towels if necessary, so food will not steam.
- Get the wok or skillet extremely hot before adding food.
- Add ingredients to the wok a little at a time. Begin by adding the densest, longest-cooking ingredients to the center of the wok; let them cook for 1 minute, then stir them up the wok's sides and add the next batch directly to the middle.
- Don't overcrowd the wok or skillet or the food will steam.

PEPPER STEAK

prep time: 30 min. • yield: 4 servings

The green, red and yellow trio of peppers looks especially pretty in this sweet-and-sour beef mixture.

4 cups hot cooked rice (cooked as directed on package)

1 cup beef broth

¼ cup hoisin sauce

1 tablespoon cornstarch

3 tablespoons ketchup

1 tablespoon rice vinegar

½ teaspoon Worcestershire sauce

¼ to ½ teaspoon coarse ground black pepper

1 tablespoon oil

1 lb. beef flank or boneless top sirloin steak, thinly sliced

1 medium onion, cut into 8 pieces

1 medium green bell pepper, cut into strips

1 medium red bell pepper, cut into strips

1 medium yellow bell pepper, cut into strips

1 While rice is cooking, in small bowl, combine broth, hoisin sauce, cornstarch, ketchup, vinegar, Worcestershire sauce and pepper; blend well. Set aside.

2 Heat oil in large skillet or wok over medium-high heat until hot. Add beef and onion; cook and stir 2 to 3 minutes or until beef is no longer pink.

3 Add bell peppers and cornstarch mixture; cook and stir 2 to 3 minutes or until vegetables are crisp-tender and sauce is bubbly and thickened. Serve over rice.

Nutrition Information Per Serving
Serving Size: ¼ of Recipe

Calories	470	Calories from Fat	120
		% Daily Value	
Total Fat	13 g	20%	
Saturated	4 g	20%	
Cholesterol	45 mg	15%	
Sodium	690 mg	29%	
Total Carbohydrate	65 g	22%	
Dietary Fiber	2 g	8%	
Sugars	13 g		
Protein	24 g		
Vitamin A	25%	Vitamin C	100%
Calcium	4%	Iron	30%

Dietary Exchanges: 3 Starch, 1 Fruit, 1 Vegetable, 2 Medium-Fat Meat OR 4 Carbohydrate, 1 Vegetable, 2 Medium-Fat Meat

PLANNING MENUS

A few simple guidelines can make daily meal planning easier, quicker and more rewarding:

- Begin with a main dish for each meal, then add appropriate side dishes, striving for complementary flavors as well as a variety of colors and textures.
- Plan two- or three-component meals, using purchased items as well as from-scratch foods.
- Be realistic about the amount of time you have for meal preparation. When you have time, freeze an extra casserole or even leftovers in individual portions.
- Develop a repertoire of quick "dress-ups" (easy additions to purchased foods) to quickly produce tasty, appetizing dishes.
- Keep your menu lists to reuse, mixing and matching recipes later on.
- Solicit ideas and input from your family.

GRILLED ROUND STEAK

prep time: 30 min. (ready in 3 hr. 30 min.) • yield: 4 servings

Marinating the steak in an oil-and-vinegar blend flavors the meat, and the vinegar serves as a tenderizer. Be aware that the vinegar will change the surface color of the meat from dark or bright red to a brownish shade.

MARINADE
1/2 cup purchased red wine vinegar and oil salad dressing or Italian salad dressing

2 tablespoons sesame seed, toasted*

1/2 to 1 teaspoon hot pepper sauce

STEAK
1 lb. boneless beef round steak (1 to 1 1/2 inches thick)

1 GRILL DIRECTIONS: In 12 × 8-inch (2-quart) baking dish or resealable food storage plastic bag, combine all marinade ingredients; mix well. Add round steak; turn to coat. Cover dish or seal bag. Refrigerate at least 3 hours, turning once.

2 Heat grill. When ready to grill, remove steak from marinade; discard marinade. Place steak on gas grill over medium heat or on charcoal grill 4 to 6 inches from medium coals. Cook 8 to 20 minutes or until of desired doneness, turning once.

TIPS: *To toast sesame seed, spread in shallow baking pan; bake at 350° F. for 6 to 8 minutes or until golden brown, stirring occasionally. Or place seed in small skillet; stir over medium heat for 8 to 10 minutes or until light golden brown.

To broil steak, place on broiler pan; broil 4 to 6 inches from heat using times above as a guide.

Nutrition Information Per Serving
Serving Size: 1/4 of Recipe

Calories	190	Calories from Fat	90
		% Daily Value	
Total Fat	10 g	15%	
Saturated	3 g	15%	
Cholesterol	60 mg	20%	
Sodium	115 mg	5%	
Total Carbohydrate	1 g	1%	
Dietary Fiber	0 g	0%	
Sugars	1 g		
Protein	23 g		
Vitamin A	0%	Vitamin C	0%
Calcium	0%	Iron	10%

Dietary Exchanges: 3 1/2 Lean Meat

PEPPER STEAKS WITH BLACKBERRY GLAZE

prep time: 25 min. • yield: 4 servings

The two-ingredient glaze is about as easy as they come. Currant or grape jelly can be used instead. The mixture also works well for baked pork chops.

GLAZE
1/2 cup blackberry jam

1/4 cup red wine vinegar

STEAKS
3 teaspoons coarse ground black pepper

4 (4-oz.) boneless beef strip steaks

1/2 cup fresh or frozen blackberries, thawed

1 GRILL DIRECTIONS: Heat grill. In small saucepan, combine jam and vinegar. Cook over medium heat until jam is melted, stirring constantly. Remove from heat.

2 Rub pepper on both sides of each steak. When ready to grill, oil grill rack. Place steaks on gas grill over medium heat or on charcoal grill 4 to 6 inches from medium-high coals. Cook 8 to

12 minutes or until of desired doneness, turning once.

3 To serve, spread steaks with glaze; top with berries.

TIP: To broil steaks, place on oiled broiler pan; broil 4 to 6 inches from heat using times above as a guide.

Nutrition Information Per Serving
Serving Size: ¼ of Recipe

Calories	250	Calories from Fat	35
		% Daily Value	
Total Fat	4 g	6%	
Saturated	1 g	5%	
Cholesterol	60 mg	20%	
Sodium	45 mg	2%	
Total Carbohydrate	30 g	10%	
Dietary Fiber	2 g	8%	
Sugars	21 g		
Protein	24 g		
Vitamin A	0%	Vitamin C	8%
Calcium	2%	Iron	15%

Dietary Exchanges: 2 Fruit, 3 ½ Very Lean Meat OR 2 Carbohydrate, 3 ½ Very Lean Meat

BLACKENED SIRLOIN WITH SOUTHWESTERN BUTTER

prep time: 30 min. (ready in 1 hr. 30 min.) • yield: 4 servings

"Blackened" meats and fish, a Cajun tradition, became popular a few years back. The technique entails generously coating meat or fish with an intense mixture of herbs and spices, then cooking it in a hot frying pan or on a grill to quickly char the outside while the inside remains moist and juicy.

SOUTHWESTERN BUTTER
6 tablespoons butter, slightly softened

¼ teaspoon cumin

¼ teaspoon dried oregano leaves

¼ teaspoon chili powder

⅛ teaspoon dried thyme leaves

⅛ teaspoon pepper

Dash ground red pepper (cayenne)

STEAK
1 lb. boneless beef sirloin steak (1 to 1½ inches thick)

1 tablespoon butter, melted

2 teaspoons blackened steak seasoning

1 GRILL DIRECTIONS: In small bowl, combine all butter ingredients; blend well. Place butter on piece of plastic wrap; shape into 4-inch log. Refrigerate 1 hour or until firm.

2 Meanwhile, using 1 tablespoon melted butter, brush both sides of steak; rub each side of steak with 1 teaspoon blackened steak seasoning. Let stand at room temperature for 30 minutes.

3 Heat grill. When ready to grill, place steak on gas grill over medium heat or on charcoal grill 4 to 6 inches from medium coals. Cook 8 to 20 minutes or until of desired doneness, turning once.

4 If necessary, let butter stand at room temperature for about 15 minutes to soften. To serve, cut steak into 4 serving pieces; place on individual serving plates. Cut butter into 4 slices; place on center of hot steaks. Serve immediately.

TIP: To broil steak, place on broiler pan; broil 4 to 6 inches from heat using times above as a guide.

Nutrition Information Per Serving
Serving Size: ¼ of Recipe

Calories	310	Calories from Fat	230
		% Daily Value	
Total Fat	25 g	38%	
Saturated	14 g	70%	
Cholesterol	115 mg	38%	
Sodium	410 mg	17%	
Total Carbohydrate	0 g	0%	
Dietary Fiber	0 g	0%	
Sugars	0 g		
Protein	21 g		
Vitamin A	15%	Vitamin C	0%
Calcium	0%	Iron	15%

Dietary Exchanges: 3 Lean Meat, 3 Fat

Cantonese Beef Chow Mein

CANTONESE BEEF CHOW MEIN

prep time: 35 min. • yield: 4 servings

An assortment of Chinese vegetables makes this sliced beef entree special. Shiitake mushrooms have a distinctive flavor, but feel free to substitute regular white mushrooms.

4 cups hot cooked instant or regular brown rice (cooked as directed on package)

¾ cup fresh shiitake mushrooms

1 tablespoon oil

1 lb. boneless beef top round steak, thinly sliced

4 oz. (1 cup) fresh snow pea pods, trimmed

2 tablespoons water

1 (8-oz.) pkg. fresh bean sprouts

1 (8-oz.) can sliced bamboo shoots, drained

¼ cup cut (1-inch) green onions

⅔ cup purchased garlic and ginger stir-fry sauce

1 While rice is cooking, remove and discard stems from mushrooms. Cut caps into thin slices; set aside.

2 Heat oil in large skillet or wok over medium-high heat until hot. Add beef; cook and stir 2 to 3 minutes or until beef is browned. Remove from skillet; cover to keep warm.

3 In same skillet, combine pea pods and water. Cover; cook 2 minutes. Add mushrooms; cook and stir 30 seconds. Add bean sprouts, bamboo shoots, onions and stir-fry sauce; cook and stir 2 to 3 minutes or until vegetables are crisp-tender. Return beef to skillet; cook and stir until thoroughly heated. Serve over rice.

Nutrition Information Per Serving
Serving Size: ¼ of Recipe

Calories	480	Calories from Fat	110
		% Daily Value	
Total Fat	12 g	18%	
Saturated	2 g	10%	
Cholesterol	60 mg	20%	
Sodium	860 mg	36%	
Total Carbohydrate	61 g	20%	
Dietary Fiber	6 g	24%	
Sugars	11 g		
Protein	32 g		
Vitamin A	0%	Vitamin C	30%
Calcium	4%	Iron	25%

Dietary Exchanges: 3 ½ Starch, 1 Vegetable, 3 Lean Meat OR 3 ½ Carbohydrate, 1 Vegetable, 3 Lean Meat

SHIITAKE MUSHROOMS

S hiitake mushrooms, widely used in Asian cooking, command a higher per pound price than ordinary white button mushrooms, but they're distinctly flavored; even a small quantity adds flavor impact. Shiitakes are available in the produce section of larger supermarkets as well as in specialty markets and Asian groceries.

The shiitake has a flat, broad brown cap and paler stem. Stems are flavorful but tough; remove them before cooking. Save the stems to flavor soup stock if the broth will be strained before serving.

Cook's Notes

PAPRIKA BEEF

prep time: 35 min. • yield: 4 servings

The blend of paprika, sour cream and mushrooms evokes the flavors of Budapest. For easier slicing, place the uncooked beef in the freezer for about 15 minutes before beginning to prepare this dish.

8 oz. (5 cups) uncooked wide egg noodles

1 tablespoon olive or vegetable oil

1 lb. boneless beef sirloin steak, cut into thin bite-sized strips

8 oz. (about 3 cups) sliced fresh mushrooms

1 large onion, sliced

2 garlic cloves, minced

3 teaspoons paprika

1 (8-oz.) can tomato sauce

¼ cup sour cream

1 teaspoon all-purpose flour

2 tablespoons chopped fresh parsley

1 Cook noodles to desired doneness as directed on package. Drain; cover to keep warm.

2 Meanwhile, heat oil in large skillet over medium-high heat until hot. If desired, sprinkle beef strips with salt and pepper. Add half of beef to skillet; cook and stir 3 to 4 minutes or until browned. Remove beef; set aside. Repeat with remaining beef strips.

3 Add mushrooms, onion and garlic to skillet; cook and stir over medium heat for 2 to 3 minutes or until vegetables are tender. Return beef to skillet. Add paprika; mix well. Cook 1 minute. Stir in tomato sauce.

4 In small bowl, combine sour cream and flour. Add to beef mixture; cook 1 minute or until thoroughly heated. If mixture becomes too thick, stir in 1 to 2 tablespoons water.

5 Add parsley to noodles; toss well. Serve beef mixture over noodles.

Nutrition Information Per Serving
Serving Size: ¼ of Recipe

Calories	470	Calories from Fat	130
		% Daily Value	
Total Fat	14 g	22%	
Saturated	5 g	25%	
Cholesterol	120 mg	40%	
Sodium	410 mg	17%	
Total Carbohydrate	54 g	18%	
Dietary Fiber	4 g	16%	
Sugars	8 g		
Protein	32 g		
Vitamin A	35%	Vitamin C	20%
Calcium	8%	Iron	35%

Dietary Exchanges: 3 Starch, 2 Vegetable, 2 ½ Lean Meat, 1 Fat OR
3 Carbohydrate, 2 Vegetable, 2 ½ Lean Meat, 1 Fat

Paprika Beef

HERBED BUTTERMILK STROGANOFF

prep time: 30 min. (ready in 1 hr. 15 min.) • yield: 5 servings

Egg noodles are the traditional accompaniment for stroganoff. Thyme and rosemary boost the flavor of the sauce.

¾ lb. boneless beef round steak, cut into 3 × ¼-inch strips

1 cup sliced fresh mushrooms

1 cup sliced onions

½ cup water

⅓ cup dry white wine or beef broth

3 tablespoons tomato juice

1 teaspoon beef-flavor instant bouillon

½ teaspoon salt

¼ teaspoon dried thyme leaves

¼ teaspoon dried rosemary leaves

⅛ teaspoon pepper

10 oz. (6 cups) uncooked wide egg noodles

2 tablespoons all-purpose flour

¾ cup buttermilk

2 tablespoons chopped fresh parsley

1 Spray large nonstick skillet with nonstick cooking spray. Heat over medium-high heat until hot. Add beef, mushrooms and onions. Cook until beef is lightly browned; drain if necessary.

2 Stir in water, wine, tomato juice, bouillon, salt, thyme, rosemary and pepper. Reduce heat to low; cover and simmer 45 minutes or until meat is tender, stirring occasionally.

3 Cook noodles to desired doneness as directed on package. Drain; cover to keep warm.

4 In small bowl, combine flour and ¼ cup of the buttermilk; beat with wire whisk until smooth. Stir in remaining ½ cup buttermilk. Stir into beef mixture. Cook over medium heat until mixture boils and thickens, stirring constantly. Serve mixture over noodles. Sprinkle with parsley.

Nutrition Information Per Serving
Serving Size: ⅕ of Recipe

Calories	360	Calories from Fat	50
		% Daily Value	
Total Fat	6 g	9%	
Saturated	2 g	10%	
Cholesterol	90 mg	30%	
Sodium	510 mg	21%	
Total Carbohydrate	49 g	16%	
Dietary Fiber	2 g	8%	
Sugars	6 g		
Protein	24 g		
Vitamin A	4%	Vitamin C	8%
Calcium	8%	Iron	25%

Dietary Exchanges: 3 Starch, 2 Lean Meat OR 3 Carbohydrate, 2 Lean Meat

BUTTERMILK

In the old days, buttermilk was the liquid left over after butter was churned. Today, it's made at the dairy processing plant by adding cultures to fresh milk. Although buttermilk has a thick texture and rich flavor, it boasts the same nonfat nutritional profile as skim milk.

In cooking, buttermilk lets you flavor and thicken sauces without adding fat.

PARSLEY-POTATO TOPPED OVEN SWISS STEAK

prep time: 20 min. (ready in 2 hr. 55 min.) • yield: 6 servings

PICTURED ON COVER

This easy version of Swiss steak (beef stewed with tomatoes) bubbles and bakes under a crown of mashed potatoes flecked with thyme and parsley.

SWISS STEAK
1 lb. boneless beef round steak (1/2 inch thick), cut into 6 pieces

2 carrots, sliced (1 cup)

1 large onion, halved, thinly sliced

1 (12-oz.) jar home-style beef gravy

1 (14.5-oz.) can diced tomatoes, undrained

1/4 teaspoon dried thyme leaves

1/8 teaspoon pepper

TOPPING
1 1/2 cups water

3 tablespoons margarine or butter

2 1/4 cups mashed potato flakes

3/4 cup milk

3 tablespoons finely chopped fresh parsley

1/4 teaspoon salt

1/4 teaspoon dried thyme leaves

1 egg, beaten

Paprika

1 Heat oven to 325°F. Arrange beef in ungreased 12 × 8-inch (2-quart) baking dish. Top with carrots and onion.

2 In medium bowl, combine gravy, tomatoes, 1/4 teaspoon thyme and pepper; mix well. Spoon over beef and vegetables. Cover with foil. Bake at 325°F. for 2 hours.

3 In medium saucepan, bring water and margarine to a boil. Remove from heat. Stir in potato flakes, milk, parsley, salt and 1/4 teaspoon thyme. Add egg; mix well.

4 Uncover baking dish; spoon or pipe potato mixture over hot mixture. Sprinkle with paprika. Bake uncovered for an additional 30 to 35 minutes or until potatoes are set and light golden brown.

Nutrition Information Per Serving
Serving Size: 1/6 of Recipe

Calories	350	Calories from Fat	120
		% Daily Value	
Total Fat	13 g	20%	
Saturated	4 g	20%	
Cholesterol	80 mg	27%	
Sodium	700 mg	29%	
Total Carbohydrate	34 g	11%	
Dietary Fiber	4 g	16%	
Sugars	6 g		
Protein	23 g		
Vitamin A	150%	Vitamin C	20%
Calcium	10%	Iron	20%

Dietary Exchanges: 2 Starch, 1 Vegetable, 2 Lean Meat, 1 Fat OR
2 Carbohydrate, 1 Vegetable, 2 Lean Meat, 1 Fat

POT ROAST AND GRAVY

prep time: 25 min. (ready in 2 hr. 40 min.) • yield: 6 servings

Slow simmering in a tightly covered pot is a classic method for transforming an inexpensive cut of beef into a tender, succulent meal. For variety, use red wine instead of bouillon.

2 tablespoons oil

1 (3- to 4-lb.) beef chuck arm, blade or 7-bone roast

½ teaspoon pepper

4 medium onions, quartered

4 stalks celery, cut into pieces

1 bay leaf

2 teaspoons beef-flavor instant bouillon or 2 beef-flavor bouillon cubes

1½ cups boiling water

6 medium potatoes, halved

6 medium carrots, cut into pieces

¼ cup cold water

3 tablespoons all-purpose flour

1 Heat oven to 325°F. In 5-quart ovenproof Dutch oven or roasting pan, heat oil over medium-high heat until hot. Add beef roast; cook about 5 minutes on each side or until browned. If desired, drain off excess fat.

2 Sprinkle pepper on both sides of beef. Add 1 of the onions, 1 of the stalks of celery and bay leaf to beef. Dissolve bouillon in boiling water; reserve ¾ cup. Pour remaining ¾ cup bouillon around beef. Bring to a boil. Cover.

3 Bake at 325°F. for 1 hour. Add remaining vegetables; cover and bake an additional 1 to 1¼ hours or until beef and vegetables are tender.

4 To prepare gravy, place beef and vegetables on warm platter; cover loosely to keep warm. Remove and discard bay leaf. Measure drippings from Dutch oven. If desired, skim off fat. Add enough of reserved ¾ cup bouillon to drippings to make 3 cups; return to Dutch oven.

5 In small jar with tight-fitting lid, combine cold water and flour; shake well. Gradually stir flour mixture into drippings. Cook over medium heat until mixture boils and thickens, stirring constantly. If desired, add salt to taste. Serve gravy with beef and vegetables.

Nutrition Information Per Serving
Serving Size: ⅙ of Recipe

Calories	510	Calories from Fat	130
		% Daily Value	
Total Fat	14 g	22%	
Saturated	4 g	20%	
Cholesterol	130 mg	43%	
Sodium	440 mg	18%	
Total Carbohydrate	49 g	16%	
Dietary Fiber	7 g	28%	
Sugars	10 g		
Protein	48 g		
Vitamin A	410%	Vitamin C	35%
Calcium	8%	Iron	40%

Dietary Exchanges: 2 ½ Starch, 2 Vegetable, 5 Lean Meat OR
2 ½ Carbohydrate, 2 Vegetable, 5 Lean Meat

SLOW-COOKED BEEF BURGUNDY

prep time: 45 min. (ready in 7 hr. 45 min.) • yield: 8 servings

Crumbled cooked bacon adds depth of flavor to this slow cooker variation of the French classic stew known as boeuf bourguignonne. Serve it with a crisp green salad, sourdough bread and goblets of burgundy wine.

4 slices bacon, crisply cooked, crumbled

2 lb. beef stew meat, cut into 1 1/2-inch cubes

2 large carrots, sliced

1 medium onion, sliced

1/2 cup all-purpose flour

1/2 teaspoon dried marjoram leaves

1/4 teaspoon pepper

1/4 teaspoon garlic powder

1 (10 1/2-oz.) can condensed beef broth

1/2 cup burgundy or dry red wine

1 tablespoon Worcestershire sauce

1 (8-oz.) pkg. fresh mushrooms, sliced

1 (16-oz.) pkg. uncooked egg noodles

2 tablespoons chopped fresh parsley

1 In 3 1/2- to 4-quart slow cooker, combine bacon, beef, carrots and onion.

2 In small bowl, combine flour, marjoram, pepper and garlic powder. With wire whisk, stir in broth, wine and Worcestershire sauce until smooth. Add to mixture in slow cooker; stir to combine.

3 Cover; cook on high setting for 1 hour. Reduce heat to low. Cook 5 to 6 hours or until meat is tender.

4 Stir in mushrooms. Cook on high setting for 30 minutes or until mushrooms are tender. Meanwhile, cook noodles to desired doneness as directed on package; drain. Serve beef mixture over noodles; sprinkle with parsley.

Nutrition Information Per Serving
Serving Size: 1/8 of Recipe

Calories	480	Calories from Fat	110
		% Daily Value	
Total Fat	12g	18%	
Saturated	4g	20%	
Cholesterol	125 mg	42%	
Sodium	340 mg	14%	
Total Carbohydrate	53g	18%	
Dietary Fiber	3g	12%	
Sugars	5g		
Protein	37g		
Vitamin A	160%	Vitamin C	6%
Calcium	4%	Iron	35%

Dietary Exchanges: 3 Starch, 2 Vegetable, 3 1/2 Lean Meat, 1/2 Fat
OR 3 Carbohydrate, 2 Vegetable, 3 1/2 Lean Meat, 1/2 Fat

COOKING WITH WINE

Wine is the key ingredient in a number of classic recipes, including *boeuf bourguignonne, coq au vin* and chicken marsala. Wine is especially favored in stews and other slow-cooked dishes, where the long cooking time lets the wine's acidic properties go to work to break down meat fibers, resulting in superbly tender meat and depth of flavor.

While you may be particular about the wine you drink, cooking with wine is another matter. Ignore the "experts" who suggest cooking with the same wine you plan to serve with dinner. Heat destroys the essential subtleties and nuances in wine as well as its alcohol, so there's little point in pouring an expensive vintage into stew. In fact, cooking is a great way to get rid of any leftover wine that's become a little "off" from exposure to air.

Wine sold as cooking wine is another possibility, but these tend to be salty; adjust the seasoning of the recipe accordingly.

Cook's Notes

CHILI CASSEROLE WITH CORNBREAD

prep time: 20 min. (ready in 40 min.) • yield: 6 servings

Here's a unique style of savory pie, with a zesty beef, bean and corn chili filling framed by cornbread.

1 lb. lean ground beef

1 (16-oz.) jar chunky style salsa

1 (15.5-oz.) can dark red kidney beans, drained

1 (14.5-oz.) can diced tomatoes, undrained

1 1/2 cups frozen whole kernel corn

3 teaspoons chili powder

1 teaspoon cumin

1 (6.5- to 8.5-oz.) pkg. cornbread mix

Milk

Margarine, if required by mix

Egg, if required by mix

1 1/3 oz. (1/3 cup) shredded Cheddar cheese

1 tablespoon sliced green onions

1 Heat oven to 400° F. In large skillet over medium-high heat, brown ground beef until thoroughly cooked; drain. Stir in salsa, kidney beans, tomatoes, corn, chili powder and cumin. Cook 3 to 4 minutes or until thoroughly heated, stirring occasionally.

2 Meanwhile, prepare cornbread as directed on package using milk and, if required, margarine and egg. Spoon cornbread batter around outside edge of ungreased 12 × 8-inch (2-quart) baking dish. Spoon hot beef mixture into center. (Casserole will be full.)

3 Bake at 400° F. for 18 minutes. Sprinkle with cheese; bake an additional 4 to 5 minutes or until cheese is melted and cornbread is deep golden brown. Just before serving, sprinkle with green onions.

Nutrition Information Per Serving
Serving Size: 1/6 of Recipe

Calories	480	Calories from Fat	170
		% Daily Value	
Total Fat	19 g	29%	
Saturated	7 g	35%	
Cholesterol	90 mg	30%	
Sodium	1330 mg	55%	
Total Carbohydrate	53 g	18%	
Dietary Fiber	7 g	28%	
Sugars	9 g		
Protein	24 g		
Vitamin A	25%	Vitamin C	15%
Calcium	15%	Iron	20%

Dietary Exchanges: 3 1/2 Starch, 2 Medium-Fat Meat, 1 Fat OR
3 1/2 Carbohydrate, 2 Medium-Fat Meat, 1 Fat

CHILI POWDER

Chili powder is a blend of ground dried chiles, cumin, oregano, garlic and, occasionally, salt or other seasonings. Chili powders range in color from bright to dark red. The dark red chili powders generally are made from milder, darker chiles. Each brand of chili powder will have its own blend of spices, so experiment to find your personal favorite—and add it judiciously at first until you can judge its heat.

Cook's Notes

BURGER BEAN BAKE

prep time: 15 min. (ready in 45 min.) •
yield: 4 (1 1/2-cup) servings

Traditional baked beans require overnight soaking of dried beans, then hours of simmering in a low-temperature oven until the beans are tender and soaked through with the molasses-pork flavor. In the recipe below, using canned beans yields similar results in less than an hour.

4 slices bacon, cut into 1-inch pieces

1 lb. ground beef

1/2 cup chopped onion

1 (16-oz.) can baked beans, undrained

1 (15.5-oz.) can kidney beans, undrained

1 (14.5-oz.) can half-inch diagonal-cut
   green beans, drained

1/2 cup ketchup

1/4 cup molasses

2 teaspoons prepared mustard

1 teaspoon Worcestershire sauce

1 Heat oven to 350°F. In large skillet over medium heat, cook bacon until crisp. Remove bacon from skillet; drain on paper towel. Discard drippings.

2 In same skillet, brown ground beef and onion until beef is thoroughly cooked. Drain. Add bacon and all remaining ingredients; mix well. Pour into ungreased 2-quart casserole; cover tightly.

3 Bake at 350°F. for 30 minutes or until bubbly.

Nutrition Information Per Serving
Serving Size: 1 1/2 Cups

Calories	650	Calories from Fat	190
		% Daily Value	
Total Fat	21 g	32%	
Saturated	8 g	40%	
Cholesterol	75 mg	25%	
Sodium	1600 mg	67%	
Total Carbohydrate	78 g	26%	
Dietary Fiber	15 g	60%	
Sugars	25 g		
Protein	37 g		
Vitamin A	15%	Vitamin C	15%
Calcium	20%	Iron	35%

Dietary Exchanges: 5 Starch, 3 Medium-Fat Meat, 1/2 Fat
OR 5 Carbohydrate, 3 Medium-Fat Meat, 1/2 Fat

GROUND BEEF

Forever popular because it's economical and quick to cook, ground beef varies in price according to the cut of meat from which it is made and the percentage of fat. Ground beef is labeled according to the ratio of fat to meat. High-fat ground beef is less costly per pound, in part because the fat cooks out and reduces the amount of cooked meat. According to USDA standards, ground beef may contain no more than 30% fat.

As consumer awareness regarding fat has increased, so have products containing less fat. Ground beef can be up to 95% lean. Commonly found in supermarkets are:

- 70 to 75% lean ground beef—Use when recipes call for browning, then draining, the meat.
- 75 to 80% lean ground beef—Use when you want the meat to hold its shape and be juicy.
- 80 to 85% lean ground beef—Use in recipes to reduce calories and fat.

TATER NUGGET HOT DISH

prep time: 20 min. (ready in 1 hr. 10 min.) •
yield: 6 (1¼-cup) servings

This meal-in-a-dish featuring ground beef and condensed soup is easy enough for the kids to help prepare. Try the casserole with frozen broccoli florets or a packaged vegetable blend instead of green beans.

1 lb. ground beef

¾ cup chopped onions

½ cup chopped celery

1 (10¾-oz.) can condensed 98% fat-free cream of mushroom soup with 30% less sodium

1 (10¾-oz.) can condensed 98% fat-free cream of chicken soup with 30% less sodium

⅛ teaspoon garlic powder

⅛ teaspoon pepper

1 cup frozen cut green beans, thawed*

1 (16-oz.) pkg. frozen potato nuggets

1 Heat oven to 375°F. In large saucepan, brown ground beef, onions and celery until beef is thoroughly cooked; drain well. Stir in soups, garlic powder, pepper and green beans. Spoon into ungreased 2-quart casserole; top with potato nuggets.

2 Bake at 375°F. for 40 to 50 minutes or until casserole is bubbly and potato nuggets are golden brown.

TIP: *To quickly thaw green beans, place in colander or strainer; rinse with warm water until thawed. Drain well.

Nutrition Information Per Serving
Serving Size: 1¼ Cups

Calories	410	Calories from Fat	230
		% Daily Value	
Total Fat	25 g	38%	
Saturated	8 g	40%	
Cholesterol	50 mg	17%	
Sodium	630 mg	26%	
Total Carbohydrate	29 g	10%	
Dietary Fiber	3 g	12%	
Sugars	3 g		
Protein	16 g		
Vitamin A	8%	Vitamin C	15%
Calcium	6%	Iron	15%

Dietary Exchanges: 2 Starch, 1½ Medium-Fat Meat, 3 Fat
OR 2 Carbohydrate, 1½ Medium-Fat Meat, 3 Fat

NACHO SKILLET CASSEROLE

prep time: 30 min. • yield: 6 (1-cup) servings

A crunchy tortilla topping highlights this mildly flavored Mexican skillet meal. To reduce the fat, purchase baked tortilla chips instead of the fried version.

1 lb. ground beef

1 medium onion, chopped

1 teaspoon sugar

½ teaspoon dried oregano leaves

½ to 1 teaspoon chili powder

1 (15.5-oz.) can kidney beans, drained

1 (15-oz.) can tomato sauce

1 (11-oz.) can vacuum-packed whole kernel corn with red and green peppers, undrained

2 cups slightly broken tortilla chips

4 oz. (1 cup) shredded Cheddar or Monterey Jack cheese

1 In large skillet, brown ground beef and onion until beef is thoroughly cooked. Drain well. Stir in sugar, oregano, chili powder, kidney beans, tomato sauce and corn. Simmer 10 to 20 minutes, stirring occasionally, until most of the liquid is absorbed.

2 Sprinkle tortilla chips evenly over meat mixture; top with cheese. Cover; simmer 2 to 3 minutes or until cheese is melted.

Nutrition Information Per Serving
Serving Size: 1 Cup

Calories	460	Calories from Fat	210
		% Daily Value	
Total Fat	23 g	35%	
Saturated	9 g	45%	
Cholesterol	65 mg	22%	
Sodium	920 mg	38%	
Total Carbohydrate	39 g	13%	
Dietary Fiber	6 g	24%	
Sugars	8 g		
Protein	24 g		
Vitamin A	20%	Vitamin C	15%
Calcium	20%	Iron	20%

Dietary Exchanges: 2 ½ Starch, 2 Medium-Fat Meat, 2 ½ Fat OR
2 ½ Carbohydrate, 2 Medium-Fat Meat, 2 ½ Fat

Nacho Skillet Casserole

BREADED VEAL CUTLETS

prep time: 10 min. (ready in 30 min.) • yield: 4 servings

An Italian restaurant favorite, breaded veal cutlets are simple to make at home. Pass Parmesan cheese and hot pepper flakes at the table.

1 egg

⅔ cup unseasoned dry bread crumbs

4 (3-oz.) veal cutlets

1 tablespoon oil

1 (15-oz.) can tomato sauce

1 teaspoon dried Italian seasoning

4 oz. (1 cup) shredded mozzarella cheese

1 In shallow bowl, beat egg slightly. Place bread crumbs in another shallow bowl. Dip each cutlet in egg; coat with bread crumbs.

2 Heat oil in large nonstick skillet over medium-high heat until hot. Add cutlets; cook on both sides until browned.

3 Reduce heat; stir in tomato sauce and Italian seasoning. Cover; simmer 12 to 17 minutes or until cutlets are tender. Sprinkle with cheese; cover and cook 1 to 2 minutes or until cheese is melted.

Breaded Veal Cutlets

Calories	350	Calories from Fat	130
		% Daily Value	
Total Fat	14 g	22%	
Saturated	5 g	25%	
Cholesterol	145 mg	48%	
Sodium	1030 mg	43%	
Total Carbohydrate	22 g	7%	
Dietary Fiber	2 g	8%	
Sugars	5 g		
Protein	34 g		
Vitamin A	30%	Vitamin C	20%
Calcium	25%	Iron	15%

Dietary Exchanges: 1 Starch, 1 Vegetable, 4 Lean Meat, ½ Fat OR
1 Carbohydrate, 1 Vegetable, 4 Lean Meat, ½ Fat

CREAMY VEAL IN APPLE JUICE

prep time: 30 min. (ready in 1 hr. 45 min.) • yield: 12 servings

This elegant dish, with its creamy, slightly sweet sauce, serves twelve and is perfect for a buffet meal.

2 tablespoons oil

3 lb. boneless veal, cut into 1-inch pieces

1 medium onion, chopped

½ teaspoon salt

½ teaspoon dried marjoram leaves

⅛ teaspoon pepper

1½ cups water

1 cup apple juice

3 cups sliced carrots

2 cups frozen sweet peas

24 oz. (12 cups) uncooked egg noodles

⅓ cup all-purpose flour

1 cup half-and-half

1 Heat oil in Dutch oven over medium-high heat until hot. Add veal; cook and stir until browned. Stir in onion, salt, marjoram, pepper, water and apple juice. Bring to a boil. Reduce heat to low; cover and simmer 45 minutes.

2 Add carrots. Cover; simmer 20 to 30 minutes or until carrots are tender. Stir in peas; simmer an additional 5 minutes.

3 Meanwhile, cook noodles to desired doneness as directed on package. Drain.

4 In small bowl, combine flour and half-and-half; blend until smooth. Carefully add to veal mixture; cook and stir over medium heat until thickened. Serve over noodles.

Nutrition Information Per Serving
Serving Size: 1/12 of Recipe

Calories	440	Calories from Fat	110
		% Daily Value	
Total Fat	12 g	18%	
Saturated	4 g	20%	
Cholesterol	135 mg	45%	
Sodium	230 mg	10%	
Total Carbohydrate	54 g	18%	
Dietary Fiber	4 g	16%	
Sugars	8 g		
Protein	29 g		
Vitamin A	180%	Vitamin C	10%
Calcium	8%	Iron	20%

Dietary Exchanges: 3 ½ Starch, 2 ½ Lean Meat, ½ Fat OR
3 ½ Carbohydrate, 2 ½ Lean Meat, ½ Fat

APPLE-BRAISED PORK CHOPS WITH NOODLES

prep time: 30 min. • yield: 4 servings

Browning the pork chops and then braising them in mustard-spiked apple juice seals in juices and keeps the meat moist and flavorful.

4 (4-oz.) boneless pork loin chops

1½ cups apple juice

1 tablespoon honey mustard

½ teaspoon salt

¼ teaspoon dried thyme leaves

⅛ teaspoon pepper

1½ cups carrots, cut into ¼-inch-thick slices

4 oz. (2½ cups) uncooked extra-wide egg noodles

2 tablespoons cornstarch

2 tablespoons water

2 tablespoons chopped fresh parsley

1 Spray large skillet with nonstick cooking spray. Heat over medium-high heat until hot. Add pork chops; cook 3 to 5 minutes or until golden brown on both sides.

2 In small bowl, combine apple juice, honey mustard, salt, thyme and pepper; mix well. Pour apple juice mixture over pork chops. Reduce heat to low; cover and simmer 10 to 15 minutes or until pork is no longer pink in center.

3 Meanwhile, bring 3 quarts water to a boil in large saucepan. Add carrots; cook over medium-high heat for 5 minutes. Add noodles; return to a boil. Cook 8 to 10 minutes or until carrots and noodles are tender, stirring occasionally. Drain.

4 Remove pork chops from skillet; cover to keep warm. In small bowl, combine cornstarch and 2 tablespoons water; blend until smooth. Add to liquid in skillet; cook and stir 1 minute or until thickened and bubbly. (Gravy can be strained, if desired.)

5 To serve, arrange carrots and noodles on serving platter. Top with pork chops and gravy. Sprinkle with parsley.

Nutrition Information Per Serving
Serving Size: ¼ of Recipe

Calories	360	Calories from Fat	90
		% Daily Value	
Total Fat	10 g	15%	
Saturated	4 g	20%	
Cholesterol	80 mg	27%	
Sodium	380 mg	16%	
Total Carbohydrate	40 g	13%	
Dietary Fiber	2 g	8%	
Sugars	13 g		
Protein	27 g		
Vitamin A	260%	Vitamin C	8%
Calcium	6%	Iron	15%

Dietary Exchanges: 2 Starch, ½ Fruit, 3 Lean Meat OR 2½ Carbohydrate, 3 Lean Meat

SERVING SIZE FOR MEATS

Current nutrition guidelines from the National Center for Nutrition and Dietetics recommend 3 ounces as a serving size for cooked boneless lean meat. An easy way to estimate serving size is to visualize a deck of playing cards. A 3-ounce serving of cooked boneless lean meat is the same size: 3½ × 2½ × ⅝ inches.

Cook's Notes

Apple-Braised Pork Chops with Noodles

PORK CHOPS ITALIAN

prep time: 10 min. (ready in 50 min.) • yield: 4 servings

Stock your freezer with quick-cooking meats such as pork chops, chicken breasts and veal cutlets. Then you'll always have something to transform into a fast supper. While the herbed chops below are baking, whip together the rest of the meal.

¼ cup chopped fresh parsley

1 teaspoon dried oregano leaves

1 teaspoon fennel seed

½ teaspoon garlic salt

½ teaspoon pepper

4 (4-oz.) boneless pork loin chops

1   Heat oven to 350°F. In small bowl, combine parsley, oregano, fennel, garlic salt and pepper; mix well. Coat pork chops with parsley mixture; place in ungreased 8-inch square (2-quart) baking dish.

2   Bake at 350°F. for 30 to 40 minutes or until pork chops are no longer pink in center.

Nutrition Information Per Serving
Serving Size: ¼ of Recipe

Calories	170	Calories from Fat	70
		% Daily Value	
Total Fat	8 g	12%	
Saturated	3 g	15%	
Cholesterol	65 mg	22%	
Sodium	280 mg	12%	
Total Carbohydrate	1 g	1%	
Dietary Fiber	1 g	2%	
Sugars	0 g		
Protein	23 g		
Vitamin A	4%	Vitamin C	6%
Calcium	4%	Iron	8%

Dietary Exchanges: 3 Lean Meat

PORK CHOPS WITH CORN STUFFING

prep time: 20 min. (ready in 6 hr. 20 min.) • yield: 6 servings

Boneless pork chops become fork-tender in the slow cooker. The stuffing mixture underneath soaks up the meat juices for a moist stuffing.

1 tablespoon oil

6 (4-oz.) boneless pork loin chops (about ¾ inch thick)

1½ teaspoons dried pork seasoning

4 cups cornbread stuffing mix

½ cup chopped celery

¼ cup chopped onion

¼ teaspoon dried sage leaves, crushed

1 (14½-oz.) can ready-to-serve chicken broth

1 (11-oz.) can vacuum-packed whole kernel corn with red and green peppers, drained

1 egg, beaten

1   Heat oil in large skillet over medium heat until hot. Add pork chops; cook until browned on both sides. Drain. Sprinkle pork with pork seasoning. In large bowl, combine all remaining ingredients; mix well.

2 Spray inside of 3½- to 4-quart slow cooker with nonstick cooking spray. Spoon stuffing mixture into sprayed slow cooker. Arrange browned pork chops in 2 layers over stuffing.

3 Cover; cook on low setting for 5 to 6 hours or until pork is no longer pink in center.

Nutrition Information Per Serving
Serving Size: ⅙ of Recipe

Calories	410	Calories from Fat	130
		% Daily Value	
Total Fat	14g	22%	
Saturated	4g	20%	
Cholesterol	105mg	35%	
Sodium	920mg	38%	
Total Carbohydrate	40g	13%	
Dietary Fiber	7g	28%	
Sugars	5g		
Protein	32g		
Vitamin A	4%	Vitamin C	4%
Calcium	6%	Iron	15%

Dietary Exchanges: 2½ Starch, 3½ Lean Meat, ½ Fat OR
2½ Carbohydrate, 3½ Lean Meat, ½ Fat

Pork Chops with Corn Stuffing

CHUNKY SAUSAGE AND POTATO SUPPER

prep time: 35 min. • yield: 6 servings

Cabbage wedges steam atop a tomato-potato-sausage stew in this homespun stovetop entree. The flavors are reminiscent of those of stuffed cabbage, but without all the work. To brighten the finished dish, sprinkle on a little chopped parsley or scallions before serving.

1 lb. fully cooked smoked sausage, cut into 1 1/2- to 2-inch chunks

6 small new red potatoes, unpeeled, quartered

1 small onion, cut into 8 wedges

1 (14.5-oz.) can stewed tomatoes, undrained

1/8 teaspoon pepper

1/2 medium head cabbage, cut into 6 wedges

1 In large skillet, combine all ingredients except cabbage; mix well. Arrange cabbage wedges over top.

2 Bring to a boil. Reduce heat to medium-low; cover and cook 15 to 20 minutes or until vegetables are tender. Spoon sauce from skillet over cabbage wedges before serving.

Nutrition Information Per Serving
Serving Size: 1/6 of Recipe

Calories	390	Calories from Fat	210
		% Daily Value	
Total Fat	23 g	35%	
Saturated	8 g	40%	
Cholesterol	55 mg	18%	
Sodium	890 mg	37%	
Total Carbohydrate	32 g	11%	
Dietary Fiber	5 g	20%	
Sugars	6 g		
Protein	14 g		
Vitamin A	10%	Vitamin C	50%
Calcium	8%	Iron	20%

Dietary Exchanges: 1 1/2 Starch, 2 Vegetable, 1 High-Fat Meat, 2 1/2 Fat OR 1 1/2 Carbohydrate, 2 Vegetable, 1 High-Fat Meat, 2 1/2 Fat

OF CABBAGES AND KINGS

It turns out that the humble cabbage, a staple food of the downtrodden in many countries, has nutritional properties fit for royalty. It's a member of the cruciferous family of vegetables, which health researchers believe play a valuable role in warding off cancer. Cabbage's cruciferous cousins include bok choy, broccoli, Brussels sprouts, collards, cauliflower, kale, kohlrabi, mustard greens, radishes, rutabagas and turnips.

HAM, EGG AND POTATO SKILLET SUPPER

prep time: 20 min. • yield: 2 (1 1/2-cup) servings

Americans tend to think of eggs as breakfast food, but in many countries, eggs are common fare at the end of the day. Bolstered with potatoes, ham and broccoli, eggs offer a hearty and economical supper alternative.

2 tablespoons margarine or butter

1 cup refrigerated diced potatoes with onions (from 1 lb. 4-oz. pkg.)

1 cup frozen cut broccoli, thawed*

1/2 cup cooked ham strips (2 × 1/4 × 1/4 inches)

4 eggs

1 tablespoon milk

1/4 teaspoon peppered seasoned salt

1 Melt margarine in medium nonstick skillet over medium heat. Add potatoes; cook over medium heat 5 to 10 minutes or until lightly browned, stirring occasionally.

2 Stir in broccoli and ham; cook and stir until broccoli is tender.

3 In medium bowl, beat eggs slightly. Add milk and seasoned salt; beat well. Add to skillet all at once. Cook 2 to 5 minutes or until eggs are set but still moist, stirring occasionally.

TIP: *To quickly thaw broccoli, place in colander or strainer; rinse with warm water until thawed. Drain well.

Nutrition Information Per Serving
Serving Size: 1 ½ Cups

Calories	360	Calories from Fat	220
		% Daily Value	
Total Fat	24 g	37%	
Saturated	6 g	30%	
Cholesterol	440 mg	147%	
Sodium	850 mg	35%	
Total Carbohydrate	14 g	5%	
Dietary Fiber	2 g	8%	
Sugars	3 g		
Protein	22 g		
Vitamin A	30%	Vitamin C	30%
Calcium	8%	Iron	15%

Dietary Exchanges: ½ Starch, 1 Vegetable, 2 ½ Medium-Fat Meat, 2 ½ Fat OR ½ Carbohydrate, 1 Vegetable, 2 ½ Medium-Fat Meat, 2 ½ Fat

LAZY-DAY OVERNIGHT LASAGNA

prep time: 20 min. (ready in 13 hr. 35 min.) •
yield: 12 servings

This unconventional cooking method eliminates the hassle of boiling the lasagna noodles and then trying to layer them in the pan before they begin to stick together. Instead, you assemble the dish a day ahead using uncooked noodles, which absorb liquid and begin to soften as they sit. The noodles become tender as the casserole bakes the next day.

1 lb. mild bulk Italian sausage or ground beef

1 (28-oz.) jar spaghetti sauce

1 cup water

1 (15-oz.) container ricotta cheese

2 tablespoons chopped fresh chives

½ teaspoon dried oregano leaves

1 egg

8 oz. uncooked lasagna noodles

1 (16-oz.) pkg. sliced mozzarella cheese

2 tablespoons grated Parmesan cheese

1 Brown sausage in large skillet over medium-high heat. Drain well. Add spaghetti sauce and water; blend well. Bring to a boil. Reduce heat to low; simmer 5 minutes.

2 In medium bowl, combine ricotta cheese, chives, oregano and egg; mix well.

3 To assemble, in ungreased 13 × 9-inch (3-quart) baking dish or lasagna pan, spread 1 ½ cups of the meat sauce. Top with half each of noodles, ricotta cheese mixture and mozzarella cheese. Repeat with 1 ½ cups meat sauce and remaining noodles, ricotta cheese mixture and mozzarella cheese. Top with remaining meat sauce. Sprinkle with Parmesan cheese. Cover; refrigerate 12 hours or overnight.

4 Heat oven to 350° F. Uncover baking dish; bake 50 to 60 minutes or until noodles are tender and casserole is bubbly. Cover; let stand 15 minutes before serving.

Nutrition Information Per Serving
Serving Size: 1/12 of Recipe

Calories	360	Calories from Fat	170
		% Daily Value	
Total Fat	19 g	29%	
Saturated	9 g	45%	
Cholesterol	70 mg	23%	
Sodium	790 mg	33%	
Total Carbohydrate	23 g	8%	
Dietary Fiber	2 g	8%	
Sugars	2 g		
Protein	24 g		
Vitamin A	15%	Vitamin C	8%
Calcium	40%	Iron	10%

Dietary Exchanges: 1 ½ Starch, 2 ½ Medium-Fat Meat, 1 Fat OR 1 ½ Carbohydrate, 2 ½ Medium-Fat Meat, 1 Fat

OVEN-ROASTED PORK 'N VEGETABLES

prep time: 20 min. (ready in 1 hr.) • yield: 8 servings

PICTURED ON PAGE 112

Tenderloin is a premium cut of pork that's thin and cylindrical. Slicing the tenderloin produces attractive medallion-shaped pieces.

- 2 to 3 boneless pork tenderloins (about 1 $\frac{1}{2}$ lb.)
- 16 to 20 new potatoes (about 2 lb.), cut in half
- 6 to 8 carrots (about 1 lb.), peeled, cut into 2-inch pieces
- 1 medium onion, cut into wedges
- 1 tablespoon olive oil
- 2 teaspoons dried rosemary leaves, crushed
- 1 teaspoon dried sage leaves, crushed
- $\frac{1}{4}$ teaspoon pepper

1 Heat oven to 450°F. Generously spray roasting pan with nonstick cooking spray. Place pork tenderloins in sprayed pan. Insert meat thermometer into thickest part of 1 tenderloin. Place potatoes, carrots and onion around tenderloin. Drizzle oil evenly over tenderloin and vegetables. Sprinkle with rosemary, sage and pepper.

2 Bake at 450°F. for 30 to 40 minutes until meat thermometer registers 165°F. and vegetables are tender, stirring vegetables occasionally. Slice the tenderloins before serving.

Nutrition Information Per Serving
Serving Size: $\frac{1}{8}$ of Recipe

Calories	270	Calories from Fat	45
		% Daily Value	
Total Fat	5 g	8%	
Saturated	1 g	5%	
Cholesterol	50 mg	17%	
Sodium	65 mg	3%	
Total Carbohydrate	36 g	12%	
Dietary Fiber	5 g	20%	
Sugars	5 g		
Protein	21 g		
Vitamin A	320%	Vitamin C	25%
Calcium	4%	Iron	15%

Dietary Exchanges: 1 $\frac{1}{2}$ Starch, 2 Vegetable, 2 Lean Meat OR
1 $\frac{1}{2}$ Carbohydrate, 2 Vegetable, 2 Lean Meat

BAKED RIBS AND SAUERKRAUT

prep time: 20 min. (ready in 2 hr. 40 min.) • yield: 6 servings

Pork ribs are very fatty. Baking them for 20 minutes before they're combined with the sauerkraut removes some of the fat and yields a somewhat leaner (but still super-moist and flavorful) meal.

- 3 lb. pork spareribs or country-style ribs
- 1 $\frac{1}{2}$ teaspoons salt
- $\frac{1}{4}$ teaspoon pepper
- 1 (32-oz.) jar sauerkraut, undrained
- $\frac{1}{4}$ cup water
- 2 tablespoons brown sugar
- 2 tart apples, peeled, chopped
- 1 small onion, chopped

1 Heat oven to 450°F. Cut ribs into serving-sized pieces. Place in ungreased 13 × 9-inch pan; sprinkle with salt and pepper. Bake at 450°F. for 20 minutes.

2 Reduce oven temperature to 350°F. Remove ribs from pan; drain and discard meat drippings. In same pan, combine sauerkraut and all remaining ingredients; spread evenly. Arrange ribs on top of sauerkraut mixture.

3 Bake at 350°F. for 1 1/2 to 2 hours or until ribs are tender.

Nutrition Information Per Serving
Serving Size: 1/6 of Recipe

Calories	430	Calories from Fat	240
		% Daily Value	
Total Fat	27 g	42%	
Saturated	10 g	50%	
Cholesterol	105 mg	35%	
Sodium	1620 mg	68%	
Total Carbohydrate	19 g	6%	
Dietary Fiber	5 g	20%	
Sugars	12 g		
Protein	27 g		
Vitamin A	0%	Vitamin C	30%
Calcium	10%	Iron	25%

Dietary Exchanges: 1 Fruit, 1 Vegetable, 3 1/2 High-Fat Meat OR
1 Carbohydrate, 1 Vegetable, 3 1/2 High-Fat Meat

PORK ROAST AND VEGETABLES WITH BROWN GRAVY

prep time: 15 min. (ready in 2 hr. 25 min.) • yield: 8 servings

Nestled into slits in the top of the roast, onion slices release their flavor directly into the meat. If you wish, add a sliver of garlic to each slit, too. The aroma as this oven meal roasts is mouthwatering.

1 (2 1/2-lb.) boneless pork loin roast

1 small onion, thinly sliced

2 teaspoons dried parsley flakes

1/2 teaspoon dried marjoram leaves

1/2 teaspoon dried rosemary leaves

1/4 teaspoon crushed red pepper flakes

1 (14 1/2-oz.) can ready-to-serve beef broth

1/8 teaspoon pepper

1 bay leaf

1 lb. fresh baby carrots

8 small red potatoes, unpeeled, quartered

4 teaspoons cornstarch

1 Heat oven to 325°F. With sharp knife, make 6 cuts down center of roast, each 2 inches long and 2 inches deep. Stuff each cut with slices of onion; reserve any remaining onion. Place roast in ovenproof Dutch oven.

2 In small bowl, combine parsley, marjoram, rosemary and red pepper flakes; sprinkle evenly over top of roast. Insert meat thermometer into thickest part of roast without touching fat. Pour 1 3/4 cups of the broth around roast; cover and refrigerate remaining broth.

3 Place reserved onion slices, pepper and bay leaf in broth in Dutch oven. Arrange carrots and potatoes around roast; cover. Bake at 325°F. for 1 3/4 to 2 hours or until meat thermometer registers 160°F.

4 Remove roast from Dutch oven; place on serving platter. With slotted spoon, remove vegetables and arrange around roast; cover to keep warm.

5 Bring pan juices in Dutch oven to a boil. Boil 10 to 12 minutes or until reduced to half. Remove and discard bay leaf.

6 In small bowl, combine remaining broth and cornstarch; blend until smooth. Add to pan juices; cook and stir until mixture is bubbly and thickened. (If desired, gravy can be strained.) Serve gravy with roast and vegetables.

Nutrition Information Per Serving
Serving Size: 1/8 of Recipe

Calories	290	Calories from Fat	45
		% Daily Value	
Total Fat	5 g	8%	
Saturated	2 g	10%	
Cholesterol	85 mg	28%	
Sodium	250 mg	10%	
Total Carbohydrate	29 g	10%	
Dietary Fiber	4 g	16%	
Sugars	5 g		
Protein	33 g		
Vitamin A	320%	Vitamin C	20%
Calcium	4%	Iron	20%

Dietary Exchanges: 1 1/2 Starch, 1 Vegetable, 3 Lean Meat OR
1 1/2 Carbohydrate, 1 Vegetable, 3 Lean Meat

SPINACH-BASIL-STUFFED TENDERLOINS

prep time: 1 hr. • yield: 6 servings

Here's a nice choice for a special-occasion supper. It's deceptively easy to prepare this pork tenderloin encasing a basil-spiked spinach mixture.

STUFFING

1 tablespoon olive or vegetable oil

1 large garlic clove, minced

1 (9-oz.) pkg. frozen spinach in a pouch, thawed, well drained*

⅓ cup chopped fresh basil or
    4½ teaspoons dried basil leaves

¼ teaspoon salt

⅛ teaspoon pepper

1 egg

PORK TENDERLOIN

2 (¾-lb.) pork tenderloins

1 tablespoon olive or vegetable oil

1 large garlic clove, minced

1 teaspoon fennel seed, crushed

1 GRILL DIRECTIONS: Heat grill. In small skillet, heat 1 tablespoon oil over medium-high heat until hot. Add 1 minced garlic clove; cook 30 to 60 seconds or until garlic is tender. In medium bowl, combine cooked garlic with oil and all remaining stuffing ingredients; mix well.

Spinach-Basil-Stuffed
Tenderloins

2 Butterfly each pork tenderloin by making lengthwise cut ¾ of the way through tenderloin, being careful not to cut tenderloin into 2 pieces. Open tenderloins; sprinkle cut sides with salt and pepper, if desired.

3 Spread stuffing evenly over cut side of 1 tenderloin. Place second tenderloin, cut side down, over stuffing. (To ensure even cooking, place wide end of 1 tenderloin over narrow end of the other.) Tie at intervals with cotton string. In small bowl, combine 1 tablespoon oil, 1 minced garlic clove and fennel seed.

4 When ready to grill, brush tenderloin with oil mixture. Place on gas grill over medium heat or on charcoal grill 4 to 6 inches from medium coals; cover grill. Cook 30 to 40 minutes or until pork is no longer pink in center, turning occasionally. (Pork is done when meat thermometer registers 150 to 160° F.)

TIP: *To quickly thaw spinach, cut small slit in center of pouch; microwave on HIGH for 2 to 3 minutes or until thawed. Remove spinach from pouch; squeeze dry with paper towels.

Nutrition Information Per Serving
Serving Size: ⅙ of Recipe

Calories	180	Calories from Fat	70
		% Daily Value	
Total Fat	8 g	12%	
Saturated	2 g	10%	
Cholesterol	100 mg	33%	
Sodium	250 mg	10%	
Total Carbohydrate	2 g	1%	
Dietary Fiber	1 g	3%	
Sugars	0 g		
Protein	26 g		
Vitamin A	30%	Vitamin C	10%
Calcium	6%	Iron	10%

Dietary Exchanges: ½ Vegetable, 3 Lean Meat

COOK'S KNOW-HOW
HOW TO STUFF AND GRILL PORK TENDERLOINS

Ever wonder how the experts create those lovely stuffed tenderloins? Now you, too, can conquer the cut! It just takes a little practice and a sharp knife. The recipe is easy enough for every day, yet the results are fine enough for the fanciest outdoor feast!

STEP 1

Butterfly each pork tenderloin by making a lengthwise cut ¾ of the way through the tenderloin, being careful not to cut the tenderloin into 2 pieces. Spread stuffing evenly over cut side of 1 tenderloin.

STEP 2

Place the second tenderloin, cut side down, over the stuffing. (To ensure even cooking, place the wide end of one tenderloin over the narrow end of the other.) Tie at intervals with cotton string.

HOT AND SWEET GLAZED RIBS

prep time: 45 min. • yield: 6 servings

The three-ingredient glaze gets its liveliness from hoisin sauce, a sweet and spicy sauce often used in Chinese cooking. A mixture of soybeans, garlic, chiles and spices, it's available in Asian markets and large supermarkets.

RIBS
3 to 4 lb. pork loin back ribs

GLAZE
1/2 cup red currant jelly

1/3 cup hoisin sauce

1/4 teaspoon hot pepper sauce

1 MICROWAVE-TO-GRILL DIRECTIONS: Heat grill. Cut ribs into serving-sized sections. Arrange ribs in layers in ungreased 12 × 8-inch (2-quart) microwave-safe dish. Cover with microwave-safe plastic wrap. Microwave on HIGH for 15 minutes or until ribs are no longer pink, rearranging and turning ribs once during cooking.

2 Meanwhile, in small saucepan, combine all glaze ingredients. Cook and stir over medium heat until jelly is melted. Remove from heat.

3 Remove ribs from microwave; immediately place on gas grill over medium-low heat or on charcoal grill 6 to 8 inches from medium coals. Cook 15 to 25 minutes or until browned, turning frequently and brushing with glaze during last 10 minutes of cooking. Heat any remaining glaze to a boil; serve with ribs.

1 BOILING WATER-TO-GRILL DIRECTIONS: Cut ribs into serving-sized sections. Place ribs in large saucepan. Add water to cover; add *1 teaspoon salt*. Bring to a boil. Reduce heat; cover and simmer 1 hour.

2 Meanwhile, prepare glaze as directed above. Drain ribs; place on grill. Continue as directed above.

1 OVEN-TO-GRILL DIRECTIONS: Heat oven to 350° F. Cut ribs into serving-sized sections. Place ribs in ungreased 13 × 9-inch pan. Bake at 350° F. for 1 hour.

2 Meanwhile, prepare glaze as directed above. Place ribs on grill. Continue as directed above.

Nutrition Information Per Serving
Serving Size: 1/6 of Recipe

Calories	570	Calories from Fat	320
		% Daily Value	
Total Fat	36 g	55%	
Saturated	13 g	65%	
Cholesterol	145 mg	48%	
Sodium	390 mg	16%	
Total Carbohydrate	26 g	9%	
Dietary Fiber	0 g	0%	
Sugars	19 g		
Protein	35 g		
Vitamin A	0%	Vitamin C	0%
Calcium	6%	Iron	15%

Dietary Exchanges: 1 1/2 Fruit, 5 High-Fat Meat OR 1 1/2 Carbohydrate, 5 High-Fat Meat

GRILLED HAM SLICE WITH PINEAPPLE SALSA

prep time: 30 min. • yield: 6 servings

It's no surprise to find ham paired with pineapple, but mixing the fruit with marmalade, cilantro, jalapeño and lime gives a whole new twist to the entree.

PINEAPPLE SALSA
1 (8-oz.) can crushed pineapple, drained

2 tablespoons orange marmalade

1 tablespoon chopped fresh cilantro

2 teaspoons chopped fresh jalapeño chile

2 teaspoons lime juice

1/4 teaspoon salt

HAM
1 (1½-lb.) fully cooked center-cut ham slice (¾ to 1 inch thick)

1 GRILL DIRECTIONS: Heat grill. In small bowl, combine all salsa ingredients; mix well.

2 When ready to grill, place ham on gas grill over medium heat or on charcoal grill 4 to 6 inches from medium coals. Cook 10 to 20 minutes or until thoroughly heated, turning 2 or 3 times. Serve with pineapple salsa.

TIP: To broil ham, place on broiler pan; broil 4 to 6 inches from heat using times above as a guide.

Nutrition Information Per Serving
Serving Size: ⅙ of Recipe

Calories	140	Calories from Fat	35
		% Daily Value	
Total Fat	4 g	6%	
Saturated	1 g	5%	
Cholesterol	40 mg	13%	
Sodium	1310 mg	55%	
Total Carbohydrate	9 g	3%	
Dietary Fiber	0 g	0%	
Sugars	6 g		
Protein	17 g		
Vitamin A	0%	Vitamin C	6%
Calcium	0%	Iron	4%

Dietary Exchanges: ½ Fruit, 2 Lean Meat OR ½ Carbohydrate, 2 Lean Meat

CILANTRO

Cilantro, also known as Chinese parsley or coriander, resembles a slightly more ruffled version of flat-leafed parsley. This aromatic herb has a flavor similar to a blend of lemon and parsley. Cilantro leaves are used in Mexican, Chinese, Indian and Moroccan dishes. Prepare it as you would parsley, by rinsing the sprigs, then pinching off and chopping the leaves. Always add the leaves close to the end of cooking time because heat diminishes their flavor. Whole sprigs make a pretty garnish. Coriander seeds, whose flavor is somewhat like orangey nutmeg or mace, are the fruit of the cilantro plant and cannot be interchanged with the fresh herb.

SKEWERED LAMB AND ONION

prep time: 15 min. (ready in 1 hr. 15 min.) • yield: 6 servings

Garnish the cooked lamb with finely minced red onion and accompany it with new potatoes and steamed sugar snap peas.

¼ cup red wine vinegar

1 teaspoon dried sage leaves, crushed

1 teaspoon olive oil

1 lb. boneless leg of lamb, cut into 1½-inch pieces

1 large red onion, cut into ½-inch pieces

1 In large bowl, combine vinegar, sage and oil; mix well. Add lamb and onion; stir gently to coat. Cover; refrigerate 1 hour to marinate.

2 Thread lamb and onion pieces on 6-inch metal skewers; reserve marinade. Broil 6 inches from heat for 8 to 10 minutes or until lamb is no longer pink, brushing frequently with marinade. (Onion pieces will remain crisp.)

Nutrition Information Per Serving
Serving Size: ⅙ of Recipe

Calories	100	Calories from Fat	35
		% Daily Value	
Total Fat	4 g	6%	
Saturated	1 g	5%	
Cholesterol	40 mg	13%	
Sodium	35 mg	1%	
Total Carbohydrate	3 g	1%	
Dietary Fiber	1 g	2%	
Sugars	1 g		
Protein	14 g		
Vitamin A	0%	Vitamin C	2%
Calcium	0%	Iron	6%

Dietary Exchanges: 1 Vegetable, 1½ Lean Meat

Chutney Lamb Chops

CHUTNEY LAMB CHOPS

prep time: 15 min. • yield: 4 servings

Lamb will be at its juiciest and most flavorful if you remove it from the grill while it is still slightly pink in the center. To test for doneness, cut a small slit near the bone and check the color.

½ cup mango chutney

2 tablespoons honey

½ teaspoon dry mustard

4 (½-inch-thick) lamb loin chops

1 GRILL DIRECTIONS: Heat grill. In small bowl, combine chutney, honey and mustard; blend well.

2 When ready to grill, place lamb chops on gas grill over medium heat or on charcoal grill 4 to 6 inches from medium coals. Cook 8 to 10 minutes or until of desired doneness, turning once and brushing with chutney mixture during last 3 to 4 minutes of cooking time.

TIP: To broil lamb chops, place on broiler pan; broil 4 to 6 inches from heat using times above as a guide.

Nutrition Information Per Serving
Serving Size: ¼ of Recipe

Calories	230	Calories from Fat	45
		% Daily Value	
Total Fat	5 g	8%	
Saturated	2 g	10%	
Cholesterol	45 mg	15%	
Sodium	310 mg	13%	
Total Carbohydrate	31 g	10%	
Dietary Fiber	0 g	0%	
Sugars	23 g		
Protein	14 g		
Vitamin A	0%	Vitamin C	0%
Calcium	0%	Iron	6%

Dietary Exchanges: 2 Fruit, 2 Lean Meat OR 2 Carbohydrate, 2 Lean Meat

CHARCOAL FIRES

To prepare a charcoal fire, start 30 to 45 minutes before beginning to cook. Mound briquettes into a pyramid; add charcoal lighter fluid and wait the time recommended on the package before lighting the mound. When coals are covered with a light gray ash, they have reached the proper grilling temperature. Arrange the coals in a single layer so they just touch, and position the rack 4 to 6 inches above the coals.

To judge the temperature of the charcoal fire, hold your hand, palm side down, over the coals at cooking height. Now count the number of seconds you can hold that position. This gives you an indication of the temperature.

- 5 seconds—low
- 4 seconds—medium
- 3 seconds—medium-high
- 2 seconds—high

Vent holes on kettle grills help control air flow and, consequently, temperature. Open the vents fully to raise the temperature; close halfway to lower it. Close the vents completely to snuff out the coals.

Italian Barbecued Halibut Steaks with Tomato Relish, page 157

FISH & SEAFOOD

Seafood is among the most popular restaurant entrees and, with the recipes in this chapter, it will be a hit at home, too. Keep it simple and plain, if you wish, with Easy Breaded Fish Fillets (page 162) or simple but slightly more exotic with Asian Grilled Halibut (page 156). Looking for other delectable choices? There's a Mussels in Wine Sauce (page 168) or zesty Margarita Shrimp (page 164) to cook on the grill.

BUTTONS AND BOWS TUNA CASSEROLE

prep time: 25 min. • yield: 3 (1 ⅓-cup) servings

Here's a quick-to-fix stovetop version of the standard tuna casserole, made with a fun combination of wagon wheel and bow tie pasta. You can also use all one pasta shape, if that's what you have on hand.

- 3 oz. (1 cup) uncooked wagon wheel pasta
- 1½ oz. (¾ cup) uncooked bow tie pasta (farfalle)
- 1 cup frozen sweet peas
- ½ cup milk
- 1 (10¾-oz.) can condensed cream of mushroom soup
- 1 (6-oz.) can water-packed tuna, drained

1 Cook pastas to desired doneness as directed on package. Drain; return to saucepan.

2 Add peas, milk, soup and tuna; mix gently until well combined. Cook over medium heat until peas are tender and mixture is thoroughly heated, stirring occasionally. If desired, top with crushed potato chips.

Nutrition Information Per Serving
Serving Size: 1 ⅓ Cups

Calories	370	Calories from Fat	90
		% Daily Value	
Total Fat	10 g	15%	
Saturated	3 g	15%	
Cholesterol	20 mg	7%	
Sodium	970 mg	40%	
Total Carbohydrate	48 g	16%	
Dietary Fiber	3 g	12%	
Sugars	6 g		
Protein	23 g		
Vitamin A	6%	Vitamin C	8%
Calcium	10%	Iron	20%

Dietary Exchanges: 3 Starch, 1 Vegetable, 1½ Very Lean Meat, 1½ Fat OR 3 Carbohydrate, 1 Vegetable, 1½ Very Lean Meat, 1½ Fat

TUNA-BROCCOLI SPAGHETTI PIE

prep time: 25 min. (ready in 1 hr. 15 min.) • yield: 6 servings

Pressed into the bottom and sides of a pie plate, cooked spaghetti enriched with cheese and eggs becomes a "crust" for a tuna-broccoli Alfredo filling.

- 6 oz. uncooked spaghetti
- 2 tablespoons margarine or butter
- ½ cup grated Parmesan cheese
- 2 eggs, slightly beaten
- 3 cups frozen cut broccoli, thawed
- 2 tablespoons all-purpose flour
- 1 (10-oz.) container refrigerated Alfredo sauce
- 1 (9¼-oz.) can water-packed tuna, drained, flaked
- ¼ cup Italian-seasoned dry bread crumbs
- 1 teaspoon margarine or butter, melted

1 In large saucepan or Dutch oven, cook spaghetti to desired doneness as directed on package. Drain; return to saucepan.

2 Meanwhile, heat oven to 350°F. Grease 10- or 9-inch deep-dish pie pan or quiche dish.

3 To cooked spaghetti, add 2 tablespoons margarine, Parmesan cheese and eggs; stir gently. Spread over bottom and up sides of greased pie pan.

4 In large bowl, combine broccoli, flour, Alfredo sauce and tuna; mix well. Spoon into spaghetti crust. In small bowl, combine bread crumbs and 1 teaspoon melted margarine; mix well. Sprinkle over tuna mixture.

5 Bake at 350°F. for 40 to 45 minutes or until spaghetti is light golden brown. Let stand 5 minutes before serving.

Nutrition Information Per Serving
Serving Size: 1/6 of Recipe

Calories	450	Calories from Fat	230
		% Daily Value	
Total Fat	25 g	38%	
Saturated	11 g	55%	
Cholesterol	120 mg	40%	
Sodium	700 mg	29%	
Total Carbohydrate	32 g	11%	
Dietary Fiber	2 g	8%	
Sugars	3 g		
Protein	23 g		
Vitamin A	10%	Vitamin C	0%
Calcium	25%	Iron	15%

Dietary Exchanges: 2 Starch, 1 Vegetable, 2 Very Lean Meat, 4 1/2 Fat OR
2 Carbohydrate, 1 Vegetable, 2 Very Lean Meat, 4 1/2 Fat

PARMESAN CHEESE

Parmesan cheese is a hard, dry granular cheese with a pale golden rind and straw-colored interior. Made from cow's milk, it has a sharp, pungent flavor. Although Parmesan cheese is made in many countries, the most highly prized is Parmigiano-Reggiano from Parma, Italy. This cheese is aged two to four years, has supreme flavor and a characteristic granular texture. It is typically more expensive than domestic varieties, but its heightened flavor means that less is needed. Parmigiano-Reggiano is available at Italian markets and in the deli departments of large supermarkets.

Parmesan cheese is primarily used grated, though restaurants sometimes "shave" it for a slightly different effect. You can purchase the cheese pre-grated in canisters. For freshest flavor, buy it in chunk form and grate it as needed, using a food processor or the fine-holed side of a hand grater.

FRESH TUNA WITH GREMOLATA

prep time: 20 min. • yield: 4 servings

Fresh tuna steaks topped with a simple mix of parsley, lemon peel, olive oil and garlic are easy enough to make for a weeknight supper and special enough for guests.

1/4 cup finely chopped fresh parsley

2 tablespoons grated lemon peel

1 teaspoon olive oil

1 garlic clove, minced

4 (4-oz.) tuna steaks (1 inch thick)

1/4 teaspoon salt

1 In small bowl, combine parsley, lemon peel, oil and garlic; mix well. Set aside.

2 Line broiler pan with foil; spray foil with non-stick cooking spray. Place tuna steaks on foil-lined pan; sprinkle with salt.

3 Broil about 4 inches from heat for 4 to 5 minutes on each side or until fish flakes easily with fork, topping fish with parsley mixture during last minute of broiling time.

Nutrition Information Per Serving
Serving Size: 1/4 of Recipe

Calories	170	Calories from Fat	60
		% Daily Value	
Total Fat	7 g	11%	
Saturated	2 g	10%	
Cholesterol	45 mg	15%	
Sodium	180 mg	8%	
Total Carbohydrate	1 g	1%	
Dietary Fiber	0 g	0%	
Sugars	0 g		
Protein	27 g		
Vitamin A	50%	Vitamin C	10%
Calcium	0%	Iron	8%

Dietary Exchanges: 4 Very Lean Meat, 1 Fat

Salmon with Rice Pilaf and Dill Sauce

SALMON WITH RICE PILAF AND DILL SAUCE

prep time: 40 min. • yield: 4 servings

Before cooking salmon fillets, run your fingers over the flesh to detect any little bones and pull them out.

DILL SAUCE
1 (8-oz.) container nonfat plain yogurt

2 tablespoons chopped green onions

$\frac{1}{2}$ teaspoon grated lemon peel

1 teaspoon dried dill weed

RICE PILAF
$1\frac{1}{3}$ cups water

$\frac{2}{3}$ cup uncooked regular long-grain white rice

1 chicken-flavor bouillon cube or
    1 teaspoon chicken-flavor instant bouillon

$\frac{1}{2}$ cup frozen sweet peas, thawed

1 teaspoon grated lemon peel

SALMON
1 small onion, sliced

1 lemon, sliced

4 to 6 peppercorns

4 (4-oz.) salmon steaks or fillets

1   In small bowl, combine all sauce ingredients; blend well. Cover; refrigerate until serving time.

2   In medium saucepan, combine $1\frac{1}{3}$ cups water, rice and bouillon. Bring to a boil. Reduce heat; cover and simmer 10 minutes. Stir in peas and lemon peel. Cover; simmer an additional 5 to 10 minutes or until rice is tender and liquid is absorbed. Keep warm.

3   Meanwhile, in large skillet, combine 4 cups water, sliced onion, lemon and peppercorns. Bring to a boil. Reduce heat; simmer 5 minutes to blend flavors. Add salmon steaks; cover and simmer 7 to 10 minutes or until fish flakes easily with fork.

4   To serve, with slotted spoon, lift fish from liquid; place on serving platter. Serve with rice pilaf and dill sauce.

Nutrition Information Per Serving
Serving Size: $\frac{1}{4}$ of Recipe

Calories	360	Calories from Fat	100
		% Daily Value	
Total Fat	11 g	17%	
Saturated	2 g	10%	
Cholesterol	85 mg	28%	
Sodium	370 mg	15%	
Total Carbohydrate	32 g	11%	
Dietary Fiber	1 g	4%	
Sugars	5 g		
Protein	33 g		
Vitamin A	6%	Vitamin C	6%
Calcium	15%	Iron	15%

Dietary Exchanges: 2 Starch, 3 $\frac{1}{2}$ Lean Meat OR 2 Carbohydrate, 3 $\frac{1}{2}$ Lean Meat

GRILLED SALMON WITH HERBED TARTAR SAUCE

prep time: 20 min. • yield: 4 servings

This three-ingredient tartar sauce can dress up any cooked frozen fish.

SAUCE

½ cup mayonnaise

2 tablespoons chopped fresh herbs (basil, dill, chives and/or parsley)

¼ teaspoon Worcestershire sauce

SALMON

2 tablespoons olive or vegetable oil

1 tablespoon lemon juice

4 (6-oz.) salmon fillets

⅛ teaspoon salt

⅛ teaspoon pepper

1 GRILL DIRECTIONS: Heat grill. In blender container or food processor bowl with metal blade, combine tartar sauce ingredients; blend at high speed until well mixed, stopping often to scrape down sides. Place in serving bowl; refrigerate.

2 In small bowl, combine oil and lemon juice; mix well.

3 When ready to grill, brush salmon fillets with lemon mixture; sprinkle with salt and pepper. Carefully oil grill rack. Place fish on gas grill over medium heat or on charcoal grill 4 to 6 inches from medium coals. Cook 8 to 12 minutes or until fish flakes easily with fork, turning once. Serve with herbed tartar sauce.

TIP: To broil salmon, place on oiled broiler pan; broil 4 to 6 inches from heat using times above as a guide.

Nutrition Information Per Serving
Serving Size: ¼ of Recipe

Calories	570	Calories from Fat	410
		% Daily Value	
Total Fat	45 g	69%	
Saturated	7 g	35%	
Cholesterol	140 mg	47%	
Sodium	330 mg	14%	
Total Carbohydrate	1 g	1%	
Dietary Fiber	0 g	0%	
Sugars	1 g		
Protein	40 g		
Vitamin A	10%	Vitamin C	2%
Calcium	0%	Iron	6%

Dietary Exchanges: 6 Lean Meat, 5 Fat

WOOD CHIPS TO FLAVOR GRILLED FOODS

Foods cooked on a covered grill take on a light woodsy taste and smoky flavor when dampened wood chips are scattered over hot coals. Hardwoods or fruit woods are the best types to use. Avoid cedar, fir, pine, spruce and eucalyptus, which give food an unpleasant resinous taste. Choose from the following:

Fruit woods	Delicate and sweet. Best for poultry, seafood and pork.
Grapevine	Delicate and sweet. Best for delicate fish or poultry.
Hickory	Popular, intense and smoky. Best for robust food such as ribs, poultry, beef.
Mesquite	Light, clean and woody. Best for meats compatible with strong flavor, such as beef, chicken and swordfish.
Nut woods	Delicate and sweet. Best for poultry and dark fish such as tuna.
Oak	Mellow and fresh. Best for meats compatible with strong flavor, such as steak, pork, chicken and salmon.

Wood chips are available at some grocery or kitchen specialty stores and can be mail-ordered from grill manufacturer's supply catalogs. A handful of soaked chips sprinkled over the briquets just before cooking is a good starter amount for moderate flavor.

For use with a gas grill, place wood chips in disposable 6 × 4-inch foil pans to prevent accumulated ash from clogging vents.

TERIYAKI SALMON AND VEGETABLES

prep time: 25 min. • yield: 4 (1-cup) servings

Serve this gingery fish and vegetable mixture over aromatic jasmine rice, available at Asian grocery stores, or basmati rice.

1 tablespoon oil

1 lb. salmon fillets, cut into 1-inch pieces

1 teaspoon purchased chopped garlic and ginger stir-fry blend

2 cups fresh broccoli florets

1½ cups thinly sliced carrots

1 cup thinly sliced celery

3 tablespoons water

½ cup purchased teriyaki baste and glaze

1 Heat oil in large skillet or wok over medium heat until hot. Add salmon and stir-fry blend; cook and stir 3 to 5 minutes or until fish flakes easily with fork. Remove fish from skillet; cover to keep warm.

2 In same skillet, combine broccoli, carrots and celery; cook and stir 3 minutes. Add water; cover and cook 3 to 4 minutes or until vegetables are crisp-tender, stirring occasionally.

3 Gently stir in fish and teriyaki baste and glaze; cook until thoroughly heated.

Nutrition Information Per Serving
Serving Size: 1 Cup

Calories	320	Calories from Fat	130
		% Daily Value	
Total Fat	14 g	22%	
Saturated	2 g	10%	
Cholesterol	85 mg	28%	
Sodium	920 mg	38%	
Total Carbohydrate	19 g	6%	
Dietary Fiber	3 g	12%	
Sugars	13 g		
Protein	29 g		
Vitamin A	290%	Vitamin C	50%
Calcium	10%	Iron	15%

Dietary Exchanges: ½ Fruit, 2 Vegetable, 3 ½ Lean Meat, 1 Fat OR
½ Carbohydrate, 2 Vegetable, 3 ½ Lean Meat, 1 Fat

SALMON

When purchasing fresh salmon fillets or steaks, select firm, moist, brighty colored fish. Salmon's color can range from bright red to pale pink or even off-white, depending on the variety.

Salmon is a moist, firm-fleshed fish, meaning that it stands up well to almost any cooking method, including broiling, grilling, poaching, microwaving or smoking. Use salmon as a main course, in pasta salads or as an appetizer. It can be served hot or cold.

Cook's Notes

GRILLED WALLEYE WITH PECAN BUTTER

prep time: 25 min. • yield: 4 servings

Grilling the fillets atop slitted foil lets the fish absorb a smoky flavor without the risk of them falling through the wires of the rack. Whitefish fillets can be substituted for walleye fillets.

¼ cup butter, softened

2 teaspoons chopped fresh chives

2 teaspoons orange juice

½ cup chopped pecans, toasted*

4 (6-oz.) walleye fillets

¼ teaspoon salt

Dash coarse ground black pepper

1 GRILL DIRECTIONS: Heat grill. Cut two 12-inch-square sheets of heavy-duty foil. With tip of sharp knife, cut 2-inch slits every 2 inches across center of foil. Spray foil with nonstick cooking spray.

2 In small bowl, combine butter, chives, orange juice and ¼ cup of the pecans; mix well.

3 When ready to grill, place foil on gas grill over medium heat or on charcoal grill 4 to 6 inches from medium coals. Sprinkle walleye fillets with salt and pepper. Place 2 fillets on each sheet of foil; cook 8 to 12 minutes or until fish flakes easily with fork, turning once. During last minute of cooking time, top fish with pecan butter. Remove fish from heat; place on serving platter. Sprinkle with remaining ¼ cup pecans.

TIPS: *To toast pecans, spread on cookie sheet; bake at 350° F. for 5 to 7 minutes or until golden brown, stirring occasionally. Or spread pecans in thin layer in microwave-safe pie pan. Microwave on HIGH for 4 to 7 minutes or until golden brown, stirring frequently.

To broil walleye, place on broiler pan sprayed with nonstick cooking spray; broil 4 to 6 inches from heat using times above as a guide and topping with pecan butter during last minute of broiling time.

Nutrition Information Per Serving
Serving Size: ¼ of Recipe

Calories	360	Calories from Fat	210
		% Daily Value	
Total Fat	23 g	35%	
Saturated	8 g	40%	
Cholesterol	175 mg	58%	
Sodium	340 mg	14%	
Total Carbohydrate	4 g	1%	
Dietary Fiber	1 g	4%	
Sugars	1 g		
Protein	34 g		
Vitamin A	10%	Vitamin C	0%
Calcium	20%	Iron	15%

Dietary Exchanges: 5 Very Lean Meat, 4 Fat

CHIVES

*C*hives, a grasslike member of the onion family, are a great "blending" agent because they complement the flavor of almost any other herb. Fresh chives are infinitely superior to the dried version, which tend to be pale and lackluster. Add fresh chives at the end of cooking time or sprinkle over each serving as a garnish.

• Onion chives (usually referred to simply as "chives") are the most common variety. Mature chives sport edible pink flower heads, which also have an onion flavor and add color to salads. The stalks of the flowers, however, are fibrous and tough.

• Chinese chives, a more pungent cousin, are larger and flatter than onion chives and range from green to yellowish. Use them as you would common chives, though perhaps with a less generous hand.

Grilled Walleye with Pecan Butter

ASIAN GRILLED HALIBUT

prep time: 25 min. (ready in 4 hr. 25 min.) • yield: 4 servings

Halibut's flavor is a good foil for this Asian-inspired ginger-soy marinade. The fish's firm texture makes it especially well suited to grilling because it can be turned without crumbling. Even so, we recommend you oil the grill rack or basket to prevent sticking.

MARINADE
1/2 cup oil

3 tablespoons soy sauce

2 tablespoons dry sherry

1 teaspoon grated gingerroot

2 garlic cloves, minced

FISH
4 (4-oz.) halibut steaks (3/4 to 1 inch thick)

1 GRILL DIRECTIONS: In 12 × 8-inch (2-quart) baking dish or resealable food storage plastic bag, combine all marinade ingredients; mix well. Place halibut in marinade; turn to coat. Cover dish or seal bag. Refrigerate 4 to 6 hours to marinate, turning occasionally.

2 Heat grill. When ready to grill, generously oil wire grill basket or carefully oil grill rack. Remove fish from marinade; reserve marinade. Place fish in well-oiled grill basket or directly on gas grill over medium heat or on charcoal grill 4 to 6 inches from medium coals. Cook 10 to 14 minutes or until fish flakes easily with fork, turning once and brushing frequently with marinade. Discard any remaining marinade.

TIP: To broil halibut, place on oiled broiler pan; broil 4 to 6 inches from heat using times above as a guide and brushing frequently with marinade.

Nutrition Information Per Serving
Serving Size: 1/4 of Recipe

Calories	180	Calories from Fat	80
		% Daily Value	
Total Fat	9 g	14%	
Saturated	1 g	5%	
Cholesterol	35 mg	12%	
Sodium	250 mg	10%	
Total Carbohydrate	1 g	1%	
Dietary Fiber	0 g	0%	
Sugars	0 g		
Protein	24 g		
Vitamin A	4%	Vitamin C	0%
Calcium	6%	Iron	6%

Dietary Exchanges: 3 1/2 Very Lean Meat, 1 1/2 Fat

CITRUS GARNISHES

A touch of citrus can brighten most chicken and fish entrees, especially if lemon, lime or orange is already used in the recipe. Two of the easiest garnishes are Citrus Twists and Cartwheels.

To make Citrus Twists, cut an unpeeled orange, lime or lemon into 1/8-inch-thick slices. Make a cut from the peel edge to the center. Twist the ends in opposite directions to form a Citrus Twist.

To make Citrus Cartwheels, hold the stem and blossom ends of an unpeeled orange, lemon or lime between your thumb and middle finger. Using a zester or peeler, pull the zester through the peel from end to end to make stripes, leaving about 1/4 to 1/2 inch between cuts. Cut the fruit into slices.

Citrus Twists and Cartwheels can themselves be garnished with sprigs of mint or parsley, whole cloves, sliced almonds or maraschino cherries.

ITALIAN BARBECUED HALIBUT STEAKS WITH TOMATO RELISH

prep time: 30 min. • **yield: 4 servings**

PICTURED ON PAGE 146

Bottled dressing makes an easy marinade for halibut steaks, and works well for boneless chicken breasts, too. The tomato-olive-herb relish can be varied as you like by stirring in items such as minced onion, capers or diced fresh mozzarella.

FISH

1/2 cup purchased fat-free Italian salad dressing

1 teaspoon paprika

1/4 teaspoon coarse ground black pepper

4 (4- to 6-oz.) halibut steaks (1 inch thick)

RELISH

1 large tomato, seeded, chopped

1 (2 1/4-oz.) can sliced ripe olives, drained

1 to 2 tablespoons chopped fresh basil or parsley

1 GRILL DIRECTIONS: In small bowl, combine dressing, paprika and pepper; mix well. Place halibut steaks in resealable food storage plastic bag. Pour dressing mixture over fish; seal bag. Turn bag to coat both sides of fish. Refrigerate 15 minutes to marinate.

2 Meanwhile, heat grill. In medium bowl, combine tomato, olives and basil; mix well.

3 When ready to grill, carefully oil grill rack. Remove fish from marinade; reserve marinade. Place fish on gas grill over medium heat or on charcoal grill 4 to 6 inches from medium-high coals. Cook 10 to 13 minutes or until fish flakes easily with fork, turning once and brushing occasionally with marinade. Discard any remaining marinade. Serve with tomato relish.

TIP: To broil halibut, place on oiled broiler pan; broil 4 to 6 inches from heat using times above as a guide and brushing occasionally with marinade.

Nutrition Information Per Serving
Serving Size: 1/4 of Recipe

Calories	220	Calories from Fat	70
		% Daily Value	
Total Fat	6 g	9%	
Saturated	1 g	5%	
Cholesterol	55 mg	18%	
Sodium	530 mg	22%	
Total Carbohydrate	6 g	2%	
Dietary Fiber	1 g	4%	
Sugars	3 g		
Protein	36 g		
Vitamin A	20%	Vitamin C	10%
Calcium	10%	Iron	15%

Dietary Exchanges: 1/2 Starch, 5 Very Lean Meat OR 1/2 Carbohydrate, 5 Very Lean Meat

TESTING FISH FOR DONENESS

Fish cooks quickly and is therefore easy to overcook. When cooked to perfection, the flesh turns from translucent to opaque or white (darker fish such as salmon or tuna don't turn white, but the flesh loses its shine). To test for doneness, insert fork tines into the thickest portion of the fish and twist gently. If it flakes easily, it's done. If the fish resists flaking and still looks shiny or translucent, continue to cook it—but check it frequently to avoid overcooking.

POACHED SOLE WITH TOMATO-MUSHROOM SAUCE

prep time: 25 min. • yield: 4 servings

Sole and flounder are flat whitefish with a mild flavor that borders on sweet. They cook more quickly than thicker round whitefish fillets such as cod or salmon.

SOLE

¼ teaspoon salt

1 tablespoon lemon juice

1 lb. sole or flounder fillets

SAUCE

2 tablespoons margarine or butter

¼ cup chopped onion

2 tomatoes, peeled, coarsely chopped

¼ cup sliced pitted green olives

1 (4.5-oz.) jar sliced mushrooms, drained

Poached Sole with
Tomato-Mushroom Sauce

1 teaspoon sugar

¼ teaspoon salt

Dash ground red pepper (cayenne)

1 In large skillet, combine 1 cup water, ¼ teaspoon salt and lemon juice. Bring to a boil. Add sole fillets. Reduce heat; cover and simmer 5 to 10 minutes or until fish flakes easily with fork.

2 Meanwhile, melt margarine in medium saucepan over medium heat. Add onion; cook and stir until tender. Stir in all remaining sauce ingredients. Cook 5 minutes, stirring occasionally.

3 To serve, with slotted spoon, carefully lift fish from liquid; place on serving platter. Serve sauce over fish.

Nutrition Information Per Serving
Serving Size: ¼ of Recipe

Calories	190	Calories from Fat	70
		% Daily Value	
Total Fat	8 g	12%	
Saturated	2 g	10%	
Cholesterol	55 mg	18%	
Sodium	730 mg	30%	
Total Carbohydrate	7 g	2%	
Dietary Fiber	2 g	8%	
Sugars	3 g		
Protein	22 g		
Vitamin A	15%	Vitamin C	15%
Calcium	4%	Iron	4%

Dietary Exchanges: 1 Vegetable, 3 Lean Meat

ITALIAN-STYLE FISH AND VEGETABLES

prep time: 35 min. • yield: 6 servings

Much of the catfish in your supermarket is likely to have been farm raised, giving it a milder flavor than that of its wild cousins. Any mild-flavored, firm-textured fish can be used in this colorful skillet entree.

2 tablespoons olive or vegetable oil

1 medium onion, sliced

1 (2.5-oz.) jar sliced mushrooms, drained

½ teaspoon dried basil leaves

½ teaspoon fennel seed

2 cups frozen mixed vegetables

1½ lb. catfish, orange roughy or sole fillets

¼ teaspoon salt

¼ teaspoon pepper

2 medium tomatoes, sliced

⅓ cup grated Parmesan cheese

1 Heat oil in large skillet over medium heat until hot. Add onion, mushrooms, basil and fennel seed; cook 4 minutes or until onion is tender, stirring occasionally.

2 Stir in frozen vegetables. Place fish over vegetables; sprinkle with salt and pepper. Arrange tomato slices over fish. Reduce heat to low; cover and cook 12 to 16 minutes or until fish flakes easily with fork.

3 Sprinkle with cheese. Remove skillet from heat; cover and let stand about 3 minutes or until cheese is melted.

Nutrition Information Per Serving
Serving Size: ⅙ of Recipe

Calories	210	Calories from Fat	80
		% Daily Value	
Total Fat	9 g	14%	
Saturated	2 g	10%	
Cholesterol	55 mg	18%	
Sodium	340 mg	14%	
Total Carbohydrate	8 g	3%	
Dietary Fiber	2 g	8%	
Sugars	2 g		
Protein	24 g		
Vitamin A	25%	Vitamin C	10%
Calcium	10%	Iron	4%

Dietary Exchanges: 2 Vegetable, 3 Very Lean Meat, 1 Fat

TANGY GRILLED FISH

prep time: 15 min. • yield: 4 servings

Purchase prepared horseradish in small quantities so it doesn't lose its zip. Discard once the horseradish begins to darken in color.

SAUCE
3 tablespoons olive or vegetable oil

3 tablespoons Dijon mustard

1 tablespoon sour cream

1 tablespoon prepared horseradish

1 teaspoon dried Italian seasoning

Dash pepper

FISH
4 (4-oz.) whitefish, haddock or orange roughy fillets

1 GRILL DIRECTIONS: Heat grill. In small bowl, combine all sauce ingredients; blend well.

Tangy Grilled Fish

2 When ready to grill, carefully oil grill rack. Place whitefish fillets on gas grill over medium heat or on charcoal grill 4 to 6 inches from medium coals. Brush with sauce. Cook 6 to 10 minutes or until fish flakes easily with fork, turning once and brushing occasionally with sauce. Bring any remaining sauce to a boil. Serve sauce with fish.

TIP: To broil whitefish, place on oiled broiler pan; broil 4 to 6 inches from heat using times above as a guide and brushing occasionally with sauce.

Nutrition Information Per Serving			
Serving Size: ¼ of Recipe			
Calories	260	Calories from Fat	170
		% Daily Value	
Total Fat	19 g	29%	
Saturated	3 g	15%	
Cholesterol	70 mg	23%	
Sodium	360 mg	15%	
Total Carbohydrate	1 g	1%	
Dietary Fiber	0 g	0%	
Sugars	1 g		
Protein	22 g		
Vitamin A	4%	Vitamin C	0%
Calcium	6%	Iron	4%

Dietary Exchanges: 3 Very Lean Meat, 3 ½ Fat

COOK'S KNOW-HOW
HOW TO GRILL FISH FILLETS

If you've ever been frustrated with fall-apart fillets, you'll appreciate this neat idea for grilling fish. It's hassle free and inexpensive. Simply use two wire cooking racks—the kind used for cooling cookies—to construct your fish grilling basket. Follow these few quick steps:

STEP 1

Brush with cooking oil or spray with nonstick cooking spray the inside cooking surfaces of both wire cooling racks.

STEP 2

Place fillets on the oiled surface of one wire rack, and place the other wire rack on top of the fillets, oiled side down. If desired, the racks can be wired together on 2 sides to form a basket.

STEP 3

Place the grill basket on a heated grill and cook the fish

according to recipe directions. Two fire-resistant heavy-duty oven mitts or 2 sets of long-handled tongs work well for turning the grill basket.

EASY BREADED FISH FILLETS

prep time: 20 min. • yield: 4 servings

The seasoned breading mixture creates a light, crisp coating for fish that cooks quickly. Serve with tartar sauce and lemon wedges.

3/4 **cup crushed seasoned croutons**

1/4 **cup grated Parmesan cheese**

2 **teaspoons dried parsley flakes**

1/4 **teaspoon paprika**

1 **egg**

1 **tablespoon water**

1 **tablespoon lemon juice**

1 **lb. fish fillets**

1 Heat oven to 350°F. Spray 15 × 10 × 1-inch baking pan with nonstick cooking spray. In shallow dish, combine croutons, Parmesan cheese, parsley flakes and paprika; blend well. In another shallow dish, combine egg, water and lemon juice; beat well.

2 Cut fish fillets into serving-sized pieces. Dip in egg mixture; coat with crouton mixture. Tuck thin ends of fish under to form pieces of uniform thickness. Place fish in sprayed pan.

3 Bake at 350°F. for 10 to 15 minutes or until fish flakes easily with fork.

Easy Breaded Fish Fillets

Nutrition Information Per Serving			
Serving Size: ¼ of Recipe			
Calories	240	Calories from Fat	70
		% Daily Value	
Total Fat	8 g	12%	
Saturated	3 g	15%	
Cholesterol	105 mg	35%	
Sodium	480 mg	20%	
Total Carbohydrate	15 g	5%	
Dietary Fiber	1 g	4%	
Sugars	2 g		
Protein	27 g		
Vitamin A	8%	Vitamin C	4%
Calcium	15%	Iron	10%

Dietary Exchanges: 1 Starch, 3 ½ Very Lean Meat, 1 Fat
OR 1 Carbohydrate, 3 ½ Very Lean Meat, 1 Fat

MICROWAVING FISH

Cooking fish is one of the areas in which the microwave excels, and fish cooked this way remains tender and moist. Arrange the fish in a microwave-safe dish with the thicker edges to the outside. Cover the dish with microwave-safe plastic wrap and cook on HIGH. Allow 3½ to 6 minutes per pound of boneless fish, rotating the dish once during cooking. In contrast to fish cooked conventionally, fish prepared in the microwave should be removed from the oven when the outer edges are opaque and the center is still slightly translucent. The fish will be firm and moist; when allowed to stand for a few minutes, it will flake easily with a fork.

Cook's Notes

CHEESY FISH AND VEGETABLES

prep time: 20 min. • yield: 4 servings

Simmering cod or halibut in liquid keeps the fish moist and flavorful, a technique that translates well to almost any mild whitefish. Thin fillets from fish such as flounder or sole, however, will cook more quickly.

1 lb. cod or halibut fillets, cut into serving-sized pieces

¼ cup dry white wine or chicken broth

1 teaspoon dried parsley flakes

1 (10-oz.) pkg. frozen broccoli, cauliflower and carrots in a pouch in cheese-flavored sauce

1 Place cod fillets in large skillet; add wine and parsley. Cover; cook 5 to 10 minutes or until fish flakes easily with fork.

2 Meanwhile, cook vegetables in pouch as directed on package.

3 Remove fish from skillet; place on warm serving platter. Add hot vegetable mixture to hot cooking liquid in skillet; mix well. Spoon mixture over fish. If desired, garnish with additional parsley.

Nutrition Information Per Serving			
Serving Size: ¼ of Recipe			
Calories	130	Calories from Fat	20
		% Daily Value	
Total Fat	2 g	3%	
Saturated	1 g	5%	
Cholesterol	50 mg	17%	
Sodium	480 mg	20%	
Total Carbohydrate	7 g	2%	
Dietary Fiber	1 g	4%	
Sugars	4 g		
Protein	22 g		
Vitamin A	30%	Vitamin C	10%
Calcium	4%	Iron	4%

Dietary Exchanges: 1 Vegetable, 3 Very Lean Meat

GRILLED SHRIMP

prep time: 25 min. • yield: 4 servings

Shrimp are done when the outside turns pink and the inside loses its slightly gray translucence, becoming an opaque white.

⅓ cup chili sauce

1 tablespoon chopped fresh parsley

1 tablespoon lemon juice

1 lb. shelled deveined uncooked medium shrimp

1 GRILL DIRECTIONS: Heat grill. In medium shallow dish, combine all ingredients except shrimp; mix well. Add shrimp; stir to coat. Cover; let stand at room temperature for 10 minutes to marinate.

2 When ready to grill, arrange shrimp on 4 (12-inch) metal skewers; reserve marinade. Place shrimp on gas grill over medium heat or on charcoal grill 4 to 6 inches from medium-high coals. Cook 4 to 6 minutes or until shrimp turn pink, turning once and brushing with marinade. Discard any remaining marinade.

TIP: To broil shrimp, place on broiler pan; broil 4 to 6 inches from heat using times above as a guide and brushing with marinade.

Nutrition Information Per Serving
Serving Size: ¼ of Recipe

Calories	110	Calories from Fat	10
		% Daily Value	
Total Fat	1 g	2%	
Saturated	0 g	0%	
Cholesterol	160 mg	53%	
Sodium	490 mg	20%	
Total Carbohydrate	6 g	2%	
Dietary Fiber	0 g	0%	
Sugars	4 g		
Protein	18 g		
Vitamin A	10%	Vitamin C	8%
Calcium	4%	Iron	15%

Dietary Exchanges: ½ Fruit, 2 ½ Very Lean Meat OR ½ Carbohydrate, 2 ½ Very Lean Meat

---

Cook's Notes

PARSLEY

Many cooks would argue that it's almost impossible to add too much parsley to a recipe. Its flavor complements just about any type of food or other herb without overpowering it. Fresh parsley will often revive the flavor of dried herbs when used in the same recipe.

This universal herb is available in two basic types: curly or Italian (flat-leaf). The flat-leaf variety is hardier and stronger in flavor, though curly parsley makes an attractive, frilly garnish.

Wrap parsley loosely in paper towels and refrigerate it in a resealable plastic bag in the vegetable drawer. Or, trim the stems and set parsley in a jar of water, bouquet style, covering the top with a plastic bag and storing it in the refrigerator door.

MARGARITA SHRIMP

prep time: 30 min. (ready in 1 hr. 30 min.) • yield: 6 servings

The tequila-and-lime cocktail struts its stuff as a marinade for grilled shrimp. Because it is cooked, the marinade yields plenty of flavor but no alcoholic jolt.

MARINADE
¼ cup tequila

1 tablespoon finely chopped fresh parsley

2 tablespoons lime juice

2 tablespoons oil

1 tablespoon honey

1 teaspoon grated orange peel

¼ teaspoon hot pepper sauce

KABOBS
24 fresh uncooked large shrimp (about 1 1/2 lb.), shelled, tails left on and deveined

2 medium limes

1 GRILL DIRECTIONS: In large nonmetal bowl or resealable food storage plastic bag, combine all marinade ingredients; blend well. Add shrimp; turn to coat. Cover dish or seal bag; refrigerate 1 to 3 hours to marinate.

2 Heat grill. Cut limes into 1/2-inch-thick slices; cut slices into fourths to make 18 pieces.

3 When ready to grill, remove shrimp from marinade; reserve marinade. On each of 6 (12- to 14-inch) metal skewers, alternate 4 shrimp and 3 lime pieces.* Carefully oil grill rack. Place kabobs on gas grill over medium heat or on charcoal grill 4 to 6 inches from medium-high coals. Cook 6 to 10 minutes or until shrimp turn pink, turning once and brushing frequently with marinade. Discard any remaining marinade.

TIP: *To prepare recipe in grill basket, cut limes into slices. Place lime slices and shrimp in oiled grill basket. Grill as directed above.

To broil shrimp, place kabobs on oiled broiler pan; broil 4 to 6 inches from heat using times above as a guide and brushing frequently with marinade.

SHRIMP

Shrimp sold in North American fish markets and grocery stores nearly always arrives at the stores frozen, where it is thawed for sale to consumers. Shrimp is typically described by "count," which indicates the approximate number of shrimp per pound. The higher the count, the smaller the shrimp. Higher-count shrimp are usually less expensive, but will take longer to peel.

To peel shrimp prior to cooking, use a small sharp knife (or your finger) to loosen the shell and peel it back. Deveining is customarily the next step, though it is optional. To devein the shrimp, use a paring knife to slit shrimp along the back (convex curved side), then pick out the dark vein with the knifepoint. Rinse away any loose bits of shell or vein under cold running water.

Watch shrimp carefully as it cooks. As soon as the outside begins to turn slightly pink, remove one shrimp and cut into it. If the center appears opaque white, remove the pan from the heat; if the middle looks grayish and still translucent, cook it a little longer, checking frequently to avoid overcooking, which toughens the shrimp.

Nutrition Information Per Serving
Serving Size: 1/6 of Recipe

Calories	110	Calories from Fat	20
		% Daily Value	
Total Fat	2 g	3%	
Saturated	0 g	0%	
Cholesterol	160 mg	53%	
Sodium	190 mg	8%	
Total Carbohydrate	3 g	1%	
Dietary Fiber	1 g	3%	
Sugars	1 g		
Protein	17 g		
Vitamin A	4%	Vitamin C	10%
Calcium	4%	Iron	15%

Dietary Exchanges: 2 1/2 Very Lean Meat

Linguine with Seafood Sauce

LINGUINE WITH SEAFOOD SAUCE

prep time: 20 min. • yield: 8 servings

This blend of linguine, shrimp and clams in a creamy sauce is the type of dish you'd order in a restaurant, but it goes together surprisingly quickly at home. A generous portion of chopped parsley adds color and fresh flavor. Garnish each serving with an herb sprig or a bit more chopped parsley.

12 oz. uncooked linguine

4 tablespoons margarine or butter

4 green onions, sliced

1 garlic clove, minced

1 (12-oz.) pkg. frozen uncooked shrimp, thawed, drained

1 (6.5-oz.) can minced clams, undrained

1 cup chicken broth

½ cup dry white wine

2 tablespoons lemon juice

¼ cup chopped fresh parsley

1 teaspoon dried basil leaves

1 teaspoon dried oregano leaves

¼ teaspoon pepper

2 tablespoons cold water

2 tablespoons cornstarch

¼ cup light sour cream

1 In large saucepan or Dutch oven, cook linguine to desired doneness as directed on package. Drain; rinse with hot water. Return to saucepan.

2 Meanwhile, melt 2 tablespoons of the margarine in large skillet over medium heat. Add onions and garlic; cook until onions are tender. Stir in shrimp, clams, broth, wine, lemon juice, parsley, basil, oregano and pepper. Bring to a boil. Reduce heat; simmer 5 minutes.

3 In small bowl, combine water and cornstarch; blend well. Slowly stir into seafood mixture. Cook until mixture boils and thickens, stirring constantly.

4 To serve, toss cooked linguine with sour cream and remaining 2 tablespoons margarine. Serve seafood sauce over linguine.

Nutrition Information Per Serving
Serving Size: ⅛ of Recipe

Calories	280	Calories from Fat	80
		% Daily Value	
Total Fat	9 g	14%	
Saturated	2 g	10%	
Cholesterol	105 mg	35%	
Sodium	390 mg	16%	
Total Carbohydrate	36 g	12%	
Dietary Fiber	2 g	8%	
Sugars	3 g		
Protein	14 g		
Vitamin A	10%	Vitamin C	8%
Calcium	6%	Iron	20%

Dietary Exchanges: 2 ½ Starch, 1 Very Lean Meat, 1 Fat OR
2 ½ Carbohydrate, 1 Very Lean Meat, 1 Fat

SHRIMP AND PASTA BAKE

prep time: 30 min. (ready in 50 min.) • yield: 6 servings

A quicker alternative to lasagna, bow tie pasta bakes under a mantle of shrimp-laden tomato sauce.

1 (16-oz.) pkg. uncooked bow tie pasta (farfalle)

1 (14.5-oz.) can diced tomatoes, undrained

1 (12-oz.) pkg. frozen shelled deveined cooked small shrimp, thawed

1 (8-oz.) can tomato sauce

1 (4.5-oz.) jar sliced mushrooms, drained

1 teaspoon dried oregano leaves

¼ teaspoon crushed red pepper flakes

¼ cup grated Parmesan cheese

1 Heat oven to 350° F. Cook pasta to desired doneness as directed on package. Drain.

2 Place cooked pasta in ungreased 13 × 9-inch (3-quart) baking dish. Stir in tomatoes, shrimp, tomato sauce, mushrooms, oregano and red pepper flakes. Sprinkle with cheese. Cover with foil.

3 Bake at 350° F. for 15 to 20 minutes or until thoroughly heated.

Nutrition Information Per Serving
Serving Size: ⅙ of Recipe

Calories	380	Calories from Fat	25
		% Daily Value	
Total Fat	3 g	5%	
Saturated	1 g	5%	
Cholesterol	115 mg	38%	
Sodium	600 mg	25%	
Total Carbohydrate	64 g	21%	
Dietary Fiber	4 g	16%	
Sugars	6 g		
Protein	25 g		
Vitamin A	20%	Vitamin C	20%
Calcium	10%	Iron	30%

Dietary Exchanges: 4 Starch, 1 Vegetable, 1½ Very Lean Meat OR 4 Carbohydrate, 1 Vegetable, 1½ Very Lean Meat

MUSSELS IN WINE SAUCE

prep time: 30 min. (ready in 50 min.) • yield: 4 servings

With their bright orange flesh, mussels make a showy main dish and they're often more economical than other shellfish. Soaking and scrubbing the shellfish before cooking is important to help remove any traces of grit.

4 lb. fresh mussels

1 teaspoon oil

2 garlic cloves, minced

2 cups dry white wine

1 teaspoon dried thyme leaves

1 teaspoon cracked black pepper

2 lemons, cut into wedges

1 In large bowl, soak mussels in cold water for 20 minutes. Remove beards from mussels; scrub well under running water. (Discard any mussels that do not close.)

2 In large saucepan, heat oil over medium heat until hot. Add garlic; cook about 1 minute. Stir in wine, thyme and pepper. Bring to a boil. Add cleaned mussels. Cover; cook about 5 minutes or until mussels are open. (Discard any mussels that do not open.) Serve mussels with lemon wedges.

Nutrition Information Per Serving
Serving Size: ¼ of Recipe

Calories	130	Calories from Fat	25
		% Daily Value	
Total Fat	3 g	5%	
Saturated	1 g	5%	
Cholesterol	35 mg	12%	
Sodium	550 mg	23%	
Total Carbohydrate	10 g	3%	
Dietary Fiber	1 g	3%	
Sugars	3 g		
Protein	16 g		
Vitamin A	4%	Vitamin C	30%
Calcium	4%	Iron	30%

Dietary Exchanges: ½ Starch, 2 Very Lean Meat, ½ Fat OR ½ Carbohydrate, 2 Very Lean Meat, ½ Fat

Mussels in Wine Sauce

Couscous with Vegetarian Spaghetti Sauce, page 173

VEGETARIAN MAIN DISHES

As family cooks around America become increasingly health-conscious, vegetarian entrees are appearing on more and more tables. In this chapter you'll find an array of "keepers" to fill out your meatless repertoire. Besides our updated version of classic macaroni and cheese (page 175), we've included the internationally flavored Risotto con Fagioli (page 178) and Vegetarian Fajitas (page 184). All of them prove that it's easy to make intriguing and satisfying meals without meat.

LINGUINE WITH ROASTED VEGETABLES

prep time: 35 min. • yield: 6 (1 ⅓-cup) servings

Oven-roasting tomatoes, eggplant, pepper, zucchini and garlic enhances the natural sweetness of each vegetable. The vegetables are the stars here, with just enough pasta to round out the entree.

6 oz. uncooked linguine

4 tomatoes, coarsely chopped

1 eggplant, unpeeled, cubed

1 red bell pepper, cut into 1-inch pieces

1 zucchini, sliced

4 garlic cloves, minced

3 tablespoons olive or vegetable oil

1 teaspoon dried basil leaves

½ teaspoon salt

⅛ teaspoon pepper

2 oz. (½ cup) shredded fresh Parmesan cheese

1 Cook linguine to desired doneness as directed on package. Drain; cover to keep warm.

2 Meanwhile, heat oven to 450°F. Spray 15 × 10 × 1-inch baking pan with nonstick cooking spray. In large bowl, combine tomatoes, eggplant, bell pepper, zucchini and garlic. Toss with 2 tablespoons of the oil, basil, salt and pepper. Place vegetables on sprayed pan.

3 Bake at 450°F. for 12 to 15 minutes or until vegetables are tender and lightly browned.

4 Place cooked linguine in serving bowl. Add remaining 1 tablespoon oil and roasted vegetables; toss gently to mix. Sprinkle with cheese.

Nutrition Information Per Serving Serving Size: 1 ⅓ Cups			
Calories	240	Calories from Fat	90
		% Daily Value	
Total Fat	10 g	15%	
Saturated	3 g	15%	
Cholesterol	5 mg	2%	
Sodium	340 mg	14%	
Total Carbohydrate	29 g	10%	
Dietary Fiber	3 g	12%	
Sugars	5 g		
Protein	9 g		
Vitamin A	30%	Vitamin C	50%
Calcium	15%	Iron	10%

Dietary Exchanges: 1 Starch, 3 Vegetable, 2 Fat OR 1 Carbohydrate, 3 Vegetable, 2 Fat

EGGPLANT

Although eggplant is generally thought to be a vegetable, it's actually a fruit—specifically, a berry! Ranging in color from deep purple to white, and in size from miniature to large, eggplant comes in many varieties. The most commonly available eggplant is large, cylindrical or pear shaped with smooth, glossy purple skin.

Choose eggplant that has firm, smooth skin and feels heavy for its size. Avoid any with soft, wrinkled or brown spots. Store eggplant in a cool, dry, dark place, using it within a day or two of purchase before it becomes bitter.

Eggplant should be cut just before cooking or serving, since the flesh discolors rapidly. If eggplant is young, the skin doesn't need to be peeled.

Cook's Notes

172 PILLSBURY: THE BEST OF CLASSIC® COOKBOOKS

PENNE PROVENÇAL

prep time: 30 min. • yield: 6 (1 ⅓-cup) servings

In this recipe, a garlicky tomato mixture is served over pasta tubes. If you have fresh-from-the garden eggplant, be sure to use it.

- 8 oz. (2 cups) uncooked penne (tube-shaped pasta)
- 3 cups diced peeled eggplant
- 2 (14.5-oz.) cans diced tomatoes, undrained
- 1 (15-oz.) can navy beans, drained, rinsed
- 3 garlic cloves, minced
- 2 teaspoons sugar
- 2 tablespoons chopped fresh Italian parsley

1 Cook penne to desired doneness as directed on package. Drain; cover to keep warm.

2 Meanwhile, in Dutch oven or large saucepan, combine eggplant, tomatoes, beans, garlic and sugar; mix well. Bring to a boil over medium-high heat. Reduce heat to low; simmer 10 to 15 minutes or until eggplant is tender. If desired, add coarse ground black pepper to taste.

3 Add cooked penne to eggplant mixture; toss gently to mix. Sprinkle with parsley.

Nutrition Information Per Serving
Serving Size: 1 ⅓ Cups

Calories	270	Calories from Fat	10
		% Daily Value	
Total Fat	1 g	2%	
Saturated	0 g	0%	
Cholesterol	0 mg	0%	
Sodium	370 mg	15%	
Total Carbohydrate	53 g	18%	
Dietary Fiber	7 g	28%	
Sugars	9 g		
Protein	12 g		
Vitamin A	20%	Vitamin C	25%
Calcium	8%	Iron	20%

Dietary Exchanges: 3 Starch, 1 Vegetable OR 3 Carbohydrate, 1 Vegetable

COUSCOUS WITH VEGETARIAN SPAGHETTI SAUCE

prep time: 15 min. • yield: 4 servings

PICTURED ON PAGE 170

Fresh parsley provides the finishing touch for this satisfying supper, which can be assembled in a jiffy from on-hand ingredients.

- 2 cups water
- 1 ⅓ cups uncooked couscous
- 1 (28-oz.) jar chunky vegetable spaghetti sauce
- 1 (15-oz.) can garbanzo beans (chickpeas), drained, rinsed
- ⅛ to ¼ teaspoon crushed red pepper flakes
- 2 tablespoons chopped fresh parsley

1 In medium saucepan, bring water to a boil. Stir in couscous. Cover; remove from heat. Let stand 5 minutes or until liquid is absorbed.

2 Meanwhile, in medium saucepan, combine spaghetti sauce, beans and red pepper flakes. Cook over medium heat for 5 to 7 minutes or until thoroughly heated, stirring occasionally.

3 Fluff couscous with fork. Serve sauce mixture over couscous; sprinkle with parsley. If desired, sprinkle with shredded fresh Parmesan cheese.

Nutrition Information Per Serving
Serving Size: ¼ of Recipe

Calories	400	Calories from Fat	25
		% Daily Value	
Total Fat	3 g	5%	
Saturated	0 g	0%	
Cholesterol	0 mg	0%	
Sodium	770 mg	32%	
Total Carbohydrate	78 g	26%	
Dietary Fiber	11 g	44%	
Sugars	15 g		
Protein	16 g		
Vitamin A	15%	Vitamin C	30%
Calcium	10%	Iron	15%

Dietary Exchanges: 5 Starch OR 5 Carbohydrate

CREAMY PASTA WITH SUMMER VEGETABLES

prep time: 30 min. • yield: 4 (1 ¾-cup) servings

The colorful array of yellow, red and green vegetables makes this a pretty choice for a "company" dish. As long as you maintain a variety of color, feel free to substitute yellow summer squash for zucchini, red or green bell pepper for yellow, and so on.

8 oz. (2 ½ cups) uncooked penne or mostaccioli (tube-shaped pasta)

1 zucchini, cut in half lengthwise, thinly sliced

1 yellow bell pepper, diced

2 teaspoons margarine or butter

½ cup chopped onion

2 garlic cloves, minced

2 cups firmly packed shredded fresh spinach

4 Italian plum tomatoes, sliced ¼ inch thick, or 10 cherry tomatoes, halved

1 cup whipping cream

¼ cup dry sherry or chicken broth

1 teaspoon prepared mustard

½ teaspoon salt

¼ cup grated Parmesan cheese

1 Cook penne to desired doneness as directed on package, adding zucchini and bell pepper during last 4 minutes of cooking time. Drain; cover to keep warm.

Creamy Pasta with Summer Vegetables

2 Meanwhile, melt margarine in large nonstick skillet over medium heat. Add onion and garlic; cook and stir 4 to 6 minutes or until onion is tender.

3 Add spinach and tomatoes; cook and stir 1 to 2 minutes or until spinach is wilted. Add cream, sherry, mustard and salt; mix well. Cook 10 to 15 minutes or until slightly thickened, stirring occasionally.

4 To serve, arrange cooked penne and vegetables on serving plate; top with cream sauce. Sprinkle with Parmesan cheese.

Nutrition Information Per Serving
Serving Size: 1 3/4 Cups

Calories	520	Calories from Fat	240
		% Daily Value	
Total Fat	27 g	42%	
Saturated	16 g	80%	
Cholesterol	85 mg	28%	
Sodium	470 mg	20%	
Total Carbohydrate	53 g	18%	
Dietary Fiber	4 g	16%	
Sugars	7 g		
Protein	13 g		
Vitamin A	70%	Vitamin C	70%
Calcium	20%	Iron	20%

Dietary Exchanges: 3 Starch, 2 Vegetable, 5 Fat OR 3 Carbohydrate, 2 Vegetable, 5 Fat

GROWN-UP MAC AND CHEESE

prep time: 30 min. (ready in 55 min.) •
yield: 4 (1 1/2-cup) servings

A childhood favorite gains distinction from a blend of cheeses—fontina, Swiss and Parmesan—that's slightly more sophisticated than the expected American cheese. Laced with wine and a dash of nutmeg, the sauce is reminiscent of the flavor of Swiss fondue.

8 oz. (2 1/2 cups) uncooked mostaccioli or penne (tube-shaped pasta)

2 tablespoons margarine or butter

2 tablespoons all-purpose flour

1/4 teaspoon salt

1/8 teaspoon white pepper

Dash nutmeg

1 1/4 cups fat-free half-and-half

2 oz. (1/2 cup) shredded fontina cheese

2 oz. (1/2 cup) shredded Swiss cheese

2 oz. (1/2 cup) shredded fresh Parmesan cheese

2 tablespoons dry white wine

2 Italian plum tomatoes, thinly sliced

1 teaspoon olive or vegetable oil

2 tablespoons sliced green onions

1 Heat oven to 350°F. Spray 1 1/2-quart casserole with nonstick cooking spray. Cook mostaccioli to desired doneness as directed on package. Drain.

2 Meanwhile, melt margarine in large saucepan over medium heat. Stir in flour, salt, pepper and nutmeg; cook and stir until bubbly. Gradually add half-and-half, stirring constantly. Cook until mixture boils and thickens, stirring frequently. Remove from heat. Stir in fontina, Swiss and Parmesan cheeses until melted. (Cheeses will be stringy.) Stir in wine.

3 Add cooked mostaccioli to cheese sauce; stir gently to coat. Pour into sprayed dish. Arrange sliced tomatoes around outside edge of dish. Brush tomatoes with oil; sprinkle with onions.

4 Bake at 350°F. for 20 to 25 minutes or until edges are bubbly and mixture is thoroughly heated.

Nutrition Information Per Serving
Serving Size: 1 1/2 Cups

Calories	520	Calories from Fat	200
		% Daily Value	
Total Fat	22 g	34%	
Saturated	11 g	55%	
Cholesterol	40 mg	13%	
Sodium	700 mg	29%	
Total Carbohydrate	56 g	19%	
Dietary Fiber	2 g	8%	
Sugars	5 g		
Protein	24 g		
Vitamin A	25%	Vitamin C	6%
Calcium	50%	Iron	15%

Dietary Exchanges: 3 1/2 Starch, 2 High-Fat Meat, 1 Fat OR 3 1/2 Carbohydrate, 2 High-Fat Meat, 1 Fat

VEGETARIAN FRIED RICE

prep time: 45 min. • yield: 3 (1 ⅓-cup) servings

Brown rice, with its slightly nutty flavor, sets off a gingery-soy blend of fresh vegetables. To add another flavor dimension, garnish each serving with minced fresh cilantro.

3 cups cooked instant brown rice (cooked as directed on package)

½ cup sliced fresh mushrooms

½ cup shredded carrot

¼ cup sliced green onions

¼ cup chopped green bell pepper

¼ teaspoon ginger

1 garlic clove, minced

2 tablespoons lite soy sauce

2 eggs, beaten

⅛ teaspoon pepper

¾ cup frozen sweet peas, thawed*

1 While rice is cooking, spray large nonstick skillet or wok with nonstick cooking spray. Heat over medium heat until hot. Add mushrooms, carrot, onions, bell pepper, ginger and garlic; cook and stir 1 minute.

2 Reduce heat to low. Stir in cooked rice and soy sauce; cook 5 minutes, stirring occasionally.

3 Push rice mixture to side of skillet; add eggs and pepper to other side. Cook over low heat for 3 to 4 minutes, stirring constantly until eggs are cooked.

4 Add peas to rice and egg mixture; stir gently to combine. Cook until thoroughly heated. If desired, serve with additional soy sauce.

TIP: *To quickly thaw peas, place in colander or strainer; rinse with warm water until thawed. Drain well.

Nutrition Information Per Serving
Serving Size: 1⅓ Cups

Calories	350	Calories from Fat	50
		% Daily Value	
Total Fat	6 g	9%	
Saturated	1 g	5%	
Cholesterol	140 mg	47%	
Sodium	540 mg	23%	
Total Carbohydrate	62 g	21%	
Dietary Fiber	6 g	24%	
Sugars	3 g		
Protein	13 g		
Vitamin A	120%	Vitamin C	20%
Calcium	4%	Iron	10%

Dietary Exchanges: 4 Starch, ½ Vegetable, ½ Fat OR 4 Carbohydrate, ½ Vegetable, ½ Fat

COOKING IN A WOK

A wok is a round-bottomed Chinese cooking pan used for stir-frying, steaming, deep-frying, braising and stewing. Flat-bottomed woks rest securely on gas or electric burners, eliminating the need for the metal "ring" on which traditional woks are placed.

Choose a wok made of heavy-gauge steel such as carbon. Aluminum and stainless steel woks don't conduct heat as evenly. Woks made of carbon steel require special care to prevent rusting. Follow the manufacturer's instructions for "seasoning" a wok prior to the initial use and after subsequent use. Electric models, usually with a nonstick finish, are also available. They're more expensive but are convenient for cooking at the table.

Vegetarian Fried Rice

Five-Spice Mushroom and Broccoli Stir-Fry, page 181

RISOTTO CON FAGIOLI

prep time: 40 min. • yield: 4 (1 ½-cup) servings

An Italian-inspired version of beans (fagioli) and rice, this hearty entree is flecked with basil and fresh parsley.

1 medium tomato, chopped (1 cup)

½ cup chopped onion

1½ cups uncooked short-grain rice (arborio)

2 (14½-oz.) cans ready-to-serve vegetable broth or fat-free chicken broth with ⅓ less sodium

1 (19-oz.) can cannellini beans, drained, rinsed

⅓ cup grated fresh Parmesan cheese

2 tablespoons chopped fresh parsley

1 tablespoon margarine or butter

¼ teaspoon dried basil leaves

¼ teaspoon pepper

1 In large saucepan, combine tomato and onion; cook and stir over medium heat 3 to 4 minutes or until onion is crisp-tender.

2 Add rice and broth. Bring to a boil. Reduce heat to low; simmer 15 minutes or until rice is tender and liquid is absorbed, stirring occasionally.

3 Stir in all remaining ingredients; cook 1 minute or until thoroughly heated. If desired, season to taste with salt.

Nutrition Information Per Serving
Serving Size: 1½ Cups

Calories	450	Calories from Fat	50
		% Daily Value	
Total Fat	6 g	9%	
Saturated	2 g	10%	
Cholesterol	5 mg	2%	
Sodium	830 mg	35%	
Total Carbohydrate	81 g	27%	
Dietary Fiber	8 g	32%	
Sugars	4 g		
Protein	18 g		
Vitamin A	10%	Vitamin C	10%
Calcium	20%	Iron	30%

Dietary Exchanges: 5 Starch, 1 Vegetable, ½ Fat OR 5 Carbohydrate, 1 Vegetable, ½ Fat

RISOTTO

Risotto is a classic dish of northern Italy where rice, not pasta, reigns supreme. The traditional cooking method entails gradually adding hot stock to arborio rice (or another short-grained rice) that has been stirred and cooked in oil or butter. The mixture is then stirred continually during cooking to give this dish its creamy texture.

Arborio rice is a fat, short-grained Italian rice with high starch content and a great capacity to absorb liquid. It's perfect for risotto because the cooking method results in grains that remain separate and firm yet creamy. Arborio rice is widely available in specialty food stores or in the rice section of most supermarkets.

EASY BLACK BEAN LASAGNA

prep time: 20 min. (ready in 1 hr. 20 min.) • yield: 10 servings

With this streamlined method, there's no need to cook the lasagna noodles before layering them with the ricotta-bean-tomato mixture; they soften in the oven as they bake with the moist filling. The dish can be assembled several hours ahead and refrigerated until baking time.

1 (15-oz.) can black beans, drained, rinsed

1 (28-oz.) can crushed tomatoes, undrained

¾ cup chopped onions

½ cup chopped green bell pepper

½ cup chunky style salsa

1 teaspoon chili powder

½ teaspoon cumin

1 cup light ricotta cheese

⅛ teaspoon garlic powder

1 egg

10 uncooked lasagna noodles

6 oz. (1½ cups) shredded Cheddar or mozzarella cheese

1 Heat oven to 350°F. Spray 13 × 9-inch (3-quart) baking dish with nonstick cooking spray. In large bowl, mash beans slightly. Stir in tomatoes, onions, bell pepper, salsa, chili powder and cumin; mix well.

2 In small bowl, combine ricotta cheese, garlic powder and egg; blend well.

3 Spread 1 cup of the tomato mixture over bottom of sprayed baking dish. Top with half of noodles, overlapping slightly. Top with half of remaining tomato mixture. Spoon ricotta mixture over top; spread carefully. Top with half of cheese, then with remaining noodles, tomato mixture and cheese. Spray sheet of foil with cooking spray; cover baking dish with foil, sprayed side down.

4 Bake at 350°F. for 40 to 45 minutes or until noodles are tender. Uncover; let stand 15 minutes before serving.

Nutrition Information Per Serving
Serving Size: ¹⁄₁₀ of Recipe

Calories	260	Calories from Fat	80
		% Daily Value	
Total Fat	9 g	14%	
Saturated	5 g	25%	
Cholesterol	45 mg	15%	
Sodium	450 mg	19%	
Total Carbohydrate	30 g	10%	
Dietary Fiber	4 g	16%	
Sugars	5 g		
Protein	14 g		
Vitamin A	15%	Vitamin C	15%
Calcium	25%	Iron	15%

Dietary Exchanges: 2 Starch, 1 High-Fat Meat OR 2 Carbohydrate, 1 High-Fat Meat

MEDITERRANEAN PASTA TORTE

prep time: 30 min. (ready in 1 hr. 25 min.) • yield: 6 servings

A trace of cinnamon complements the tomato sauce in an almost imperceptible way, deepening the flavor without overpowering it. Chunky with vegetables, this casserole is a good choice for supper with friends. It's economical and requires no last-minute fussing.

12 oz. (3 cups) uncooked ziti (long tubular pasta)

2½ cups cubed (½-inch) peeled eggplant (8 oz.)

1 medium onion, chopped

1 (15-oz.) can chunky tomato sauce with onions, celery and green bell peppers, undrained

½ teaspoon cinnamon

½ teaspoon dried oregano leaves, crushed

2 cups milk

2 tablespoons all-purpose flour

¼ teaspoon salt

⅛ teaspoon pepper

2 eggs

½ cup grated Parmesan cheese

3 tablespoons unseasoned dry bread crumbs

2 teaspoons margarine or butter, melted

1 Heat oven to 350°F. Spray 12 × 8-inch (2-quart) baking dish and 14 × 12-inch sheet of foil with nonstick cooking spray. Set aside.

2 In Dutch oven or large saucepan, cook ziti to desired doneness as directed on package. Drain; return to Dutch oven. Cover to keep warm.

3 Meanwhile, in medium saucepan, combine eggplant, onion, tomato sauce, cinnamon and oregano; mix well. Bring to a boil. Reduce heat; simmer 10 to 15 minutes or until onion and eggplant are crisp-tender, stirring frequently.

4 In another medium saucepan, combine ½ cup of the milk, flour, salt and pepper; mix with wire whisk until smooth. Stir in remaining 1½ cups milk. Cook over medium heat until mixture boils and thickens, stirring constantly. Boil and stir 1 minute. Remove from heat.

5 In medium bowl, beat eggs; gradually add half of the hot milk mixture to beaten eggs, stirring constantly. Stir egg mixture back into mixture in saucepan. Add cheese; mix well. Add to cooked ziti; toss gently to coat evenly.

6 Place half of ziti mixture in sprayed dish. Spoon tomato sauce over ziti. Top with remaining ziti mixture. Cover tightly with sprayed foil.

7 Bake at 350°F. for 35 to 45 minutes or until casserole is bubbly. In small bowl, combine bread crumbs and melted margarine; mix well. Sprinkle over top; bake uncovered for an additional 5 minutes. Let stand 5 minutes before serving.

Nutrition Information Per Serving
Serving Size: ⅙ of Recipe

Calories	390	Calories from Fat	80
		% Daily Value	
Total Fat	9 g	14%	
Saturated	4 g	20%	
Cholesterol	85 mg	28%	
Sodium	740 mg	31%	
Total Carbohydrate	61 g	20%	
Dietary Fiber	4 g	16%	
Sugars	11 g		
Protein	17 g		
Vitamin A	20%	Vitamin C	15%
Calcium	25%	Iron	20%

Dietary Exchanges: 3 ½ Starch, 2 Vegetable, 1 ½ Fat OR
3 ½ Carbohydrate, 2 Vegetable, 1 ½ Fat

FIVE-SPICE MUSHROOM AND BROCCOLI STIR-FRY

prep time: 35 min. • yield: 4 servings

PICTURED ON PAGE 177

This dish offers a change of pace from spaghetti with tomato sauce but doesn't take much longer to prepare. Thin noodles make a bed for a vegetable mélange topped with a spiced orange sweet-and-hot sauce.

1 (7-oz.) pkg. uncooked vermicelli

½ cup orange juice

1 tablespoon cornstarch

¾ teaspoon Chinese five-spice powder

⅛ to ¼ teaspoon crushed red pepper flakes

2 tablespoons soy sauce

2 teaspoons honey

8 large mushrooms (12 oz.), cut into ¼-inch-thick slices

1 cup fresh baby carrots, quartered lengthwise

1 medium onion, cut into thin wedges

1 garlic clove, minced

3 cups small broccoli florets (about 6 oz.)

1 Cook vermicelli to desired doneness as directed on package. Drain; cover to keep warm.

2 Meanwhile, in small bowl, combine orange juice, cornstarch, five-spice powder, red pepper flakes, soy sauce and honey; stir until well blended. Set aside.

3 Spray large nonstick skillet with nonstick cooking spray. Heat over medium-high heat until hot. Add mushrooms, carrots, onion and garlic; cook and stir 4 minutes.

4 Add broccoli; cover and cook 2 to 4 minutes or until vegetables are crisp-tender, stirring occasionally. Add orange juice mixture; cook and stir 2 to 3 minutes or until bubbly and thickened. Serve over cooked vermicelli.

Nutrition Information Per Serving
Serving Size: ¼ of Recipe

Calories	300	Calories from Fat	20
		% Daily Value	
Total Fat	2 g	3%	
Saturated	0 g	0%	
Cholesterol	0 mg	0%	
Sodium	550 mg	23%	
Total Carbohydrate	59 g	20%	
Dietary Fiber	6 g	24%	
Sugars	13 g		
Protein	11 g		
Vitamin A	180%	Vitamin C	90%
Calcium	6%	Iron	25%

Dietary Exchanges: 3 ½ Starch, 1 Vegetable OR 3 ½ Carbohydrate, 1 Vegetable

ONIONS

Called the "king of vegetables," the onion has a dominant flavor and is extremely versatile. There are two general flavors—mild and pungent—and two shapes: round and elongated. Onions can also be grouped by the time of year they're available.

- Spring/summer onions are available April through August. They have a mild sweet flavor and are more fragile than fall/-winter onions. Vidalia and Walla Walla are two popular spring/summer onions.
- Fall/winter onions are available August through March. They have a robust flavor and may be white, yellow or red in color. They are firm and store well in a cool, dry, dark place that's well ventilated.
- Green onions, which are immature onions picked before the bulbs develop, are available year-round.

Fresh Vegetable Curry

FRESH VEGETABLE CURRY

prep time: 30 min. • yield: 4 servings

Stirring the curry powder into hot oil releases the fragrance of the spice blend for this chunky, Indian-inspired rendition of rice and beans.

1 tablespoon oil

3 to 4 teaspoons curry powder

1 large onion, cut into 8 wedges

3 cups fresh cauliflower florets

1 (14 1/2-oz.) can ready-to-serve vegetable broth

1 cup uncooked instant brown rice

2 small zucchini, cut into 3/8-inch slices (2 cups)

1 (15-oz.) can garbanzo beans (chickpeas), drained, rinsed

4 Italian plum tomatoes, quartered, seeded

1 Heat oil in large nonstick skillet or wok over medium heat until hot. Add curry powder; cook and stir 30 seconds. Add onion; cook and stir 2 minutes. Add cauliflower and 3/4 cup of the broth. Bring to a boil. Reduce heat to low; cover and simmer 5 minutes or until cauliflower is crisp-tender.

2 Meanwhile, in medium saucepan, bring remaining broth to a boil. Add rice. Reduce heat; cover and simmer 10 minutes or until broth is absorbed. Remove from heat; cover and let stand 5 minutes.

3 Add zucchini to cauliflower mixture; cook and stir 2 minutes. Add garbanzo beans and tomatoes; cook 4 minutes, stirring occasionally. Fluff rice with fork. Serve vegetable mixture over rice.

Nutrition Information Per Serving			
Serving Size: 1/4 of Recipe			
Calories	310	Calories from Fat	60
		% Daily Value	
Total Fat	7 g	11%	
Saturated	1 g	5%	
Cholesterol	0 mg	0%	
Sodium	650 mg	27%	
Total Carbohydrate	50 g	17%	
Dietary Fiber	10 g	40%	
Sugars	8 g		
Protein	11 g		
Vitamin A	15%	Vitamin C	60%
Calcium	8%	Iron	15%

Dietary Exchanges: 3 Starch, 1 Vegetable, 1 Fat OR 3 Carbohydrate, 1 Vegetable, 1 Fat

CURRY

The spice mixture known as curry powder originated in India, where knowledge of spice blending is key to becoming a good cook. In India, cooks blend spices fresh nearly every day, varying components and proportions to complement a particular meal. In the United States, basic curry powder usually consists of a pulverized blend of dried red chiles, coriander seeds, cumin seeds, mustard seeds, ginger, turmeric and black pepper.

Cook's Notes

COCONUT CURRIED VEGETABLES WITH RICE

prep time: 20 min. • yield: 4 servings

Coconut milk contributes an exotic nuance and creamy texture to this main-course rice dish.

3 cups hot cooked rice (cooked as directed on package)

2 tablespoons all-purpose flour

1½ teaspoons curry powder

½ teaspoon salt

⅛ teaspoon pepper

1 (14-oz.) can light coconut milk

1 teaspoon lime juice

1 (1-lb.) pkg. frozen broccoli florets, carrots and cauliflower

1 cup frozen sweet peas

1 While rice is cooking, in small bowl, combine flour, curry powder, salt, pepper and ¼ cup of the coconut milk; beat with wire whisk until smooth. Stir in remaining coconut milk and lime juice. Set aside.

2 In large saucepan, combine frozen vegetables, peas and ½ cup water. Bring to a boil. Reduce heat to low; cover and simmer 6 to 8 minutes or until vegetables are crisp-tender. Drain; set aside.

3 Pour coconut milk mixture into same saucepan. Bring to a boil, stirring constantly. Boil and stir 1 minute. Stir in vegetables. Cook over medium heat until thoroughly heated, stirring frequently. Serve over rice.

Nutrition Information Per Serving
Serving Size: ¼ of Recipe

Calories	310	Calories from Fat	50
		% Daily Value	
Total Fat	6 g	9%	
Saturated	5 g	25%	
Cholesterol	0 mg	0%	
Sodium	420 mg	18%	
Total Carbohydrate	55 g	18%	
Dietary Fiber	5 g	20%	
Sugars	9 g		
Protein	8 g		
Vitamin A	60%	Vitamin C	35%
Calcium	6%	Iron	35%

Dietary Exchanges: 2 Starch, 1 Fruit, 2 Vegetable, 1 Fat
OR 3 Carbohydrate, 2 Vegetable, 1 Fat

VEGETARIAN FAJITAS

prep time: 15 min. • yield: 8 fajitas

To intensify the Southwestern character of this dish, sprinkle the vegetables with a bit of ground cumin or chili powder as they cook.

2 tablespoons oil

1 green bell pepper, sliced

1 yellow bell pepper, sliced

1 medium onion, sliced

1 (11-oz.) can vacuum-packed whole kernel corn, drained

1 large tomato, chopped

¼ teaspoon salt

⅛ teaspoon pepper

8 (8-inch) flour tortillas, warmed

Guacamole, sour cream and/or salsa, if desired

1 Heat oil in large skillet or wok over medium-high heat until hot. Add bell peppers and onion; cook and stir 2 to 3 minutes or until vegetables are crisp-tender. Add corn, tomato, salt and pepper; cook until thoroughly heated.

2 To serve, place ½ cup vegetable mixture in center of each warmed tortilla. Top with desired toppings; fold or roll up.

Nutrition Information Per Serving
Serving Size: 1 Fajita

Calories	260	Calories from Fat	100
		% Daily Value	
Total Fat	11 g	17%	
Saturated	4 g	20%	
Cholesterol	5 mg	2%	
Sodium	540 mg	23%	
Total Carbohydrate	34 g	11%	
Dietary Fiber	3 g	12%	
Sugars	6 g		
Protein	6 g		
Vitamin A	8%	Vitamin C	40%
Calcium	8%	Iron	8%

Dietary Exchanges: 2 Starch, 1 Vegetable OR 2 Carbohydrate, 1 Vegetable

CHEESE POLENTA WITH SPICY CHILI TOPPING

prep time: 40 min. • yield: 6 servings

Polenta, a home-style Italian cornmeal specialty, is enjoyed in two different ways: as soft-textured cornmeal mush and as firm slices, used here.

POLENTA
1 cup yellow cornmeal

3½ cups water

½ teaspoon garlic salt

⅛ teaspoon pepper

4 oz. (1 cup) shredded sharp Cheddar cheese

TOPPING
1 (15-oz.) can spicy chili beans, undrained

¾ cup chunky style salsa

1 In medium saucepan, combine cornmeal and 1 cup of the water; beat with wire whisk until well blended. Add remaining 2½ cups water, garlic salt and pepper; mix well. Bring to a boil over medium-high heat, stirring constantly. Reduce heat to medium-low. Cover; cook 10 to 15 minutes or until very thick, stirring frequently.

2 Remove polenta from heat; stir in cheese. Spread in ungreased 9-inch pie pan.

3 In small saucepan, combine beans and salsa. Cook over medium heat for 5 minutes, stirring occasionally, or until thoroughly heated.

4 To serve, cut polenta into wedges; place on individual serving plates. Spoon topping over wedges. If desired, sprinkle with additional cheese.

Nutrition Information Per Serving
Serving Size: ⅙ of Recipe

Calories	220	Calories from Fat	70
		% Daily Value	
Total Fat	8 g	12%	
Saturated	4 g	20%	
Cholesterol	20 mg	7%	
Sodium	690 mg	29%	
Total Carbohydrate	29 g	10%	
Dietary Fiber	4 g	16%	
Sugars	3 g		
Protein	9 g		
Vitamin A	10%	Vitamin C	6%
Calcium	15%	Iron	10%

Dietary Exchanges: 2 Starch, ½ High-Fat Meat, ½ Fat OR 2 Carbohydrate, ½ High-Fat Meat, ½ Fat

SALSA AND PICANTE SAUCES

*S*alsa is the Spanish word for "sauce." Salsas are generally chunky in texture and almost always contain chiles. Salsas add zest to meats, poultry and fish as well as serving as a dip for chips or vegetables and a topping for meatless entrees.

Picante is a Spanish word that means "hot" or "spicy." Picante sauces are made with similar ingredients as salsa, but are often smoother in texture and thinner in consistency.

Salsas and picante sauces can be used interchangeably, but the recipe's texture may be affected.

Cook's Notes

HARVEST RATATOUILLE WITH BLACK BEANS

prep time: 30 min. • yield: 4 (1 ¼-cup) servings

The vegetables in ratatouille can vary according to the cook, but this popular dish from Provence usually contains eggplant, tomatoes, onions, bell peppers and garlic cooked in olive oil.

2 tablespoons olive or vegetable oil

½ cup chopped onion

½ cup chopped green bell pepper

1½ cups diced eggplant

1½ cups diced zucchini

1½ cups diced yellow summer squash

2 cups chopped tomatoes

½ teaspoon garlic powder

½ teaspoon dried oregano leaves

¼ teaspoon salt

1 (15-oz.) can black beans, drained

2 tablespoons grated Parmesan cheese

1 tablespoon chopped fresh parsley

1 Heat oil in large skillet over medium-high heat until hot. Add onion and bell pepper; cook and stir 2 to 3 minutes or until crisp-tender.

2 Stir in eggplant, zucchini and yellow squash; cook and stir 4 to 5 minutes or until crisp-tender.

3 Stir in tomatoes, garlic powder, oregano, salt and black beans. Bring to a boil. Reduce heat to low; simmer 5 minutes, stirring occasionally. Sprinkle with Parmesan cheese and parsley.

Nutrition Information Per Serving
Serving Size: 1 ¼ Cups

Calories	220	Calories from Fat	70
		% Daily Value	
Total Fat	8 g	12%	
Saturated	2 g	10%	
Cholesterol	0 mg	0%	
Sodium	410 mg	17%	
Total Carbohydrate	27 g	9%	
Dietary Fiber	8 g	32%	
Sugars	7 g		
Protein	9 g		
Vitamin A	20%	Vitamin C	50%
Calcium	10%	Iron	10%

Dietary Exchanges: 1½ Starch, 1 Vegetable, 1½ Fat OR
1½ Carbohydrate, 1 Vegetable, 1½ Fat

ONION MATH

*U*nlike baking, where precise measurements dramatically affect the outcome of the finished recipe, soups, stews and the like are more easygoing. A little more or less onion or chopped bell pepper won't affect the quality of dinner. Nonetheless, here's a list of approximate equivalencies:

1 small onion = ⅓ cup chopped

1 medium onion = ½ cup chopped

1 large onion = 1 cup chopped

1 green onion = 2 tablespoons sliced

Cook's Notes

Harvest Ratatouille with Black Beans

MEATLESS JAMBALAYA

prep time: 1 hr. 20 min. • yield: 6 (1 ¼-cup) servings

Stirring fennel seed, red pepper and Italian seasoning into this savory stew evokes the flavor of sausage without the fat and calories. Each serving has only 3 grams of fat and 280 calories.

1 tablespoon oil

½ cup coarsely chopped onion

½ cup coarsely chopped green bell pepper

2 garlic cloves, minced

2 cups water

1 (14.5-oz.) can stewed tomatoes, undrained, cut up

1 (8-oz.) can tomato sauce

½ teaspoon dried Italian seasoning

¼ teaspoon ground red pepper (cayenne)

⅛ teaspoon fennel seed, crushed

1 cup uncooked regular long-grain white rice

1 (15.5-oz.) can butter beans, drained, rinsed

1 (15.5-oz.) can red beans or kidney beans, drained, rinsed

1 Heat oil in large skillet over medium-high heat until hot. Add onion, bell pepper and garlic; cook and stir 2 to 3 minutes or until crisp-tender.

2 Stir in water, tomatoes, tomato sauce, Italian seasoning, ground red pepper and fennel. Bring to a boil; add rice. Reduce heat to low; cover and simmer 25 to 35 minutes or until rice is tender, stirring occasionally.

3 Stir in beans. Cover; simmer an additional 5 to 10 minutes or until thoroughly heated, stirring occasionally.

Nutrition Information Per Serving
Serving Size: 1 ¼ Cups

Calories	280	Calories from Fat	25
		% Daily Value	
Total Fat	3 g	5%	
Saturated	0 g	0%	
Cholesterol	0 mg	0%	
Sodium	630 mg	26%	
Total Carbohydrate	52 g	17%	
Dietary Fiber	7 g	28%	
Sugars	5 g		
Protein	10 g		
Vitamin A	15%	Vitamin C	25%
Calcium	8%	Iron	20%

Dietary Exchanges: 3 Starch, 1 Vegetable, ½ Fat OR 3 Carbohydrate, 1 Vegetable, ½ Fat

SKILLET CORN FRITTATA

prep time: 40 min. • yield: 8 servings

Eggs can be the solution for many a supper "emergency" when the refrigerator is bare. Here, a cheesy-egg mixture encases a blend of herbed corn, tomatoes and bell pepper. If you wish, garnish each serving with a sprig of fresh parsley or a spoonful of purchased salsa.

3 tablespoons margarine or butter

1 (1-lb.) pkg. frozen whole kernel corn

¼ cup sliced green onions

10 eggs

½ cup half-and-half

1 teaspoon dried basil leaves

½ teaspoon salt

⅛ teaspoon pepper

2 tomatoes, peeled, sliced

1 green bell pepper, cut into rings

4 oz. (1 cup) shredded Swiss cheese

1 Melt margarine in large skillet over medium heat. Add frozen corn and onions; cook and stir 5 minutes or until vegetables are crisp-tender. Reduce heat to low.

2 In large bowl, beat eggs well. Add half-and-half, basil, salt and pepper; blend well. Pour over vegetables. Cook over low heat 6 minutes.

3 As edges set, run spatula around edge of skillet, gently lifting vegetable mixture to allow uncooked egg to flow to bottom of skillet. Cover; cook an additional 6 minutes or until top is almost set. (Top will be moist.)

4 Arrange tomato slices and bell pepper rings around outer edge of skillet; sprinkle with cheese. Cover; cook an additional 5 minutes or until cheese is melted. Remove from heat; let stand 5 minutes. Cut into wedges to serve.

Nutrition Information Per Serving
Serving Size: 1/8 of Recipe

Calories	270	Calories from Fat	150
		% Daily Value	
Total Fat	17 g	26%	
Saturated	6 g	30%	
Cholesterol	285 mg	95%	
Sodium	340 mg	14%	
Total Carbohydrate	14 g	5%	
Dietary Fiber	2 g	8%	
Sugars	4 g		
Protein	14 g		
Vitamin A	20%	Vitamin C	20%
Calcium	20%	Iron	8%

Dietary Exchanges: 1 Starch, 1 1/2 Medium-Fat Meat, 1 1/2 Fat OR
1 Carbohydrate, 1 1/2 Medium-Fat Meat, 1 1/2 Fat

SPEEDY RAVIOLI BAKE

prep time: 30 min. • yield: 6 servings

Purchased ravioli and spaghetti sauce bake under a blanket of shredded mozzarella, yielding an entree that's long on flavor but short on work for the cook.

2 (9-oz.) pkg. refrigerated uncooked cheese-filled ravioli

1 (28-oz.) jar chunky spaghetti sauce

1 teaspoon dried basil leaves

8 oz. (2 cups) shredded mozzarella cheese

1 Heat oven to 400° F. In large saucepan or Dutch oven, cook ravioli to desired doneness as directed on package. Drain; set aside.

2 In same saucepan, combine spaghetti sauce and basil. Cook over medium heat 5 minutes or until thoroughly heated, stirring occasionally. Stir in ravioli. Pour into ungreased 13 × 9-inch (3-quart) glass baking dish. Sprinkle with cheese.

3 Bake at 400° F. for 10 minutes or until sauce is bubbly and cheese is melted.

Nutrition Information Per Serving
Serving Size: 1/6 of Recipe

Calories	470	Calories from Fat	170
		% Daily Value	
Total Fat	19 g	29%	
Saturated	9 g	45%	
Cholesterol	95 mg	32%	
Sodium	1150 mg	48%	
Total Carbohydrate	48 g	16%	
Dietary Fiber	4 g	16%	
Sugars	2 g		
Protein	26 g		
Vitamin A	20%	Vitamin C	15%
Calcium	50%	Iron	15%

Dietary Exchanges: 3 Starch, 2 1/2 Medium-Fat Meat, 1 Fat
OR 3 Carbohydrate, 2 1/2 Medium-Fat Meat, 1 Fat

Home-Style
Roasted Vegetables

HOME-STYLE ROASTED VEGETABLES

prep time: 15 min. (ready in 1 hr.) • yield: 4 servings

In the oven, vegetables take on an appealing golden brown exterior and a greater depth of flavor.

2 tablespoons olive or vegetable oil

1 teaspoon seasoned salt

¼ teaspoon dried marjoram leaves

¼ teaspoon pepper

4 medium russet potatoes, unpeeled, cut into 1½-inch chunks

2 medium carrots, cut into 2 × ¼ × ¼-inch strips (1 to 1½ cups)

1 to 2 parsnips, peeled, cut into 2 × ¼ × ¼-inch strips (1 to 1½ cups)

1 red onion, cut into 8 wedges

1 medium green bell pepper, cut into 8 pieces

1 Heat oven to 450° F. In large bowl, combine oil, seasoned salt, marjoram and pepper; mix well. Add all remaining ingredients; toss to coat. Spread in ungreased 15 × 10 × 1-inch baking pan.

2 Bake at 450° F. for 20 minutes. Turn and stir vegetables. Bake an additional 20 to 25 minutes or until vegetables are tender, stirring once.

Nutrition Information Per Serving
Serving Size: ¼ of Recipe

Calories	270	Calories from Fat	60
		% Daily Value	
Total Fat	7 g	11%	
Saturated	1 g	5%	
Cholesterol	0 mg	0%	
Sodium	410 mg	17%	
Total Carbohydrate	47 g	16%	
Dietary Fiber	7 g	28%	
Sugars	8 g		
Protein	4 g		
Vitamin A	200%	Vitamin C	50%
Calcium	4%	Iron	15%

Dietary Exchanges: 2 ½ Starch, 1 Vegetable, 1 Fat OR 2 ½ Carbohydrate, 1 Vegetable, 1 Fat

HOW TO ROAST VEGETABLES

Roasting is enjoying a resurgence in popularity. This high-temperature cooking technique adds rich, robust flavor to vegetables, meats, garlic and potatoes.

STEP 1

In a large bowl, combine oil, seasoned salt, marjoram and pepper; mix well. Add cut vegetables; toss to coat. Spread vegetables in an ungreased 15 × 10 × 1-inch baking pan.

STEP 2

Bake vegetables in a preheated 450° F. oven for 20 minutes. Turn and stir vegetables. Bake vegetables an additional 20 to 25 minutes or until tender, stirring once.

ROASTED VEGETABLE PIZZAS

prep time: 30 min. • yield: 4 pizzas

Vinaigrette-splashed roasted vegetables combine in this change-of-pace pizza. Serve an individual pie to each person for lunch or supper, or cut pies into wedges for an easy hot appetizer.

VEGETABLES
1 small red bell pepper, seeded, cut into 1-inch pieces (1 cup)

1 small zucchini, cut into ¼-inch-thick slices (¾ cup)

1 small yellow summer squash, cut into ¼-inch-thick slices (¾ cup)

1 small red onion, thinly sliced (1 cup)

VINAIGRETTE
1 tablespoon oil

1 tablespoon red wine vinegar

1 teaspoon dried Italian seasoning

⅛ teaspoon pepper

PIZZAS
2 (8-oz.) pkg. prebaked Italian pizza crusts (4 crusts)

2 oz. (½ cup) shredded mozzarella cheese

2 tablespoons grated Parmesan cheese

1 Heat oven to 450°F. In large bowl, combine all vegetables. In small bowl, combine all vinaigrette ingredients; mix well. Pour over vegetables; toss gently to coat. Place in ungreased 15 × 10 × 1-inch baking pan. Bake at 450°F. for 10 minutes.

Three-Pepper Pizza

2 Meanwhile, place pizza crusts on ungreased cookie sheet. Stir vegetables; spoon onto crusts. Bake at 450° F. for 4 to 6 minutes or until vegetables are tender and pizza crusts are hot.

3 Sprinkle mozzarella and Parmesan cheeses over vegetables. Bake an additional 2 to 3 minutes or until cheese is melted.

Nutrition Information Per Serving
Serving Size: 1 Pizza

Calories	430	Calories from Fat	120
		% Daily Value	
Total Fat	13 g	20%	
Saturated	5 g	25%	
Cholesterol	20 mg	7%	
Sodium	730 mg	30%	
Total Carbohydrate	57 g	19%	
Dietary Fiber	3 g	12%	
Sugars	7 g		
Protein	20 g		
Vitamin A	20%	Vitamin C	40%
Calcium	30%	Iron	20%

Dietary Exchanges: 3 Starch, 2 Vegetable, 1 High-Fat Meat, 1 Fat OR
3 Carbohydrate, 2 Vegetable, 1 High-Fat Meat, 1 Fat

THREE-PEPPER PIZZA

prep time: 25 min. • yield: 3 servings

If red and yellow bell peppers are overly expensive in your market, vary the three-color scheme to include thin slices of fresh plum tomato and skinny rounds of yellow summer squash.

1 (10-oz.) can refrigerated pizza crust

6 oz. (1½ cups) shredded mozzarella cheese

½ teaspoon dried Italian seasoning

1 medium green bell pepper, chopped

1 medium red bell pepper, chopped

1 medium yellow bell pepper, chopped

MOZZARELLA

This soft, white cheese has a mild, delicate flavor. Because it melts easily, mozzarella is most often used on pizzas or in baked dishes. It can also be sliced for sandwiches. Prepackaged mozzarella, in either whole-milk or part-skim versions, is available in the dairy case in blocks or preshredded.

Fresh mozzarella is somewhat softer and less stringy when melted. It's typically sold immersed in water in Italian specialty shops or at the deli counter of large supermarkets. The fresh cheese is more perishable than the prepackaged variety; use it within a day or two. Fresh mozzarella plus sliced garden-ripe tomatoes and shredded fresh basil tossed with balsamic vinaigrette is a simple, heavenly summer dish.

1 Heat oven to 425° F. Lightly grease 12-inch pizza pan or 13 × 9-inch pan. Unroll dough; place in greased pan. Starting at center, press out with hands. Bake at 425° F. for 4 to 6 minutes or just until crust begins to brown.

2 Top crust with ½ cup of the cheese; sprinkle with Italian seasoning. Arrange peppers evenly over top. Sprinkle with remaining 1 cup cheese.

3 Bake at 425° F. for 8 to 12 minutes or until crust is deep golden brown and cheese is melted.

Nutrition Information Per Serving
Serving Size: ⅓ of Recipe

Calories	420	Calories from Fat	120
		% Daily Value	
Total Fat	13 g	20%	
Saturated	7 g	35%	
Cholesterol	30 mg	10%	
Sodium	940 mg	39%	
Total Carbohydrate	51 g	17%	
Dietary Fiber	3 g	12%	
Sugars	8 g		
Protein	24 g		
Vitamin A	40%	Vitamin C	130%
Calcium	40%	Iron	15%

Dietary Exchanges: 3 Starch, 1 Vegetable, 2 Medium-Fat Meat OR
3 Carbohydrate, 1 Vegetable, 2 Medium-Fat Meat

LENTIL RICE LOAF

prep time: 45 min. (ready in 2 hr.) • yield: 6 servings

Lentils and rice join forces for a flavorful meatless loaf topped with spaghetti sauce. Serve steamed spinach on the side.

3 cups water

¾ cup uncooked lentils, sorted, rinsed

1 cup uncooked regular long-grain white rice

½ cup finely chopped onion

½ teaspoon salt

1 (14-oz.) jar spaghetti sauce

½ cup unseasoned dry bread crumbs

½ cup shredded carrot

⅛ teaspoon coarsely ground black pepper

1 egg, slightly beaten

1 In medium saucepan, combine water and lentils. Bring to a boil. Reduce heat; cover and simmer 5 minutes. Add rice, onion and salt; mix well. Cover; simmer an additional 15 to 18 minutes or until liquid is absorbed and lentils and rice are tender. Remove from heat; cool 10 minutes.

2 Heat oven to 350°F. Grease 8 × 4-inch loaf (1½-quart) baking dish. (Do not use metal pan.) Add ¼ cup of the spaghetti sauce and remaining ingredients to lentil mixture; mix well, mashing mixture slightly while mixing. Press mixture firmly in greased dish.

3 Bake at 350°F. for 40 to 45 minutes or until top is golden brown and loaf is firm. Remove from oven; cool 10 minutes. Loosen edges with knife, if necessary; invert loaf onto serving platter.

4 In small saucepan, heat remaining spaghetti sauce for 3 to 4 minutes or until hot. To serve, slice loaf; place on individual serving plates. Spoon warm sauce over each slice.

Nutrition Information Per Serving
Serving Size: ⅙ of Recipe

Calories	290	Calories from Fat	25
		% Daily Value	
Total Fat	3 g	5%	
Saturated	1 g	5%	
Cholesterol	35 mg	12%	
Sodium	540 mg	23%	
Total Carbohydrate	52 g	17%	
Dietary Fiber	10 g	40%	
Sugars	3 g		
Protein	13 g		
Vitamin A	60%	Vitamin C	10%
Calcium	6%	Iron	25%

Dietary Exchanges: 3 Starch, 2 Vegetable OR 3 Carbohydrate, 2 Vegetable

LENTILS

Lentils, small disk-shaped legumes about the size of peas, are the oldest cultivated legume, with references dating back to around 2400 B.C. Unlike other dried legumes, lentils require no soaking; they become tender in 30 to 40 minutes of cooking. Lentils are a plant source of incomplete protein, so are best paired with grains such as rice to provide a complete, higher quality protein. A ½-cup serving of cooked lentils is an excellent source of fiber and folic acid and a good source of iron as well as lesser amounts of other vitamins and minerals.

Dried lentils are widely available and should be stored tightly covered at room temperature. They will keep up to eight months. Red, brown, yellow or green lentils can be used interchangeably in cooking.

THREE-BEAN CASSOULET

prep time: 15 min. (ready in 6 hr. 45 min.) •
yield: 6 (1-cup) servings

Prepare this high-fiber meatless main dish in an oven or slow cooker according to your timetable. Because it reheats well, the cassoulet is a good candidate to make a day or two in advance.

1 (15.5-oz.) can butter beans, drained

1 (15.5-oz.) can great northern beans, drained

1 (15-oz.) can garbanzo beans (chickpeas), drained

1 (14.5-oz.) can stewed tomatoes, undrained, cut up

1 cup finely chopped carrots

1 cup chopped onions

2 garlic cloves, minced

2 teaspoons dried parsley flakes

1 teaspoon dried basil leaves

½ teaspoon dried thyme leaves

½ teaspoon salt

⅛ teaspoon pepper

1 bay leaf

1 In 3½- to 4-quart slow cooker, combine all ingredients. Cover; cook on high setting for 30 minutes.

2 Reduce heat to low. Cook 5 to 6 hours or until vegetables are tender. Remove bay leaf.

TIP: To bake in oven, combine ingredients in ungreased 2-quart casserole. Bake at 350° F. for 35 to 45 minutes.

Nutrition Information Per Serving
Serving Size: 1 Cup

Calories	210	Calories from Fat	20
		% Daily Value	
Total Fat	2 g	3%	
Saturated	0 g	0%	
Cholesterol	0 mg	0%	
Sodium	690 mg	29%	
Total Carbohydrate	37 g	12%	
Dietary Fiber	10 g	40%	
Sugars	5 g		
Protein	11 g		
Vitamin A	120%	Vitamin C	15%
Calcium	15%	Iron	15%

Dietary Exchanges: 2 Starch, 1 Vegetable, ½ Very Lean Meat OR
2 Carbohydrate, 1 Vegetable, ½ Very Lean Meat

THYME

Thyme, a member of the mint family, is related to basil, marjoram and oregano. The stems of the plant are twiglike with small oval leaves. For most dishes, strip leaves from stems, though whole sprigs can be used in soups and stews if they're removed before serving. Thyme blends well with other herbs, enhancing but not overpowering them. The slightly pungent, spicy flavor is especially good with dried bean recipes. Dried thyme is available in whole-leaf or ground versions.

Chicken Biscuit Stew, page 213

SOUPS, CHILIES, STEWS & SANDWICHES

C ASUAL COOKS, THIS CHAPTER IS FOR YOU! SERVE UP A BOWL OF SOUP, STEW OR CHILI WHEN YOU NEED A SIMPLE, HEARTY MEAL. MANY ARE GOOD CANDIDATES FOR FREEZING, SO YOU CAN STOCK YOUR FREEZER WITH READY-MADE DINNERS. ROUNDING OUT THE CHAPTER, OUR SANDWICHES (SOME SERVED WARM) TRANSFORM A CASUAL PRE-PARATION INTO A SATISFYING MEAL.

HARVEST CHICKEN NOODLE SOUP

prep time: 20 min. (ready in 45 min.) •
yield: 4 (1 ¼-cup) servings

Long, skinny noodles are natural partners for chicken soup, but you can also choose alphabet macaroni, orzo (rice-shaped pasta) or ditalini (short macaroni tubes). Garnish the soup with a sprinkling of Parmesan cheese, chopped parsley or finely chopped green onions.

½ cup sliced celery

½ cup chopped carrot

¼ cup chopped onion

1 small zucchini, coarsely chopped

½ teaspoon dried thyme leaves

2 (14½-oz.) cans ready-to-serve chicken broth

½ cup water

6 oz. (2 cups) frozen egg noodles

1 cup cubed cooked chicken

1 In large saucepan, combine all ingredients except noodles and chicken; mix well. Bring to a boil.

2 Stir in noodles and chicken. Reduce heat; simmer 25 minutes or until noodles and vegetables are tender.

Harvest Chicken Noodle Soup

Nutrition Information Per Serving
Serving Size: 1¼ Cups

Calories	230	Calories from Fat	45
		% Daily Value	
Total Fat	5 g	8%	
Saturated	1 g	5%	
Cholesterol	90 mg	30%	
Sodium	710 mg	30%	
Total Carbohydrate	27 g	9%	
Dietary Fiber	2 g	8%	
Sugars	3 g		
Protein	18 g		
Vitamin A	90%	Vitamin C	6%
Calcium	4%	Iron	15%

Dietary Exchanges: 1½ Starch, 1 Vegetable, 1½ Lean Meat OR
1½ Carbohydrate, 1 Vegetable, 1½ Lean Meat

LIGHT CHICKEN—WILD RICE SOUP

prep time: 30 min. • yield: 6 (1½-cup) servings

The addition of skim milk blended with flour thickens this soup and gives the illusion, but not the extra fat and calories, of a broth made with heavy cream.

2 (14½-oz.) cans ready-to-serve fat-free chicken broth with ⅓ less sodium

3 boneless, skinless chicken breast halves, cut into ¾-inch pieces

1 (6.2-oz.) pkg. quick-cooking long-grain and wild rice mix (with seasoning packet)

4 cups skim milk

¾ cup all-purpose flour

4 slices bacon, crisply cooked, crumbled

1½ teaspoons diced pimientos

1 tablespoon dry sherry, if desired

1 In nonstick Dutch oven or large saucepan, combine broth, chicken, rice and seasoning packet; mix well. Bring to a boil. Reduce heat; cover and simmer 5 to 10 minutes or until rice is tender.

2 In small jar with tight-fitting lid, combine 1 cup of the milk and flour; shake until well blended.

3 Add flour mixture, remaining 3 cups milk, bacon, pimientos and sherry to rice mixture; cook and stir over medium heat until soup is bubbly and thickened and chicken is no longer pink. If desired, add salt and pepper to taste.

Nutrition Information Per Serving
Serving Size: 1½ Cups

Calories	310	Calories from Fat	35
		% Daily Value	
Total Fat	4 g	6%	
Saturated	1 g	5%	
Cholesterol	45 mg	15%	
Sodium	840 mg	35%	
Total Carbohydrate	42 g	14%	
Dietary Fiber	1 g	4%	
Sugars	9 g		
Protein	27 g		
Vitamin A	8%	Vitamin C	2%
Calcium	20%	Iron	15%

Dietary Exchanges: 3 Starch, 2½ Very Lean Meat OR 3 Carbohydrate,
2½ Very Lean Meat

SKIMMING FAT FROM SOUPS

During cooking, the fat in meat and poultry liquefies and rises to the surface of broths and soups. To skim this fat from hot broth and soup, use a skimmer, spoon or baster to siphon off the oily layer at the top. If there's time to chill the broth or soup, the fat will solidify and easily lift off.

Cook's Notes

GOLDEN SPLIT PEA SOUP

prep time: 25 min. (ready in 1 hr. 25 min.) •
yield: 7 (1-cup) servings

Here's a lovely golden soup that's very thick and satisfying. Green split peas can be substituted for the yellow, if you prefer, but may need a slightly longer cooking time. A dollop of plain yogurt or sour cream for a garnish provides a tangy contrast to the earthy soup.

1 (16-oz.) pkg. dry yellow split peas, sorted, rinsed and drained

7 cups water

1 cup sliced carrots

$\frac{1}{2}$ cup chopped onion

$\frac{1}{2}$ cup chopped celery

1 tablespoon chicken-flavor instant bouillon

1 teaspoon salt

$\frac{1}{2}$ teaspoon hot pepper sauce

1 cup chopped cooked ham, if desired

1 In Dutch oven or large saucepan, combine all ingredients except ham. Bring to a boil over medium-high heat. Reduce heat to low; simmer 45 to 60 minutes or until peas and vegetables are very tender.

2 In blender container or food processor bowl with metal blade, blend half of soup until smooth. Return to Dutch oven; stir in ham. Cook over medium-low heat until thoroughly heated, stirring frequently.

Nutrition Information Per Serving
Serving Size: 1 Cup

Calories	270	Calories from Fat	20
		% Daily Value	
Total Fat	2 g	3%	
Saturated	1 g	5%	
Cholesterol	10 mg	3%	
Sodium	1030 mg	43%	
Total Carbohydrate	43 g	14%	
Dietary Fiber	16 g	64%	
Sugars	4 g		
Protein	20 g		
Vitamin A	100%	Vitamin C	4%
Calcium	4%	Iron	15%

Dietary Exchanges: 3 Starch, 1 $\frac{1}{2}$ Very Lean Meat OR 3 Carbohydrate, 1 $\frac{1}{2}$ Very Lean Meat

INSTANT BOUILLON

Instant bouillon is a commercially prepared dehydrate that's a quick, easy way to flavor soups and stews. Instant beef, chicken and vegetable bouillon is available in jars as granules or cubes and is found in the soup section of supermarkets. Instant bouillon can be substituted for canned or homemade broth by dissolving 1 teaspoon of granules or 1 cube per cup of hot water.

Cook's Notes

VEGETABLE-BEEF-BARLEY SOUP

prep time: 35 min. • yield: 4 (1 $\frac{1}{2}$-cup) servings

Mixed vegetables round out the time-honored soup pairing of beef and barley. This soup freezes well, if you care to make a double batch.

$\frac{1}{2}$ lb. extra-lean ground beef

1 (14 $\frac{1}{2}$-oz.) can ready-to-serve beef broth

1 (14.5-oz.) can stewed tomatoes, cut up, undrained

1 (9-oz.) pkg. frozen mixed vegetables in a pouch

1 (8-oz.) can no-salt-added tomato sauce

$\frac{1}{3}$ cup uncooked quick-cooking barley

1 In large saucepan, brown ground beef until thoroughly cooked. Drain.

2 Stir in all remaining ingredients. Bring to a boil. Reduce heat to medium; cover and cook 10 to 15 minutes or until vegetables and barley are tender, stirring occasionally.

Nutrition Information Per Serving
Serving Size: 1 1/2 Cups

Calories	230	Calories from Fat	70
		% Daily Value	
Total Fat	8 g	12%	
Saturated	3 g	15%	
Cholesterol	35 mg	12%	
Sodium	690 mg	29%	
Total Carbohydrate	23 g	8%	
Dietary Fiber	4 g	16%	
Sugars	6 g		
Protein	16 g		
Vitamin A	35%	Vitamin C	30%
Calcium	6%	Iron	15%

Dietary Exchanges: 1 Starch, 2 Vegetable, 1 1/2 Lean Meat, 1/2 Fat OR
1 Carbohydrate, 2 Vegetable, 1 1/2 Lean Meat, 1/2 Fat

Cook's Notes

BROTH SUBSTITUTIONS

Here are some convenient substitutions for beef or chicken broth:

- A 14 1/2-ounce can ready-to-serve beef or chicken broth equals 1 3/4 cups broth
- A 10 1/2-ounce can condensed beef or 10 3/4-ounce can condensed chicken broth diluted with 1 soup can water equals 2 2/3 cups broth
- 1 beef- or chicken-flavor bouillon cube, 1 teaspoon instant beef or chicken bouillon dissolved in 1 cup water or 1 teaspoon beef or chicken base diluted with 1 cup water equals 1 cup broth

ITALIAN SAUSAGE-PASTA SOUP

prep time: 35 min. • yield: 6 (1 1/2-cup) servings

2 oz. (3/4 cup) uncooked pasta nuggets (radiatore)

3/4 lb. Italian sausage links, cut into 1/4-inch slices

1 cup chopped onions

1 green bell pepper, chopped

3 garlic cloves, minced

1 (19-oz.) can cannellini beans, drained, rinsed

1 (14.5-oz.) can diced tomatoes, undrained

1 (14 1/2-oz.) can ready-to-serve beef broth

1 (14-oz.) jar pizza sauce

1 Cook pasta nuggets to desired doneness as directed on package. Drain.

2 Meanwhile, in large saucepan, brown sausage over medium-high heat. Add onions, bell pepper and garlic; cook 1 to 2 minutes. Stir in beans, tomatoes, broth and pizza sauce; simmer 10 to 15 minutes.

3 Add cooked pasta nuggets to soup; cook until thoroughly heated.

Nutrition Information Per Serving
Serving Size: 1 1/2 Cups

Calories	300	Calories from Fat	120
		% Daily Value	
Total Fat	13 g	20%	
Saturated	4 g	20%	
Cholesterol	30 mg	10%	
Sodium	1180 mg	49%	
Total Carbohydrate	30 g	10%	
Dietary Fiber	6 g	24%	
Sugars	9 g		
Protein	16 g		
Vitamin A	10%	Vitamin C	25%
Calcium	6%	Iron	20%

Dietary Exchanges: 2 Starch, 1 1/2 High-Fat Meat OR 2 Carbohydrate,
1 1/2 High-Fat Meat

TOMATO PARMESAN SOUP

prep time: 25 min. • yield: 4 (1 ½-cup) servings

Using canned plum tomatoes for this cream-style soup gives a tomato flavor that's more true than that of many prepared canned soups. Mini pasta adds texture and makes the soup more filling.

2 oz. (½ cup) uncooked mini bow tie pasta (farfalle), orzo or rosamarina (rice-shaped pasta)

2 tablespoons butter

1 medium onion, chopped

1 (28-oz.) can Italian plum tomatoes, undrained, cut up

1 cup water

⅓ cup whipping cream

1⅓ oz. (⅓ cup) shredded fresh Parmesan cheese

1 Cook pasta to desired doneness as directed on package. Drain.

2 Meanwhile, melt butter in large saucepan over medium heat. Add onion; cook and stir 4 to 5 minutes or until tender. Add tomatoes and water; simmer 10 minutes, stirring occasionally. Add cream; simmer 5 minutes.

3 Add cooked pasta to soup. If desired, add salt and pepper to taste. To serve, ladle soup into individual soup bowls. Top each serving with cheese.

Nutrition Information Per Serving
Serving Size: 1 ½ Cups

Calories	250	Calories from Fat	140
		% Daily Value	
Total Fat	16 g	25%	
Saturated	10 g	50%	
Cholesterol	50 mg	17%	
Sodium	420 mg	18%	
Total Carbohydrate	20 g	7%	
Dietary Fiber	2 g	8%	
Sugars	5 g		
Protein	7 g		
Vitamin A	25%	Vitamin C	25%
Calcium	15%	Iron	8%

Dietary Exchanges: 1 Starch, 1 Vegetable, 3 Fat OR 1 Carbohydrate, 1 Vegetable, 3 Fat

SOUP NOODLES

Add cooked pasta to soups just before serving to prevent them from disintegrating and making the soup "gluey." Choose a size and shape that will add body and satisfaction without transforming the soup into a pasta dish. Some favorites for adding to soups:

• Mini bow ties (farfalle)
• Mini lasagna noodles (mafalda)
• Alphabet noodles
• Orzo (rosamarina or rice-shaped pasta)
• Ditalini (tiny tubes)
• Skinny egg noodles
• Mini stars

Cook's Notes

FRENCH ONION SOUP GRATINÉE

prep time: 25 min. (ready in 50 min.) • yield: 6 (1-cup) servings

A favorite appetizer in restaurants, French onion soup pairs an intense oniony broth with a rich topping of melted cheese and a toasted bread "crouton."

3 tablespoons margarine or butter

4 cups thinly sliced onions

5 cups beef broth

1 beef-flavor bouillon cube or 1 teaspoon beef-flavor instant bouillon

1 teaspoon Worcestershire sauce

Dash pepper

4 oz. (1 cup) shredded Swiss cheese

¼ cup grated Parmesan cheese

6 slices French bread, toasted

1 Melt margarine in Dutch oven or large saucepan over low heat. Add onions; cook 15 minutes or until onions are golden brown and tender, stirring occasionally.

2 Add broth, bouillon cube, Worcestershire sauce and pepper. Bring to a boil. Reduce heat; cover and simmer 20 to 25 minutes.

3 Meanwhile, in medium bowl, combine Swiss and Parmesan cheeses.

4 To serve, place 6 ovenproof individual soup bowls on cookie sheet for ease in broiling. Ladle soup into bowls. Top each with slice of toasted bread; sprinkle each with about 2 tablespoons cheese mixture.

5 Broil about 3 to 5 inches from heat for 1 to 3 minutes or until cheese is bubbly.

Nutrition Information Per Serving
Serving Size: 1 Cup

Calories	250	Calories from Fat	120
		% Daily Value	
Total Fat	13 g	20%	
Saturated	6 g	30%	
Cholesterol	20 mg	7%	
Sodium	1150 mg	48%	
Total Carbohydrate	21 g	7%	
Dietary Fiber	2 g	8%	
Sugars	5 g		
Protein	13 g		
Vitamin A	8%	Vitamin C	6%
Calcium	30%	Iron	6%

Dietary Exchanges: 1 Starch, 1 Vegetable, 1 High-Fat Meat, 1 Fat OR
1 Carbohydrate, 1 Vegetable, 1 High-Fat Meat, 1 Fat

Corn and Clam Chowder

CORN AND CLAM CHOWDER

prep time: 25 min. (ready in 45 min.) •
yield: 5 (1 1/2-cup) servings

While Manhattan-style clam chowder is made with tomatoes, New Englanders prefer theirs in a creamy broth. Our version is made with skim milk to lower the fat content.

2 slices bacon, cut up

3 medium potatoes, peeled, cut into
   1/2-inch cubes (3 cups)

3/4 cup chopped onions

1/2 cup chopped celery

2 cups skim milk

2 (6.5-oz.) cans minced clams, drained,
   reserving liquid

3/4 teaspoon dried thyme leaves

1/8 to 1/4 teaspoon pepper

1 (15-oz.) can cream-style corn

1 (11-oz.) can vacuum-packed whole
   kernel corn, drained

1 In large saucepan or Dutch oven, cook bacon over medium heat until brown and crisp. With slotted spoon, transfer bacon to paper towel to drain. Remove all but 1 tablespoon pan drippings from saucepan.

2 Add potatoes, onions and celery to drippings in saucepan; cook and stir 5 minutes. Add milk, reserved clam liquid, thyme and pepper; mix well. Reduce heat to medium-low; cover and simmer 15 to 20 minutes or until vegetables are tender.

3 Carefully transfer 2 cups hot mixture to food processor bowl with metal blade or blender container; process until smooth. Return mixture to saucepan. Stir in cream-style corn, whole kernel corn and clams. Return to a boil. Reduce heat; simmer 4 to 6 minutes or until thoroughly heated, stirring occasionally.

4 To serve, ladle chowder into individual soup bowls. Crumble reserved bacon; sprinkle over chowder.

Nutrition Information Per Serving
Serving Size: 1 1/2 Cups

Calories	280	Calories from Fat	45
		% Daily Value	
Total Fat	5 g	8%	
Saturated	2 g	10%	
Cholesterol	10 mg	3%	
Sodium	730 mg	30%	
Total Carbohydrate	49 g	16%	
Dietary Fiber	4 g	16%	
Sugars	17 g		
Protein	9 g		
Vitamin A	8%	Vitamin C	20%
Calcium	15%	Iron	6%

Dietary Exchanges: 3 Starch, 1 Fat OR 3 Carbohydrate, 1 Fat

WHITE BEAN-TURKEY MEATBALL CHILI

prep time: 30 min. (ready in 50 min.) •

yield: 5 (1½-cup) servings

Ground turkey is a good choice for meatballs with good flavor and texture but less fat than those made with ground beef and/or pork. A touch of sugar in the chili brings out the flavor of the vegetables.

MEATBALLS

1 lb. lean ground turkey

¼ cup unseasoned dry bread crumbs

¼ cup chopped onion

¼ teaspoon seasoned salt

1 egg

CHILI

1 medium zucchini, cut into 1 × ¼ × ¼-inch strips

2 garlic cloves, minced

1 (28-oz.) can whole tomatoes, undrained, cut up

1 (15.5-oz.) can great northern beans, drained

1 (14½-oz.) can ready-to-serve chicken broth

1 teaspoon sugar

1 teaspoon cumin

3 teaspoons chili powder

¼ teaspoon pepper

⅛ teaspoon salt

1 In medium bowl, combine all meatball ingredients; mix well. Shape into 24 (1½-inch) balls.

2 Spray large skillet with nonstick cooking spray. Heat over medium heat until hot. Add meatballs; cook 8 to 10 minutes or until browned on all sides and no longer pink in center.

3 In Dutch oven or large saucepan, combine all chili ingredients; mix well. Bring to a boil. Reduce heat; add meatballs. Simmer 10 to 15 minutes or until thoroughly heated.

Nutrition Information Per Serving
Serving Size: 1½ Cups

Calories	340	Calories from Fat	140
		% Daily Value	
Total Fat	15 g	23%	
Saturated	5 g	25%	
Cholesterol	100 mg	33%	
Sodium	930 mg	39%	
Total Carbohydrate	26 g	9%	
Dietary Fiber	6 g	24%	
Sugars	6 g		
Protein	26 g		
Vitamin A	35%	Vitamin C	20%
Calcium	15%	Iron	25%

Dietary Exchanges: 1½ Starch, 1 Vegetable, 3 Lean Meat, 1 Fat OR 1½ Carbohydrate, 1 Vegetable, 3 Lean Meat, 1 Fat

WHAT IS A DUTCH OVEN?

A Dutch oven is a heavyweight cooking pot with a lid for slow simmering. The standard size is 5 quarts. Dutch ovens can be cast iron, aluminum alloy or stainless steel, and some have a nonstick finish. Choose a Dutch oven with a heavy bottom, a tight-fitting cover and, if possible, ovenproof handles. You'll find it's the pot you reach for when preparing stews, chilies, sauces and more.

Cook's Notes

White Bean-Turkey Meatball Chili

WHITE CHICKEN CHILI

prep time: 30 min. • yield: 9 (1-cup) servings

Chili doesn't have to be red. Here, cannellini beans and chicken join forces in this chili, topped with shredded cheese and cilantro.

1 tablespoon oil

1 cup chopped onions

2 garlic cloves, minced

1 lb. boneless, skinless chicken breasts, cut into bite-sized pieces

3 (14 1/2-oz.) cans ready-to-serve chicken broth

2 (15-oz.) cans cannellini beans, drained

2 (4.5-oz.) cans chopped green chiles, drained

1 teaspoon dried oregano leaves

1/2 teaspoon cumin

Dash ground red pepper (cayenne), if desired

6 oz. (1 1/2 cups) shredded Monterey Jack cheese

Chopped fresh cilantro, if desired

1 Heat oil in large saucepan or Dutch oven over medium-high heat until hot. Add onions, garlic and chicken; cook and stir until chicken is no longer pink.

2 Stir in all remaining ingredients except cheese and cilantro. Bring to a boil. Reduce heat; simmer 10 to 15 minutes to blend flavors, stirring occasionally.

3 To serve, ladle chili into individual soup bowls. Top each serving with cheese and cilantro.

Nutrition Information Per Serving			
Serving Size: 1 Cup			
Calories	250	Calories from Fat	90
		% Daily Value	
Total Fat	10 g	15%	
Saturated	4 g	20%	
Cholesterol	45 mg	15%	
Sodium	670 mg	28%	
Total Carbohydrate	17 g	6%	
Dietary Fiber	4 g	16%	
Sugars	3 g		
Protein	23 g		
Vitamin A	8%	Vitamin C	60%
Calcium	20%	Iron	10%

Dietary Exchanges: 1 Starch, 3 Very Lean Meat, 1 1/2 Fat
OR 1 Carbohydrate, 3 Very Lean Meat, 1 1/2 Fat

SLOW-COOKED CHILI

prep time: 20 min. (ready in 8 hr. 20 min.) •
yield: 6 (1 1/2-cup) servings

If you're planning a buffet, slow-cooker dishes such as this beef chili are ideal. You can complete all the prep ahead of time, leaving you free to tend to other details.

1/2 lb. bulk Italian sausage

1 lb. lean ground beef

1/2 cup chopped onion

1 (28-oz.) can whole tomatoes, undrained, cut up

1 (15-oz.) can tomato sauce

1 teaspoon sugar

1 to 1 1/2 teaspoons cumin

2 teaspoons chili powder

1 teaspoon dried oregano leaves

1 (15-oz.) can spicy chili beans, undrained

1 (15-oz.) can garbanzo beans (chickpeas), drained, rinsed

1 In large skillet, cook sausage, ground beef and onion until beef is browned and thoroughly cooked. Drain.

2 In 3½- or 4-quart slow cooker, combine browned meat and onion with all remaining ingredients; mix well. Cover; cook on low setting for 7 to 8 hours.

Nutrition Information Per Serving
Serving Size: 1½ Cups

Calories	420	Calories from Fat	170
		% Daily Value	
Total Fat	19 g	29%	
Saturated	7 g	35%	
Cholesterol	70 mg	23%	
Sodium	1300 mg	54%	
Total Carbohydrate	35 g	12%	
Dietary Fiber	9 g	36%	
Sugars	8 g		
Protein	28 g		
Vitamin A	40%	Vitamin C	35%
Calcium	10%	Iron	30%

Dietary Exchanges: 2 Starch, 1 Vegetable, 3 Lean Meat, 1½ Fat OR
2 Carbohydrate, 1 Vegetable, 3 Lean Meat, 1½ Fat

OREGANO

Popularly known as the "pizza" herb, oregano is similar in flavor to marjoram, only stronger. A member of the mint family, its small, soft leaves dry quickly and hold their flavor well. Oregano is used to season pasta sauces and salad dressings, as well as to flavor meat, fish, poultry and egg dishes.

Oregano is a satisfying "crop" for a neglectful gardener, as it thrives unattended. When the plant goes to flower, use the flowers for cooking—they have the same flavor as the leaves.

QUICK AND EASY CHILI

prep time: 35 min. • **yield: 4 (1½-cup) servings**

Serve the chili with assorted fixin's: chopped jalapeño chiles, shredded cheese, sour cream (or nonfat plain yogurt), chopped tomatoes and/or sliced olives.

1 lb. lean ground beef

⅔ cup chopped onions

½ cup chopped green bell pepper

½ cup water

2 (15.5-oz.) cans dark red kidney beans, drained, rinsed

1 (10½-oz.) can condensed beef broth

1 (8-oz.) can tomato sauce

1 (6-oz.) can tomato paste

3 teaspoons chili powder

1 In large saucepan, brown ground beef, onions and bell pepper; cook until beef is thoroughly cooked. Drain.

2 Stir in all remaining ingredients. Bring to a boil. Reduce heat; simmer 15 minutes, stirring occasionally.

Nutrition Information Per Serving
Serving Size: 1½ Cups

Calories	470	Calories from Fat	140
		% Daily Value	
Total Fat	16 g	25%	
Saturated	6 g	30%	
Cholesterol	70 mg	23%	
Sodium	1400 mg	58%	
Total Carbohydrate	46 g	15%	
Dietary Fiber	12 g	48%	
Sugars	7 g		
Protein	36 g		
Vitamin A	45%	Vitamin C	45%
Calcium	15%	Iron	35%

Dietary Exchanges: 2 Starch, 3 Vegetable, 3½ Lean Meat, 1 Fat OR
2 Carbohydrate, 3 Vegetable, 3½ Lean Meat, 1 Fat

EASY OVEN STEW

prep time: 10 min. (ready in 7 hr. 10 min.) •
yield: 12 (1-cup) servings

*Let the enticing aroma of beef and onions fill your
house. This no-fuss stew requires a long, slow bake in
the oven.*

3 lb. beef stew meat

3 large onions, cut into eighths

1 (14.5- or 16-oz.) can whole tomatoes,
undrained, chopped

2 cups water

¼ cup instant tapioca or cornstarch

1 tablespoon beef-flavor instant bouillon

1 tablespoon brown sugar

2 teaspoons salt

1 teaspoon pepper

2 bay leaves

1 (1-lb.) pkg. fresh baby carrots

1 (1-lb.) pkg. frozen cut green beans

1 Heat oven to 300° F. In large Dutch oven or
roasting pan, combine all ingredients except carrots and green beans; mix well. Cover.

2 Bake at 300° F. for 6 to 7 hours, stirring occasionally and adding carrots and green beans during last hour of cooking time. Remove bay leaves
before serving.

Easy Oven Stew

TIPS: To freeze stew, cool completely in refrigerator. Place in 3 ovenproof casseroles or freezer containers following directions for *How to Freeze a Casserole* (below). When ready to use, place in original baking dish. Thaw in refrigerator; reheat at 350° F. for 45 to 55 minutes.

Stew can be prepared in slow cooker. Combine all ingredients except carrots and green beans in slow cooker; mix well. Cover; cook on high setting for 6 to 7 hours, stirring occasionally and adding carrots and green beans during last hour of cooking. Remove bay leaves before serving.

Nutrition Information Per Serving			
Serving Size: 1 Cup			
Calories	320	Calories from Fat	100
		% Daily Value	
Total Fat	11 g	17%	
Saturated	4 g	20%	
Cholesterol	95 mg	32%	
Sodium	670 mg	28%	
Total Carbohydrate	18 g	6%	
Dietary Fiber	3 g	12%	
Sugars	6 g		
Protein	36 g		
Vitamin A	70%	Vitamin C	20%
Calcium	4%	Iron	20%

Dietary Exchanges: 3 Vegetable, 4 ½ Lean Meat

HOW TO FREEZE A CASSEROLE

When you've got the time, tuck an extra casserole or two away in your freezer for those inevitable rushed-day dinners. So that you don't tie up your baking dishes, here's a simple way to freeze a casserole meal in aluminum foil.

STEP 1

Lightly grease an ovenproof casserole or baking dish. Line the dish with a sheet of foil large enough to bring the edges together to fold and seal. Place the casserole mixture in the foil-lined dish. Bake it according to the recipe directions, or leave it unbaked.

After the casserole or stew has cooled, bring the edges of foil together and seal tightly, making sure the foil touches the top of the mixture to shut out any air. Freeze it until firm.

STEP 2

Lift the frozen casserole from the dish. For additional protection, wrap the casserole in foil or place it in a freezer bag. Label the outer wrap with casserole name, date frozen, "use by" date,

number of servings and reheating or baking instructions. Return the labeled casserole to the freezer.

When ready to use the casserole, place it in the original baking dish. Thaw in refrigerator, reheat or bake. (Note: When using microwave oven to bake or reheat, remove the foil first.)

GROUND BEEF STEW

prep time: 15 min. (ready in 45 min.) •
yield: 5 (1 ½-cup) servings

Using ground beef instead of beef chunks speeds prep time and makes this an economical family meal.

1 lb. ground beef

½ teaspoon salt

¼ teaspoon pepper

3 carrots, cut into ½-inch pieces

2 medium potatoes, cut into ¾-inch chunks

1 medium onion, cut into 8 wedges

1 (14½-oz.) can ready-to-serve beef broth

1 medium zucchini, sliced

1 (14.5-oz.) can diced tomatoes, undrained

1 (6-oz.) jar sliced mushrooms, drained

½ teaspoon dried thyme leaves

1 tablespoon Worcestershire sauce

¼ cup water

2 tablespoons all-purpose flour

1 In Dutch oven or large saucepan, combine ground beef, salt and pepper; cook over medium-high heat until beef is browned and thoroughly cooked. Drain.

2 Add carrots, potatoes, onion and broth. Bring to a boil. Reduce heat; cover and simmer 15 to 20 minutes or until vegetables are almost tender.

3 Stir in zucchini, tomatoes, mushrooms, thyme and Worcestershire sauce. Cook 5 to 10 minutes or until zucchini is tender.

4 In small jar with tight-fitting lid, combine water and flour; shake well to blend. Gradually add to stew, stirring constantly; cook and stir until bubbly and thickened.

Nutrition Information Per Serving
Serving Size: 1 ½ Cups

Calories	310	Calories from Fat	120
		% Daily Value	
Total Fat	13 g	20%	
Saturated	5 g	25%	
Cholesterol	55 mg	18%	
Sodium	920 mg	38%	
Total Carbohydrate	28 g	9%	
Dietary Fiber	5 g	20%	
Sugars	7 g		
Protein	20 g		
Vitamin A	260%	Vitamin C	30%
Calcium	6%	Iron	20%

Dietary Exchanges: 1 ½ Starch, 1 Vegetable, 2 Medium-Fat Meat, ½ Fat OR
1 ½ Carbohydrate, 1 Vegetable, 2 Medium-Fat Meat, ½ Fat

FORMING GROUND BEEF PATTIES

U nless you plan to use ground beef within a day of purchase, form it into patties for easy freezer storage and retrieval. Use your hands or one of several patty-making devices available in housewares departments, home plastics parties or the supermarket's kitchen equipment aisle. Handle the meat gently and as little as possible to keep the texture tender. If you wish, blend in seasonings before forming into patties.

Keep the size of the patties uniform: ¼ pound is convenient. Wrap each patty individually in plastic wrap (for later defrosting in the microwave), then package all into a resealable plastic freezer bag. The plastic bag serves as an extra defense against freezer burn and helps prevent stray patties from getting "lost" at the back of the freezer.

CHICKEN BISCUIT STEW

prep time: 20 min. (ready in 45 min.) •
yield: 5 (1½-cup) servings

PICTURED ON PAGE 196

Refrigerated biscuits garnished with poppy seed offer an easy, flaky version of dumplings for this chicken stew.

¼ cup margarine or butter

⅓ cup all-purpose flour

Dash pepper

1 (10½-oz.) can condensed chicken broth

¾ cup milk

2 cups cubed cooked chicken

1 cup frozen sweet peas

1 cup fresh baby carrots

⅓ cup chopped onion

1 (12-oz.) can refrigerated flaky biscuits

Poppy seed, if desired

1 Heat oven to 375° F. Melt margarine in 10-inch ovenproof skillet. Stir in flour and pepper; cook, stirring constantly, for 1 minute or until smooth and bubbly.

2 Gradually stir in broth and milk; cook until mixture boils and thickens, stirring constantly. Add chicken, peas, carrots and onion; cook until hot and bubbly.

3 Separate dough into 10 biscuits. Arrange biscuits over hot chicken mixture in skillet; sprinkle with poppy seed.

4 Bake at 375° F. for 20 to 25 minutes or until biscuits are golden brown.

Nutrition Information Per Serving
Serving Size: 1½ Cups

Calories	500	Calories from Fat	220
		% Daily Value	
Total Fat	24 g	37%	
Saturated	5 g	25%	
Cholesterol	55 mg	18%	
Sodium	1330 mg	55%	
Total Carbohydrate	44 g	15%	
Dietary Fiber	3 g	12%	
Sugars	9 g		
Protein	27 g		
Vitamin A	150%	Vitamin C	6%
Calcium	10%	Iron	20%

Dietary Exchanges: 3 Starch, 2½ Lean Meat, 3 Fat OR 3 Carbohydrate, 2½ Lean Meat, 3 Fat

STEW

A stew most often contains meat or fish, vegetables and a thick broth. Stewing, which means to cook by simmering slowly, tenderizes ingredients as well as creates a delicious blend of flavors.

The thickness of a stew can vary widely, sparking the question, Do you eat stew with a spoon or a fork? A spoon seems appropriate when the stew is served in a bowl and has a thin gravy. A fork seems best when the stew is served on a plate and has a thicker, saucelike liquid.

Cook's Notes

CHICKEN RATATOUILLE STEW

prep time: 20 min. (ready in 8 hr. 20 min.) •
yield: 6 (1¾-cup) servings

Chicken enriches this traditional stew.

- 4 boneless, skinless chicken breast halves, cut into 1-inch pieces

- 1 (28- to 30-oz.) jar spaghetti sauce

- 1 medium eggplant, peeled, coarsely chopped

- 2 tomatoes, coarsely chopped

- 2 small zucchini, sliced

- 1 green bell pepper, cut into 1-inch pieces

- 1 large onion, chopped

- 3 garlic cloves, minced

- 1 teaspoon dried basil leaves

- 1 teaspoon dried oregano leaves

1 In 3½- or 4-quart slow cooker, combine all ingredients; mix well.

2 Cover; cook on low setting for 8 to 10 hours or until chicken is no longer pink.

Nutrition Information Per Serving
Serving Size: 1¾ Cups

Calories	220	Calories from Fat	45
		% Daily Value	
Total Fat	5 g	8%	
Saturated	1 g	5%	
Cholesterol	50 mg	17%	
Sodium	630 mg	26%	
Total Carbohydrate	21 g	7%	
Dietary Fiber	5 g	20%	
Sugars	4 g		
Protein	22 g		
Vitamin A	25%	Vitamin C	45%
Calcium	8%	Iron	15%

Dietary Exchanges: 1 Starch, 1 Vegetable, 2½ Very Lean Meat, ½ Fat OR
1 Carbohydrate, 1 Vegetable, 2½ Very Lean Meat, ½ Fat

SLOW-COOKED CHICKEN AND SAUSAGE STEW

prep time: 15 min. (ready in 8 hr. 25 min.) •
yield: 4 (1½-cup) servings

Sit down at the end of a busy day to a home-style stew. This one combines baked beans, chicken and sausage with a sweet and tangy sauce that includes a hint of mustard.

- ½ lb. kielbasa sausage, cut into ¼-inch slices

- 2 boneless, skinless chicken breast halves, cut into thin bite-sized strips

- ½ cup thinly sliced carrot

- 1 medium onion, thinly sliced, separated into rings

- 1 (16-oz.) can baked beans, undrained

- 2 tablespoons brown sugar

- 1 teaspoon dry mustard

- ½ cup ketchup

- 1 tablespoon vinegar

- 1 (8-oz.) pkg. frozen cut green beans in a pouch, thawed*

1 In 3½- or 4-quart slow cooker, combine all ingredients except green beans; mix well. Cover; cook on low setting at least 8 hours or until chicken is no longer pink and carrot slices are tender.

2 Ten minutes before serving, stir in green beans. Increase heat to high setting; cover and cook 10 minutes or until green beans are crisp-tender.

TIP: *To quickly thaw green beans, remove from pouch and place in colander or strainer; rinse with warm water until thawed. Drain well.

Nutrition Information Per Serving
Serving Size: 1 ½ Cups

Calories	460	Calories from Fat	160
		% Daily Value	
Total Fat	18 g	28%	
Saturated	6 g	30%	
Cholesterol	75 g	25%	
Sodium	1520 mg	63%	
Total Carbohydrate	47 g	16%	
Dietary Fiber	8 g	32%	
Sugars	20 g		
Protein	28 g		
Vitamin A	100%	Vitamin C	20%
Calcium	15%	Iron	15%

Dietary Exchanges: 2 Starch, 1 Fruit, 3 Lean Meat, 1 ½ Fat OR
3 Carbohydrate, 3 Lean Meat, 1 ½ Fat

FAMILY-STYLE PORK AND POTATO STEW

prep time: 30 min. (ready in 1 hr. 10 min.) •
yield: 6 (1 ½-cup) servings

Serve this stew with baking powder biscuits and a tossed green salad. For variety, replace half of the carrots with cut parsnips.

1 tablespoon oil

1 lb. pork tenderloin, cut into 1-inch slices

1 cup julienne-cut (2 × ⅛ × ⅛-inch) carrots

1 cup sliced onions

4 medium baking potatoes, peeled, cubed

3 tablespoons chicken-flavor instant bouillon

1 teaspoon dried pork seasoning

1 tablespoon cider vinegar

4¼ cups water

3 tablespoons all-purpose flour

2 cups thinly sliced cabbage

1 Heat oil in Dutch oven over medium heat until hot. Add pork, carrots and onions; cook until pork is browned. Drain.

2 Add potatoes, bouillon, pork seasoning, vinegar and 4 cups of the water; mix well. Simmer 30 minutes, stirring occasionally.

3 In small bowl, combine remaining ¼ cup water and flour; beat with wire whisk until well blended. Add flour mixture and cabbage to stew; mix well. Cover; simmer an additional 10 minutes or until stew is thickened, stirring occasionally.

Nutrition Information Per Serving
Serving Size: 1 ½ Cups

Calories	250	Calories from Fat	50
		% Daily Value	
Total Fat	6 g	9%	
Saturated	2 g	10%	
Cholesterol	45 mg	15%	
Sodium	1530 mg	64%	
Total Carbohydrate	30 g	10%	
Dietary Fiber	4 g	16%	
Sugars	5 g		
Protein	20 g		
Vitamin A	120%	Vitamin C	25%
Calcium	4%	Iron	15%

Dietary Exchanges: 2 Starch, 2 Lean Meat OR 2 Carbohydrate, 2 Lean Meat

FREEZING COMBINATION DISHES CONTAINING POTATOES

Combination dishes (soups, stews, casseroles) that contain potatoes freeze with varying degrees of success. The potato pieces may discolor or lose their texture. You can try to get around this by omitting the potatoes when preparing the dish to be frozen, then adding potatoes during reheating. Canned Irish potatoes retain their texture and can sometimes be substituted in soup and stew recipes.

Lentil and Bean Stew

LENTIL AND BEAN STEW

prep time: 15 min. (ready in 1 hr. 10 min.) •
yield: 5 (1½-cup) servings

*Unlike other dried legumes, lentils require no soaking
or precooking to become tender. They pair well with
garbanzo beans (chickpeas) and potatoes in this
meatless soup.*

1 (28-oz.) can whole tomatoes, undrained,
   cut up

1 (15-oz.) can garbanzo beans
   (chickpeas), undrained

2 cups cubed peeled potatoes

1 cup dry lentils, sorted, rinsed and
   drained

1 cup thinly sliced carrots

½ cup chopped onion

½ cup chopped green bell pepper

3 to 6 teaspoons chili powder

1 teaspoon garlic salt

1 In 4-quart saucepan or Dutch oven, combine
all ingredients; mix well. Bring to a boil.

2 Reduce heat; cover and simmer 45 to 55 minutes or until vegetables and lentils are tender.

Nutrition Information Per Serving
Serving Size: 1½ Cups

Calories	330	Calories from Fat	20
		% Daily Value	
Total Fat	2 g	3%	
Saturated	0 g	0%	
Cholesterol	0 mg	0%	
Sodium	910 mg	38%	
Total Carbohydrate	60 g	20%	
Dietary Fiber	20 g	80%	
Sugars	8 g		
Protein	18 g		
Vitamin A	180%	Vitamin C	50%
Calcium	10%	Iron	35%

Dietary Exchanges: 3 ½ Starch, 1 Vegetable, ½ Lean Meat OR
3 ½ Carbohydrate, 1 Vegetable, ½ Lean Meat

POTATO POINTERS

A favorite comfort food, potatoes may be
the most versatile vegetable in the
world. Familiar potatoes found in the supermarket include:

• Idaho or russet potatoes, which have
  superior baking and frying qualities.
• All-purpose potatoes, which include
  round potatoes with white or red skins
  and long potatoes with white skins. These
  potatoes are excellent for boiling, mashing
  and salad making.
• New potatoes, which are young red or
  white potatoes small enough to cook
  whole, are blessed with tender skin that
  doesn't require peeling. They're a good
  choice for potato salads and pan-roasted
  potatoes.

Other varieties may be available in your
area. These include buttery-tasting yellow
Yukon Gold potatoes, snack-sized Texas
Finger potatoes and purple potatoes.

Store potatoes in a cool, dark, well-
ventilated place. Refrigerating potatoes
causes them to become unnaturally sweet
and turn dark. Warm temperatures encourage sprouting and shriveling.

FESTIVE OYSTER STEW

prep time: 45 min. • yield: 8 (1½-cup) servings

Oyster stew, a must for Christmas in some families, gains extra flavor from the liquid in which the canned oysters are packed.

2 (8-oz.) cans whole oysters

1 red bell pepper, chopped

¾ cup chopped onions

¼ cup margarine or butter

½ cup all-purpose flour

1 teaspoon salt

¼ teaspoon white pepper

4 cups half-and-half

4 cups milk

2 cups frozen Southern-style hash-brown potatoes

½ teaspoon hot pepper sauce

1 cup chopped fresh spinach

1 Drain oysters, reserving liquid. Cut oysters in half. Set liquid and oysters aside.

2 In Dutch oven or large saucepan, cook bell pepper and onions in margarine until tender. Stir in flour, salt and pepper. Cook over medium heat for 1 minute, stirring constantly.

3 Gradually stir in half-and-half, milk and reserved oyster liquid. Add potatoes and hot pepper sauce; mix well. Cook over medium heat until slightly thickened and potatoes are tender, stirring frequently.

4 Stir in oysters and spinach. Cook over medium heat until thoroughly heated, stirring frequently.

Nutrition Information Per Serving			
Serving Size: 1½ Cups			
Calories	380	Calories from Fat	220
		% Daily Value	
Total Fat	24 g	37%	
Saturated	12 g	60%	
Cholesterol	85 mg	28%	
Sodium	520 mg	22%	
Total Carbohydrate	26 g	9%	
Dietary Fiber	1 g	4%	
Sugars	12 g		
Protein	14 g		
Vitamin A	45%	Vitamin C	30%
Calcium	30%	Iron	25%

Dietary Exchanges: 1½ Starch, 1½ Lean Meat, 4 Fat OR
1½ Carbohydrate, 1½ Lean Meat, 4 Fat

BARBECUED BEEF IN BUNS

prep time: 20 min. (ready in 4 hr. 5 min.) • yield: 24 sandwiches

In the South, barbecued meats cook slowly over a wood fire until they're fork-tender and steeped in flavor. In this stovetop version, long, slow simmering yields a similar result.

1 (4-lb.) boneless beef chuck roast, trimmed of fat

4 cups water

½ cup firmly packed brown sugar

2 tablespoons dry mustard

½ teaspoon pepper

⅓ cup vinegar

2 cups ketchup

2 tablespoons Worcestershire sauce

24 sandwich buns, split

1 Place roast in Dutch oven; add water. Bring to a boil. Reduce heat to low; cover and simmer 2 to 3 hours or until tender.

2 Drain beef, reserving 3 cups liquid. Shred beef; return to Dutch oven. Add brown sugar, mustard, pepper, vinegar and reserved 3 cups liquid. Bring to a boil. Reduce heat to low; cover and simmer 20 minutes.

3 Add ketchup and Worcestershire sauce to beef mixture. Simmer, uncovered, for 20 to 25 minutes or until of desired consistency. Serve ⅓ cup beef mixture in each bun.

Nutrition Information Per Serving
Serving Size: 1 Sandwich

Calories	240	Calories from Fat	45
		% Daily Value	
Total Fat	5 g	8%	
Saturated	2 g	10%	
Cholesterol	35 mg	12%	
Sodium	550 mg	23%	
Total Carbohydrate	33 g	11%	
Dietary Fiber	1 g	4%	
Sugars	12 g		
Protein	15 g		
Vitamin A	4%	Vitamin C	4%
Calcium	8%	Iron	15%

Dietary Exchanges: 1½ Starch, ½ Fruit, 1½ Lean Meat
OR 2 Carbohydrate, 1½ Lean Meat

SLOPPY JOE TURNOVERS

prep time: 20 min. (ready in 40 min.) • yield: 5 sandwiches

Part of the pleasure of sloppy Joes is the way the saucy beef soaks into the bread. Serve these turnovers with a knife and fork.

½ lb. lean ground beef

2 tablespoons chopped onion

¼ cup ketchup

2 tablespoons sour cream

¼ teaspoon salt

⅛ teaspoon garlic powder

1 (6-oz.) can refrigerated buttermilk flaky biscuits

1 Heat oven to 375°F. In large skillet, brown ground beef and onion until beef is thoroughly cooked. Drain. Stir in ketchup, sour cream, salt and garlic powder. Simmer 2 minutes.

2 Separate dough into 5 biscuits. Press or roll each biscuit into a 4 × 4-inch square. Place about ¼ cup beef mixture on center of each square. Fold over one corner of each biscuit to form triangles; seal edges firmly with fork. Place on ungreased cookie sheet. Cut two ½-inch slits in top of each.

3 Bake at 375°F. for 12 to 18 minutes or until golden brown.

Nutrition Information Per Serving
Serving Size: 1 Sandwich

Calories	220	Calories from Fat	110
		% Daily Value	
Total Fat	12 g	18%	
Saturated	4 g	20%	
Cholesterol	30 mg	10%	
Sodium	640 mg	27%	
Total Carbohydrate	18 g	6%	
Dietary Fiber	1 g	3%	
Sugars	3 g		
Protein	11 g		
Vitamin A	4%	Vitamin C	2%
Calcium	2%	Iron	8%

Dietary Exchanges: 1 Starch, 1 Lean Meat, 2 Fat OR 1 Carbohydrate, 1 Lean Meat, 2 Fat

TORTILLA-WRAPPED MEXICAN SANDWICHES

prep time: 20 min. • yield: 6 sandwiches

Because they can be made in advance and are more interesting than plain meat-on-bread, these Mexican sandwiches make good party fare. Serve one per person or slice them into several pieces for party-tray appetizers.

6 (8-inch) flour tortillas

1 (6-oz.) container frozen avocado dip, thawed

1 (3-oz.) pkg. cream cheese, softened

8 oz. thinly sliced cooked roast beef or turkey

6 leaves leaf lettuce

4 oz. (1 cup) shredded Monterey Jack cheese

1 cup alfalfa sprouts

1/3 cup salsa or taco sauce

1 Heat tortillas as directed on package. Meanwhile, in small bowl, combine avocado dip and cream cheese; blend well.

2 Spread avocado mixture evenly over each warm tortilla to within 1/2 inch of edge. Arrange beef, lettuce, cheese and sprouts over avocado mixture. Top with salsa. (If sandwiches are made ahead, omit salsa inside tortillas; serve as a dip with sandwiches.)

3 Roll up each tortilla; secure with toothpicks. Serve immediately, or wrap securely in plastic wrap and refrigerate until serving time.

Nutrition Information Per Serving
Serving Size: 1 Sandwich

Calories	370	Calories from Fat	180
		% Daily Value	
Total Fat	20 g	31%	
Saturated	10 g	50%	
Cholesterol	70 mg	23%	
Sodium	650 mg	27%	
Total Carbohydrate	24 g	8%	
Dietary Fiber	2 g	8%	
Sugars	2 g		
Protein	23 g		
Vitamin A	10%	Vitamin C	0%
Calcium	20%	Iron	15%

Dietary Exchanges: 1 1/2 Starch, 2 1/2 Lean Meat, 2 1/2 Fat OR
1 1/2 Carbohydrate, 2 1/2 Lean Meat, 2 1/2 Fat

LOW-FAT SANDWICH TOPPINGS

Improvise tortilla fillings to add flavor and crunch without piling on the calories:

- Bean or alfalfa sprouts
- Radicchio or other specialty lettuces
- Sliced cucumbers
- Thinly sliced onions, especially Vidalias and other sweet varieties
- Sliced tomatoes
- Shredded carrots
- Sliced radishes
- Thinly sliced fresh mushrooms
- Chopped hot or sweet cherry peppers
- Roasted bell peppers (not the kind packed in oil)
- Purchased coleslaw blend

Cook's Notes

ITALIAN MEATBALL SUBS

prep time: 40 min. • yield: 4 sandwiches

For uniformly sized meatballs, invest in a meatball maker. It's an inexpensive gadget that resembles tongs.

½ lb. ground beef

½ lb. bulk Italian pork sausage

¼ cup unseasoned dry bread or cracker crumbs

1 small onion, chopped

1 egg

1 (15-oz.) can pizza sauce

4 hoagie buns, split

4 oz. (1 cup) shredded mozzarella cheese

1 In medium bowl, combine ground beef, sausage, bread crumbs, onion and egg; mix well. Shape into 16 (1½-inch) balls.

2 In medium skillet, cook meatballs over medium heat for 5 minutes or until browned, turning frequently. Drain. Add pizza sauce. Reduce heat; cover and simmer 15 minutes or until meatballs are no longer pink in center.

3 Place 4 meatballs in each hoagie bun. Spoon sauce over meatballs. Sprinkle with cheese.

Nutrition Information Per Serving
Serving Size: 1 Sandwich

Calories	700	Calories from Fat	290
		% Daily Value	
Total Fat	32 g	49%	
Saturated	12 g	60%	
Cholesterol	135 mg	45%	
Sodium	1910 mg	80%	
Total Carbohydrate	65 g	22%	
Dietary Fiber	5 g	20%	
Sugars	9 g		
Protein	37 g		
Vitamin A	15%	Vitamin C	8%
Calcium	35%	Iron	30%

Dietary Exchanges: 4 Starch, 1 Vegetable, 2 Medium-Fat Meat, 3 Fat OR 4 Carbohydrate, 1 Vegetable, 3 Medium-Fat Meat, 3 Fat

HAWAIIAN HAM SALAD PITAS

prep time: 10 min. • yield: 6 sandwiches

A sweet glaze of pineapple and mustard is traditional with baked ham and these flavors work well for sandwiches, too. Fat-free mayonnaise and honey mustard bind the ingredients together nicely.

6 oz. 96% fat-free cooked ham, diced

1 (8-oz.) can pineapple tidbits in unsweetened juice, drained

½ cup chopped carrot

¼ cup fat-free mayonnaise or salad dressing

1 tablespoon honey mustard

3 (6-inch) pita (pocket) breads, halved

6 lettuce leaves

1 In medium bowl, combine all ingredients except pita breads and lettuce; mix well.

2 Line each pita bread half with lettuce leaf. Fill with scant ⅓ cup ham salad.

Nutrition Information Per Serving
Serving Size: 1 Sandwich

Calories	150	Calories from Fat	20
		% Daily Value	
Total Fat	2 g	3%	
Saturated	1 g	5%	
Cholesterol	15 mg	5%	
Sodium	730 mg	30%	
Total Carbohydrate	24 g	8%	
Dietary Fiber	2 g	8%	
Sugars	5 g		
Protein	9 g		
Vitamin A	60%	Vitamin C	8%
Calcium	4%	Iron	8%

Dietary Exchanges: 1 Starch, ½ Fruit, 1 Lean Meat OR 1½ Carbohydrate, 1 Lean Meat

CASHEW CHICKEN SANDWICH LOAF

prep time: 30 min. (ready in 2 hr. 30 min.) •
yield: 12 servings

Layers of bread and chicken salad with a cheesy topping make a pretty loaf that's a good choice for a spring luncheon buffet.

LOAF
1 (1-lb.) unsliced loaf whole wheat or
    white sandwich bread, crusts removed*

½ cup margarine or butter, softened

FILLING
2½ cups finely chopped cooked chicken

½ cup finely chopped celery

2 tablespoons finely chopped onion

½ cup chopped cashews

½ cup mayonnaise or salad dressing

¼ teaspoon salt

⅛ teaspoon pepper

TOPPING
2 (8-oz.) pkg. cream cheese, softened

½ cup half-and-half

1 Cut loaf lengthwise into 4 slices. Spread 3 slices with margarine. In small bowl, combine all filling ingredients; mix well. Spread ⅓ of filling over margarine on each slice of bread. Stack slices on serving plate, placing plain slice on top.

2 In large bowl, combine cream cheese and half-and-half; mix well. Spread over sides and top of loaf. Cover carefully with plastic wrap; refrigerate at least 2 hours.

3 Just before serving, garnish with chopped parsley and cashews, if desired. Store in refrigerator.

TIP: *Sandwich loaf can be made with alternating white and whole wheat slices; use remaining slices for a second sandwich loaf or other party sandwiches.

Nutrition Information Per Serving
Serving Size: 1/12 of Recipe

Calories	440	Calories from Fat	320
		% Daily Value	
Total Fat	35 g	54%	
Saturated	13 g	65%	
Cholesterol	75 mg	25%	
Sodium	490 mg	20%	
Total Carbohydrate	15 g	5%	
Dietary Fiber	2 g	8%	
Sugars	3 g		
Protein	15 g		
Vitamin A	20%	Vitamin C	0%
Calcium	8%	Iron	10%

Dietary Exchanges: 1 Starch, 1 ½ Lean Meat, 6 Fat OR 1 Carbohydrate,
1 ½ Lean Meat, 6 Fat

REDUCED-FAT CREAM CHEESE

To lower the fat content of recipes calling for cream cheese, look for reduced-fat versions in the supermarket's dairy section. Neufchâtel, known as the "cream cheese" of Switzerland and France, is also a good alternative. It's a soft, white unripened cheese that's good in desserts, dips, sauces and spreads. Though sometimes considered a lighter form of cream cheese, Neufchâtel is a variety all its own. American Neufchâtel contains less fat and more moisture than the European type. Find Neufchâtel in the dairy section along with the cream cheese.

SIZZLING SEAFOOD SANDWICHES

prep time: 15 min. • yield: 4 sandwiches

The deli comes to the rescue with prepared seafood salad that you can easily "doctor" to make an original and delicious sandwich. If you wish, garnish each portion with a sprig of fresh dill.

4 kaiser rolls, split

2 tablespoons margarine or butter, softened

½ teaspoon dried dill weed

2 cups seafood salad (from deli)

1 oz. (¼ cup) shredded fresh Parmesan cheese

¼ cup cocktail sauce, if desired

1 Spread cut sides of kaiser rolls with margarine; sprinkle with dill. Place on ungreased cookie sheet. Broil 4 to 6 inches from heat for 1 to 2 minutes or until lightly browned. Set top halves aside.

2 Spoon seafood salad onto bottom half of each roll. Sprinkle with cheese. Broil 1 to 2 minutes or until cheese is melted. Drizzle cocktail sauce over salad mixture. Cover with top halves of rolls.

Nutrition Information Per Serving
Serving Size: 1 Sandwich

Calories	480	Calories from Fat	230
		% Daily Value	
Total Fat	26 g	40%	
Saturated	5 g	25%	
Cholesterol	65 mg	22%	
Sodium	1260 mg	53%	
Total Carbohydrate	39 g	13%	
Dietary Fiber	3 g	12%	
Sugars	6 g		
Protein	22 g		
Vitamin A	10%	Vitamin C	6%
Calcium	25%	Iron	15%

Dietary Exchanges: 2 ½ Starch, 2 Very Lean Meat, 4 ½ Fat OR
2 ½ Carbohydrate, 2 Very Lean Meat, 4 ½ Fat

CHILE RELLEÑO GRILLED SANDWICHES

prep time: 20 min. • yield: 4 sandwiches

A cross between a Mexican stuffed pepper and the all-American grilled cheese sandwich, this zesty sandwich pairs nicely with a mug of soup.

1 (4-oz.) can whole green chiles, drained

8 slices white bread

4 (1-oz.) slices Monterey Jack cheese

4 (1-oz.) slices Cheddar cheese

3 tablespoons margarine or butter, softened

1 Heat electric skillet or griddle to 375° F. Cut each chile into 4 pieces.

2 To assemble sandwiches, top each of 4 slices of bread with 1 slice Monterey Jack cheese, ¼ of chiles and 1 slice Cheddar cheese. Top with remaining bread slices. Spread margarine on outside of each sandwich.

3 Grill sandwiches in skillet at 375° F. (medium heat) for 2 to 4 minutes on each side or until bread is golden brown and cheese is melted.

Nutrition Information Per Serving
Serving Size: 1 Sandwich

Calories	440	Calories from Fat	250
		% Daily Value	
Total Fat	28 g	43%	
Saturated	13 g	65%	
Cholesterol	55 mg	18%	
Sodium	700 mg	29%	
Total Carbohydrate	27 g	9%	
Dietary Fiber	1 g	4%	
Sugars	4 g		
Protein	19 g		
Vitamin A	20%	Vitamin C	60%
Calcium	50%	Iron	10%

Dietary Exchanges: 2 Starch, 2 High-Fat Meat, 2 Fat OR 2 Carbohydrate,
2 High-Fat Meat, 2 Fat

Dilled Cream Cheese Garden Sandwiches

DILLED CREAM CHEESE GARDEN SANDWICHES

prep time: 10 min. • yield: 4 sandwiches

The cream cheese/yogurt spread, enhanced with pecans and dill, doubles as a dip for crackers, pita triangles or raw vegetables.

4 oz. cream cheese, softened

2 tablespoons plain yogurt

¼ cup chopped pecans

2 tablespoons chopped fresh dill or
    2 teaspoons dried dill weed

¼ teaspoon pepper

⅛ teaspoon salt

8 slices whole grain bread

1 cup loosely packed fresh spinach leaves

4 oz. thinly sliced Cheddar cheese

1 cup thinly sliced cucumber

1 tomato, thinly sliced

1 cup alfalfa sprouts

1 In small bowl, combine cream cheese and yogurt; blend until smooth. Stir in pecans, dill, pepper and salt.

2 Spread about 1½ tablespoons mixture on each slice of bread. Top 4 slices of bread with spinach, cheese, cucumber, tomato and sprouts. Cover with remaining slices of bread.

Nutrition Information Per Serving
Serving Size: 1 Sandwich

Calories	430	Calories from Fat	230
		% Daily Value	
Total Fat	26 g	40%	
Saturated	13 g	65%	
Cholesterol	60 mg	20%	
Sodium	600 mg	25%	
Total Carbohydrate	31 g	10%	
Dietary Fiber	5 g	20%	
Sugars	5 g		
Protein	17 g		
Vitamin A	40%	Vitamin C	25%
Calcium	30%	Iron	20%

Dietary Exchanges: 2 Starch, ½ Vegetable, 1½ High-Fat Meat, 2½ Fat OR 2 Carbohydrate, ½ Vegetable, 1½ High-Fat Meat, 2½ Fat

VEGGIE BAGEL SANDWICHES

prep time: 10 min. • yield: 4 sandwiches

Enjoy these toppings on a flavored bagel such as sun-dried tomato or onion.

4 oz. garden vegetable cream cheese
    spread

4 large soft bagels, split

1 tomato, thinly sliced

½ medium green bell pepper, thinly sliced

½ medium cucumber, thinly sliced

1 cup alfalfa sprouts

Spread cream cheese spread evenly on cut sides of bagels. Top bottom halves of bagels with tomato, bell pepper, cucumber and sprouts. Cover with top halves of bagels.

Nutrition Information Per Serving
Serving Size: 1 Sandwich

Calories	350	Calories from Fat	100
		% Daily Value	
Total Fat	11 g	17%	
Saturated	6 g	30%	
Cholesterol	30 mg	10%	
Sodium	580 mg	24%	
Total Carbohydrate	51 g	17%	
Dietary Fiber	3 g	12%	
Sugars	3 g		
Protein	12 g		
Vitamin A	15%	Vitamin C	25%
Calcium	10%	Iron	20%

Dietary Exchanges: 3 Starch, 1 Vegetable, 2 Fat OR 3 Carbohydrate, 1 Vegetable, 2 Fat

FRESH VEGETABLE-EGG SALAD POCKETS

prep time: 25 min. (ready in 1 hr. 25 min.) •
yield: 4 sandwiches

Put the "salad" back in "egg salad" with a mixture of crisp and crunchy fresh vegetables seasoned with dill.

4 eggs

½ cup thinly sliced celery

½ cup shredded carrot

½ cup sliced zucchini

2 tablespoons sliced green onions

⅓ cup reduced-calorie mayonnaise or
salad dressing

1 tablespoon chopped fresh dill or
1 teaspoon dried dill weed

1 teaspoon Dijon mustard

⅛ teaspoon salt

2 (6-inch) pita (pocket) breads, halved

Lettuce leaves

1 Place eggs in medium saucepan; cover with cold water. Bring to a boil. Reduce heat; simmer about 15 minutes. Immediately drain; run cold water over eggs to stop cooking. Peel eggs and chop; place in medium bowl.

2 Add all remaining ingredients except pita breads and lettuce; mix well. Cover; refrigerate at least 1 hour to blend flavors.

3 To serve, line each pita bread half with lettuce; fill each with about ½ cup egg mixture.

Nutrition Information Per Serving
Serving Size: 1 Sandwich

Calories	240	Calories from Fat	110
		% Daily Value	
Total Fat	12 g	18%	
Saturated	3 g	15%	
Cholesterol	220 mg	73%	
Sodium	490 mg	20%	
Total Carbohydrate	22 g	7%	
Dietary Fiber	2 g	8%	
Sugars	2 g		
Protein	10 g		
Vitamin A	90%	Vitamin C	10%
Calcium	6%	Iron	10%

Dietary Exchanges: 1½ Starch, 1 Medium-Fat Meat, 1 Fat OR
1½ Carbohydrate, 1 Medium-Fat Meat, 1 Fat

FRENCH BLT SANDWICHES

prep time: 10 min. • yield: 4 sandwiches

Brie is a particularly good cheese for warm sandwiches because it melts very smoothly and isn't stringy.

4 oz. Brie cheese, cut into ¼-inch slices

4 French rolls or mini baguettes, split
lengthwise, toasted

4 tomato slices

Leaf lettuce

1 Place ¼ of the cheese on bottom half of each toasted roll. Place on ungreased cookie sheet.

2 Broil 4 to 6 inches from heat for 1 to 2 minutes or until cheese is melted. Top with tomato slices, lettuce leaves and top halves of rolls.

Nutrition Information Per Serving
Serving Size: 1 Sandwich

Calories	200	Calories from Fat	80
		% Daily Value	
Total Fat	9 g	14%	
Saturated	5 g	25%	
Cholesterol	30 mg	10%	
Sodium	410 mg	17%	
Total Carbohydrate	21 g	7%	
Dietary Fiber	1 g	4%	
Sugars	2 g		
Protein	9 g		
Vitamin A	10%	Vitamin C	6%
Calcium	8%	Iron	6%

Dietary Exchanges: 1½ Starch, 1 High-Fat Meat OR 1½ Carbohydrate,
1 High-Fat Meat

French BLT Sandwiches

Corn-Stuffed Zucchini, page 238, and Spicy Corn and Black Beans, page 237

VEGETABLES & SIDE DISHES

EVERYONE KNOWS THAT VEGETABLES ARE GOOD FOR YOU—HERE'S HOW TO MAKE THEM ESPECIALLY GOOD TASTING, TOO. SPICES AND GLAZES PLAY UP THE NATURAL SWEETNESS OF CARROTS, ACORN SQUASH AND MORE, WHILE GARLIC, SAVORY HERBS AND CITRUS ACCENT THE STRONGER FLAVORS OF BROCCOLI, EGGPLANT AND ASPARAGUS. YOU'LL ALSO FIND AN ASSORTMENT OF HEARTY SIDES FEATURING POTATOES, PASTA AND RICE.

229

LEMON-BUTTERED ASPARAGUS

prep time: 20 min. • yield: 4 servings

Hints of lemon and butter bring out the flavor of this springtime vegetable. Save leftover asparagus to cut up and toss with a green salad or sprinkle with vinaigrette for a sandwich topper.

1 lb. fresh asparagus

3 tablespoons butter

1 tablespoon lemon juice

½ teaspoon grated lemon peel

1 Snap off tough ends of asparagus. Rinse spears thoroughly to remove any sand from tips. In large skillet, combine asparagus spears and ½ cup water. Bring to a boil over medium heat. Cook 5 to 10 minutes or until crisp-tender. Drain.

Lemon-Buttered
Asparagus

2 Meanwhile, melt butter in small saucepan. Stir in lemon juice and lemon peel.

3 Place asparagus on serving platter; pour butter mixture over spears. Garnish as desired.

Nutrition Information Per Serving
Serving Size: ¼ of Recipe

Calories	110	Calories from Fat	80
		% Daily Value	
Total Fat	9 g	14%	
Saturated	5 g	25%	
Cholesterol	25 mg	8%	
Sodium	90 mg	4%	
Total Carbohydrate	5 g	2%	
Dietary Fiber	2 g	8%	
Sugars	2 g		
Protein	2 g		
Vitamin A	20%	Vitamin C	15%
Calcium	2%	Iron	4%

Dietary Exchanges: 1 Vegetable, 2 Fat

ASPARAGUS

When purchasing asparagus, look for straight, bright green spears that are firm and crisp. Tips should be tightly closed and dry, with stem ends moist. Asparagus stalks vary in thickness; whether you choose thick or thin is a matter of personal preference. Thickness does not correspond to sweetness or quality. Purchase spears of uniform thickness to ensure even cooking.

Refrigerate asparagus, set upright if possible, in a container holding an inch of water; cover the container loosely with a plastic bag or plastic wrap. Or, wrap stem ends in wet paper towels and place the asparagus in a plastic bag in the refrigerator.

COOK'S KNOW-HOW
HOW TO MICROWAVE ASPARAGUS

When asparagus pushes its bright green tips up through the soil, it is crisp, tender and succulent. But overcooking can make this fabulous spring veggie pale and limp. To keep asparagus as fresh as a spring day, follow these two simple cooking steps.

STEP 1

Just before cooking, cut or snap off tough ends of asparagus. Rinse spears thoroughly to remove any sand from tips.

STEP 2

Arrange spears with their tips toward the center in a 12 × 8-inch or 2-quart microwave-safe dish. Add ¼ cup water and cover with microwave-safe plastic wrap. Microwave on HIGH for 4 to 8 minutes or until asparagus is crisp-tender. Rearrange spears once during cooking. Drain.

Broccoli Two-Pepper Stir-Fry

BROCCOLI TWO-PEPPER STIR-FRY

prep time: 20 min. • yield: 8 (½-cup) servings

Garlic, ginger and soy lend some bite to broccoli and peppers. Cook the broccoli just until it is crisp-tender and serve the dish right away for the brightest color.

- 1 tablespoon oil
- 3 cups bite-sized fresh broccoli florets
- ½ teaspoon minced gingerroot
- 1 garlic clove, minced
- 2 tablespoons water
- 1 small red bell pepper, cut into ¼-inch strips
- 1 small yellow bell pepper, cut into ¼-inch strips
- 1 tablespoon reduced-sodium soy sauce

1 Heat oil in large skillet or wok over medium-high heat until hot. Add broccoli, gingerroot and garlic; cook and stir 1 minute.

2 Add water; cover and cook 2 minutes. Add bell peppers; cook and stir 1 minute. Stir in soy sauce.

Nutrition Information Per Serving
Serving Size: ½ Cup

Calories	35	Calories from Fat	20
		% Daily Value	
Total Fat	2 g	3%	
Saturated	0 g	0%	
Cholesterol	0 mg	0%	
Sodium	90 mg	4%	
Total Carbohydrate	3 g	1%	
Dietary Fiber	1 g	4%	
Sugars	1 g		
Protein	1 g		
Vitamin A	25%	Vitamin C	60%
Calcium	0%	Iron	2%

Dietary Exchanges: ½ Vegetable, ½ Fat

PEAS AND MUSHROOMS

prep time: 10 min. • yield: 5 (½-cup) servings

Instead of being boiled, frozen peas are defrosted, then sautéed with mushrooms, onion, celery and pimientos.

- 2 tablespoons margarine or butter
- ¼ cup chopped celery
- 2 tablespoons finely chopped onion
- 1 (2.5-oz.) jar sliced mushrooms, drained
- 2 cups frozen sweet peas, thawed*
- 1 (2-oz.) jar diced pimientos, drained

1 Melt margarine in medium saucepan over medium heat. Stir in celery and onion; cook 3 to 4 minutes or until crisp-tender.

2 Stir in all remaining ingredients; cook 3 to 5 minutes or until thoroughly heated.

TIP: *To quickly thaw peas, place in colander or strainer; rinse with warm water until thawed. Drain well.

Nutrition Information Per Serving
Serving Size: ½ Cup

Calories	100	Calories from Fat	45
		% Daily Value	
Total Fat	5 g	8%	
Saturated	1 g	5%	
Cholesterol	0 mg	0%	
Sodium	180 mg	8%	
Total Carbohydrate	10 g	3%	
Dietary Fiber	3 g	12%	
Sugars	2 g		
Protein	3 g		
Vitamin A	15%	Vitamin C	20%
Calcium	0%	Iron	6%

Dietary Exchanges: ½ Starch, 1 Vegetable, 1 Fat OR ½ Carbohydrate, 1 Vegetable, 1 Fat

GREEN BEANS WITH ROASTED RED PEPPERS

prep time: 20 min. • yield: 4 (⅔-cup) servings

Southern cooks often enhance vegetables with bacon or other types of pork. Old-fashioned recipes called for cooking the vegetables until they were practically mush. Here, the beans cook until just tender, retaining their color and character.

2 slices bacon, cut into ½-inch pieces

2 cups cut (1-inch) fresh green beans (8 oz.)

¼ cup chopped shallots

2 tablespoons chopped roasted red bell peppers (from 7.25-oz. jar)

1 In medium skillet over medium heat, cook bacon until crisp. Remove bacon from skillet; drain on paper towels.

2 Reserve 1 tablespoon drippings in skillet. Add green beans and shallots; cover and cook 8 to 10 minutes or until beans are tender, stirring occasionally. Stir in roasted peppers; sprinkle with cooked bacon.

Nutrition Information Per Serving
Serving Size: ⅔ Cup

Calories	80	Calories from Fat	45
		% Daily Value	
Total Fat	5 g	8%	
Saturated	2 g	10%	
Cholesterol	5 mg	2%	
Sodium	55 mg	2%	
Total Carbohydrate	6 g	2%	
Dietary Fiber	2 g	8%	
Sugars	2 g		
Protein	2 g		
Vitamin A	15%	Vitamin C	20%
Calcium	2%	Iron	4%

Dietary Exchanges: 1 Vegetable, 1 Fat

SHALLOTS

Shallots have been referred to as the aristocrats of the onion family. The bulbs have several distinct cloves, similar to garlic bulbs. Their flavor, somewhere between that of onion and garlic, is often described as sophisticated. Shallots are used successfully in sauces because their flavor is more delicate and their texture more tender than either onion or garlic.

APRICOT-GLAZED CARROTS

prep time: 15 min. • yield: 8 (½-cup) servings

Melted apricot preserves transform cooked julienned carrots into an elegant side dish.

5 cups julienne-cut (2 × ⅛ × ⅛-inch) carrots

¼ teaspoon salt

¼ cup apricot preserves

1 In medium saucepan, combine carrots and ¾ cup water; bring to a boil. Reduce heat to low; cover and simmer until carrots are tender. Drain.

2 Add salt and apricot preserves; stir to coat. Cook over low heat for 1 to 2 minutes or until thoroughly heated.

Nutrition Information Per Serving
Serving Size: ½ Cup

Calories	60	Calories from Fat	0
		% Daily Value	
Total Fat	0 g	0%	
Saturated	0 g	0%	
Cholesterol	0 mg	0%	
Sodium	100 mg	4%	
Total Carbohydrate	14 g	5%	
Dietary Fiber	2 g	8%	
Sugars	10 g		
Protein	1 g		
Vitamin A	430%	Vitamin C	10%
Calcium	2%	Iron	2%

Dietary Exchanges: ½ Fruit, 1 Vegetable OR ½ Carbohydrate, 1 Vegetable

STEAMED VEGETABLES WITH CHILE-LIME BUTTER

prep time: 20 min. • yield: 6 (¾-cup) servings

The outer layer of citrus peel contains oils that contribute intense bursts of flavor. A fine-holed grater or citrus zester (a tool similar to a vegetable peeler but with several small sharp holes instead of a long blade) makes short work of removing the peel. Don't include the white pith underneath, which is bitter.

- 2 tablespoons butter

- 1 small garlic clove, minced

- 1 teaspoon grated lime peel

- 1 teaspoon finely chopped serrano or jalapeño chile

- 1 tablespoon fresh lime juice

- 3 cups cut-up fresh vegetables (such as broccoli florets, cauliflower florets and/or sliced carrots)

1 Melt butter in small saucepan over low heat. Add garlic; cook and stir about 20 seconds. Add lime peel, chile and lime juice; mix well. Set aside.

2 Place steamer basket in large saucepan. Add 1 cup water; bring to a boil. Add cut-up vegetables to basket; cook 4 to 5 minutes or until crisp-tender.

3 To serve, place vegetables in serving bowl. Add butter mixture; toss gently to coat.

Nutrition Information Per Serving
Serving Size: ¾ Cup

Calories	60	Calories from Fat	35
		% Daily Value	
Total Fat	4 g	6%	
Saturated	2 g	10%	
Cholesterol	10 mg	3%	
Sodium	55 mg	2%	
Total Carbohydrate	4 g	1%	
Dietary Fiber	1 g	4%	
Sugars	2 g		
Protein	1 g		
Vitamin A	130%	Vitamin C	30%
Calcium	0%	Iron	0%

Dietary Exchanges: 1 Vegetable, 1 Fat

STEAMING VEGETABLES

Steaming is a healthy, easy way to cook fresh vegetables. The technique requires no added fat, and vitamins remain in the vegetables instead of leaching into the water, as can happen with boiling.

There are two main types of "add on" steamers designed for stovetop use. Collapsible metal steamers, available in houseware stores or kitchenware departments, expand to fit the saucepan. Bamboo steamers, sold in Asian markets and houseware stores, look like round baskets and fit over a skillet or inside a wok. They usually come as a set of two baskets that can be stacked, with denser foods cooking in the bottom closest to the heat and more delicate foods on the top.

Bring the water underneath the steamer to a boil before adding food to the basket, then cover the pot and cook until the vegetables are crisp-tender and still brightly colored. The timing will depend on the density and size of the vegetables.

Cook's Notes

ZUCCHINI WITH TOMATOES AND BASIL

prep time: 15 min. • yield: 5 (½-cup) servings

In summer, when gardens are overflowing with produce, make this dish with fresh tomatoes. In winter, substitute canned plum tomatoes.

4 small zucchini (½ lb.), cut into ½-inch-thick slices

1 cup coarsely chopped tomatoes

2 tablespoons chopped fresh basil

¼ teaspoon salt

⅛ teaspoon pepper

2 teaspoons lemon juice

2 tablespoons shredded fresh Parmesan cheese, if desired

1 In medium saucepan, combine zucchini and ¼ cup water. Cook over medium heat for 3 to 4 minutes or until crisp-tender. Drain well.

2 Add tomatoes, basil, salt, pepper and lemon juice; mix well. Cook and stir about 1 minute or until thoroughly heated. Sprinkle with cheese.

Nutrition Information Per Serving
Serving Size: ½ Cup

Calories	30	Calories from Fat	10
		% Daily Value	
Total Fat	1 g	2%	
Saturated	0 g	0%	
Cholesterol	0 mg	0%	
Sodium	150 mg	6%	
Total Carbohydrate	3 g	1%	
Dietary Fiber	1 g	4%	
Sugars	2 g		
Protein	2 g		
Vitamin A	8%	Vitamin C	15%
Calcium	4%	Iron	2%

Dietary Exchanges: 1 Vegetable

Zucchini with Tomatoes and Basil

SPICY CORN AND BLACK BEANS

prep time: 15 min. • yield: 6 (½-cup) servings

PICTURED ON PAGE 228

Here's a colorful vegetable dish laced with Southwestern flavors. In summer, substitute 1½ cups cooked fresh sweet-corn kernels for the canned corn.

1 tablespoon oil

½ cup chopped onion

1 (11-oz.) can vacuum-packed whole kernel corn, undrained

1 (15-oz.) can black beans, drained, rinsed

1 (4.5-oz.) can chopped green chiles, undrained

1 tablespoon chopped fresh cilantro

1 teaspoon cumin

¼ teaspoon salt

⅛ teaspoon crushed red pepper flakes

1 Heat oil in large saucepan over medium–high heat until hot. Add onion; cook 2 to 3 minutes or until onion is tender, stirring occasionally.

2 Add all remaining ingredients; mix well. Reduce heat to medium; cook 3 to 4 minutes or until thoroughly heated, stirring occasionally.

Nutrition Information Per Serving
Serving Size: ½ Cup

Calories	140	Calories from Fat	25
		% Daily Value	
Total Fat	3 g	5%	
Saturated	1 g	5%	
Cholesterol	0 mg	0%	
Sodium	470 mg	20%	
Total Carbohydrate	22 g	7%	
Dietary Fiber	5 g	20%	
Sugars	4 g		
Protein	5 g		
Vitamin A	0%	Vitamin C	8%
Calcium	4%	Iron	8%

Dietary Exchanges: 1½ Starch, ½ Fat OR 1½ Carbohydrate, ½ Fat

SCALLOPED CORN

prep time: 20 min. (ready in 1 hr.) • yield: 6 (½-cup) servings

A family favorite, this custard-style corn casserole is also a good choice for guests. It's easily made with canned cream-style corn.

¼ cup margarine or butter

½ cup chopped onion

1 green bell pepper, chopped

1 (15-oz.) can cream-style corn

½ cup Italian-style dry bread crumbs

2 eggs, beaten

1 Heat oven to 375°F. Grease 1-quart casserole. Melt margarine in medium saucepan over medium heat. Add onion and bell pepper; cook 3 to 4 minutes or until crisp-tender.

2 Stir in all remaining ingredients. Pour into greased casserole.

3 Bake at 375°F. for 35 to 40 minutes or until knife inserted in center comes out clean.

Nutrition Information Per Serving
Serving Size: ½ Cup

Calories	200	Calories from Fat	90
		% Daily Value	
Total Fat	10 g	15%	
Saturated	2 g	10%	
Cholesterol	70 mg	23%	
Sodium	610 mg	25%	
Total Carbohydrate	22 g	7%	
Dietary Fiber	2 g	8%	
Sugars	8 g		
Protein	5 g		
Vitamin A	10%	Vitamin C	15%
Calcium	2%	Iron	4%

Dietary Exchanges: 1 Starch, 1 Vegetable, 2 Fat OR 1 Carbohydrate, 1 Vegetable, 2 Fat

CORN-STUFFED ZUCCHINI

prep time: 15 min. (ready in 45 min.) • yield: 8 servings

PICTURED ON PAGE 228

Tangy feta cheese and sweet-corn kernels combine to make a zesty filling for hollowed-out zucchini "boats."

4 medium zucchini, cut in half lengthwise

½ cup chopped onion

2½ oz. (½ cup) crumbled feta cheese or shredded farmer cheese

1 (11-oz.) can vacuum-packed whole kernel corn with red and green peppers

1⅓ oz. (⅓ cup) shredded Cheddar cheese

1 Heat oven to 375°F. Using teaspoon, scoop out zucchini seeds and pulp, leaving a ¼- to ⅓-inch wall. Chop ½ cup of the zucchini pulp.

2 In medium bowl, combine zucchini pulp, onion, feta cheese and corn; mix well. Spoon about ¼ cup mixture into each zucchini half, mounding slightly. Place stuffed zucchini in ungreased 13 × 9-inch pan.

3 Bake at 375°F. for 25 to 30 minutes or until stuffing is thoroughly heated and zucchini is crisp-tender. Sprinkle with Cheddar cheese. Bake an additional 1 to 2 minutes or until cheese is melted.

Nutrition Information Per Serving
Serving Size: ⅛ of Recipe

Calories	100	Calories from Fat	35
		% Daily Value	
Total Fat	4 g	6%	
Saturated	2 g	10%	
Cholesterol	15 mg	5%	
Sodium	350 mg	15%	
Total Carbohydrate	11 g	4%	
Dietary Fiber	2 g	8%	
Sugars	5 g		
Protein	4 g		
Vitamin A	8%	Vitamin C	10%
Calcium	10%	Iron	4%

Dietary Exchanges: ½ Starch, 1 Vegetable, ½ Fat OR ½ Carbohydrate, 1 Vegetable, ½ Fat

CORN ON THE COB WITH TACO BUTTER

prep time: 25 min. • yield: 6 servings

Cooked on the grill, corn on the cob takes on smoky, chewy goodness. Double the recipe and toss leftover kernels with pasta salad or stir into homemade salsa.

⅓ cup butter, melted

2 tablespoons chopped fresh cilantro

1 tablespoon 40%-less-sodium taco seasoning mix (from 1¼-oz. pkg.)

6 ears corn, husks removed, cleaned and dried

1 GRILL DIRECTIONS: Heat grill. In small bowl, combine melted butter, cilantro and taco seasoning mix; mix well. Brush each ear of corn with butter mixture.

2 When ready to grill, place corn on gas grill over medium heat or on charcoal grill 4 to 6 inches from medium-high coals. Cook 15 to 18 minutes or until tender, turning and brushing frequently with butter mixture.

TIP: To broil corn, place on broiler pan; broil 4 to 6 inches from heat using times above as a guide.

Nutrition Information Per Serving
Serving Size: ⅙ of Recipe

Calories	140	Calories from Fat	35
		% Daily Value	
Total Fat	4 g	6%	
Saturated	2 g	10%	
Cholesterol	5 mg	2%	
Sodium	60 mg	3%	
Total Carbohydrate	23 g	8%	
Dietary Fiber	3 g	12%	
Sugars	2 g		
Protein	3 g		
Vitamin A	6%	Vitamin C	6%
Calcium	0%	Iron	4%

Dietary Exchanges: 1½ Starch, ½ Fat OR 1½ Carbohydrate, ½ Fat

SWISS VEGETABLE CASSEROLE

prep time: 20 min. (ready in 50 min.) • yield: 8 (½-cup) servings

Shredded Swiss cheese enriches this variation on the classic white sauce made with butter, flour and milk. Topped with crushed crackers and more cheese, this casserole bakes in the oven until bubbly and golden.

2 tablespoons margarine or butter

6 green onions, cut into ½-inch pieces (½ cup)

2 tablespoons all-purpose flour

¼ teaspoon salt

⅛ teaspoon pepper

1½ cups milk

4 oz. (1 cup) shredded Swiss cheese

1 (1-lb.) pkg. frozen broccoli florets, carrots and cauliflower, cooked, drained

¼ cup crushed round buttery crackers

1 Heat oven to 350°F. Grease 1- to 1½-quart casserole. Melt margarine in medium saucepan over medium heat. Add onions; cook and stir 2 to 3 minutes or until tender.

2 Stir in flour, salt and pepper; mix well. Gradually add milk, stirring constantly. Cook and stir until mixture is bubbly and thickened. Remove from heat.

3 Add ¾ cup of the cheese; stir until melted. Stir in cooked vegetables. Spoon mixture into greased casserole. Sprinkle with crushed crackers and remaining ¼ cup cheese.

4 Bake at 350°F. for 25 to 30 minutes or until topping is golden brown and casserole is bubbly.

Nutrition Information Per Serving
Serving Size: ½ Cup

Calories	130	Calories from Fat	50
		% Daily Value	
Total Fat	6 g	9%	
Saturated	2 g	10%	
Cholesterol	10 mg	3%	
Sodium	190 mg	8%	
Total Carbohydrate	10 g	3%	
Dietary Fiber	2 g	8%	
Sugars	4 g		
Protein	8 g		
Vitamin A	50%	Vitamin C	15%
Calcium	25%	Iron	4%

Dietary Exchanges: 2 Vegetable, ½ High-Fat Meat, ½ Fat

VEGETABLE AND HERB PAIRINGS

Is your garden overflowing with summer vegetables and fresh herbs? Here are ideas for compatible pairings:

- Basil—asparagus, beans, broccoli, cabbage, carrots, celery, cucumbers, eggplant, onions, peas, potatoes, spinach, squash
- Chives—artichokes, asparagus, carrots, cauliflower, corn, onions, peas, potatoes, spinach, tomatoes
- Cilantro—corn, peppers, squash, sweet potatoes, tomatoes
- Dill—beets, cabbage, carrots, cauliflower, celery, green beans, parsnips, peas, potatoes
- Parsley—beets, cabbage, carrots, cauliflower, celery, eggplant, onions, potatoes, tomatoes, turnips
- Tarragon—asparagus, beets, carrots, green beans, mushrooms, onions, potatoes
- Thyme—asparagus, beets, carrots, green beans, onion, potatoes, squash

Cook's Notes

MIXED VEGETABLE GRILL

prep time: 30 min. • yield: 6 servings

Pattypan squash, mushrooms and bell peppers marinate in purchased Italian dressing before being grilled or broiled to perfection.

- 6 pattypan squash (about 2 inches in diameter)
- 3 medium red, green or yellow bell peppers, halved lengthwise, seeded
- 6 jumbo mushrooms
- 1 (8-oz.) bottle Italian salad dressing

1 GRILL DIRECTIONS: Place all ingredients in resealable food storage plastic bag or ungreased 13 × 9-inch (3-quart) baking dish; turn vegetables to coat all sides. Seal bag or cover dish. Let stand at room temperature for at least 1 hour to marinate, turning vegetables occasionally.

2 Heat grill. When ready to grill, drain vegetables, reserving marinade. Place vegetables on gas grill over medium heat or on charcoal grill 4 to 6 inches from medium coals. Cook vegetables 10 to 15 minutes or until crisp-tender, turning occasionally and brushing frequently with marinade.

TIP: To broil vegetables, place on broiler pan; broil 4 to 6 inches from heat using times above as a guide.

Mixed Vegetable Grill

Nutrition Information Per Serving
Serving Size: 1/6 of Recipe

Calories	220	Calories from Fat	170
		% Daily Value	
Total Fat	19 g	29%	
Saturated	3 g	15%	
Cholesterol	0 mg	0%	
Sodium	300 mg	13%	
Total Carbohydrate	10 g	3%	
Dietary Fiber	2 g	8%	
Sugars	7 g		
Protein	2 g		
Vitamin A	45%	Vitamin C	90%
Calcium	0%	Iron	4%

Dietary Exchanges: 1/2 Starch, 1 Vegetable, 3 1/2 Fat OR 1/2 Carbohydrate, 1 Vegetable, 3 1/2 Fat

PORTABLE COOKING

It's a truism of summer cooking that everything tastes better when cooked on a grill, and sometimes you can heighten the fun by grilling away from home, too. When camping or picnicking in a new area, check to make sure fires are allowed. If fireplaces, firepits or firewood are not available, several options exist:

- Hibachis and small portable grills can be packed for making charcoal fires. A hibachi is a small cast iron container with a grill on top. It's good for cooking small amounts of food at a time because grill space is limited. Bring along charcoal, lighter fluid and matches.

- Kits containing a disposable foil container, grill and charcoal briquettes are also available in larger supermarkets. This is a convenient and an economical way to try out camping or outdoor cooking.

- Folding camp stoves (a good investment for those who camp often) are compact and easy to tote. These stoves use liquid fuel, and most of them have two burners that function like conventional gas burners, allowing you to cook with regular pots and pans.

SLOW-COOKED BEANS

prep time: 15 min. (ready in 8 hr. 15 min.) •
yield: 18 (1/2-cup) servings

These baked beans made with canned beans come together quickly, then the slow cooker steps in and blends the flavors over six or more hours.

1/2 lb. bacon, diced

1/2 cup firmly packed brown sugar

1/4 cup cornstarch

1 teaspoon dry mustard

1/2 cup molasses

1 tablespoon vinegar

4 (16-oz.) cans baked beans

1 medium onion, chopped

1 green bell pepper, chopped

1 In large skillet over medium heat, cook bacon until crisp. Drain, reserving 2 tablespoons drippings.

2 In 3 1/2- to 4-quart slow cooker, combine bacon, reserved drippings and all remaining ingredients; mix well. Cover; cook on high setting for 1 hour.

3 Reduce heat to low setting; cook an additional 5 to 7 hours.

Nutrition Information Per Serving
Serving Size: 1/2 Cup

Calories	180	Calories from Fat	20
		% Daily Value	
Total Fat	2 g	3%	
Saturated	1 g	5%	
Cholesterol	3 mg	1%	
Sodium	460 mg	19%	
Total Carbohydrate	35 g	12%	
Dietary Fiber	5 g	20%	
Sugars	17 g		
Protein	6 g		
Vitamin A	4%	Vitamin C	8%
Calcium	8%	Iron	6%

Dietary Exchanges: 2 Starch, 1/2 Fruit OR 2 1/2 Carbohydrate

BAKED SQUASH WITH PECAN BRITTLE

prep time: 15 min. (ready in 1 hr. 10 min.) • yield: 4 servings

Make the most of your oven's heat and bake the squash along with a casserole or roasted chicken. Brown sugar and pecans enhance the sweetness of the squash.

2 tablespoons chopped pecans

1 tablespoon brown sugar

1 tablespoon orange juice

2 teaspoons margarine or butter, melted

$\frac{1}{8}$ teaspoon cinnamon

1 ($1\frac{1}{2}$-lb.) buttercup or acorn squash

1 Heat oven to 350°F. Line 8-inch square pan with foil; spray foil with nonstick cooking spray.

2 In small bowl, combine all ingredients except squash; mix well. Spread in sprayed foil-lined pan. Bake at 350°F. for 8 to 10 minutes or until bubbly and deep golden brown, stirring once. Cool 15 minutes or until completely cooled.

3 Meanwhile, quarter squash; remove seeds. Place squash, cut side up, in ungreased 13 × 9-inch pan. Pour $\frac{1}{2}$ cup water into pan; cover with foil. Bake at 350°F. for 45 to 50 minutes or until tender.

4 To serve, arrange squash on serving platter. Crumble pecan mixture; sprinkle over squash.

Nutrition Information Per Serving Serving Size: $\frac{1}{4}$ of Recipe			
Calories	120	Calories from Fat	35
		% Daily Value	
Total Fat	4 g	6%	
Saturated	1 g	5%	
Cholesterol	0 mg	0%	
Sodium	30 mg	1%	
Total Carbohydrate	20 g	7%	
Dietary Fiber	5 g	20%	
Sugars	8 g		
Protein	2 g		
Vitamin A	10%	Vitamin C	15%
Calcium	6%	Iron	6%

Dietary Exchanges: $\frac{1}{2}$ Fruit, 2 Vegetable, 1 Fat OR $\frac{1}{2}$ Carbohydrate, 2 Vegetable, 1 Fat

---

HERBED MASHED POTATOES

prep time: 25 min. (ready in 45 min.) • yield: 4 (1-cup) servings

Although the warmth of the potatoes melts the butter during mashing, experienced cooks prefer to heat the milk, butter and herbs together. Gradually pouring in the mixture while mashing helps keep the mixture piping hot for serving.

4 medium russet or Idaho baking potatoes (about $1\frac{1}{2}$ lb.), peeled, cut into quarters

1 teaspoon salt

2 tablespoons chopped fresh parsley

1 tablespoon margarine or butter

2 teaspoons chopped fresh basil or $\frac{1}{2}$ teaspoon dried basil leaves

$\frac{1}{4}$ to $\frac{1}{2}$ cup milk

1 Place potatoes in large saucepan; add enough water to cover. Add $\frac{1}{2}$ teaspoon of the salt. Bring to a boil. Reduce heat to medium-low; cover loosely and boil gently for 15 to 20 minutes or until potatoes break apart easily when pierced with fork. Drain well.

2 Return potatoes to saucepan; shake saucepan gently over low heat for 1 to 2 minutes to evaporate any excess moisture.

3 Mash potatoes with potato masher until no lumps remain. Add parsley, margarine, basil and remaining ½ teaspoon salt. Continue mashing, gradually adding enough milk until potatoes are smooth and creamy.

Nutrition Information Per Serving
Serving Size: 1 Cup

Calories	200	Calories from Fat	35
		% Daily Value	
Total Fat	4 g	6%	
Saturated	1 g	5%	
Cholesterol	2 mg	1%	
Sodium	460 mg	19%	
Total Carbohydrate	36 g	12%	
Dietary Fiber	3 g	12%	
Sugars	3 g		
Protein	4 g		
Vitamin A	6%	Vitamin C	25%
Calcium	6%	Iron	10%

Dietary Exchanges: 2 ½ Starch OR 2 ½ Carbohydrate

CHEESY GARLIC AND CHIVE SMASHED POTATOES

prep time: 20 min. (ready in 45 min.) • yield: 8 (½-cup) servings

Instead of perfectly smooth mashed potatoes, leave some of the spuds in chunks for a side dish with character.

4 medium russet or Idaho baking potatoes (about 1 ½ lb.), unpeeled, cut into 1-inch cubes

2 garlic cloves, quartered

½ cup warm buttermilk or milk

1 ⅓ oz. (⅓ cup) shredded Cheddar cheese

1 tablespoon chopped fresh chives or 1 teaspoon freeze-dried chopped chives

¼ teaspoon salt

1 Place potatoes and garlic in large saucepan; add enough water to cover. Bring to a boil. Reduce heat to medium-low; cover loosely and boil gently 15 to 20 minutes or until potatoes break apart easily when pierced with fork. Drain well.

2 Return potatoes and garlic to saucepan; shake saucepan gently over low heat for 1 to 2 minutes to evaporate any excess moisture.

3 Mash potatoes and garlic with back of spoon or potato masher, leaving some potato pieces in chunks. Add all remaining ingredients; mix gently.

Nutrition Information Per Serving
Serving Size: ½ Cup

Calories	90	Calories from Fat	20
		% Daily Value	
Total Fat	2 g	3%	
Saturated	1 g	5%	
Cholesterol	5 mg	2%	
Sodium	120 mg	5%	
Total Carbohydrate	16 g	5%	
Dietary Fiber	1 g	4%	
Sugars	1 g		
Protein	3 g		
Vitamin A	0%	Vitamin C	10%
Calcium	6%	Iron	4%

Dietary Exchanges: 1 Starch OR 1 Carbohydrate

SHEAR GENIUS

Kitchen shears, or scissors, make quick work of many tasks. Use them to:

- Snip chives and other fresh herbs.
- Cut up canned whole tomatoes right in the can before adding to soups and sauces.
- Cut chicken breasts in half along the breast bone before cooking.
- Cut pizza into serving-sized slices.
- Snip grapes into serving-sized clusters.

Be sure to wash the shears in hot soapy water and dry thoroughly to store.

Cook's Notes

OUTSTANDING OVEN-BROWNED POTATOES

prep time: 15 min. (ready in 1 hr. 15 min.) • yield: 8 servings

As they bake, the potatoes become an appealing golden brown. Slice leftovers and heat them in a buttered skillet for home fries to accompany scrambled eggs.

4 medium baking potatoes, peeled, halved lengthwise

$^1/_3$ cup margarine or butter

$^1/_2$ teaspoon garlic powder

2 tablespoons grated Parmesan cheese

2 tablespoons unseasoned dry bread crumbs

1 Heat oven to 350°F. Generously grease 13 × 9-inch (3-quart) baking dish. Cut deep slits in rounded side of potatoes at $^1/_4$-inch intervals. Place potatoes, slit side up, in greased baking dish.

2 Melt margarine in small saucepan. Stir in garlic powder. Spoon margarine mixture evenly over potatoes. Bake at 350°F. for 40 minutes.

3 Brush potatoes with margarine mixture from bottom of baking dish. Sprinkle evenly with cheese and bread crumbs. Bake an additional 10 to 20 minutes or until potatoes are fork-tender.

Nutrition Information Per Serving
Serving Size: $^1/_8$ of Recipe

Calories	150	Calories from Fat	100
		% Daily Value	
Total Fat	8 g	12%	
Saturated	2 g	10%	
Cholesterol	0 mg	0%	
Sodium	130 mg	5%	
Total Carbohydrate	17 g	6%	
Dietary Fiber	2 g	8%	
Sugars	1 g		
Protein	2 g		
Vitamin A	6%	Vitamin C	10%
Calcium	4%	Iron	6%

Dietary Exchanges: 1 Starch, 1 $^1/_2$ Fat OR 1 Carbohydrate, 1 $^1/_2$ Fat

FOIL-WRAPPED POTATOES

prep time: 15 min. (ready in 1 hr. 10 min.) • yield: 4 servings

To vary the flavor, tuck a sprig of fresh thyme or dill into each packet along with the parsley.

4 medium unpeeled potatoes, cubed (4 cups)

$^1/_2$ cup chopped onion

4 teaspoons chopped fresh parsley

$^1/_2$ teaspoon salt

$^1/_8$ teaspoon pepper

4 tablespoons margarine or butter

1 GRILL DIRECTIONS: Heat grill. Cut four 18 × 12-inch pieces of heavy-duty foil. Place $^1/_4$ of potatoes and onion on each piece of foil. Sprinkle each with $^1/_4$ of parsley, salt and pepper; top each with 1 tablespoon margarine. Wrap each packet securely using double-fold seals, allowing room for heat expansion.

2 When ready to grill, place foil packets on gas grill over medium heat or on charcoal grill 4 to 6 inches from medium coals. Cook 45 to 55 minutes or until potatoes are tender, rearranging packets several times during cooking. Open packets carefully to allow hot steam to escape.

TIP: To bake packets in oven, prepare packets as directed above; place on cookie sheet. Bake at 350°F. for 45 to 55 minutes.

Nutrition Information Per Serving
Serving Size: 1/4 of Recipe

Calories	250	Calories from Fat	110
		% Daily Value	
Total Fat	12 g	18%	
Saturated	2 g	10%	
Cholesterol	0 mg	0%	
Sodium	410 mg	17%	
Total Carbohydrate	33 g	11%	
Dietary Fiber	3 g	12%	
Sugars	2 g		
Protein	3 g		
Vitamin A	10%	Vitamin C	20%
Calcium	2%	Iron	10%

Dietary Exchanges: 2 Starch, 2 Fat OR 2 Carbohydrate, 2 Fat

THYME AU GRATIN POTATOES

prep time: 20 min. (ready in 2 hr.) •

yield: 12 (1/2-cup) servings

Creamy and comforting, potatoes au gratin go well with roast beef, chops or burgers. This easy version of the classic casserole uses cream of celery soup, sour cream and Cheddar cheese.

5 oz. (1 1/4 cups) finely shredded Cheddar cheese

1/2 cup sour cream

1 (10 3/4-oz.) can condensed cream of celery soup

1/4 to 1/2 teaspoon dried thyme leaves

1/4 teaspoon pepper

6 medium russet potatoes, cooked, peeled and diced

1/4 cup sliced green onions

1/2 cup seasoned croutons, crushed

1 Heat oven to 350°F. Grease 1 1/2-quart casserole. In greased casserole, combine 1 cup of the cheese, sour cream, soup, thyme and pepper; mix well. Stir in potatoes and onions; cover. Bake at 350°F. for 45 minutes.

2 In small bowl, combine crushed croutons and remaining 1/4 cup cheese. Uncover casserole; sprinkle with crouton mixture. Bake uncovered for an additional 10 to 15 minutes or until bubbly and golden brown.

Nutrition Information Per Serving
Serving Size: 1/2 Cup

Calories	160	Calories from Fat	70
		% Daily Value	
Total Fat	8 g	12%	
Saturated	4 g	20%	
Cholesterol	20 mg	7%	
Sodium	290 mg	12%	
Total Carbohydrate	16 g	5%	
Dietary Fiber	1 g	4%	
Sugars	2 g		
Protein	5 g		
Vitamin A	6%	Vitamin C	10%
Calcium	10%	Iron	4%

Dietary Exchanges: 1 Starch, 2 Fat OR 1 Carbohydrate, 2 Fat

CASSEROLE COLOR

Most casseroles have a decidedly down-home appearance. To dress them up, try a colorful garnish:

- Chopped fresh herbs
- Fresh herb sprigs
- Sliced ripe olives
- Sprinkled paprika or chili powder
- Ground mixed peppercorns
- Diced pimiento or fresh bell pepper
- Spoonful of salsa

Cook's Notes

LEMON RICE PILAF

prep time: 10 min. (ready in 30 min.) • yield: 4 (²/₃-cup) servings

Flavored with lemon and parsley, this pilaf makes a good accompaniment for fish or chicken.

2 tablespoons butter

½ cup uncooked regular long-grain white rice

2 oz. uncooked vermicelli, broken into 1-inch pieces (½ cup)

1¾ cups chicken broth

1 tablespoon grated lemon peel

1 tablespoon chopped fresh parsley or 1 teaspoon dried parsley flakes

1 Melt butter in medium saucepan over medium heat. Add rice and vermicelli; cook and stir until golden brown.

2 Add broth; bring to a boil. Reduce heat to low; cover and simmer 15 to 20 minutes or until liquid is absorbed. Stir in lemon peel and parsley.

Nutrition Information Per Serving
Serving Size: ²/₃ Cup

Calories	210	Calories from Fat	60
		% Daily Value	
Total Fat	7 g	11%	
Saturated	4 g	20%	
Cholesterol	15 mg	5%	
Sodium	400 mg	17%	
Total Carbohydrate	30 g	10%	
Dietary Fiber	1 g	3%	
Sugars	1 g		
Protein	6 g		
Vitamin A	6%	Vitamin C	4%
Calcium	0%	Iron	10%

Dietary Exchanges: 2 Starch, 1 Fat OR 2 Carbohydrate, 1 Fat

VEGETABLE FRIED RICE

prep time: 25 min. • yield: 6 (¾-cup) servings

This colorful dish, seasoned with ginger and soy, goes equally well with an Asian-accented entree or a simple main course such as broiled chicken breasts.

3 tablespoons margarine or butter

1 cup uncooked regular long-grain white rice

½ cup chopped onion

½ cup sliced celery

½ cup sliced carrot

2 cups water

2 tablespoons chopped fresh parsley or 2 teaspoons dried parsley flakes

2 teaspoons chicken-flavor instant bouillon

½ teaspoon sugar

¼ teaspoon ginger

2 tablespoons soy sauce

1 (9-oz.) pkg. frozen sweet peas in a pouch

1 Melt margarine in large skillet over medium-high heat. Add rice, onion, celery and carrot; cook and stir 4 to 5 minutes or until rice is golden brown.

2 Stir in water, parsley, bouillon, sugar, ginger and soy sauce. Reduce heat to low; cover and simmer 20 minutes.

3 Stir in frozen peas; cook an additional 5 to 10 minutes or until liquid is absorbed and peas are tender.

Nutrition Information Per Serving
Serving Size: ¾ Cup

Calories	210	Calories from Fat	50
		% Daily Value	
Total Fat	6 g	9%	
Saturated	1 g	5%	
Cholesterol	0 mg	0%	
Sodium	840 mg	35%	
Total Carbohydrate	34 g	11%	
Dietary Fiber	3 g	12%	
Sugars	5 g		
Protein	5 g		
Vitamin A	70%	Vitamin C	8%
Calcium	4%	Iron	10%

Dietary Exchanges: 2 Starch, 1 Vegetable, 1 Fat OR 2 Carbohydrate,
1 Vegetable, 1 Fat

QUICK BROWN RICE PILAF

prep time: 15 min. • yield: 5 (½-cup) servings

Shredded carrot adds color and vitamins to the brown rice. To reduce the fat, omit the margarine from the cooking liquid.

- 1¼ cups chicken broth
- 1 tablespoon margarine or butter
- 1 to 1½ cups uncooked instant brown rice*
- ½ cup shredded carrot
- ⅓ cup sliced green onions
- ½ teaspoon dried rosemary or marjoram leaves

1 In medium saucepan, combine broth and margarine. Bring to a boil. Stir in all remaining ingredients. Reduce heat to low; cover and simmer 5 minutes.

2 Remove saucepan from heat; stir. Cover; let stand 5 minutes. Fluff mixture with fork before serving.

TIP: *Use amount of rice indicated on package to make 4 servings.

Nutrition Information Per Serving
Serving Size: ½ Cup

Calories	140	Calories from Fat	35
		% Daily Value	
Total Fat	4 g	6%	
Saturated	1 g	5%	
Cholesterol	0 mg	0%	
Sodium	230 mg	10%	
Total Carbohydrate	22 g	7%	
Dietary Fiber	2 g	8%	
Sugars	1 g		
Protein	4 g		
Vitamin A	60%	Vitamin C	2%
Calcium	0%	Iron	2%

Dietary Exchanges: 1 Starch, 1 Vegetable, 1 Fat OR 1 Carbohydrate,
1 Vegetable, 1 Fat

BROWN RICE

Brown rice is the whole rice grain with only the inedible outer husk removed. The high-fiber bran covering has a nutty flavor and chewy texture.

Brown rice can be boiled, steamed, baked or microwaved and can be substituted for white rice in most recipes. Brown rice takes 40 to 45 minutes to cook, about twice as long as regular white rice, though instant brown rice is ready in about 10 minutes.

Brown rice will keep up to six months if stored in an airtight container in a cool, dark, dry place. For longer storage, it can be refrigerated in an airtight container.

Cook's Notes

LIGHT FETTUCCINE ALFREDO

prep time: 30 min. • yield: 8 servings

Using half-and-half instead of heavy cream in this favorite pasta dish reduces the fat somewhat without sacrificing the rich, creamy sauce. The touch of nutmeg deepens the flavor without being readily recognizable as a sweet spice.

8 oz. uncooked fettuccine

1/3 cup margarine or butter

1 1/2 teaspoons all-purpose flour

1/4 teaspoon white or black pepper

1/8 to 1/4 teaspoon nutmeg, if desired

1/2 cup half-and-half

2 oz. (1/2 cup) shredded fresh Parmesan cheese

1 tablespoon chopped fresh parsley, if desired

1 Cook fettuccine to desired doneness as directed on package. Drain; cover to keep warm.

2 Meanwhile, melt margarine in large skillet over low heat. Stir in flour, pepper and nutmeg. Gradually stir in half-and-half. Cook over low heat for 5 minutes or until mixture thickens slightly, stirring frequently.

3 Stir in cheese; cook just until cheese is melted, stirring constantly. Immediately stir in cooked fettuccine; toss to coat with sauce. Sprinkle with parsley.

Nutrition Information Per Serving
Serving Size: 1/8 of Recipe

Calories	220	Calories from Fat	110
		% Daily Value	
Total Fat	12 g	18%	
Saturated	4 g	20%	
Cholesterol	35 mg	12%	
Sodium	180 mg	8%	
Total Carbohydrate	22 g	7%	
Dietary Fiber	1 g	3%	
Sugars	2 g		
Protein	6 g		
Vitamin A	10%	Vitamin C	0%
Calcium	8%	Iron	8%

Dietary Exchanges: 1 1/2 Starch, 2 Fat OR 1 1/2 Carbohydrate, 2 Fat

FRESH PASTA

In addition to the wide variety of dry pasta available, more types of fresh pasta have come into the market. Look for fresh pasta in Italian groceries or in the refrigerated or deli section of most supermarkets.

Fresh pasta is moist and soft, so its cooking time is shorter than that of dried pasta. Follow the cooking times on individual packages. Because it is perishable, fresh pasta must be stored airtight in the refrigerator. Use it within four days unless the package shows a different "use by" date. It can be frozen up to a month.

Cook's Notes

NOODLES WITH BREAD CRUMBS

prep time: 25 min. • yield: 5 (1-cup) servings

Pasta served with oil and bread crumbs is as Italian as pasta sauce with garlic. In some regions of Italy, bread is toasted, then grated into crumbs. In other regions, soft bread is made into crumbs, as in the recipe below. Commercially prepared bread crumbs, with their flourlike smoothness, would not work in this recipe.

8 oz. (4 cups) uncooked extra-wide egg noodles

4 tablespoons butter

1 cup soft whole wheat bread crumbs

½ cup finely chopped onion

½ teaspoon dried marjoram leaves

¼ teaspoon salt

⅛ teaspoon pepper

1 Cook noodles to desired doneness as directed on package. Drain; cover to keep warm.

2 Melt 3 tablespoons of the butter in medium skillet over medium-high heat. Add bread crumbs and onion; cook 3 to 5 minutes or until onion is crisp-tender, stirring constantly.

3 Stir in marjoram, salt, pepper, cooked egg noodles and remaining 1 tablespoon butter. Cook until thoroughly heated, stirring frequently.

Nutrition Information Per Serving
Serving Size: 1 Cup

Calories	290	Calories from Fat	110
		% Daily Value	
Total Fat	12 g	18%	
Saturated	6 g	30%	
Cholesterol	70 mg	23%	
Sodium	260 mg	11%	
Total Carbohydrate	38 g	13%	
Dietary Fiber	2 g	8%	
Sugars	3 g		
Protein	8 g		
Vitamin A	8%	Vitamin C	0%
Calcium	2%	Iron	15%

Dietary Exchanges: 2 ½ Starch, 2 Fat OR 2 ½ Carbohydrate, 2 Fat

Frosted
Cranberry-
Cherry Pie,
page 276

DESSERTS

KIDS ADMIT IT OPENLY AND MANY GROWNUPS SECRETLY AGREE: DESSERT IS THE BEST PART OF THE MEAL! WE'RE PROUD TO PRESENT SELECTIONS FROM OUR ALL-TIME BEST SWEETS. THE CHAPTER IS DIVIDED TO HIGHLIGHT COOKIES, BARS, CAKES, PIES AND MORE, THE LATTER INCLUDING A SPECTACULAR CHOCOLATE-ORANGE CHEESECAKE (PAGE 282), HOT FUDGE PUDDING CAKE (PAGE 285) AND LEMON TRUFFLE PIE (PAGE 278)!

CHOCOLATE CHUNK COOKIES

prep time: 50 min. • yield: 3 dozen cookies

Although you can certainly make this recipe with semi-sweet chips, the big chunks of chocolate are especially satisfying and indulgent.

¾ cup firmly packed brown sugar

½ cup sugar

½ cup margarine or butter, softened

½ cup shortening

1½ teaspoons vanilla

1 egg

1¾ cups all-purpose flour

1 teaspoon baking soda

½ teaspoon salt

8 oz. semi-sweet chocolate, coarsely chopped

1 cup chopped nuts

1 Heat oven to 375°F. In large bowl, combine brown sugar, sugar, margarine and shortening; beat until light and fluffy. Add vanilla and egg; blend well.

2 Add flour, baking soda and salt; mix well. Stir in chocolate and nuts. Drop by tablespoonfuls 2 inches apart onto ungreased cookie sheets.

3 Bake at 375°F. for 9 to 12 minutes or until light golden brown. Cool 1 minute; remove from cookie sheets.

High Altitude (Above 3,500 feet):
Increase flour to 2 cups. Bake as directed above.

Nutrition Information Per Serving
Serving Size: 1 Cookie

Calories	160	Calories from Fat	90
		% Daily Value	
Total Fat	10 g	15%	
Saturated	3 g	15%	
Cholesterol	5 mg	2%	
Sodium	85 mg	4%	
Total Carbohydrate	17 g	6%	
Dietary Fiber	1 g	3%	
Sugars	11 g		
Protein	1 g		
Vitamin A	2%	Vitamin C	0%
Calcium	0%	Iron	4%

Dietary Exchanges: ½ Starch, ½ Fruit, 2 Fat OR 1 Carbohydrate, 2 Fat

FREEZING COOKIES AND BARS

Most baked, cooled cookies and bars freeze well for up to six months, with the exception of meringue-type cookies, which do not freeze well.

- Freezer should be at 0°F. (Refrigerator freezers are often not this cold.)
- Freeze each kind of cookie separately to keep flavors from mixing.
- Place smaller amounts in resealable plastic bags. Use metal tins or plastic freezer containers for larger amounts. Cardboard boxes are not recommended for cookies and bars.
- Freeze cookies and bars unfrosted, then glaze them as desired once they're thawed. If you prefer, freeze a single layer of glazed or frosted cookies and bars just until frozen. Place between sheets of waxed paper in an airtight container. Remove from the freezer and separate the layers before thawing to prevent sticking.
- Label the container with the name of the cookies and the date frozen.

Cook's Notes

CHOCOLATE PIXIES

prep time: 1 hr. 15 min. (ready in 2 hr. 15 min.) •
yield: 4 dozen cookies

In this recipe, balls of cookie dough are heavily coated with powdered sugar before baking. Like the molasses cookies of old, the pixies emerge from the oven with crackled tops.

¼ cup margarine or butter

4 oz. unsweetened chocolate, cut into pieces

2 cups all-purpose flour

2 cups sugar

½ cup chopped walnuts or pecans

2 teaspoons baking powder

½ teaspoon salt

4 eggs

Powdered sugar

1 In large saucepan over low heat, melt margarine and chocolate, stirring constantly until smooth. Remove from heat; cool slightly.

2 Add flour, sugar, walnuts, baking powder, salt and eggs; mix well. Cover with plastic wrap; refrigerate at least 1 hour for easier handling.

3 Heat oven to 300°F. Shape dough into 1-inch balls; roll in powdered sugar, coating heavily. Place 2 inches apart on ungreased cookie sheets.

4 Bake at 300°F. for 13 to 18 minutes or until set. Immediately remove from cookie sheets. Cool 15 minutes or until completely cooled. Store in tightly covered container.

High Altitude (Above 3,500 feet):
Increase flour to 2 ¼ cups. Bake as directed above.

Nutrition Information Per Serving
Serving Size: 1 Cookie

Calories	90	Calories from Fat	25
		% Daily Value	
Total Fat	3 g	5%	
Saturated	1 g	5%	
Cholesterol	20 mg	7%	
Sodium	60 mg	3%	
Total Carbohydrate	15 g	5%	
Dietary Fiber	1 g	2%	
Sugars	10 g		
Protein	1 g		
Vitamin A	0%	Vitamin C	0%
Calcium	0%	Iron	2%

Dietary Exchanges: ½ Starch, ½ Fruit, ½ Fat OR 1 Carbohydrate, ½ Fat

COOKIE BAKING TIPS

- Use shiny, heavy-gauge stainless steel or aluminum cookie sheets. Dark cookie sheets absorb heat, so check cookies at the minimum baking time.
- Parchment or baking paper is convenient for lining cookie sheets. It eliminates greasing, allows for easy cookie removal and speeds cleanup.
- Cool cookie sheets before reusing them to prevent excessive spreading of cookies during baking.
- Make sure there are at least 2 inches between the cookie sheet and the oven's sides and door so hot air can circulate.

Cook's Notes

FROSTED CASHEW COOKIES

prep time: 1 hr. 15 min. • yield: 4 dozen cookies

Cashews turn basic brown sugar dough into an elegant cookie that would be good for a holiday dessert tray or formal tea party. The nuts provide a salty, crunchy counterpoint to the sweet cookie dough.

COOKIES
1 cup firmly packed brown sugar

1/2 cup butter, softened

1/2 teaspoon vanilla

1 egg

2 cups all-purpose flour

3/4 teaspoon baking powder

3/4 teaspoon baking soda

1/3 cup sour cream

3/4 cup coarsely chopped salted cashews

FROSTING
1/2 cup butter (do not use margarine)

2 cups powdered sugar

3 tablespoons half-and-half or milk

1/2 teaspoon vanilla

1 Heat oven to 375°F. Lightly grease cookie sheets. In large bowl, combine brown sugar and 1/2 cup butter; beat until light and fluffy. Add 1/2 teaspoon vanilla and egg; blend well.

2 Add flour, baking powder, baking soda and sour cream; mix well. Stir in cashews. Drop dough by rounded teaspoonfuls 2 inches apart onto greased cookie sheets.

3 Bake at 375°F. for 8 to 10 minutes or until golden brown. Immediately remove from cookie sheets. Cool 15 minutes or until completely cooled.

4 Meanwhile, in medium saucepan over medium heat, heat 1/2 cup butter until light golden brown, stirring constantly. Remove from heat. Stir in powdered sugar, half-and-half and 1/2 teaspoon vanilla; beat until smooth. Frost cooled cookies.

High Altitude (Above 3,500 feet): No change.

Nutrition Information Per Serving
Serving Size: 1 Cookie

Calories	110	Calories from Fat	45
		% Daily Value	
Total Fat	5 g	8%	
Saturated	3 g	15%	
Cholesterol	15 mg	5%	
Sodium	85 mg	4%	
Total Carbohydrate	14 g	5%	
Dietary Fiber	0 g	0%	
Sugars	10 g		
Protein	1 g		
Vitamin A	4%	Vitamin C	0%
Calcium	0%	Iron	2%

Dietary Exchanges: 1/2 Starch, 1/2 Fruit, 1 Fat OR 1 Carbohydrate, 1 Fat

FUNFETTI COOKIES

prep time: 40 min. • yield: 3 dozen cookies

Cooking with kids takes planning and patience; an easy-to-fix recipe goes a long way toward ensuring success. Here, packaged cake mix streamlines preparation, and the kids will enjoy decorating the frosted cookies with sprinkles.

1 (1 lb. 2.9-oz.) pkg. pudding-included white cake mix with candy bits

1/3 cup oil

2 eggs

1/2 (15.6-oz.) can pink vanilla frosting with candy bits

1 Heat oven to 375°F. In large bowl, combine cake mix, oil and eggs; stir with spoon until thoroughly moistened. Shape dough into 1-inch balls; place 2 inches apart on ungreased cookie sheets. With bottom of glass dipped in flour, flatten to 1/4-inch thickness.

2 Bake at 375° F. for 6 to 8 minutes or until edges are light golden brown. Cool 1 minute; remove from cookie sheets.

3 Spread frosting over warm cookies. Immediately sprinkle each with candy bits from frosting. Let stand until set. Store in tightly covered container.

High Altitude (Above 3,500 feet):
Add ½ cup flour to dry cake mix. Bake as directed above.

Nutrition Information Per Serving
Serving Size: 1 Cookie

Calories	110	Calories from Fat	45
		% Daily Value	
Total Fat	5 g	8%	
Saturated	1 g	5%	
Cholesterol	10 mg	3%	
Sodium	105 mg	4%	
Total Carbohydrate	16 g	5%	
Dietary Fiber	0 g	0%	
Sugars	11 g		
Protein	1 g		
Vitamin A	0%	Vitamin C	0%
Calcium	0%	Iron	0%

Dietary Exchanges: ½ Starch, ½ Fruit, 1 Fat OR 1 Carbohydrate, 1 Fat

Funfetti Cookies

WHITE CHOCOLATE-MACADAMIA NUT COOKIES

prep time: 1 hr. 10 min. • yield: 4 dozen cookies

An updated variation on America's beloved chocolate chip cookies, these golden treats contain vanilla chips and macadamia nuts.

¾ cup firmly packed brown sugar

½ cup sugar

½ cup margarine or butter, softened

½ cup shortening

2 teaspoons vanilla

1 egg

1¾ cups all-purpose flour

1 teaspoon baking soda

½ teaspoon salt

1⅓ cups white vanilla chips or 8 oz. vanilla-flavored candy coating, coarsely chopped

1 (3½-oz.) jar macadamia nuts, coarsely chopped

1 Heat oven to 375°F. In large bowl, combine brown sugar, sugar, margarine and shortening; beat until light and fluffy. Add vanilla and egg; blend well.

2 Stir in flour, baking soda and salt; mix well. Stir in vanilla chips and macadamia nuts. Drop dough by tablespoonfuls 3 inches apart onto ungreased cookie sheets.

3 Bake at 375°F. for 8 to 10 minutes or until light golden brown. Cool 1 minute; remove from cookie sheets.

High Altitude (Above 3,500 feet): Decrease margarine to 6 tablespoons; decrease baking soda to ¾ teaspoon. Bake as directed above.

Nutrition Information Per Serving
Serving Size: 1 Cookie

Calories	120	Calories from Fat	60
		% Daily Value	
Total Fat	7 g	11%	
Saturated	2 g	10%	
Cholesterol	5 mg	2%	
Sodium	80 mg	3%	
Total Carbohydrate	12 g	4%	
Dietary Fiber	0 g	0%	
Sugars	9 g		
Protein	1 g		
Vitamin A	0%	Vitamin C	0%
Calcium	0%	Iron	0%

Dietary Exchanges: 1 Fruit, 1½ Fat OR 1 Carbohydrate, 1½ Fat

MINT PETITES

prep time: 1 hr. • yield: 3½ dozen cookies

Cool mint pairs wonderfully with chocolate in these cookies that are great with coffee or tea.

¼ cup sugar

1 cup margarine or butter, softened

¼ to ½ teaspoon peppermint extract

½ teaspoon vanilla

2 cups all-purpose flour

11 foil-wrapped rectangular chocolate mints

½ cup milk chocolate frosting (from 16-oz. can)

1 Heat oven to 375°F. In large bowl, combine sugar and margarine; beat until light and fluffy. Add peppermint extract and vanilla; blend well.

2 Add flour; mix well. Shape dough into 1-inch balls. Place on ungreased cookie sheets; flatten slightly.

3 Bake at 375°F. for 10 to 12 minutes or until edges are lightly browned. Cool 1 minute; remove from cookie sheets. Cool 15 minutes or until completely cooled.

4 Unwrap chocolate mints; cut mints crosswise, then diagonally in half to form small triangles. Frost cookies; top each with chocolate mint triangle.

High Altitude (Above 3,500 feet): No change.

Nutrition Information Per Serving
Serving Size: 1 Cookie

Calories	80	Calories from Fat	45
		% Daily Value	
Total Fat	5 g	8%	
Saturated	1 g	5%	
Cholesterol	0 mg	0%	
Sodium	55 mg	2%	
Total Carbohydrate	8 g	3%	
Dietary Fiber	0 g	0%	
Sugars	3 g		
Protein	1 g		
Vitamin A	4%	Vitamin C	0%
Calcium	0%	Iron	0%

Dietary Exchanges: ½ Fruit, 1 Fat OR ½ Carbohydrate, 1 Fat

OATMEAL CHIP COOKIES

prep time: 1 hr. 25 min. • yield: 6 dozen cookies

Brown sugar cookie dough gains texture and flavor from rolled oats and chopped almonds, which lend a welcome crunch to these favorites.

1 cup sugar

1 cup firmly packed brown sugar

½ cup margarine or butter, softened

½ cup shortening

2 eggs

2 cups all-purpose flour

1 teaspoon baking soda

1 teaspoon salt

1½ cups quick-cooking rolled oats

1 cup chopped almonds

1 (6-oz.) pkg. (1 cup) semi-sweet chocolate chips

1 Heat oven to 375° F. In large bowl, combine sugar, brown sugar, margarine and shortening; beat until light and fluffy. Add eggs; blend well.

2 Add flour, baking soda and salt; mix well. Add oats, almonds and chocolate chips; blend well. Drop dough by rounded teaspoonfuls 2 inches apart onto ungreased cookie sheets.

3 Bake at 375° F. for 9 to 11 minutes or until light golden brown. Immediately remove from cookie sheets.

High Altitude (Above 3,500 feet): No change.

Nutrition Information Per Serving
Serving Size: 1 Cookie

Calories	80	Calories from Fat	35
		% Daily Value	
Total Fat	4 g	6%	
Saturated	1 g	5%	
Cholesterol	5 mg	2%	
Sodium	65 mg	3%	
Total Carbohydrate	11 g	4%	
Dietary Fiber	1 g	2%	
Sugars	7 g		
Protein	1 g		
Vitamin A	0%	Vitamin C	0%
Calcium	0%	Iron	2%

Dietary Exchanges: ½ Starch, 1 Fat OR ½ Carbohydrate, 1 Fat

STORING COOKIES

- Cool cookies completely before storing.
- Store each kind of cookie in a separate container to prevent flavors from mixing.
- To keep soft cookies soft, store them in a container with a tight-fitting cover. Place sheets of waxed paper between layers so the cookies won't stick together.
- To keep crisp cookies crisp, store them in a container with a loose-fitting cover. If, however, the weather is humid, use a tight-fitting cover. If crisp cookies become soggy after storage, reheat them in a 300° F. oven for a few minutes.
- Frosted cookies should be stored after the frosting has set. Separate the layers with waxed paper and stack only two or three layers deep.

Whole Wheat Sugar Cookies

WHOLE WHEAT SUGAR COOKIES

prep time: 45 min. (ready in 1 hr. 15 min.) •
yield: 3 dozen cookies

Whole wheat flour gives these cookies an appealing nutty flavor that combines nicely with the lemon and sweet spices.

1 cup sugar

½ cup margarine or butter, softened

2 tablespoons milk

1 teaspoon grated lemon peel

1 teaspoon vanilla

1 egg

1¾ cups whole wheat flour

1 teaspoon baking powder

½ teaspoon baking soda

½ teaspoon salt

½ teaspoon nutmeg

2 tablespoons sugar

½ teaspoon cinnamon

1 In large bowl, combine 1 cup sugar and margarine; beat until light and fluffy. Add milk, lemon peel, vanilla and egg; blend well. Add flour, baking powder, baking soda, salt and nutmeg; mix well. Cover with plastic wrap; refrigerate 30 minutes for easier handling.

2 Heat oven to 375°F. In small bowl, combine 2 tablespoons sugar and cinnamon. Shape dough into 1-inch balls; roll in sugar-cinnamon mixture. Place 2 inches apart on ungreased cookie sheets.

3 Bake at 375°F. for 7 to 10 minutes or until light golden brown. Cool 1 minute; remove from cookie sheets.

High Altitude (Above 3,500 feet):
Increase flour to 2 cups. Bake as directed above.

Nutrition Information Per Serving
Serving Size: 1 Cookie

Calories	80	Calories from Fat	25
		% Daily Value	
Total Fat	3 g	5%	
Saturated	1 g	5%	
Cholesterol	5 mg	2%	
Sodium	95 mg	4%	
Total Carbohydrate	11 g	4%	
Dietary Fiber	1 g	3%	
Sugars	6 g		
Protein	1 g		
Vitamin A	2%	Vitamin C	0%
Calcium	0%	Iron	0%

Dietary Exchanges: ½ Fruit, 1 Fat OR ½ Carbohydrate, 1 Fat

DECORATING COOKIES WITH PURCHASED FROSTING

After cookies are baked and cooled, give them character with purchased frosting. Use it right from the container or try one of these quick ideas:

- Colored frosting: Tint vanilla frosting with food color.
- Icing glaze: Place ½ cup purchased frosting in a microwave-safe bowl and microwave on HIGH for 10 to 15 seconds or until glaze is smooth; stir. Quickly spread over cookies and allow to dry.
- Marbleized glaze: Spread cookies with one color of icing glaze. Quickly drizzle another color on top; marble the two colors with a toothpick.
- Easy icing lines: Place ¾ cup purchased frosting in a heavy resealable plastic bag. Snip off a tiny tip of one corner; close the top and gently squeeze the frosting through the hole to make thin lines, squiggles, etc.

ALMOST CANDY BARS

prep time: 15 min. (ready in 1 hr. 30 min.) • yield: 48 bars

Here's some temptation for lovers of rich, gooey desserts. Dry cake mix blended with margarine forms a crust for butterscotch chips, chocolate chips, coconut and nuts.

$\frac{1}{2}$ cup margarine or butter

1 (1 lb. 2.25-oz.) pkg. pudding-included devil's food cake mix

1 cup butterscotch chips

1 (6-oz.) pkg. (1 cup) semi-sweet chocolate chips

1 cup coconut

1 cup chopped nuts

1 (14-oz.) can sweetened condensed milk (not evaporated)

1 Heat oven to 350°F. In large bowl, cut margarine into cake mix with fork or pastry blender until crumbly. Sprinkle evenly over bottom of ungreased 15 × 10 × 1-inch baking pan; press lightly.

2 Sprinkle with butterscotch chips, chocolate chips, coconut and nuts. Pour sweetened condensed milk evenly over all ingredients.

3 Bake at 350°F. for 20 to 30 minutes or until light golden brown. Cool 45 minutes or until completely cooled. Cut into bars.

High Altitude (Above 3,500 feet): No change.

Nutrition Information Per Serving
Serving Size: 1 Bar

Calories	160	Calories from Fat	70
		% Daily Value	
Total Fat	8 g	12%	
Saturated	3 g	15%	
Cholesterol	3 mg	1%	
Sodium	125 mg	5%	
Total Carbohydrate	19 g	6%	
Dietary Fiber	1 g	3%	
Sugars	14 g		
Protein	2 g		
Vitamin A	2%	Vitamin C	0%
Calcium	2%	Iron	4%

Dietary Exchanges: $\frac{1}{2}$ Starch, 1 Fruit, 1$\frac{1}{2}$ Fat OR 1$\frac{1}{2}$ Carbohydrate, 1$\frac{1}{2}$ Fat

CUTTING BAR COOKIES

Bar cookies can be easily cut into rectangles or squares. For a more festive look, cut into diamonds or triangles. Use a thin, sharp knife or a serrated knife for easier cutting.

• To cut triangles, cut bar cookies into squares (2 to 2$\frac{1}{2}$ inches), then simply cut each square in half diagonally.

• To cut diamonds, begin by cutting straight parallel lines down the length of the pan, about 1$\frac{1}{2}$ inches apart. Next, make diagonal cuts across the straight cuts 1$\frac{1}{2}$ inches apart, keeping the lines as even as possible. At each end of the pan, you'll end up with irregularly shaped pieces that are great for nibbling!

Cook's Notes

PINEAPPLE-NUT BARS

prep time: 30 min. (ready in 2 hr. 50 min.) • yield: 36 bars

The pairing of rum with tropical ingredients such as pineapple and coconut is a delicious tradition. Here, rum extract is introduced in the glaze.

BASE
1 cup all-purpose flour

½ cup sugar

½ cup margarine or butter

FILLING
1 (8-oz.) pkg. cream cheese, softened

2 tablespoons sugar

2 tablespoons milk

1 teaspoon vanilla

1 egg

1 (8-oz.) can crushed pineapple, well drained

1 cup coconut

½ cup chopped macadamia nuts or almonds

1 tablespoon margarine or butter, melted

GLAZE
½ cup powdered sugar

¼ teaspoon rum extract

3 to 4 teaspoons milk

1 Heat oven to 350°F. In medium bowl, combine flour and ½ cup sugar; mix well. With pastry blender or fork, cut in ½ cup margarine until mixture resembles coarse crumbs. Press in bottom of ungreased 9-inch square pan. Bake at 350°F. for 10 minutes.

2 Meanwhile, in small bowl, combine cream cheese, 2 tablespoons sugar, 2 tablespoons milk, vanilla and egg; beat until smooth. Stir in pineapple. Spread over partially baked base. In small bowl, combine coconut, nuts and 1 tablespoon margarine; mix well. Sprinkle evenly over pineapple mixture.

3 Bake at 350°F. for 18 to 20 minutes or until coconut is golden brown and filling appears set. Cool 1 hour or until completely cooled.

4 In small bowl, combine all glaze ingredients, adding enough milk for desired drizzling consistency. Drizzle over cooled bars. Refrigerate 1 hour or until set. Cut into bars. Store in refrigerator.

High Altitude (Above 3,500 feet): No change.

Nutrition Information Per Serving
Serving Size: 1 Bar

Calories	110	Calories from Fat	60
		% Daily Value	
Total Fat	7 g	11%	
Saturated	3 g	15%	
Cholesterol	15 mg	5%	
Sodium	60 mg	3%	
Total Carbohydrate	10 g	3%	
Dietary Fiber	0 g	0%	
Sugars	7 g		
Protein	1 g		
Vitamin A	4%	Vitamin C	0%
Calcium	0%	Iron	0%

Dietary Exchanges: ½ Starch, 1½ Fat OR ½ Carbohydrate, 1½ Fat

BAKING BARS IN JELLY ROLL PANS

A standard jelly roll pan is a rectangular pan measuring 15 × 10 inches with 1-inch-deep sides. Some baking pans have sides that are less than 1 inch deep; these should not be used for baking bar cookies because batter can spill over the edges during baking.

Cook's Notes

NO-BAKE CEREAL BARS

prep time: 20 min. (ready in 35 min.) • yield: 36 bars

Make these for the children, but save a couple for yourself! They're great with coffee or milk.

- 1 cup light corn syrup
- 1 cup sugar
- 1 cup peanut butter
- 6 cups toasted oat cereal
- 1 (12-oz.) pkg. (2 cups) semi-sweet chocolate chips

1 Lightly grease 13 × 9-inch pan. In large saucepan, combine corn syrup and sugar. Bring to a boil, stirring constantly. Cook until sugar is dissolved; remove from heat.

2 Add peanut butter; stir until mixture is smooth. Add cereal; mix well. Immediately press in greased pan.

3 In medium saucepan over low heat, melt chocolate chips, stirring constantly. Spread evenly over bars. Refrigerate 10 to 15 minutes or cool completely at room temperature until chocolate is set. Cut into bars.

1 MICROWAVE DIRECTIONS: Lightly grease 13 × 9-inch pan. Place corn syrup and sugar in 8-cup microwave-safe measuring cup or 2-quart bowl. Microwave on HIGH for 4 to 5 minutes or until mixture comes to a full boil and sugar is dissolved, stirring once during cooking.

2 Add peanut butter; stir until mixture is smooth. Add cereal; mix well. Immediately press in greased pan.

3 Place chocolate chips in 4-cup microwave-safe measuring cup. Microwave on MEDIUM for 3 to 5 minutes, stirring once halfway through cooking. Stir again until smooth. Spread evenly over bars. Refrigerate 10 to 15 minutes or cool completely at room temperature until chocolate is set. Cut into bars.

Nutrition Information Per Serving
Serving Size: 1 Bar

Calories	160	Calories from Fat	60
		% Daily Value	
Total Fat	7 g	11%	
Saturated	3 g	15%	
Cholesterol	0 mg	0%	
Sodium	80 mg	3%	
Total Carbohydrate	22 g	7%	
Dietary Fiber	1 g	4%	
Sugars	14 g		
Protein	3 g		
Vitamin A	4%	Vitamin C	4%
Calcium	0%	Iron	8%

Dietary Exchanges: 1 Starch, 1/2 Fruit, 1 Fat OR 1 1/2 Carbohydrate, 1 Fat

LINING BAKING PANS WITH FOIL

For easier cutting and quicker cleanup when baking bars, thoroughly moisten the inside of the baking pan with a wet cloth or paper towel. Line the pan with foil, extending the foil up and over the sides of the pan and making sure corners fit snugly. Grease and/or flour the foil as directed in the recipe. When the bars are baked and cooled, lift the foil and bars out of the pan and invert onto a cutting board. Peel the foil back and cut the bars.

Cook's Notes

No-Bake Cereal Bars

Oatmeal Carmelitas

OATMEAL CARMELITAS

prep time: 30 min. (ready in 2 hr. 55 min.) • yield: 36 bars

Caramel ice cream topping plus chocolate chips and chopped nuts become a wonderfully rich filling for the chewy oatmeal–brown sugar crust.

BASE

2 cups all-purpose flour

2 cups quick-cooking rolled oats

1½ cups firmly packed brown sugar

1 teaspoon baking soda

½ teaspoon salt

1¼ cups margarine or butter, softened

FILLING

1 (12.5-oz.) jar (1 cup) caramel ice cream topping

3 tablespoons all-purpose flour

1 (6-oz.) pkg. (1 cup) semi-sweet chocolate chips

½ cup chopped nuts

1 Heat oven to 350°F. Grease 13 × 9-inch pan. In large bowl, combine all base ingredients; mix at low speed until crumbly. Reserve half of crumb mixture (about 3 cups) for topping. Press remaining crumb mixture in bottom of greased pan. Bake at 350°F. for 10 minutes.

2 Meanwhile, in small bowl, combine caramel topping and 3 tablespoons flour. Remove partially baked base from oven; sprinkle with chocolate chips and nuts. Drizzle evenly with caramel mixture; sprinkle with reserved crumb mixture.

3 Bake at 350°F. for an additional 18 to 22 minutes or until golden brown. Cool 1 hour or until completely cooled. Refrigerate 1 to 2 hours or until filling is set. Cut into bars.

High Altitude (Above 3,500 feet): No change.

Nutrition Information Per Serving
Serving Size: 1 Bar

Calories	200	Calories from Fat	80
		% Daily Value	
Total Fat	9 g	14%	
Saturated	2 g	10%	
Cholesterol	0 mg	0%	
Sodium	180 mg	8%	
Total Carbohydrate	28 g	9%	
Dietary Fiber	1 g	4%	
Sugars	17 g		
Protein	2 g		
Vitamin A	6%	Vitamin C	0%
Calcium	2%	Iron	6%

Dietary Exchanges: 1 Starch, 1 Fruit, 1½ Fat OR 2 Carbohydrate, 1½ Fat

ROLLED OATS

Rolled oats can be purchased in three varieties: old-fashioned, quick-cooking and instant.

• Old-fashioned rolled oats are whole oats that have been hulled, steamed and flattened by rollers into flakes.

• Quick-cooking rolled oats have been cut into smaller pieces before rolling, yielding thinner flakes that cook more quickly.

• Instant oats have been cut into even smaller pieces, precooked and dried so they cook very fast.

Old-fashioned and quick-cooking oats can usually be used interchangeably in a recipe unless a particular variety is specified. However, old-fashioned rolled oats result in a firm-textured, chewier product. Instant oats are rarely used for baking; most instant oat products include sugar, salt or flavorings, and are primarily used as cereal.

PUMPKIN BARS

prep time: 30 min. (ready in 1 hr. 45 min.) • yield: 48 bars

Cream cheese frosting, expected with carrot cake, complements the spicy flavor of these pumpkin bars, too. Serve them with a mug of hot apple cider.

BARS
2 cups all-purpose flour

2 cups sugar

2 teaspoons baking powder

1 teaspoon baking soda

1 teaspoon cinnamon

1 teaspoon nutmeg

$\frac{1}{2}$ teaspoon salt

$\frac{1}{2}$ teaspoon cloves

1 cup oil

1 (16-oz.) can (2 cups) pumpkin

4 eggs

$\frac{1}{2}$ cup chopped nuts

$\frac{1}{2}$ cup raisins

FROSTING
2 cups powdered sugar

$\frac{1}{3}$ cup margarine or butter, softened

1 (3-oz.) pkg. cream cheese, softened

1 tablespoon milk

1 teaspoon vanilla

1 Heat oven to 350°F. Grease 15 × 10 × 1-inch baking pan. In large bowl, combine all bar ingredients except nuts and raisins; beat at low speed until moistened. Beat 2 minutes at medium speed. Stir in nuts and raisins. Pour into greased pan.

2 Bake at 350°F. for 25 to 30 minutes or until toothpick inserted in center comes out clean. Cool 45 minutes or until completely cooled.

3 In small bowl, combine all frosting ingredients; beat until smooth. Spread over cooled bars. Cut into bars. Store in refrigerator.

High Altitude (Above 3,500 feet):
Decrease baking soda to $\frac{1}{2}$ teaspoon. Bake at 375°F. for 30 to 35 minutes.

Nutrition Information Per Serving
Serving Size: 1 Bar

Calories	160	Calories from Fat	70
		% Daily Value	
Total Fat	8 g	12%	
Saturated	1 g	5%	
Cholesterol	20 mg	7%	
Sodium	95 mg	4%	
Total Carbohydrate	20 g	7%	
Dietary Fiber	1 g	2%	
Sugars	15 g		
Protein	2 g		
Vitamin A	45%	Vitamin C	0%
Calcium	2%	Iron	4%

Dietary Exchanges: $\frac{1}{2}$ Starch, 1 Fruit, 1 $\frac{1}{2}$ Fat OR 1 $\frac{1}{2}$ Carbohydrate, 1 $\frac{1}{2}$ Fat

ROCKY ROAD CRESCENT BARS

prep time: 15 min. (ready in 2 hr. 15 min.) • yield: 36 bars

"Rocky road" desserts get their pebbly texture from a combination of marshmallows, nuts and chocolate.

1 (8-oz.) can refrigerated crescent dinner rolls

$\frac{1}{2}$ cup sugar

$\frac{3}{4}$ cup peanut butter

1 (8-oz.) pkg. cream cheese, softened

$\frac{1}{2}$ cup corn syrup

1 teaspoon vanilla

1 egg

1 $\frac{1}{2}$ cups miniature marshmallows

$\frac{3}{4}$ cup salted peanuts or other nuts, chopped

1 (6-oz.) pkg. (1 cup) semi-sweet chocolate chips

1 Heat oven to 375°F. Separate dough into 2 long rectangles. Place in ungreased 13 × 9-inch pan; press over bottom and ½ inch up sides to form crust. Firmly press perforations to seal. Bake at 375°F. for 5 minutes.

2 Meanwhile, in medium bowl, combine sugar, peanut butter and cream cheese; blend until smooth. Stir in corn syrup, vanilla and egg; mix well.

3 Pour mixture over partially baked crust; spread evenly. Sprinkle with marshmallows, peanuts and chocolate chips.

4 Bake at 375°F. for 25 to 30 minutes or until filling is firm to the touch. Cool 30 minutes or until completely cooled. Refrigerate at least 1 hour or until filling is set. Cut into bars. Store in refrigerator.

High Altitude (Above 3,500 feet): No change.

Nutrition Information Per Serving
Serving Size: 1 Bar

Calories	150	Calories from Fat	80
		% Daily Value	
Total Fat	9 g	14%	
Saturated	3 g	15%	
Cholesterol	15 mg	5%	
Sodium	125 mg	5%	
Total Carbohydrate	15 g	5%	
Dietary Fiber	1 g	4%	
Sugars	9 g		
Protein	3 g		
Vitamin A	0%	Vitamin C	0%
Calcium	0%	Iron	4%

Dietary Exchanges: 1 Starch, 1½ Fat OR 1 Carbohydrate, 1½ Fat

CHOCOLATE-CHERRY BARS

prep time: 15 min. (ready in 2 hr.) • yield: 48 bars

In the tradition of Germany's famous "Black Forest" pairing of chocolate and cherries, Frances Jerzak of Porter, Minnesota, enriched a chocolate cake mix with cherry pie filling and almond flavoring to win the $25,000 Grand Prize at the 1974 Pillsbury Bake-Off® Contest.

BARS

1 (1 lb. 2.25-oz.) pkg. pudding-included devil's food cake mix

1 (21-oz.) can cherry pie filling

1 teaspoon almond extract

2 eggs, beaten

FROSTING

1 cup sugar

⅓ cup milk

5 tablespoons margarine or butter

1 (6-oz.) pkg. (1 cup) semi-sweet chocolate chips

1 Heat oven to 350°F. Grease and flour 15 × 10 × 1-inch baking pan or 13 × 9-inch pan. In large bowl, combine all bar ingredients; stir until well blended. Spread in greased and floured pan.

2 Bake at 350°F. Bake 15 × 10 × 1-inch pan 20 to 30 minutes; bake 13 × 9-inch pan 25 to 30 minutes or until toothpick inserted in center comes out clean.

3 In small saucepan, combine sugar, milk and margarine. Bring to a boil. Boil 1 minute, stirring constantly. Remove from heat; stir in chocolate chips until smooth. Pour and spread over warm bars. Cool 1¼ hours or until completely cooled. Cut into bars.

High Altitude (Above 3,500 feet):
Bake at 375°F. as directed above.

Nutrition Information Per Serving
Serving Size: 1 Bar

Calories	110	Calories from Fat	35
		% Daily Value	
Total Fat	4 g	6%	
Saturated	1 g	5%	
Cholesterol	10 mg	3%	
Sodium	100 mg	4%	
Total Carbohydrate	18 g	6%	
Dietary Fiber	1 g	2%	
Sugars	13 g		
Protein	1 g		
Vitamin A	0%	Vitamin C	0%
Calcium	0%	Iron	2%

Dietary Exchanges: ½ Starch, ½ Fruit, 1 Fat OR 1 Carbohydrate, 1 Fat

APPLE PECAN LAYER CAKE

prep time: 35 min. (ready in 2 hr. 10 min.) •
yield: 12 servings

Sweet and spicy, this layered apple cake is topped with a browned butter frosting. You won't want to substitute margarine: Butter browns best and offers the most flavor.

CAKE
2½ cups all-purpose flour

2 cups sugar

1 teaspoon baking powder

1 teaspoon baking soda

1 teaspoon salt

1 teaspoon cinnamon

1½ cups applesauce

¾ cup oil

2 eggs

½ cup chopped pecans

APPLE BROWN BUTTER FROSTING
½ cup butter (do not use margarine)

4½ cups powdered sugar

6 to 8 tablespoons apple juice

1 Heat oven to 350°F. Grease and flour two 9-inch round cake pans. In large bowl, combine flour, sugar, baking powder, baking soda, salt and cinnamon; mix well. Add applesauce, oil and eggs; blend at low speed until moistened. Beat 2 minutes at high speed. Stir in pecans. Pour batter into greased and floured pans.

2 Bake at 350°F. for 30 to 40 minutes or until toothpick inserted in center comes out clean. Cool 10 minutes. Remove from pans; cool 45 minutes or until completely cooled.

3 In small heavy saucepan over medium heat, heat butter until light golden brown, stirring constantly. Remove from heat; cool. In large bowl, combine powdered sugar, 4 tablespoons of the apple juice and the browned butter; blend at low speed until moistened. Continue beating until well blended, adding additional apple juice for desired spreading consistency.

4 To assemble cake, place 1 cake layer, top side down, on serving plate; spread evenly with about ¼ of frosting. Top with remaining cake layer, top side up. Spread sides and top of cake with remaining frosting. Garnish with purchased brittle, if desired.

High Altitude (Above 3,500 feet):
Decrease sugar to 1¾ cups. Bake at 375°F. for 25 to 35 minutes.

Nutrition Information Per Serving
Serving Size: ¹⁄₁₂ of Recipe

Calories	680	Calories from Fat	230
		% Daily Value	
Total Fat	26 g	40%	
Saturated	7 g	35%	
Cholesterol	55 mg	18%	
Sodium	410 mg	17%	
Total Carbohydrate	107 g	36%	
Dietary Fiber	2 g	8%	
Sugars	84 g		
Protein	4 g		
Vitamin A	8%	Vitamin C	0%
Calcium	4%	Iron	10%

Dietary Exchanges: 1½ Starch, 5½ Fruit, 5 Fat OR 7 Carbohydrate, 5 Fat

BAKING CAKES

For best results, always preheat the oven before baking a cake. If only one pan is used, place it in the center of the oven. Two pans should be staggered on the same rack at least 1 inch apart and 1 inch from the sides of the oven for even baking.

Cook's Notes

Apple Pecan Layer Cake

BLACK BOTTOM CUPS

prep time: 20 min. (ready in 1 hr. 35 min.) •
yield: 18 cupcakes

Before the cupcakes go into the oven, the cocoa-flavored batter is topped with a mixture of cream cheese, sugar, egg and chocolate chips, which bakes into a rich filling that eliminates the need for frosting.

2 (3-oz.) pkg. cream cheese, softened

$\frac{1}{3}$ cup sugar

1 egg

1 (6-oz.) pkg. (1 cup) semi-sweet chocolate chips

$1\frac{1}{2}$ cups all-purpose flour

1 cup sugar

$\frac{1}{4}$ cup unsweetened cocoa

1 teaspoon baking soda

$\frac{1}{2}$ teaspoon salt

1 cup water

$\frac{1}{3}$ cup oil

1 tablespoon vinegar

1 teaspoon vanilla

$\frac{1}{2}$ cup chopped almonds, if desired

2 tablespoons sugar, if desired

1 Heat oven to 350° F. Line 18 muffin cups with paper baking cups. In small bowl, combine cream cheese, $\frac{1}{3}$ cup sugar and egg; mix well. Stir in chocolate chips; set aside.

2 In large bowl, combine flour, 1 cup sugar, cocoa, baking soda and salt; mix well. Add water, oil, vinegar and vanilla; beat 2 minutes at medium speed. Fill paper-lined muffin cups half full.

3 Top each with 1 tablespoon cream cheese mixture. Combine almonds and 2 tablespoons sugar; sprinkle evenly over cream cheese mixture.

Black Bottom Cups

4 Bake at 350° F. for 20 to 30 minutes or until cream cheese mixture is light golden brown. Cool 15 minutes. Remove from pans; cool 30 minutes or until completely cooled. Store in refrigerator.

High Altitude (Above 3,500 feet): No change.

Nutrition Information Per Serving
Serving Size: 1 Cupcake

Calories	260	Calories from Fat	120
		% Daily Value	
Total Fat	13 g	20%	
Saturated	5 g	25%	
Cholesterol	20 mg	7%	
Sodium	160 mg	7%	
Total Carbohydrate	32 g	11%	
Dietary Fiber	2 g	8%	
Sugars	22 g		
Protein	3 g		
Vitamin A	4%	Vitamin C	0%
Calcium	2%	Iron	6%

Dietary Exchanges: 1 Starch, 1 Fruit, 2 ½ Fat OR 2 Carbohydrate, 2 ½ Fat

PIÑA COLADA PARTY CAKE

prep time: 30 min. (ready in 1 hr. 30 min.) • yield: 12 servings

Enjoy piña colada flavors in a cake!

CAKE
1 cup coconut

1 (1 lb. 2.25-oz.) pkg. pudding-included white cake mix

½ cup water

½ cup pineapple juice

⅓ cup oil

¼ cup rum*

4 egg whites

½ cup pineapple juice

½ cup sugar

FROSTING
1 (16-oz.) can vanilla frosting

1 tablespoon rum or ½ teaspoon rum extract

½ cup reserved toasted coconut

1 Heat oven to 350° F. Sprinkle 1 cup coconut on cookie sheet. Bake at 350° F. for 5 to 7 minutes or until toasted.

2 Meanwhile, grease and flour 13 × 9-inch pan. In large bowl, combine cake mix, water, ½ cup pineapple juice, oil, ¼ cup rum and egg whites; beat at low speed until moistened. Beat 2 minutes at high speed.

3 Stir in ½ cup of the toasted coconut; reserve remaining ½ cup for frosting. Pour into greased and floured pan.

4 Bake at 350° F. for 25 to 35 minutes or until toothpick inserted in center comes out clean. Cool 10 minutes.

5 In small saucepan, combine ½ cup pineapple juice and sugar; bring to a boil. With long-tined fork, prick cake at ½-inch intervals. Pour hot pineapple mixture over cake. Cool 1 hour or until completely cooled.

6 In small bowl, combine frosting and 1 tablespoon rum; blend well. Frost cake. Sprinkle with reserved ½ cup coconut. Refrigerate until serving time.

TIP: *To substitute for rum, use ¼ cup water plus 1 teaspoon rum extract.

High Altitude (Above 3,500 feet):
Add 3 tablespoons flour to dry cake mix; increase water to ½ cup plus 1 tablespoon. Bake at 375° F. for 25 to 35 minutes.

Nutrition Information Per Serving
Serving Size: 1/12 of Recipe

Calories	500	Calories from Fat	180
		% Daily Value	
Total Fat	20 g	31%	
Saturated	6 g	30%	
Cholesterol	0 mg	0%	
Sodium	330 mg	14%	
Total Carbohydrate	74 g	25%	
Dietary Fiber	1 g	4%	
Sugars	55 g		
Protein	3 g		
Vitamin A	6%	Vitamin C	2%
Calcium	0%	Iron	6%

Dietary Exchanges: 1 Starch, 4 Fruit, 4 Fat OR 5 Carbohydrate, 4 Fat

VANILLA-BUTTER CAKE

prep time: 30 min. (ready in 2 hr. 30 min.) •
yield: 12 servings

A hot butter sauce is poured over the top and soaks into the dessert, "frosting" the cake.

CAKE
1 (1 lb. 2.25-oz.) pkg. pudding-included
    butter flavor yellow cake mix

1 (3.4-oz.) pkg. instant vanilla pudding
    and pie filling mix

1 cup water

½ cup butter, softened

4 eggs

BUTTER SAUCE
¾ cup sugar

⅓ cup butter

3 tablespoons water

1 to 2 teaspoons vanilla

GARNISH
2 to 3 teaspoons powdered sugar

1 Heat oven to 350°F. Generously grease and flour 12-cup Bundt® pan or 10-inch tube pan. In large bowl, combine all cake ingredients; beat at low speed until moistened. Beat 2 minutes at high speed. Pour batter into greased and floured pan.

2 Bake at 350°F. for 50 to 60 minutes or until toothpick inserted in center comes out clean.

3 In small saucepan, combine all sauce ingredients except vanilla; cook over medium heat, stirring constantly until mixture boils. Boil 1 minute. Stir in vanilla.

4 With long-tined fork, pierce cake 10 to 12 times. Slowly pour hot sauce over warm cake. Let stand 10 to 15 minutes or until sauce is absorbed.

Invert cake onto serving plate. Cool 1 hour or until completely cooled.

5 Just before serving, sprinkle with powdered sugar. If desired, serve with whipped cream.

High Altitude (Above 3,500 feet):
Add ⅓ cup flour to dry cake mix; increase water to 1¼ cups. Bake as directed above.

Nutrition Information Per Serving
Serving Size: ¹⁄₁₂ of Recipe

Calories	400	Calories from Fat	160
		% Daily Value	
Total Fat	18 g	28%	
Saturated	9 g	45%	
Cholesterol	105 mg	35%	
Sodium	540 mg	23%	
Total Carbohydrate	56 g	19%	
Dietary Fiber	0 g	0%	
Sugars	40 g		
Protein	3 g		
Vitamin A	10%	Vitamin C	0%
Calcium	10%	Iron	6%

Dietary Exchanges: 1 Starch, 2 ½ Fruit, 3 ½ Fat OR 3 ½ Carbohydrate, 3 ½ Fat

CHOCOLATE PRALINE CAKE

prep time: 25 min. (ready in 2 hr. 15 min.) •
yield: 15 servings

In this upside-down cake, a praline mixture of cream, butter, brown sugar and pecans bakes underneath the batter at the bottom of the cake pan, becoming a moist, rich topping when the cake is inverted onto a platter.

CAKE
½ cup butter or margarine

¼ cup whipping cream

1 cup firmly packed brown sugar

¾ cup coarsely chopped pecans

1 (1 lb. 2.25-oz.) pkg. pudding-included
    devil's food cake mix

1¼ cups water

⅓ cup oil

3 eggs

TOPPING

1¾ cups whipping cream

¼ cup powdered sugar

¼ teaspoon vanilla

1 Heat oven to 325°F. In small, heavy saucepan, combine butter, ¼ cup whipping cream and brown sugar; cook over low heat just until butter is melted, stirring occasionally. Pour into ungreased 13 × 9-inch pan; sprinkle evenly with chopped pecans.

2 In large bowl, combine all remaining cake ingredients; beat at low speed until moistened. Beat 2 minutes at high speed. Carefully spoon about half of batter over pecan mixture around edges of pan; spoon remaining batter into center of pan.

3 Bake at 325°F. for 50 to 60 minutes or until cake springs back when touched lightly in center.

Cool 5 minutes. Invert onto serving platter; cool 45 minutes or until completely cooled.

4 In small bowl, beat 1¾ cups whipping cream until soft peaks form. Add powdered sugar and vanilla; beat until stiff peaks form. Pipe whipped cream onto cake. Serve with any remaining whipped cream. Store in refrigerator.

High Altitude (Above 3,500 feet):
Add ¼ cup flour to dry cake mix.
Bake at 350°F. for 50 to 60 minutes.

Nutrition Information Per Serving
Serving Size: ¹⁄₁₅ of Recipe

Calories	480	Calories from Fat	280
		% Daily Value	
Total Fat	31 g	48%	
Saturated	14 g	70%	
Cholesterol	100 mg	33%	
Sodium	360 mg	15%	
Total Carbohydrate	45 g	15%	
Dietary Fiber	1 g	4%	
Sugars	31 g		
Protein	4 g		
Vitamin A	15%	Vitamin C	0%
Calcium	4%	Iron	10%

Dietary Exchanges: 1½ Starch, 1½ Fruit, 6 Fat. OR 3 Carbohydrate, 6 Fat

Chocolate Praline Cake

BUSTER SUNDAE PIE

prep time: 25 min. (ready in 3 hr. 55 min.) • yield: 8 servings

This fancy pie, easily assembled from purchased ice cream and toppings, makes a refreshing alternative to cake for hot-weather birthdays. In summer, substitute your favorite fresh berries for the maraschino cherries.

1 refrigerated pie crust (from 15-oz. pkg.)

1 quart (4 cups) vanilla ice cream, slightly softened

1/2 cup caramel ice cream topping

1/2 cup fudge ice cream topping

3/4 cup Spanish peanuts

1/2 cup whipping cream, whipped and sweetened

8 maraschino cherries with stems, if desired

1 Heat oven to 450° F. Prepare pie crust as directed on package for one-crust baked shell using 9-inch pie pan. Bake at 450° F. for 9 to 11 minutes or until light golden brown. Cool 30 minutes or until completely cooled.

2 Spoon and spread 2 cups ice cream in cooled baked shell. Drizzle with half of the caramel topping and half of the fudge topping. Sprinkle with peanuts. Layer remaining 2 cups ice cream over peanuts. Drizzle with remaining caramel and fudge toppings.

3 Freeze at least 3 hours or overnight. Garnish with whipped cream and cherries.

Nutrition Information Per Serving
Serving Size: 1/8 of Recipe

Calories		540	Calories from Fat	260
			% Daily Value	
Total Fat		29 g	45%	
Saturated		13 g	65%	
Cholesterol		60 mg	20%	
Sodium		320 mg	13%	
Total Carbohydrate		62 g	21%	
Dietary Fiber		2 g	8%	
Sugars		37 g		
Protein		8 g		
Vitamin A	10%		Vitamin C	0%
Calcium	15%		Iron	4%

Dietary Exchanges: 3 Starch, 1 Fruit, 5 1/2 Fat OR 4 Carbohydrate, 5 1/2 Fat

PEANUTS

Peanuts are commonly considered a nut; however, they're actually a legume. At one stage of growth, the peanut plant resembles a garden pea vine. Goober, earth-nut, ground pea and ground nut are other names for the peanut because the plant buries its pods in the ground after flowering and the peanuts develop underground like potatoes.

Raw peanuts are somewhat soft and bland; roasting brings out the flavor we've come to expect and love. Peanuts require proper storage to remain fresh tasting. Store unshelled peanuts airtight in a cool, dry place for up to six months. Store shelled peanuts in the refrigerator airtight for up to three months. Like other nuts, peanuts freeze well and can be stored in the freezer for up to six months.

Cook's Notes

CHOCOLATE-DATE-PECAN PIE

prep time: 20 min. (ready in 1 hr. 20 min.) • yield: 10 servings

How do you make an already delicious dessert classic even better? Add chocolate! We took a Southern favorite, pecan pie, and stirred in chocolate chips and chopped dates.

CRUST
1 refrigerated pie crust (from 15-oz. pkg.)

FILLING
1 cup firmly packed brown sugar

½ cup all-purpose flour

½ cup butter, softened

1 teaspoon vanilla

2 eggs

1 (6-oz.) pkg. (1 cup) semi-sweet chocolate chips

1 cup chopped pecans

1 cup chopped dates

Whipped cream, if desired

1 Prepare pie crust as directed on package for one-crust filled pie using 9-inch pie pan.

2 Heat oven to 325°F. In large bowl, combine brown sugar, flour, butter, vanilla and eggs; beat well. Stir in chocolate chips, pecans and dates. Spread evenly in crust-lined pan.

3 Bake at 325°F. for 55 to 60 minutes or until deep golden brown. Cover edge of crust with strips of foil after 15 to 20 minutes of baking to prevent excessive browning. Serve warm with whipped cream. Garnish as desired.

BAKING A PIE CRUST WITHOUT A FILLING

To bake a pie crust without a filling (called "blind baking"), generously prick the bottom and sides of the dough before baking to prevent blistering and rising. Or, cut a circle of foil 2 inches larger than the diameter of the pie plate. Fit the foil into the crust-lined pie pan (it will overlap 1 inch) and fill the foil with dried beans or rice to support the sides of the pie crust and keep it from shrinking into the center while it bakes. Metal or ceramic pie weights from gourmet specialty shops can also be used. Remove the weights and foil a few minutes before the baking time is over to allow the crust to brown evenly.

Cool the crust completely before adding the filling, which should ideally be at room temperature. If the filling is too hot, the crust may become soggy.

Cook's Notes

FROSTED CRANBERRY-CHERRY PIE

prep time: 30 min. (ready in 2 hr. 20 min.) • yield: 8 servings

PICTURED ON PAGE 250

Wake up the flavor of a regular cherry pie by spiking the filling with cranberry sauce.

CRUST
1 (15-oz.) pkg. refrigerated pie crusts

FILLING
1 (21-oz.) can cherry pie filling

1 (16-oz.) can whole berry cranberry
   sauce

3 tablespoons cornstarch

¼ teaspoon cinnamon

GLAZE AND TOPPING
½ cup powdered sugar

1 tablespoon light corn syrup

3 to 4 teaspoons water

¼ cup almond slices

1 Prepare pie crust as directed on package for two-crust pie using 9-inch pie pan.

2 Heat oven to 400° F. In large bowl, combine all filling ingredients; mix well. Spoon into crust-lined pan. Top with second crust; seal edges and flute. Cut slits in several places in top crust.

3 Bake at 400° F. for 40 to 50 minutes or until crust is golden brown. Cover edge of crust with strips of foil after 15 to 20 minutes of baking to prevent excessive browning.

4 Remove pie from oven. Immediately, in small bowl, blend powdered sugar, corn syrup and enough water for desired drizzling consistency. Drizzle over hot pie. Decorate or sprinkle with almonds. Cool at least 1 hour before serving.

Nutrition Information Per Serving
Serving Size: ⅛ of Recipe

Calories	480	Calories from Fat	140
		% Daily Value	
Total Fat	15 g	23%	
Saturated	6 g	30%	
Cholesterol	15 mg	5%	
Sodium	230 mg	10%	
Total Carbohydrate	83 g	28%	
Dietary Fiber	2 g	8%	
Sugars	49 g		
Protein	2 g		
Vitamin A	4%	Vitamin C	4%
Calcium	2%	Iron	4%

Dietary Exchanges: ½ Starch, 5 Fruit, 3 Fat OR 5 ½ Carbohydrate, 3 Fat

FREEZING PIES

Some pies, like pumpkin and pecan, must be baked before storing; fruit pies can be frozen baked or unbaked. Custard and cream pies or pies with meringue toppings are not recommended for freezing. To store baked pies, cool quickly.

For unbaked pies, brush bottom crust with egg white before filling to prevent sogginess. Cover pie with inverted foil pie pan; wrap tightly. To serve a baked pie, unwrap and heat it in 325° F. oven for 45 minutes until thawed and warm. For an unbaked pie, unwrap and bake at 425° F. for 15 minutes, then at 375° F. for 45 minutes or until the center is bubbly. For a chiffon pie, unwrap and thaw in the refrigerator 2 to 4 hours.

Cook's Notes

EASY APPLE PIE FOLDOVER

prep time: 20 min. (ready in 1 hr. 15 min.) • yield: 4 servings

Is it a little apple pie or a large apple turnover? Whichever way you view it, this recipe makes just the right amount for a small family.

1½ cups (2 medium) thinly sliced, peeled apples

¼ cup firmly packed brown sugar

1 tablespoon water

1 teaspoon lemon juice

1 tablespoon all-purpose flour

1 tablespoon sugar

¼ teaspoon salt

½ teaspoon vanilla

1 tablespoon margarine or butter

1 refrigerated pie crust (from 15-oz. pkg.)

1 tablespoon water

1 egg

1 In medium saucepan, combine apples, brown sugar, 1 tablespoon water and lemon juice. Cook over medium heat until bubbly, stirring occasionally. Reduce heat to low; cover and cook 6 to 8 minutes or until apples are tender, stirring occasionally.

2 In small bowl, combine flour, sugar and salt; stir into apple mixture. Cook until mixture thickens, stirring constantly. Remove from heat; stir in vanilla and margarine. Cool 15 to 20 minutes.

3 Heat oven to 375° F. Let pie crust pouch stand at room temperature for 15 to 20 minutes.

4 Remove pie crust from pouch. Unfold crust; remove plastic sheets. Place on ungreased cookie sheet. Press out fold lines.

5 Spoon fruit mixture evenly on half of crust to within ½ inch of edge. In small bowl, beat 1 tablespoon water and egg; brush over edges of pastry. Fold remaining side of crust over fruit turnover fashion; press edges firmly to seal.* Flute edge; cut small slits in top of pastry. Brush top with egg mixture.

6 Bake at 375° F. for 25 to 35 minutes or until crust is golden brown. Serve warm or cool.

TIP: *If desired, cut out decorative shapes from remaining side of crust before folding crust over fruit. Omit slits in crust.

Nutrition Information Per Serving
Serving Size: ¼ of Recipe

Calories	380	Calories from Fat	160
		% Daily Value	
Total Fat	18 g	28%	
Saturated	6 g	30%	
Cholesterol	65 mg	22%	
Sodium	390 mg	16%	
Total Carbohydrate	51 g	17%	
Dietary Fiber	1 g	4%	
Sugars	23 g		
Protein	3 g		
Vitamin A	4%	Vitamin C	4%
Calcium	4%	Iron	6%

Dietary Exchanges: 1 Starch, 2 ½ Fruit, 3 ½ Fat OR 3 ½ Carbohydrate, 3 ½ Fat

LEMON TRUFFLE PIE

prep time: 50 min. (ready in 2 hr. 50 min.) •
yield: 10 servings

Savor each forkful of this smooth, light yet rich dessert. Lemon juice and lemon peel provide a bright bit of tartness to balance the sweet filling.

CRUST
1 refrigerated pie crust (from 15-oz. pkg.)

FILLING
1 cup sugar

2 tablespoons cornstarch

2 tablespoons all-purpose flour

1 cup water

2 egg yolks, beaten

1 tablespoon margarine or butter

½ teaspoon grated lemon peel

¼ cup lemon juice

6 oz. (1 cup) white vanilla chips or chopped white chocolate baking bar

1 (8-oz.) pkg. ⅓-less-fat cream cheese (Neufchatel), softened

½ cup whipping cream

1 tablespoon sliced almonds, toasted*

Lemon Truffle Pie

1 Heat oven to 450° F. Prepare pie crust as directed on package for one-crust baked shell using 9-inch pie pan. Bake at 450° F. for 9 to 11 minutes or until light golden brown. Cool 30 minutes or until completely cooled.

2 In medium saucepan, combine sugar, cornstarch and flour; mix well. Gradually stir in water until smooth. Cook over medium heat until mixture boils, stirring constantly. Reduce heat; cook 2 minutes, stirring constantly.

3 Remove from heat. Stir about ¼ cup of hot mixture into egg yolks; blend well. Add egg yolk mixture to mixture in saucepan. Cook over low heat until mixture boils, stirring constantly. Cook 2 minutes, stirring constantly.

4 Remove from heat. Stir in margarine, lemon peel and lemon juice. Transfer ⅓ cup of hot filling to small saucepan; cool remaining lemon mixture 15 minutes. Add vanilla chips to hot filling in small saucepan; stir over low heat just until chips are melted.

5 In small bowl, beat cream cheese until fluffy. Add melted vanilla chip mixture; beat until well blended. Spread over bottom of cooled baked shell. Spoon lemon mixture over cream cheese layer. Refrigerate 2 to 3 hours or until set.

6 In another small bowl, beat whipping cream until stiff peaks form. Pipe or spoon over pie. Garnish with toasted almonds. Store in refrigerator.

TIP: *To toast almonds, spread on cookie sheet; bake at 350° F. for 5 to 7 minutes or until light golden brown, stirring occasionally. Or spread in thin layer in microwave-safe pie pan. Microwave on HIGH for 4 to 7 minutes or until light golden brown, stirring frequently.

Nutrition Information Per Serving
Serving Size: ¹⁄₁₀ of Recipe

Calories	410	Calories from Fat	210
		% Daily Value	
Total Fat	23 g	35%	
Saturated	12 g	60%	
Cholesterol	85 mg	28%	
Sodium	210 mg	9%	
Total Carbohydrate	45 g	15%	
Dietary Fiber	0 g	0%	
Sugars	32 g		
Protein	5 g		
Vitamin A	10%	Vitamin C	2%
Calcium	8%	Iron	2%

Dietary Exchanges: 1½ Starch, 1½ Fruit, 4½ Fat OR 3 Carbohydrate, 4½ Fat

WHAT IS WHITE CHOCOLATE?

White "chocolate" is usually a blend of cocoa butter, sugar, milk and flavorings. (Actually, white chocolate doesn't meet the Food and Drug Administration's definition of chocolate because it doesn't contain chocolate liquor from the cocoa bean.) Similar products known as confectionary coatings are made from coconut, soybean or palm kernel oil but no cocoa butter. White chocolate and coatings are available in several different forms:

- White chocolate baking bar
- Vanilla-flavored candy coating or almond bark
- White vanilla chips

These products have a mild flavor similar to that of milk chocolate and can be found in specialty food shops and the baking section of most supermarkets.

STRAWBERRY-LEMON TART

prep time: 25 min. (ready in 1 hr. 50 min.) •
yield: 10 servings

Melting jelly to glaze fruit tarts is a bakery secret. In place of the apple jelly called for in this recipe, peach or apricot jelly could be used for equally good results.

CRUST
1 cup all-purpose flour

1 tablespoon sugar

1 teaspoon grated lemon peel

⅛ teaspoon salt

¼ cup margarine or butter

1 egg, slightly beaten

2 to 6 teaspoons water

FILLING
2 eggs, slightly beaten

¾ cup sugar

2 tablespoons all-purpose flour

2 teaspoons grated lemon peel

½ teaspoon baking powder

2 tablespoons lemon juice

TOPPING
2 cups strawberries, halved

2 tablespoons apple jelly, melted

1 Heat oven to 375° F. In medium bowl, combine 1 cup flour, 1 tablespoon sugar, 1 teaspoon lemon peel and salt; mix well. With pastry blender or fork, cut in margarine until mixture resembles coarse crumbs. With fork, stir in egg and enough water for mixture to form a ball. Press in bottom and up sides of 9½- or 10-inch tart pan with removable bottom. Bake at 375° F. for 15 minutes.

2 Reduce oven temperature to 350° F. In medium bowl, combine all filling ingredients except lemon juice; blend well. Stir in lemon juice. Pour mixture over warm crust.

3 Bake at 350° F. for 20 to 25 minutes or until top is light golden brown. Cool 1 hour or until completely cooled.

4 Just before serving, arrange strawberries over top of tart. Brush with melted jelly. Store in refrigerator.

High Altitude (Above 3,500 feet): No change.

Nutrition Information Per Serving
Serving Size: ¹⁄₁₀ of Recipe

Calories	200	Calories from Fat	50
		% Daily Value	
Total Fat	6 g	9%	
Saturated	1 g	5%	
Cholesterol	65 mg	22%	
Sodium	125 mg	5%	
Total Carbohydrate	32 g	11%	
Dietary Fiber	1 g	4%	
Sugars	20 g		
Protein	4 g		
Vitamin A	6%	Vitamin C	25%
Calcium	4%	Iron	6%

Dietary Exchanges: 1½ Starch, ½ Fruit, 1 Fat OR 2 Carbohydrate, 1 Fat

Strawberry-Lemon Tart

CHOCOLATE-ORANGE CHEESECAKE

prep time: 25 min. (ready in 4 hr. 35 min.) •
yield: 16 servings

Swirled through the creamy batter, melted chocolate marbles this rich cheesecake. This is a good make-ahead dessert: Refrigerating for several hours (preferably overnight) firms up the texture for easier slicing.

- 1/3 cup graham cracker crumbs (about 5 to 6 squares)
- 4 (8-oz.) pkg. cream cheese, softened
- 1 1/3 cups sugar
- 4 eggs
- 2 tablespoons orange-flavored liqueur or orange juice
- 1 teaspoon grated orange peel
- 3 oz. semi-sweet chocolate, melted

1 Heat oven to 325°F. Lightly grease bottom and sides of 9-inch springform pan. Sprinkle graham cracker crumbs over bottom and sides of pan.

2 In large bowl, beat cream cheese at medium speed until smooth and creamy. Gradually add sugar, beating until smooth. At low speed, add eggs 1 at a time, beating just until blended. Add liqueur and orange peel; beat 2 minutes at medium speed, scraping sides of bowl occasionally.

3 In small bowl, reserve 1 1/2 cups of batter. Pour remaining batter into crumb-lined pan. Slowly blend melted chocolate into reserved batter. Spoon chocolate batter by teaspoonfuls onto batter in pan, forming 9 drops around outside and 5 drops in center, using all the batter. Starting in center of one outer drop, run knife through center of outer drops; run knife through inner drops, forming 2 circles of hearts.

4 Bake at 325°F. for 1 hour or until set.* Cool 1 hour. Refrigerate at least 3 hours or overnight.

COOK'S KNOW-HOW

HOW TO MAKE A DECORATIVE CHEESECAKE

A double ring of chocolate hearts adorn this decadent cheesecake. While the technique is easy, the impressive results will earn rave reviews from cheesecake aficionados everywhere.

STEP 1

Spoon chocolate batter by teaspoonfuls onto batter in pan, forming 9 drops around outside and 5 drops in center, using all the batter.

STEP 2

Starting in center of one outer drop, run knife through centers of outer drops; run knife through inner drops, forming 2 circles of hearts.

Store in refrigerator. Just before serving, remove sides of pan.

Tip: *To minimize cracks in cheesecake, place a shallow pan half full of water on bottom of oven during baking time.

Nutrition Information Per Serving
Serving Size: 1/16 of Recipe

Calories	320	Calories from Fat	210
		% Daily Value	
Total Fat	23 g	35%	
Saturated	14 g	70%	
Cholesterol	115 mg	38%	
Sodium	190 mg	8%	
Total Carbohydrate	23 g	8%	
Dietary Fiber	0 g	0%	
Sugars	21 g		
Protein	6 g		
Vitamin A	20%	Vitamin C	0%
Calcium	6%	Iron	6%

Dietary Exchanges: 1 1/2 Starch, 4 1/2 Fat OR 1 1/2 Carbohydrate, 4 1/2 Fat

Chocolate-Orange Cheesecake

FRESH PEAR CROSTATA

prep time: 25 min. (ready in 1 hr.) • yield: 8 servings

Although apples are the all-American choice for pie, pears are delicious in baked desserts as well. Easy to assemble with purchased pie crust, this one-crust dessert makes an elegant finish for a company meal.

1 refrigerated pie crust (from 15-oz. pkg.)

½ cup sugar

3 tablespoons all-purpose flour

4 cups chopped peeled ripe pears

1 teaspoon sugar

2 tablespoons sliced almonds

1 Let pie crust pouch stand at room temperature for 15 to 20 minutes.

2 Meanwhile, heat oven to 450° F. In medium bowl, combine ½ cup sugar and flour; blend well. Add pears; toss gently.

3 Remove pie crust from pouch. Unfold crust; remove plastic sheets. Place in ungreased 15 × 10 × 1-inch baking pan. Press out fold lines.

4 Spoon pear mixture onto center of crust, leaving 2-inch border. Fold edge of crust 2 inches over pear mixture; crimp crust slightly. Sprinkle crust edge with 1 teaspoon sugar.

5 Bake at 450° F. for 14 to 20 minutes or until crust is golden brown and pears are tender, sprinkling almonds over pear mixture during last 5 minutes of baking time. Cool at least 15 minutes before serving.

Fresh Pear Crostata

HOT FUDGE PUDDING CAKE

prep time: 15 min. (ready in 1 hr.) • yield: 8 servings

As it bakes, this pudding cake separates into a moist, rich cake layer and a fudgy sauce. Serve the cake warm with whipped cream or ice cream.

1 1/4 cups all-purpose flour

3/4 cup sugar

2 tablespoons unsweetened cocoa

1 1/2 teaspoons baking powder

1/2 teaspoon salt

1/2 cup milk

2 tablespoons margarine or butter, melted

1 teaspoon vanilla

1 cup sugar

2 tablespoons unsweetened cocoa

Dash salt

1 1/3 cups water, heated to 115 to 120° F.

1 Heat oven to 350° F. In small bowl, combine flour, 3/4 cup sugar, 2 tablespoons cocoa, baking powder and 1/2 teaspoon salt; mix well. Stir in milk, margarine and vanilla; blend well. Spread batter in ungreased 9-inch round or square pan.

2 In small bowl, combine 1 cup sugar, 2 tablespoons cocoa and dash salt; mix well. Sprinkle evenly over cake batter. Pour hot water over sugar mixture.

3 Bake at 350° F. for 35 to 45 minutes or until center is set and firm to the touch. Serve warm.

High Altitude (Above 3,500 feet): No change.

CHANTILLY CREAM

Chantilly cream is a French term for sweetened, flavored whipped cream. For each cup of whipping cream, any of the following can be added with the sugar:

- 1 to 2 tablespoons unsweetened cocoa
- 1 tablespoon finely grated orange, lemon or lime peel
- 1/2 to 1 teaspoon instant coffee
- 1/4 teaspoon ginger or cinnamon
- 2 teaspoons liqueur or liquor
- 1 teaspoon vanilla
- 1/4 teaspoon peppermint extract
- 1/4 teaspoon almond extract

"Christmas Classics with a Twist" Menu for 8, pages 288–290

HOLIDAY SPECIALTIES

CHANCES ARE GOOD THAT YOUR EARLIEST HOLIDAY MEMORIES INCLUDE SPECIAL RECIPES—PERHAPS A FANCY CAKE YOUR GRANDMOTHER MADE ONCE A YEAR OR ELABORATE COOKIES YOU HELPED SHAPE AND DECORATE. SOME OF THE RECIPES IN THIS CHAPTER MAY PROMPT YOU TO RECALL THE FLAVORS OF THOSE BYGONE DAYS, WHILE OTHERS ARE LIKELY TO BECOME NEW FAMILY TRADITIONS. REMEMBER TO MAKE PLENTY: HOLIDAY GOODIES ARE MEANT TO BE SHARED!

BAKED HAM WITH ORANGE-MUSTARD GLAZE

prep time: 20 min. (ready in 3 hr.) • yield: 16 servings

Sherry or orange juice in the bottom of the roasting pan helps keep the meat moist while boosting flavor. The sweet-sharp marmalade and mustard glaze can also be used for fresh pork roast.

1 (6- to 8-lb.) fully cooked bone-in ham half

1 cup water

1 cup dry sherry or orange juice

²⁄₃ cup orange marmalade

¹⁄₃ cup stone-ground mustard

3 teaspoons dry mustard

1 Heat oven to 325°F. Place ham, fat side up, in disposable roasting pan (place on baking pan) or on rack in shallow roasting pan. Pour water into pan. Bake at 325°F. for 1 hour.

2 Remove ham from oven. Add sherry to roasting pan. If necessary, trim fat from ham. Score ham diagonally at 1-inch intervals, cutting about ¹⁄₄ inch deep; score in opposite direction to form diamond shapes. Insert meat thermometer so bulb reaches center of thickest part of ham but does not rest in fat or on bone.

3 In small bowl, combine marmalade and mustards; mix well. Brush half of marmalade mixture over ham; baste with pan juices. Return to oven; bake 1 to 1¹⁄₂ hours or until meat thermometer registers 140°F., basting frequently with pan juices and brushing with remaining marmalade mixture.

4 Let ham stand covered in pan for 15 minutes before carving, basting frequently with pan juices.

Nutrition Information Per Serving
Serving Size: ¹⁄₁₆ of Recipe

Calories	200	Calories from Fat	60
		% Daily Value	
Total Fat	7 g	11%	
Saturated	2 g	10%	
Cholesterol	70 mg	23%	
Sodium	1770 mg	74%	
Total Carbohydrate	3 g	1%	
Dietary Fiber	0 g	0%	
Sugars	2 g		
Protein	32 g		
Vitamin A	0%	Vitamin C	0%
Calcium	0%	Iron	6%

Dietary Exchanges: 4 Lean Meat

CARROT-POTATO BAKE

prep time: 30 min. (ready in 1 hr. 45 min.) •
yield: 8 (²⁄₃-cup) servings

Immediately submerging the potatoes in cold water as they're peeled and shredded prevents discoloration. The potatoes and shredded carrots cook together in the oven, bathed in a rich cream sauce.

6 to 8 potatoes

1¹⁄₂ cups shredded carrots

¹⁄₂ cup finely chopped onion

2 cups half-and-half or whipping cream

1 to 1¹⁄₂ teaspoons salt

Dash pepper

1 tablespoon margarine or butter

¹⁄₂ cup soft bread crumbs

2 tablespoons chopped fresh parsley

1 Heat oven to 325°F. Lightly grease 12 × 8-inch (2-quart) baking dish. Peel and shred into cold water enough potatoes to make 6 cups. Drain thoroughly; pat dry with paper towels.

2 In large bowl, combine potatoes, carrots, onion, half-and-half, salt and pepper; mix well. Spoon into greased baking dish.

3 Melt margarine in small saucepan over low heat. Stir in bread crumbs and parsley. Sprinkle over potato mixture.

4 Bake at 325° F. for 60 to 70 minutes or until vegetables are tender. Let stand 5 minutes before serving.

Nutrition Information Per Serving			
Serving Size: ⅔ Cup			
Calories	210	Calories from Fat	80
		% Daily Value	
Total Fat	9 g	14%	
Saturated	5 g	25%	
Cholesterol	20 mg	7%	
Sodium	470 mg	20%	
Total Carbohydrate	27 g	9%	
Dietary Fiber	2 g	8%	
Sugars	5 g		
Protein	4 g		
Vitamin A	120%	Vitamin C	20%
Calcium	8%	Iron	4%

Dietary Exchanges: 1½ Starch, 1 Vegetable, 1½ Fat OR
1½ Carbohydrate, 1 Vegetable, 1½ Fat

CHRISTMAS CLASSICS WITH A TWIST

Here's an elegant menu that's grounded in tradition but served with contemporary flair. Each dish features delightful contrasts of color, texture and flavor.

─── MENU FOR 8 ───

PICTURED ON PAGE 286

Spinach and Pear Salad, p. 290

**Baked Ham with
Orange-Mustard Glaze**

Cranberry-Mango Relish, p. 290

Carrot-Potato Bake

Holiday Vegetable Sauté

Dinner Rolls

Yuletide Red Velvet Cake, p. 313

Milk, Wine and/or Coffee

HOLIDAY VEGETABLE SAUTÉ

prep time: 25 min. • yield: 8 (½-cup) servings

The mix of seasonal colors—green beans, red bell pepper and white onions—makes this a beautiful as well as delicious dish.

1 lb. fresh green beans, trimmed, halved crosswise

1 cup frozen small whole onions

2 tablespoons butter

1 red bell pepper, cut into ¼-inch-wide strips

1 garlic clove, minced

1 teaspoon chopped fresh thyme or ¼ teaspoon dried thyme leaves

⅛ teaspoon salt

1 In medium saucepan, combine green beans and enough water to cover. Bring to a boil. Cook 5 minutes. Drain.

2 In large skillet, combine cooked beans and all remaining ingredients. Cook and stir over medium heat for 6 to 8 minutes or until vegetables are crisp-tender.

Nutrition Information Per Serving			
Serving Size: ½ Cup			
Calories	60	Calories from Fat	25
		% Daily Value	
Total Fat	3 g	5%	
Saturated	2 g	10%	
Cholesterol	10 mg	3%	
Sodium	65 mg	3%	
Total Carbohydrate	6 g	2%	
Dietary Fiber	2 g	8%	
Sugars	2 g		
Protein	1 g		
Vitamin A	20%	Vitamin C	30%
Calcium	2%	Iron	4%

Dietary Exchanges: 1 Vegetable, ½ Fat

SPINACH AND PEAR SALAD

prep time: 25 min. • yield: 8 servings

Heartier salads are appreciated in winter. Here, radicchio and spinach showcase a pleasing combination of pears, walnuts and feta cheese.

4 firm ripe pears

⅓ cup fresh lime juice

1 teaspoon grated lime peel

⅓ cup honey

3 tablespoons olive or vegetable oil

⅛ teaspoon pepper

4 cups torn fresh spinach

¾ cup torn radicchio

½ cup coarsely chopped walnuts

4 oz. (1 cup) crumbled feta cheese

1 Core each pear and cut lengthwise into 8 wedges. Toss with 1 tablespoon of the lime juice to prevent browning.

2 In small jar with tight-fitting lid, combine remaining lime juice, lime peel, honey, oil and pepper; shake well.

3 Arrange spinach and radicchio on individual salad plates. Fan 4 pear wedges on each plate. Sprinkle with walnuts and cheese. Spoon dressing over salads.

Nutrition Information Per Serving
Serving Size: ⅛ of Recipe

Calories	250	Calories from Fat	120
		% Daily Value	
Total Fat	13 g	20%	
Saturated	3 g	15%	
Cholesterol	15 mg	5%	
Sodium	180 mg	8%	
Total Carbohydrate	28 g	9%	
Dietary Fiber	3 g	12%	
Sugars	21 g		
Protein	4 g		
Vitamin A	40%	Vitamin C	25%
Calcium	10%	Iron	8%

Dietary Exchanges: 2 Fruit, ½ Medium-Fat Meat, 2 Fat OR 2 Carbohydrate, ½ Medium-Fat Meat, 2 Fat

Cook's Notes

CRANBERRY-MANGO RELISH

prep time: 15 min. (ready in 1 hr. 45 min.) • yield: 3 cups

For a change of pace from the usual cranberry-orange concoctions, try this pairing of cranberries and mango. Save leftovers to spread on sandwiches.

½ cup sugar

½ cup firmly packed brown sugar

1 cup water

3 cups fresh or frozen cranberries

1 cup diced fresh or canned mango, drained

1 tablespoon Dijon mustard

1 In medium saucepan, combine sugar, brown sugar and water. Bring to a boil over medium heat.

2 Add cranberries; return to a boil. Reduce heat to low; simmer 10 minutes or until cranberries pop and mixture is slightly thickened, stirring occasionally. Cool completely.

3 Stir in mango and mustard. Cover; refrigerate until serving time.

Nutrition Information Per Serving
Serving Size: 1 Tablespoon

Calories	25	Calories from Fat	0
		% Daily Value	
Total Fat	0 g	0%	
Saturated	0 g	0%	
Cholesterol	0 mg	0%	
Sodium	10 mg	0%	
Total Carbohydrate	6 g	2%	
Dietary Fiber	0 g	0%	
Sugars	5 g		
Protein	0 g		
Vitamin A	2%	Vitamin C	2%
Calcium	0%	Iron	0%

Dietary Exchanges: ½ Fruit OR ½ Carbohydrate

DICKENS CHRISTMAS SUPPER

The rich, hearty flavors of a traditional English holiday dinner are streamlined for the American kitchen.

— MENU FOR 8 —

PICTURED ON PAGE 292

Burgundy, Tawny Port or Zinfandel Wine

Standing Rib Roast

Yorkshire Pudding, p. 292

Apricot-Glazed Carrots, p. 234

Green Bean–Hazelnut Salad, p. 293

Chocolate-Date-Pecan Pie, p. 275

Tea with Milk, Sugar and/or Lemon Slices

STANDING RIB ROAST

prep time: 15 min. (ready in 4 hr. 15 min.) •
yield: 12 servings

Horseradish sauce is a traditional condiment for rib roast. To improvise an easy version, stir prepared horseradish (to taste) into approximately 2 cups of non-fat plain yogurt.

1 (4- to 6-lb.) standing beef rib roast

1 Heat oven to 325°F. Place roast, fat side up, on rack in shallow roasting pan. Insert meat thermometer so bulb reaches center of thickest part of meat but does not rest in fat or on bone.

2 Bake at 325°F. for 2 to 4 hours or until of desired doneness.*

3 Let roast stand covered for 10 to 15 minutes before carving. To carve, slice from outside toward rib bone and then cut along bone to remove slice of meat. If desired, season to taste with salt and pepper.

TIP: *Roast beef to 140°F. for rare, 160°F. for medium and 170°F. for well-done.

Nutrition Information Per Serving
Serving Size: 1/12 of Recipe

Calories	230	Calories from Fat	120
		% Daily Value	
Total Fat	13 g	20%	
Saturated	5 g	25%	
Cholesterol	80 mg	27%	
Sodium	75 mg	3%	
Total Carbohydrate	0 g	0%	
Dietary Fiber	0 g	0%	
Sugars	0 g		
Protein	28 g		
Vitamin A	0%	Vitamin C	0%
Calcium	0%	Iron	15%

Dietary Exchanges: 4 Lean Meat

YORKSHIRE PUDDING

prep time: 45 min. • **yield: 8 servings**

In England, roast beef wouldn't be the same without Yorkshire pudding! The pudding, a cross between a pop-over and a soufflé, is baked with drippings from the beef and should be eaten as soon as it emerges from the oven.

¼ cup roast beef drippings*

2 eggs

1 cup all-purpose flour

½ teaspoon salt

1 cup milk

1 Heat oven to 425° F. Pour beef drippings into ungreased 9-inch square pan; tilt pan to coat bottom and sides. Place pan in oven to heat about 2 minutes.

2 In small bowl, beat eggs slightly. Add flour, salt and milk; beat just until blended. DO NOT OVERBEAT. Pour batter into hot pan.

3 Bake at 425° F. for 15 minutes. Reduce oven temperature to 350° F.; bake an additional 10 to 15 minutes or until puffed and golden brown. Serve immediately.

TIP: *One-fourth cup shortening, melted, can be substituted for roast beef drippings.

"Dickens Christmas Supper"
Menu for 8, pages 291–293

Calories	110	Calories from Fat	35
		% Daily Value	
Total Fat	4 g	6%	
Saturated	2 g	10%	
Cholesterol	60 mg	20%	
Sodium	180 mg	8%	
Total Carbohydrate	14 g	5%	
Dietary Fiber	0 g	0%	
Sugars	2 g		
Protein	5 g		
Vitamin A	2%	Vitamin C	0%
Calcium	4%	Iron	6%

Dietary Exchanges: 1 Starch, 1/2 Fat OR 1 Carbohydrate, 1/2 Fat

GREEN BEAN-HAZELNUT SALAD

prep time: 15 min. (ready in 2 hr. 15 min.) •
yield: 8 (3/4-cup) servings

Toasted hazelnuts and cherry tomatoes elevate a green bean salad to holiday side-dish status. It can be assembled in advance, making it perfect for entertaining.

1/3 cup oil

1/4 cup cider vinegar

2 teaspoons sugar

1/4 teaspoon salt

1/8 teaspoon dried basil leaves

1 teaspoon Dijon mustard

2 (8-oz.) pkg. frozen cut green beans in a pouch, cooked, drained

2 cups cherry tomatoes, halved

1 cup hazelnuts (filberts), toasted*

1 In large bowl, combine oil, vinegar, sugar, salt, basil and mustard; blend well. Add cooked beans; toss to coat well. Cover; refrigerate 2 hours or overnight.

2 Just before serving, stir in tomatoes and hazelnuts.

TIP: *To toast hazelnuts, spread on cookie sheet; bake at 350° F. for 5 to 10 minutes or until light golden brown; cool. To remove skins, gently rub hazelnuts between fingers.

Calories	230	Calories from Fat	180
		% Daily Value	
Total Fat	20 g	31%	
Saturated	2 g	10%	
Cholesterol	0 mg	0%	
Sodium	150 mg	6%	
Total Carbohydrate	9 g	3%	
Dietary Fiber	3 g	12%	
Sugars	4 g		
Protein	3 g		
Vitamin A	10%	Vitamin C	15%
Calcium	6%	Iron	6%

Dietary Exchanges: 2 Vegetable, 4 Fat

HAZELNUTS

Hazelnuts, also known as filberts, are sweet, rich, grape-sized nuts. Hazelnuts have a bitter brown skin that is best removed by heating them at 350°F. for 8 to 10 minutes until the skin begins to crack and flake. Place a handful of warm nuts between layers of a clean dishtowel and rub vigorously to remove the skins. Hazelnuts are usually packaged whole, and can be used whole, chopped or ground in bread and dessert recipes and in a variety of main dishes, salads and side dishes.

Cook's Notes

FESTIVE HOLIDAY BARK

prep time: 15 min. (ready in 45 min.) •
yield: 42 (1 ½ × 1 ½-inch) pieces

Pretzel twists are the surprise here; the saltiness sets off the sweet candy coating.

16 oz. vanilla-flavored candy coating, chopped

2 cups small pretzel twists

½ cup red and green candy-coated chocolate pieces

1 Line cookie sheet with waxed paper. In medium saucepan, melt candy coating over low heat, stirring constantly.

2 Add remaining ingredients; toss to coat. Spread mixture thinly on waxed paper–lined cookie sheet. Cool 30 minutes or until set. Break into pieces.

Nutrition Information Per Serving
Serving Size: 1 Piece

Calories	80	Calories from Fat	35
		% Daily Value	
Total Fat	4 g	6%	
Saturated	2 g	10%	
Cholesterol	3 mg	1%	
Sodium	70 mg	3%	
Total Carbohydrate	11 g	4%	
Dietary Fiber	0 g	0%	
Sugars	8 g		
Protein	1 g		
Vitamin A	0%	Vitamin C	0%
Calcium	2%	Iron	0%

Dietary Exchanges: ½ Fruit, 1 Fat OR ½ Carbohydrate, 1 Fat

MICROWAVE ALMOND BRITTLE

prep time: 15 min. (ready in 45 min.) • yield: 15 ounces

Almond brittle is a delightfully old-fashioned snack. Handle the sugar mixture carefully: It is extremely hot and may foam up when the baking soda is added.

1 cup sugar

½ cup light corn syrup

1 cup whole blanched almonds

1 teaspoon butter

1 teaspoon almond extract

1 teaspoon baking soda

1 MICROWAVE DIRECTIONS: Line cookie sheet with foil; lightly butter. In 8-cup microwave-safe measuring cup or medium microwave-safe bowl, combine sugar and corn syrup; mix well.

2 Microwave on HIGH for 4 minutes; stir. Add almonds; blend well. Microwave on HIGH for 3½ to 4½ minutes or until mixture is very light brown. Stir in butter and almond extract. Microwave on HIGH for 1 minute.

3 Add baking soda; stir quickly to blend. Pour immediately onto buttered, foil-lined cookie sheet, spreading mixture quickly with wooden spoon. Cool 30 minutes. Break into pieces. Store in tightly covered container.

Nutrition Information Per Serving
Serving Size: 1 Ounce

Calories	150	Calories from Fat	45
		% Daily Value	
Total Fat	5 g	8%	
Saturated	1 g	5%	
Cholesterol	0 mg	0%	
Sodium	100 mg	4%	
Total Carbohydrate	24 g	8%	
Dietary Fiber	1 g	4%	
Sugars	18 g		
Protein	2 g		
Vitamin A	0%	Vitamin C	0%
Calcium	2%	Iron	2%

Dietary Exchanges: 1 1/2 Fruit, 1 Fat OR 1 1/2 Carbohydrate, 1 Fat

PEPPERMINT SWIRL FUDGE

prep time: 25 min. (ready in 1 hr. 25 min.) • yield: 36 squares

Prepared vanilla frosting streamlines preparation of this minty-cool fudge that's beautifully marbled with red food color.

1 (12-oz.) pkg. (2 cups) white vanilla chips

1 (16-oz.) can vanilla frosting

1/2 teaspoon peppermint extract

4 drops red food color

2 tablespoons peppermint candies, crushed

1 Line 8-inch square pan with foil so foil extends over sides of pan; lightly butter foil. Melt vanilla chips in large saucepan over very low heat, stirring until smooth.*

2 Remove saucepan from heat; stir in frosting and peppermint extract. Spread in buttered foil-lined pan.

3 Drop food color over fudge. Pull knife through mixture to marble. Sprinkle with crushed candy; press lightly. Refrigerate about 1 hour or until firm.

4 Remove fudge from pan by lifting foil; remove foil from sides of fudge. With long knife, cut fudge into squares.

TIP: *To melt vanilla chips in microwave, place chips in large microwave-safe bowl; microwave on HIGH for 1 to 2 minutes. Stir until smooth.

Nutrition Information Per Serving
Serving Size: 1 Square

Calories	90	Calories from Fat	35
		% Daily Value	
Total Fat	4 g	6%	
Saturated	2 g	10%	
Cholesterol	0 mg	0%	
Sodium	30 mg	1%	
Total Carbohydrate	13 g	4%	
Dietary Fiber	0 g	0%	
Sugars	12 g		
Protein	0 g		
Vitamin A	0%	Vitamin C	0%
Calcium	0%	Iron	0%

Dietary Exchanges: 1 Fruit, 1/2 Fat OR 1 Carbohydrate, 1/2 Fat

TRIPLE CHOCOLATE FUDGE

prep time: 40 min. (ready in 1 hr. 40 min.) • yield: 60 squares

Chocolate chips, sweet baking chocolate and unsweetened chocolate team up to make this fudge three times the treat.

4½ cups sugar

½ cup butter

1 (12-oz.) can (1½ cups) evaporated milk

4½ cups miniature marshmallows

1 (12-oz.) pkg. (2 cups) semi-sweet chocolate chips

12 oz. sweet baking chocolate, cut into pieces

2 oz. unsweetened chocolate, cut into pieces

2 teaspoons vanilla

¼ teaspoon almond extract

1 cup chopped walnuts or pecans

Colored sugar, if desired

1 Line 15 × 10 × 1-inch baking pan with foil so foil extends over sides of pan; grease foil. In large saucepan, combine sugar, butter and evaporated milk; cook and stir over medium heat until sugar is dissolved. Bring to a full boil, stirring constantly. Boil uncovered over medium heat without stirring for 5 minutes.

2 Remove saucepan from heat. Add marshmallows; stir until melted. Add chocolate chips, sweet chocolate and unsweetened chocolate, stirring constantly until all chocolate is melted and mixture is smooth. Stir in vanilla, almond extract and walnuts. Quickly spread mixture in greased foil-lined pan. Sprinkle with colored sugar. Cool 1 hour or until completely cooled.

3 Remove fudge from pan by lifting foil; remove foil from sides of fudge. With long knife, cut fudge into squares.

Nutrition Information Per Serving
Serving Size: 1 Square

Calories	170	Calories from Fat	60
		% Daily Value	
Total Fat	7 g	11%	
Saturated	4 g	20%	
Cholesterol	5 mg	2%	
Sodium	25 mg	1%	
Total Carbohydrate	26 g	9%	
Dietary Fiber	1 g	4%	
Sugars	23 g		
Protein	1 g		
Vitamin A	0%	Vitamin C	0%
Calcium	2%	Iron	2%

Dietary Exchanges: ½ Starch, 1 Fruit, 1½ Fat OR 1½ Carbohydrate, 1½ Fat

FRUIT AND FUDGE COMBO

Arrange squares of Triple Chocolate Fudge in a holiday box or tin. Place the box or tin in a basket and surround it with several pieces of fruit—red apples and green pears, for instance—and add a holiday candle and holder. Include some seasonal greenery such as pine or balsam and a large bow. You've created a lovely gift!

Cook's Notes

CHERRY-CHOCOLATE BISCOTTI

prep time: 40 min. (ready in 1 hr. 10 min.) •
yield: 3 dozen cookies

Italian biscotti (literally, "twice cooked") bake first in a loaf, then in individual slices. They're traditionally dunked in coffee or sweet wine before eating.

¾ cup sugar

½ cup margarine or butter, softened

2 teaspoons almond extract

3 eggs

3 cups all-purpose flour

2 teaspoons baking powder

½ cup chopped candied cherries

½ cup miniature chocolate chips

3 tablespoons chocolate chips, melted, if desired

3 tablespoons white vanilla chips, melted, if desired

1 Heat oven to 350°F. Lightly grease cookie sheet. In large bowl, combine sugar and margarine; beat until well blended. Add almond extract and eggs; blend well. Add flour and baking powder; mix well. Stir in cherries and miniature chocolate chips. Shape dough into two 10-inch rolls. Place rolls 5 inches apart on greased cookie sheet; flatten each to 3-inch width.

2 Bake at 350°F. for 20 to 25 minutes or until set and light golden brown. Remove from cookie sheet; place on wire racks. Cool 10 minutes.

3 With serrated knife, cut rolls diagonally into ½-inch-thick slices. Arrange slices, cut side down, on ungreased cookie sheets.

4 Bake at 350°F. for 8 to 10 minutes or until bottoms begin to brown. Turn cookies over; bake an additional 5 minutes or until browned and crisp. Remove from cookie sheets; cool 15 minutes or until completely cooled.

5 Drizzle cookies with melted chocolate and vanilla chips. Store in tightly covered container.

High Altitude (Above 3,500 feet): No change.

Nutrition Information Per Serving
Serving Size: 1 Cookie

Calories	110	Calories from Fat	35
		% Daily Value	
Total Fat	4 g	6%	
Saturated	1 g	5%	
Cholesterol	20 mg	7%	
Sodium	70 mg	3%	
Total Carbohydrate	17 g	6%	
Dietary Fiber	0 g	0%	
Sugars	8 g		
Protein	2 g		
Vitamin A	2%	Vitamin C	0%
Calcium	2%	Iron	4%

Dietary Exchanges: 1 Fruit, 1 Fat OR 1 Carbohydrate, 1 Fat

WRAPPING SUGGESTIONS FOR GIFTS FROM THE KITCHEN

Wrappings:
- Decorative boxes, bags, tins or mugs
- Baskets of all shapes, sizes and colors
- Assorted tissue, patterned or foil papers
- Clear or patterned cellophane
- Colorful kitchen towels
- Attractive cording or ribbons

Attachments:
- Personalized labels
- Recipe cards
- Gift or enclosure cards
- Small cookie cutters or kitchen gadgets
- Sample packs of specialty coffee or tea

EASY SANTA COOKIES

prep time: 1 hr. (ready in 2 hr.) • yield: 34 cookies

Decorated with powdered sugar icing and assorted trimmings, round sugar cookies take on the appearance of the jolly old elf himself.

COOKIES
1 (18-oz.) pkg. refrigerated sugar cookies

FROSTING
2 cups powdered sugar

2 tablespoons margarine or butter, softened

2 to 3 tablespoons milk

2 to 3 drops red food color

68 semi-sweet chocolate chips (about ¼ cup)

34 cinnamon candies

⅔ cup coconut

34 miniature marshmallows

1 Freeze cookie dough for at least 1 hour.

2 Heat oven to 350°F. Cut frozen dough into ¼-inch-thick slices. (Return dough to freezer if it becomes too soft to cut.) Place slices 3 inches apart on ungreased cookie sheets.

3 Bake at 350°F. for 8 to 12 minutes or until golden brown. Cool 2 minutes; remove from cookie sheets. Cool completely.

4 Meanwhile, in small bowl, combine powdered sugar, margarine and enough milk for desired spreading consistency; beat until smooth. Place half of frosting in small bowl. Add red food color; stir until blended.

5 Frost top ⅓ of each cooled cookie with red frosting; frost bottom ⅓ with white frosting. Pipe white frosting along bottom edge of red frosting for fur on hat.

6 Use small amount of frosting to attach chocolate chips for eyes and cinnamon candy for nose. Gently press coconut into white frosting for beard. Press marshmallow into red frosting for tassel on cap. Let stand until frosting is set. Store between sheets of waxed paper in tightly covered container.

Nutrition Information Per Serving
Serving Size: 1 Cookie

Calories	110	Calories from Fat	35
		% Daily Value	
Total Fat	4 g	6%	
Saturated	1 g	5%	
Cholesterol	0 mg	0%	
Sodium	70 mg	3%	
Total Carbohydrate	18 g	6%	
Dietary Fiber	0 g	0%	
Sugars	13 g		
Protein	1 g		
Vitamin A	0%	Vitamin C	0%
Calcium	0%	Iron	0%

Dietary Exchanges: 1 Starch, ½ Fat OR 1 Carbohydrate, ½ Fat

Easy Santa Cookies

PACKING COOKIES, BROWNIES AND BARS FOR SHIPPING

Best choices for sending:

- Unfrosted crispy or chewy bars
- Chewy or fudgy brownies
- Firm cut-out cookies
- Drop cookies

Poor choices:

- Cakelike brownies or bars
- Soft cookies
- Cookies or bars with soft frosting
- Fragile or delicate cookies
- Cookies or bars with ingredients that might melt or spoil

How to pack:

- Use plastic or metal containers
- Line containers with plastic wrap, waxed paper or aluminum foil
- Cushion cookies with crumpled waxed paper so they won't shift
- Wrap tender cookies individually in plastic wrap or in back-to-back pairs

How to ship:

- Pack each container of cookies, brownies or bars in a strong cardboard shipping box
- Tuck crumpled newspaper or waxed paper around container to prevent shifting
- Label box carefully
- Mark the shipping box "perishable" to encourage careful handling

EGGNOG CUT-OUT COOKIES

prep time: 1 hr. 50 min. (ready in 2 hr. 20 min.) •
yield: 8 dozen (2½- to 3-inch) cookies

"Paint" made of egg yolk and liquid food color dresses up this cookie dough.

COOKIES
1 cup butter, softened

2 cups sugar

2 eggs

⅓ cup eggnog

1 teaspoon vanilla

4 cups all-purpose flour

1 teaspoon nutmeg

2 teaspoons baking powder

EGG YOLK PAINT
2 egg yolks

½ teaspoon water

Assorted colors of liquid food color

1 In large bowl, combine butter, sugar and eggs; beat until light and fluffy. Stir in eggnog and vanilla. In medium bowl, combine flour, nutmeg and baking powder; mix well. Add flour mixture to butter mixture; blend well. Cover with plastic wrap; refrigerate 30 minutes for easier handling.

2 Meanwhile, in small bowl, combine egg yolks and water; blend well. Divide mixture into several small cups; tint with food color. If paint thickens, add a few drops water.

3 Heat oven to 350° F. Divide dough in half. On lightly floured surface, roll half of dough to ⅛-inch thickness. Cut with assorted cookie cutters. Place 2 inches apart on ungreased cookie sheets. Using small paint brush, paint designs on cookies with egg yolk paint.

4 Bake at 350° F. for 7 to 10 minutes or until light golden brown. Immediately remove from cookie sheets.

High Altitude (Above 3,500 feet):
Increase flour to 4 ¼ cups. Bake as directed above.

Nutrition Information Per Serving
Serving Size: 1 Cookie

Calories	50	Calories from Fat	20
		% Daily Value	
Total Fat	2 g	3%	
Saturated	1 g	5%	
Cholesterol	15 mg	5%	
Sodium	30 mg	1%	
Total Carbohydrate	8 g	3%	
Dietary Fiber	0 g	0%	
Sugars	4 g		
Protein	1 g		
Vitamin A	0%	Vitamin C	0%
Calcium	0%	Iron	0%

Dietary Exchanges: ½ Starch OR ½ Carbohydrate

NUTMEG COOKIE LOGS

prep time: 1 hr. 30 min. (ready in 2 hr.) •
yield: 5 dozen cookies

For the freshest-tasting spice, purchase whole nutmeg and grate it using a small, specially designed grater.

COOKIES
¾ cup sugar

1 cup margarine or butter, softened

2 teaspoons vanilla

2 teaspoons rum extract

1 egg

3 cups all-purpose flour

1 teaspoon nutmeg

FROSTING
2 cups powdered sugar

3 tablespoons margarine or butter, softened

¾ teaspoon rum extract

¼ teaspoon vanilla

2 to 3 tablespoons half-and-half or milk

Nutmeg

1 In large bowl, combine sugar, 1 cup margarine, 2 teaspoons vanilla, 2 teaspoons rum extract and egg; beat until light and fluffy. Stir in flour and 1 teaspoon nutmeg; mix well. Cover with plastic wrap; refrigerate 30 to 45 minutes for easier handling.

2 Heat oven to 350° F. Divide dough into 6 pieces. On lightly floured surface, shape each piece of dough into long rope, ½ inch in diameter. Cut into 3-inch lengths; place on ungreased cookie sheets.

3 Bake at 350° F. for 12 to 15 minutes or until light golden brown. Immediately remove from cookie sheets. Cool completely.

4 In small bowl, combine all frosting ingredients except nutmeg, adding enough half-and-half for desired spreading consistency. Spread on top and sides of cookies. If desired, mark frosting with tines of fork to resemble bark. Sprinkle lightly with nutmeg. Let stand until frosting is set. Store in tightly covered container.

High Altitude (Above 3,500 feet): No change.

Nutrition Information Per Serving
Serving Size: 1 Cookie

Calories	80	Calories from Fat	35
		% Daily Value	
Total Fat	4 g	6%	
Saturated	1 g	5%	
Cholesterol	4 mg	1%	
Sodium	45 mg	2%	
Total Carbohydrate	11 g	4%	
Dietary Fiber	0 g	0%	
Sugars	6 g		
Protein	1 g		
Vitamin A	4%	Vitamin C	0%
Calcium	0%	Iron	0%

Dietary Exchanges: ½ Starch, 1 Fat OR ½ Carbohydrate, 1 Fat

TWO-IN-ONE HOLIDAY BARS

prep time: 15 min. (ready in 1 hr. 40 min.) • yield: 4 bars

Get double mileage out of one recipe by topping half of the batter with candied fruit, half with chocolate chips and nuts. If you wish, vary the glaze by mixing the powdered sugar with orange juice or liqueur instead of milk.

BASE

1 cup sugar

¾ cup margarine or butter, softened

1 teaspoon vanilla

1 egg

2 cups all-purpose flour

1 cup diced mixed candied fruit

½ cup semi-sweet chocolate chips

½ cup chopped pecans

GLAZE

1 cup powdered sugar

1 to 2 tablespoons milk

1. Heat oven to 350° F. In large bowl, combine sugar and margarine; beat until light and fluffy. Add vanilla and egg; blend well. Add flour; mix well. Spread dough in ungreased 15 × 10 × 1-inch baking pan.

2. Sprinkle half of dough with candied fruit; sprinkle other half with chocolate chips and pecans. Press lightly into dough.

3. Bake at 350° F. for 25 to 30 minutes or until edges are light golden brown. Cool 1 hour or until completely cooled.

4. In small bowl, combine powdered sugar and enough milk for desired drizzling consistency; blend until smooth. Drizzle over cooled bars. Let stand until set. Cut into bars.

High Altitude (Above 3,500 feet):
Increase flour to 2 ¼ cups. Bake as directed above.

Nutrition Information Per Serving
Serving Size: 1 Bar with Fruit

Calories	90	Calories from Fat 25
		% Daily Value
Total Fat	3 g	5%
Saturated	1 g	5%
Cholesterol	4 mg	1%
Sodium	55 mg	2%
Total Carbohydrate	16 g	5%
Dietary Fiber	0 g	0%
Sugars	11 g	
Protein	1 g	
Vitamin A	2%	Vitamin C 10%
Calcium	0%	Iron 0%

Dietary Exchanges: ½ Starch, ½ Fruit, ½ Fat OR 1 Carbohydrate, ½ Fat

Nutrition Information Per Serving
Serving Size: 1 Bar with Chips and Nuts

Calories	110	Calories from Fat 50
		% Daily Value
Total Fat	6 g	9%
Saturated	1 g	5%
Cholesterol	4 mg	1%
Sodium	35 mg	1%
Total Carbohydrate	13 g	4%
Dietary Fiber	1 g	2%
Sugars	9 g	
Protein	1 g	
Vitamin A	2%	Vitamin C 0%
Calcium	0%	Iron 2%

Dietary Exchanges: ½ Starch, ½ Fruit, 1 Fat OR 1 Carbohydrate, 1 Fat

CANDY CANE COFFEE CAKE

prep time: 20 min. (ready in 1 hr. 15 min.) • yield: 12 servings

Clever snipping and tucking transforms refrigerated crescent roll dough into a candy cane shape with cherry-flavored filling peeping through.

COFFEE CAKE

1 (3-oz.) pkg. cream cheese, softened

2 tablespoons sugar

1 teaspoon almond extract

¼ cup chopped almonds

¼ cup chopped maraschino cherries, drained

1 (8-oz.) can refrigerated crescent dinner rolls

1 egg, slightly beaten

GLAZE

½ cup powdered sugar

2 teaspoons milk or maraschino cherry liquid

1 Heat oven to 375°F. Grease cookie sheet. In small bowl, combine cream cheese and sugar; beat until light and fluffy. Stir in almond extract, almonds and cherries. Set aside.

2 On greased cookie sheet, unroll dough into 2 long rectangles. Overlap long sides to form 13 × 7-inch rectangle; firmly press perforations and edges to seal. Spoon cream cheese mixture down center third of rectangle.

3 On each long side of rectangle, make cuts 1 inch apart to edge of filling. Fold opposite strips of dough over filling to form a braided appearance. Seal ends. Form braid into candy cane shape. Brush top of braid with beaten egg.

4 Bake at 375°F. for 18 to 22 minutes or until golden brown. Cool 30 minutes or until completely cooled.

5 In small bowl, combine glaze ingredients; blend until smooth. Drizzle over coffee cake. If desired, garnish with additional cherries. Store in refrigerator.

Nutrition Information Per Serving			
Serving Size: ¹⁄₁₂ of Recipe			
Calories	150	Calories from Fat	70
		% Daily Value	
Total Fat	8 g	12%	
Saturated	3 g	15%	
Cholesterol	25 mg	8%	
Sodium	170 mg	7%	
Total Carbohydrate	16 g	5%	
Dietary Fiber	1 g	2%	
Sugars	9 g		
Protein	3 g		
Vitamin A	2%	Vitamin C	0%
Calcium	2%	Iron	4%

Dietary Exchanges: ½ Starch, ½ Fruit, 1 ½ Fat OR 1 Carbohydrate, 1 ½ Fat

Quick Holiday
Cranberry Bread

QUICK HOLIDAY CRANBERRY BREAD

prep time: 15 min. (ready in 2 hr. 35 min.)

• **yield: 1 (12-slice) loaf**

Short on time? Doctor up a purchased cranberry bread mix with nuts and grated orange peel. To keep the loaf tender, don't overmix the batter.

1 (15.6-oz.) pkg. cranberry quick bread mix

½ cup chopped nuts

1 tablespoon grated orange peel

½ cup orange juice

½ cup water

2 tablespoons oil

1 egg

1 Heat oven to 350°F. Grease and flour bottom only of 8 × 4- or 9 × 5-inch loaf pan. In large bowl, combine all ingredients. Stir 50 to 75 strokes with spoon until mix is moistened. Pour batter into greased and floured pan.

2 Bake at 350°F. for 55 to 65 minutes or until toothpick inserted in center comes out clean. Cool 15 minutes; remove from pan. Cool 1 hour or until completely cooled. Wrap tightly and store in refrigerator.

High Altitude (Above 3,500 feet):
Add 1 tablespoon flour to dry quick bread mix. Bake at 375°F. for 35 to 45 minutes.

Nutrition Information Per Serving
Serving Size: 1 Slice

Calories	200	Calories from Fat	60
		% Daily Value	
Total Fat	7 g	11%	
Saturated	1 g	5%	
Cholesterol	20 mg	7%	
Sodium	160 mg	7%	
Total Carbohydrate	32 g	11%	
Dietary Fiber	1 g	4%	
Sugars	17 g		
Protein	3 g		
Vitamin A	0%	Vitamin C	6%
Calcium	0%	Iron	8%

Dietary Exchanges: 1 Starch, 1 Fruit, 1½ Fat OR 2 Carbohydrate, 1½ Fat

CITRUS PEEL

The thin, colored outer peel of oranges, lemons and limes contains flavorful oils, while the white pith underneath is bitter. Be sure to remove just the colored part of the peel. To accomplish this, use the fine holes of a regular grater or invest in a citrus zester, a tool that resembles a vegetable peeler except it has a horizontal row of small holes instead of a long vertical blade. A zester removes longer strands of the peel or "zest." Another technique, although a bit more cumbersome, is to shave off the outer peel with a sharp paring knife or vegetable peeler, then use a chef's knife to chop it into shreds.

TANNENBAUM COFFEE CAKES

prep time: 45 min. (ready in 2 hr. 45 min.) •
yield: 2 (24-slice) coffee cakes

COFFEE CAKES
5 to 6 cups all-purpose flour

$\frac{1}{2}$ cup sugar

2 teaspoons salt

2 pkg. active dry yeast

$1\frac{1}{2}$ cups milk

$\frac{1}{2}$ cup margarine or butter

2 eggs

FILLING
4 tablespoons margarine or butter, melted

1 cup sugar

$\frac{1}{2}$ cup chopped nuts

1 tablespoon cinnamon

TOPPING
1 cup powdered sugar

2 to 3 tablespoons milk

Candied cherries

1 In large bowl, combine 2 cups flour, $\frac{1}{2}$ cup sugar, salt and yeast; mix well. In medium saucepan, heat $1\frac{1}{2}$ cups milk and $\frac{1}{2}$ cup margarine until very warm (120 to 130° F.). Add warm liquid and eggs to flour mixture; blend at low speed until moistened. Beat 3 minutes at medium speed. By hand, stir in an additional 2 to $2\frac{1}{2}$ cups flour to form a stiff dough.

2 On floured surface, knead in 1 to $1\frac{1}{2}$ cups flour until dough is smooth and elastic, 5 to 8 minutes. Place dough in greased bowl; cover loosely with greased plastic wrap and cloth towel. Let rise in warm place (80 to 85° F.) until light and doubled in size, 1 to $1\frac{1}{4}$ hours.

3 Generously grease two $15 \times 10 \times 1$-inch baking pans. Punch down dough several times to

COOK'S KNOW-HOW

HOW TO SHAPE TANNENBAUM COFFEE CAKES

Bake your best for the holidays with this recipe for cinnamon and nut–filled coffee cakes. The dough is shaped into two beautiful tree-shaped breads—one to give as a gift and one to enjoy with your family on Christmas morning.

STEP 1

Roll half of the dough into a triangle with two 15-inch sides and a 12-inch base. Brush with 1 tablespoon of the melted margarine; sprinkle with half of the filling.

STEP 2

Fold 15-inch sides of triangle to meet in center, completely covering filling. Press all seams to seal. Invert, seam side down, onto greased pan.

STEP 3

Make 12 slits (1 inch apart) along outside edges to within $\frac{1}{2}$ inch of center of dough. Twist each strip so cut side is up to show filling.

remove all air bubbles. Divide dough into 2 equal parts. On lightly floured surface, roll one part into a triangle with two 15-inch sides and a 12-inch base.* Brush with 1 tablespoon of the melted margarine.

4 In small bowl, combine 2 tablespoons melted margarine, 1 cup sugar, nuts and cinnamon; mix well. Sprinkle half of filling mixture evenly over dough.

5 To shape tree, starting at top point of dough triangle, fold 15-inch sides to meet in center, pressing all seams to seal. Invert, seam side down, onto greased pan.

6 With scissors or sharp knife, make 12 slits about 1 inch apart along each long outside edge of tree, cutting to within ½ inch of center of dough. Starting at bottom of tree, twist each strip so cut side is up to show filling. Cover; let rise in warm place until light and doubled in size, 30 to 40 minutes. Repeat with remaining dough and filling to make second coffee cake.

7 Heat oven to 350° F. Uncover dough. Bake 20 to 30 minutes or until golden brown. Cool 5 minutes. Remove from pans; cool on wire racks for 30 minutes or until completely cooled. In small bowl, blend powdered sugar and enough milk for desired drizzling consistency. Drizzle over coffee cakes. Garnish with candied cherries.

TIP: *For easier shaping of each coffee cake, roll dough on lightly floured cookie sheet. When ready to place on baking pan, invert baking pan over tree on cookie sheet. Invert again; remove cookie sheet.

High Altitude (Above 3,500 feet): No change.

Nutrition Information Per Serving
Serving Size: 1 Slice

Calories		130	Calories from Fat	35
			% Daily Value	
Total Fat		4 g	6%	
Saturated		1 g	5%	
Cholesterol		10 mg	3%	
Sodium		135 mg	6%	
Total Carbohydrate		22 g	7%	
Dietary Fiber		1 g	3%	
Sugars		10 g		
Protein		2 g		
Vitamin A		4%	Vitamin C	0%
Calcium		0%	Iron	6%

Dietary Exchanges: 1 Starch, ½ Fruit, ½ Fat OR 1 ½ Carbohydrate, ½ Fat

Tannenbaum Coffee Cakes

TREE-SHAPED BREADSTICKS

prep time: 30 min. • yield: 8 breadsticks

An "eggwash" of egg and water brushed on the dough promotes browning and gives the breadsticks a shiny top. It also helps the seeds adhere to the dough.

1 (11-oz.) can refrigerated breadsticks

1 egg

1 tablespoon water

Sesame or poppy seed

1 Heat oven to 350° F. Lightly grease cookie sheets. Separate dough into 8 pieces. Unroll each breadstick into an 18-inch rope. Cut off 1 inch of each breadstick for tree trunk.

2 On greased cookie sheet, shape each breadstick into a tree. Place trunk at base of tree.

3 In small bowl, combine egg and water; blend well. Brush over trees; sprinkle with sesame seed.

4 Bake at 350° F. for 14 to 16 minutes or until golden brown. Serve warm.

Nutrition Information Per Serving
Serving Size: 1 Breadstick

Calories	120	Calories from Fat	25
		% Daily Value	
Total Fat	3 g	5%	
Saturated	1 g	5%	
Cholesterol	25 mg	8%	
Sodium	290 mg	12%	
Total Carbohydrate	19 g	6%	
Dietary Fiber	1 g	3%	
Sugars	3 g		
Protein	4 g		
Vitamin A	0%	Vitamin C	0%
Calcium	0%	Iron	6%

Dietary Exchanges: 1 Starch, ½ Fat OR 1 Carbohydrate, ½ Fat

Tree-Shaped Breadsticks

RASPBERRY RAZZLE-DAZZLE

prep time: 30 min. (ready in 7 hr. 15 min.) •
yield: 15 servings

Cassis, a specialty of France's Dijon area, is a sweet, pungent liqueur made with black currants. It adds depth of flavor to a beautiful red-purple sauce that's spooned over this frozen raspberry-vanilla dessert.

DESSERT
30 chocolate-covered graham cracker cookies, finely crushed (about 2 cups crumbs)

1 quart (4 cups) vanilla ice cream, slightly softened

1 pint (2 cups) raspberry sherbet, slightly softened

1 (4-oz.) container (1½ cups) frozen whipped topping, thawed

SAUCE
½ cup cranberry juice cocktail

2 tablespoons sugar

2 teaspoons cornstarch

¼ cup crème de cassis or cranberry juice cocktail

1 (12-oz.) pkg. frozen raspberries without syrup, thawed

1 Heat oven to 375°F. Spray 13 X 9-inch pan with nonstick cooking spray. Press cookie crumbs in bottom of sprayed pan. Bake at 375°F. for 7 minutes. Place in refrigerator or freezer until cool.

2 Spoon ice cream over cooled crust. Place spoonfuls of sherbet randomly over ice cream; swirl gently into ice cream. If necessary, smooth top with knife. If ice cream is very soft, freeze 20 minutes. Spread whipped topping over top. Cover with foil or plastic wrap; freeze 6 hours or overnight.

3 In medium saucepan, combine cranberry juice cocktail, sugar and cornstarch; blend well. Cook over medium heat until mixture boils and thickens, stirring constantly. Remove from heat; cool 15 minutes. Stir in crème de cassis and raspberries. Cool 30 minutes or until completely cooled.

4 Just before serving, let dessert stand at room temperature for 10 to 15 minutes. Cut into squares; place on individual plates. Spoon sauce over each serving. If desired, garnish each with additional frozen whipped topping and chocolate filigree.*

TIP: *To make chocolate filigrees, draw desired 1½-inch design on a square of white paper. Place pattern on cookie sheet; place square of waxed paper (cut one for each filigree) over pattern. Place 2 to 3 tablespoons of chocolate chips in small resealable plastic bag. Seal bag tightly; place in bowl of hot water until chips are melted. Wipe bag; cut off tiny corner to create small opening. Pipe chocolate onto waxed paper, tracing pattern. (Chocolate lines should be about ¼ inch wide.) Carefully remove pattern piece. Make additional filigrees on separate squares of waxed paper. Refrigerate 30 minutes or until serving time. Carefully remove waxed paper.

Nutrition Information Per Serving
Serving Size: 1/15 of Recipe

Calories	310	Calories from Fat	120
		% Daily Value	
Total Fat	13 g	20%	
Saturated	7 g	35%	
Cholesterol	15 mg	5%	
Sodium	125 mg	5%	
Total Carbohydrate	44 g	15%	
Dietary Fiber	2 g	8%	
Sugars	26 g		
Protein	3 g		
Vitamin A	6%	Vitamin C	10%
Calcium	8%	Iron	6%

Dietary Exchanges: 1 Starch, 2 Fruit, 2½ Fat OR 3 Carbohydrate, 2½ Fat

HOLIDAY FRUITCAKE

prep time: 30 min. (ready in 11 hr. 30 min.) •
yield: 36 servings

This moist, delicious cake, replete with nuts, raisins, and candied fruits, can be made well in advance.

2 eggs

2 cups water

¼ cup oil

2 (1 lb. 0.6- or 15.4-oz.) pkg. date or nut quick bread mix

2 cups pecans (halves or chopped)

2 cups raisins

2 cups (12 to 13 oz.) candied cherries, halved

1 cup cut-up candied pineapple

Corn syrup, if desired

1 Heat oven to 350°F. Grease and flour bottom and sides of 12-cup Bundt® pan or 10-inch tube pan. In large bowl, combine eggs, water and oil; beat well. Add all remaining ingredients except corn syrup; stir by hand until combined. Pour into greased and floured pan.

2 Bake at 350°F. for 80 to 90 minutes or until toothpick inserted in center comes out clean. Cool in pan 30 minutes; loosen edges and remove from pan. Cool 1 hour or until completely cooled.

3 Wrap in plastic wrap or foil; refrigerate at least 8 hours. Can be stored in refrigerator for up to 2 weeks or in freezer for up to 3 months.

4 Heat corn syrup until warm. Brush over fruitcake before serving. If desired, decorate with additional candied fruits and nuts.

High Altitude (Above 3,500 feet):
Add ¼ cup flour to dry bread mix. Bake as directed above.

Nutrition Information Per Serving
Serving Size: 1/36 of Recipe

Calories	240	Calories from Fat	60
		% Daily Value	
Total Fat	7 g	11%	
Saturated	1 g	5%	
Cholesterol	10 mg	3%	
Sodium	140 mg	6%	
Total Carbohydrate	41 g	14%	
Dietary Fiber	2 g	8%	
Sugars	25 g		
Protein	2 g		
Vitamin A	0%	Vitamin C	0%
Calcium	0%	Iron	6%

Dietary Exchanges: 1 Starch, 1½ Fruit, 1½ Fat OR 2½ Carbohydrate, 1½ Fat

ORANGE CHEESECAKE WITH RASPBERRY SAUCE

prep time: 40 min. (ready in 8 hr. 15 min.) •
yield: 16 servings

CRUST
1 (9-oz.) pkg. chocolate wafer cookies, crushed

6 tablespoons margarine or butter, melted

FILLING
4 (8-oz.) pkg. cream cheese, softened

1⅓ cups sugar

4 eggs

2 tablespoons orange-flavored liqueur or orange juice

1 teaspoon grated orange peel

SAUCE
1 (10-oz.) pkg. frozen red raspberries in syrup, thawed

3 tablespoons sugar

1 teaspoon cornstarch

1 Heat oven to 325°F. In medium bowl, combine crust ingredients; mix well. Press in bottom and 2 inches up sides of ungreased 9-inch springform pan.

2 In large bowl, beat cream cheese at medium speed until smooth and creamy. Gradually add 1⅓ cups sugar, beating until smooth. At low speed, add eggs 1 at a time, beating just until blended. Add liqueur and orange peel; beat 2 minutes at medium speed, scraping sides of bowl occasionally. Pour mixture into crust.

3 Bake at 325°F. for 55 to 65 minutes or until almost set. Cool 2½ hours or until completely cooled. Refrigerate at least 4 hours or overnight.

4 In food processor bowl with metal blade or blender container, process raspberries with syrup until smooth. If desired, place strainer over medium bowl; pour raspberry puree into strainer.

Press puree with back of spoon through strainer to remove seeds; discard seeds.

5 In small saucepan, combine 3 tablespoons sugar and cornstarch; stir in raspberry puree. Cook and stir over medium heat until mixture boils and thickens. Cool to room temperature.

6 Just before serving, carefully remove sides of pan. Serve cheesecake with sauce. Garnish with fresh raspberries and mint leaves, if desired. Store in refrigerator.

Nutrition Information Per Serving
Serving Size: 1/16 of Recipe

Calories	440	Calories from Fat	250
		% Daily Value	
Total Fat	28 g	43%	
Saturated	14 g	70%	
Cholesterol	115 mg	38%	
Sodium	330 mg	14%	
Total Carbohydrate	38 g	13%	
Dietary Fiber	1 g	4%	
Sugars	31 g		
Protein	7 g		
Vitamin A	20%	Vitamin C	4%
Calcium	6%	Iron	10%

Dietary Exchanges: 2 Starch, ½ Fruit, 5 ½ Fat OR 2 ½ Carbohydrate, 5 ½ Fat

Orange Cheesecake with Raspberry Sauce

Yuletide Red Velvet Cake

YULETIDE RED VELVET CAKE

prep time: 40 min. (ready in 2 hr. 30 min.) •
yield: 16 servings

Food color keeps this festive cake deep red, even after the mix is enriched with sour cream. The intensely vanilla frosting gains extra smoothness from the unique cooked flour-milk base.

CAKE
1 (1 lb. 2.25-oz.) pkg. pudding-included
    German chocolate cake mix

1 cup sour cream

1/2 cup water

1/4 cup oil

1 (1-oz.) bottle red food color

3 eggs

FROSTING
1/2 cup all-purpose flour

1 1/2 cups milk

1 1/2 cups sugar

1 1/2 cups margarine or butter, softened

1 tablespoon vanilla

1 Heat oven to 350° F. Grease and flour two 9-inch round cake pans. In large bowl, combine all cake ingredients; beat at low speed until moistened. Beat 2 minutes at medium speed. Pour batter into greased and floured pans.

2 Bake at 350° F. for 25 to 35 minutes or until cake springs back when touched lightly in center. Cool 15 minutes. Remove from pans. Cool 1 hour or until completely cooled.

3 Meanwhile, in medium saucepan, combine flour and milk. Cook over medium heat until mixture is very thick, stirring constantly. Cover surface with plastic wrap; cool 30 minutes or until completely cooled.

4 In large bowl, combine sugar and margarine; beat until light and fluffy. Gradually add flour mixture by tablespoonfuls, beating at high speed until smooth. Beat in vanilla.

5 Place 1 cake layer, top side down, on serving plate; spread with 1 cup frosting. Top with second layer, top side up. Frost sides and top of cake with frosting. Store in refrigerator.

High Altitude (Above 3,500 feet):
Add 1/4 cup flour to dry cake mix. Bake as directed above.

Nutrition Information Per Serving
Serving Size: 1/16 of Recipe

Calories	470	Calories from Fat	250
		% Daily Value	
Total Fat	28 g	43%	
Saturated	7 g	35%	
Cholesterol	50 mg	17%	
Sodium	440 mg	18%	
Total Carbohydrate	49 g	16%	
Dietary Fiber	1 g	3%	
Sugars	34 g		
Protein	5 g		
Vitamin A	20%	Vitamin C	0%
Calcium	8%	Iron	4%

Dietary Exchanges: 1 1/2 Starch, 2 Fruit, 5 Fat OR 3 1/2 Carbohydrate, 5 Fat

FROSTING A LAYER CAKE

To frost a layer cake, place the first layer, top side down, on the serving plate. Spread about 1/3 to 1/2 cup of the frosting over the layer to within 1/4 inch of the edge. Place the second layer, top side up, over the first layer. Thinly frost the sides to seal in crumbs. Gradually add more frosting, building up a slight rim around the top edge. With the remaining frosting, frost the top of the cake.

Cook's Notes

TREE-SHAPED BROWNIE TORTE

prep time: 40 min. (ready in 3 hr.) • yield: 18 servings

Chocolate stars and red and green candy-coated choco-late pieces decorate a double-layer brownie tree graced with shiny glaze. Vanilla frosting holds top and bottom tiers together.

BROWNIES
1 (1 lb. 3.5-oz.) pkg. fudge brownie mix

½ cup oil

¼ cup water

2 eggs

FROSTING
2 cups powdered sugar

⅓ cup margarine or butter, softened

½ teaspoon vanilla

1 to 3 tablespoons milk

GLAZE AND GARNISH
½ cup whipping cream

1 (6-oz.) pkg. (1 cup) semi-sweet
    chocolate chips

40 chocolate star candies (from 8 to
    12-oz. pkg.)

1 tablespoon red and green candy-coated
    chocolate pieces

1 Heat oven to 350°F. Line 13 × 9-inch pan with foil, extending foil over edges; grease foil. In large bowl, combine all brownie ingredients; beat 50 strokes with spoon. Spread batter in greased foil-lined pan.

2 Bake at 350°F. for 28 to 30 minutes or until set. DO NOT OVERBAKE. Cool 30 minutes or until completely cooled. Freeze brownies 30 minutes.

3 Meanwhile, in small bowl, blend all frosting ingredients, adding enough milk for desired spreading consistency. Set aside.

4 Using foil, lift brownies from pan; place on cutting board. To cut tree shape from brownies, starting at center of 1 short side, make 2 cuts diagonally to corners of opposite short side, forming a triangular piece in center. (See diagram.)

5 Place 2 side pieces together on foil-lined serving tray to form tree shape. Spread with frosting. Top with whole tree shape. Trim if necessary to line up edges.

6 In small saucepan, bring whipping cream to a boil. Remove from heat. Stir in chocolate chips until melted. Let stand about 30 minutes or until spreadable.

7 Spread glaze evenly over sides and top of brownie torte. Immediately top with star candies, starting at base with 2 rows of 6, followed by 2 rows of 5, 2 rows of 4, 2 rows of 3, 1 row of 2 and 2 rows of 1. Arrange candy-coated chocolate pieces between star candies. Let stand 15 minutes or until set.

8 To serve, slice crosswise between rows of can-dies; cut each slice into pieces with 2 or 3 candies each.

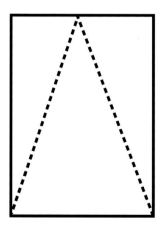

High Altitude (Above 3,500 feet):
See package for directions.

Nutrition Information Per Serving
Serving Size: 1/18 of Recipe

Calories	390	Calories from Fat	180
		% Daily Value	
Total Fat	20 g	31%	
Saturated	7 g	35%	
Cholesterol	35 mg	12%	
Sodium	140 mg	6%	
Total Carbohydrate	50 g	17%	
Dietary Fiber	2 g	8%	
Sugars	40 g		
Protein	3 g		
Vitamin A	6%	Vitamin C	0%
Calcium	4%	Iron	6%

Dietary Exchanges: 1 Starch, 2 1/2 Fruit, 3 1/2 Fat OR
3 1/2 Carbohydrate, 3 1/2 Fat

SCENTED CINNAMON CUTOUTS

prep time: 30 min. (ready in 3 days) •
yield: about 32 (2-inch) ornaments

Cinnamon, nutmeg and cloves give these charming decorations the sweet smell of Christmas. For best results, use small cookie cutters.

1 (4-oz.) can (about 1 cup) cinnamon

3 teaspoons cloves

3 teaspoons nutmeg

3/4 cup applesauce

2 tablespoons white glue

1 drinking straw

Ribbon

1 In medium bowl, combine cinnamon, cloves and nutmeg; mix well. Add applesauce and glue; stir to combine. Work mixture with hands for 2 to 3 minutes or until dough is smooth and ingredients are thoroughly mixed.

2 Divide dough into 4 equal portions. Roll out each portion to 1/4-inch thickness. Cut dough with 2-inch cookie cutters of desired shapes.

3 With drinking straw, make small hole in top of each ornament. Place cutouts on wire racks; let dry at room temperature for 3 days, turning over once each day for more even drying.

4 Insert ribbon through hole in each ornament; tie with knot or bow. DO NOT EAT.

DECORATING IDEAS

Some ideas for using the Scented Cinnamon Cutouts:

• Hang them on the Christmas tree or use them to add flair to indoor evergreen wreaths or garlands.

• Tie them onto presents or onto the handle of gift baskets or bags.

• Suspend ornaments on ribbons of varying lengths in a window.

• Instead of making a hole for a ribbon in the ornament dough, press a thin wooden skewer or craft stick into some of the ornaments. After they're dried, group the ornaments into a small vase or jar for a fragrant "bouquet."

Cook's Notes

INDEX

CONVERSION CHART

EQUIVALENT IMPERIAL AND METRIC MEASUREMENTS

American cooks use standard containers, the 8-ounce cup and a tablespoon that takes exactly 16 level fillings to fill that cup level. Measuring by cup makes it very difficult to give weight equivalents, as a cup of densely packed butter will weigh considerably more than a cup of flour. The easiest way therefore to deal with cup measurements in recipes is to take the amount by volume rather than by weight. Thus the equation reads:

1 cup = 240 ml = 8 fl. oz.   ½ cup = 120 ml = 4 fl. oz.

It is possible to buy a set of American cup measures in major stores around the world.

In the States, butter is often measured in sticks. One stick is the equivalent of 8 tablespoons. One tablespoon of butter is therefore the equivalent to ½ ounce/15 grams.

LIQUID MEASURES

Fluid Ounces	U.S.	Imperial	Milliliters
	1 teaspoon	1 teaspoon	5
¼	2 teaspoons	1 dessertspoon	10
½	1 tablespoon	1 tablespoon	14
1	2 tablespoons	2 tablespoons	28
2	¼ cup	4 tablespoons	56
4	½ cup		110
5		¼ pint or 1 gill	140
6	¾ cup		170
8	1 cup		225
9			250, ¼ liter
10	1¼ cups	½ pint	280
12	1½ cups		340
15		¾ pint	420
16	2 cups		450
18	2¼ cups		500, ½ liter
20	2½ cups	1 pint	560
24	3 cups		675
25		1¼ pints	700
27	3½ cups		750
30	3¾ cups	1½ pints	840
32	4 cups or 1 quart		900
35		1¾ pints	980
36	4½ cups		1000, 1 liter
40	5 cups	2 pints or 1 quart	1120

SOLID MEASURES

U.S. and Imperial Measures		Metric Measures	
Ounces	Pounds	Grams	Kilos
1		28	
2		56	
3½		100	
4	¼	112	
5		140	
6		168	
8	½	225	
9		250	¼
12	¾	340	
16	1	450	
18		500	½
20	1¼	560	
24	1½	675	
27		750	¾
28	1¾	780	
32	2	900	
36	2¼	1000	1
40	2½	1100	
48	3	1350	
54		1500	1½

OVEN TEMPERATURE EQUIVALENTS

Fahrenheit	Celsius	Gas Mark	Description
225	110	¼	Cool
250	130	½	
275	140	1	Very Slow
300	150	2	
325	170	3	Slow
350	180	4	Moderate
375	190	5	
400	200	6	Moderately Hot
425	220	7	Fairly Hot
450	230	8	Hot
475	240	9	Very Hot
500	250	10	Extremely Hot

Any broiling recipes can be used with the grill of the oven, but beware of high-temperature grills.

all-purpose flour—plain flour
baking sheet—oven tray
buttermilk—ordinary milk
cheesecloth—muslin
coarse salt—kitchen salt
confectioners' sugar—icing sugar

cornstarch—cornflour
light cream—single cream
heavy cream—double cream
granulated sugar—caster sugar
half and half—12% fat milk
parchment paper—greaseproof paper

plastic wrap—cling film
shortening—white fat
unbleached flour—strong, white flour
vanilla bean—vanilla pod
zest—rind